RÉGIS DEBRAY was born in France in 1941 and studied at the Ecole Normale Supérieure, where his teachers included the Marxist philospher Louis Althusser. In 1961 he travelled to Cuba, and from there to many Latin American countries, afterwards writing classic studies of the guerrilla strategies then being developed by the left there. Five years later, Debray returned to Cuba to take up a chair of philosophy in the University of Havana; his *Revolution in the Revolution*? appeared in 1967. The same year Debray left Cuba for Bolivia, having been commissioned by the Mexican weekly *Sucesos* and the Paris publishing house Maspero to report on the newly opened guerrilla fronts. In the course of his journalistic work there he was arrested and charged with aiding the guerrillas. He was sentenced to thirty years imprisonment but was released after three years, in 1970.

Since his return to France, Debray has continued to write prolifically and has considerably broadened the formal and thematic range of his work. As well as works of political theory such as *Strategy for Revolution* and *A Critique of Arms*, with its successor volume, *The Revolution on Trial*, he has also written several highly acclaimed works of fiction, among them *Undesirable Alien*. He is at present a foreign policy adviser to the Mitterrand government. Régis Debray's *Teachers, Writers, Celebrities* was published by Verso in 1981, with an introduction by Francis Mulhern.

Régis Debray

Verso

Critique of Political Reason

Translated by David Macey

First published as *Critique de la raison politique*
by Gallimard, Paris 1981
© Gallimard 1981

This abridged translation first published by Verso Editions and NLB, ·
15 Greek Street, London W1, 1983
© NLB, 1983

Typeset by Comset Graphic Designs

Printed in Great Britain by
The Thetford Press Ltd
Thetford, Norfolk

SBN 86091 063 6 Cloth
SBN 86091 763 0 Paper

Contents

BOOK ONE
DIALECTIC

Introduction

Publishing one's first work at an advanced age (after a number of assorted hors d'oeuvre) is an incongruity due to wisdom after the events as much as to the hard times in which we live. As the two things are not unrelated, I think the time has come for me to explain myself by giving an overview of my 'educational background.' Of course, this is not quite the done thing—first of all because it involves talking about oneself. An intellectual never says 'I'. Quite apart from the vulgar soliciting it implies, any attempt to mitigate the shortcomings of a demonstration with the emotions of confidentiality presupposes a mixture of genres rejected by our profession. Let me make it quite clear that narrative is here used to introduce a discourse so that it does not have to be introduced *into* it at a later stage. I am not looking for attention, pity or love but simply trying to make myself understood. If a work of this kind is primarily the work of time, a rational order should already be apparent in the succession of chance events that led the author to write it.

Then there is the social impropriety. The current mode of existence and communication of ideas has definitely made a 'connecting thread' obsolete and incoherence profitable. Every writer knows the advantages of saying one thing one day and the opposite the next provided of course that he remains silent about the motives that led him to contradict himself. He can then be sure of the effect he will produce, surprise making the news and the news making what is new.

Since I know that a result is abstract without its genesis, and that a rational exposition becomes an assertion of authority if no trace remains of the fumbling approaches that made it possible, I intend to ignore the conventions of academia and advertising alike. The reader should therefore excuse the autobiographical element in these landmarks, chosen as they are simply to outline the internal logic of a discursive discovery in which there has been no break but only an uphill progression. To trace back one's course is not the same as to retrace one's steps. For knowledge of where you have come from does give you a better idea of where you are going.

I was in prison when I began to reflect on the phenomenon of politics towards the middle of 1967, some ten years after my first acts of political 'commitment'. Not that there is anything unusual about the time lag between experience and consciousness. But the actual *being* (or nature) of politics might never have seemed a problem if I had not found myself materially incapable of political activity for years on end. Until then I had simultaneously been pursuing a normal arts education (philosophy, literature, history) and a normal involvement in public activities of the day (first agitation and then action). It had never occurred to me to establish any relationship between the two norms: between study at school and experience on the streets, between textual exegesis and a look at the newspapers. I attached no practical importance to the monuments of written history, which only concerned me as a student facing exams, while my one obsession, the twists and turns of the other history that is made and unmade from day to day, did not appear as an object of theoretical consideration. Whether or not my epoch succeeded in entering the future—the future which our world-view assigned it—depended upon the vicissitudes of current events. Biding one's time was such a waste of time.

The past was the past—a museum of familiar and therefore useless objects. The present was explored in conjectures or analysed in the heat of the moment, all the sharper in that moments had to be urgently recognized on pain of falling into error or a 'fatal' lag. The socialist future was awaited on the plane of certainties, the first of which was that it would be unprecedented and therefore unrecognizable. The concept of the 'epistemological break' arrived at just the right moment to set the seal of Science on these lunatic divisions, making the theoretician's schizophrenia both a strict requirement and a guarantee of objectivity. We, the bearers of the new science of history, were already walking the New World in the rue d'Ulm of the sixties, somewhat in advance of the real breaks that would soon divide human history into two. In short, politics hid the political from me for a long time, just as adherence to a singularly logical ideology hid the general logic of ideological adherence. The idea that 'the infinite time of human development' might obey a few immutable laws that had been stated over and over again, albeit none too clearly and in poor translation, would have seemed the mark of a typically bourgeois mental confusion. By what right could one imagine that Latin mythology or studies in classical anthropology had anything to tell us about the 'ideological struggles' of the conjuncture or the organization of 'revolutionary combat units'? Virgil and Marcel Mauss were on one side, Gramsci and Che Guevara on the other. As were magic and the 'new man', or the founding of Rome and the setting up of 'liberated areas'. Between heaven and earth there was the mystery of the Incarnation; between skin and flesh, 'the present situation and our current tasks'. The two orders did deserve equal respect, despite the unequal attention I actually gave them, so long as they never connected in theory or in practice.

The parallel lines met for the first time when I was in prison. I will never be able to say how much I owe to those four years or so of 'self-communion'. Everything in this *Critique of Political Reason* stems from my ruminations at that time and from the rough drafts I have kept. By publishing it, I am acquitting myself of an old debt to the privilege that a period behind bars represents for any intellectual worker. The short-term rhythm of current events erodes and may even shatter the long, slow time of philosophical gestation; it encourages a polemical *presto*, and citizens at liberty always feel somewhat ashamed to rid themselves of it. Imprisonment is a form of liberation, allowing the most to be made of the long nights and a few viable ideas.

By chance—but we all know about 'primitive man's refusal to believe that anything happens by chance'—the Franciscan chaplain in Camiri gave me a faded *Don Quixote* and the tattered remains of a biography of Gregory VII (presumably a Spanish translation of Morghen) when he was finally allowed to visit me. It was quite an event to receive my first two books. Don Quixote provided me with some escapism, while Hildebrand (1020–1085), the hero of the quarrel over episcopal appointments, showed me the world in which I lived. Far from revealing the inanity of 'present tasks', this digression gave them a content and a definite outline. The real danger in the organization of social amnesia is not, as some argue, that we will be marooned from our past, but that we will fail to understand our immediate present, especially when we think it most original. If men walked backwards into the future, instead of turning their back on the practices of the past, they would not open the wrong door so often.

Profiting from the dedication of my few visitors, I directed my subsequent requests for reading matter towards the history of religion—an area free from censorship—not forgetting to obtain the great classics of the labour movement in false bindings. Slowly and confusedly, I began to weave together the threads of different eras and vocabularies, discovering the web of the 'profane' and the 'sacred' even in contemporary history. I had to spend May '68 in the company of Lucien Febvre, Huizinga and Festugière (*La Religion de Rabelais*, *The Decline of the Middle Ages* and Hermes Trismegistus)—an unfortunate accident which, though perhaps obscuring the novelties of the day, may conceivably have given me a head's start in understanding them. In Paris, Marxist theory was then all the rage, 'all powerful because it is true'. Its place has now been taken by the sacred and the return to the spiritual, in no less terrorist a form. 'Heaven inside our heads' has eclipsed the earth, and the Holy Scriptures have pushed aside the duplicated leaflets. Yet the heads are still the same, as is the intensity of fashion. The chopping and changing is all too easy to explain, since it allows each aspect to be forgotten at the point when its complementary aspect is taken up. The confusion is no less damaging, however, given that we only understand our daily lives if the two registers are brought together, if we look at both the back and front of real societies. Totally absorbed in handling their political disappoint-ments, our retired militants heap scorn on the mechanisms of militancy, as if they have only to gaze heavenward in order to drive them from the face of the earth. If I have been spared the 'great disappointment' and all its inverted illusions, it is, I think, because I took seriously the realities of religion and the nation as early as I did. How could I have avoided them when we constantly came up against them in our struggles? Haltingly, I trained myself to con-front both the City and the gods (on paper of course), scribbling rough notes in exercise books. I later published some of the theoretical notes in a journal and the literary notes in the form of a book.[1] It was doubtless too soon in 1970 to think religion by talking politics, and by 1980 it was too late to think politics by talking religion. What does it matter if, as I hope, this *Critique* is basically far enough removed from current events not to make anyone who reads it in the year 2080 burst out laughing?

Cut off from his normal horizons, a militant turns his eyes on his own way of looking at the world. Locked up and deprived of future, I began by returning to the mental universe from which I had come. With all the objectivity that comes of having nothing to do, I applied to it a mixture of critical suspicion and floating attention born of the sometimes productive clash between the familiar and the unfamiliar, the lived and the learned. We all know that information of a rare kind suddenly appears when banal and apparently unrelated things are brought into relation with one another. In asking myself how to weight unknown and familiar elements in the history that we were, I experienced some curious inversions of form and essence in the most stereotyped figures of my 'ideology': clichés, mechanical residues, forgotten corners of official discourse.

The religious nature or coloration of national and social liberation struggles is an undeniable fact of history past and present. From Engels to Ernst Bloch, from Landernari to Jacques Berque, interpretations of this have become classic texts. In the East, it is plain for all to see that Islam provides the coherence and dynamic of the people's encounter with their ruined identity. In the West, and not only in Poland, Christianity works both on the surface and deep beneath it, unbeknown to the most evidently atheist vanguards. In Latin America, Christian culture goes beyond Christianity itself and outlives it in 'scientific socialism'. Over and above the patent messianism of its thirst for justice and its belief in the Kingdom, the sacrifical morality of duty inspires militants who are confronted with imminent martyrdom. Redemption through suffering, salvation in death and expiation of the past, although derived from the Spanish mystics, the 'Apostle' Marti or even Seneca, are dressed up in a Marxist-Leninist vocabulary that would have left Marx and Lenin quite bewildered. As we know, Zapata was a devotee of the Virgin; Sandino a theosophist. National liberation as the *redemption* of the poor, revolution as *rebirth*, commitment as a *vocation*, discipline as *devotion*, *el hombre nuevo* as the vanquisher of Old Adam—all these themes figure prominently in the early Havana manifestos (1960-1962) and are still the common language of those who fall in armed struggle in Central America. Blood is the seed of nations—an image common to Tertullian and our funeral orations—and dying for the cause is the supreme reward. One day some *'latino'* Max Weber will write a book on it: The Catholic Ethic and the Spirit of Revolution. Salvation through grace did a lot for capitalism, once Calvin had made interest-bearing loans acceptable and demonstrated that a good businessman was not necessarily a bad Christian. Today, salvation through good works is doing a great deal for the social movement in Latin American countries, where it goes without saying that a bad Catholic will never make a good fighter. We cannot here analyse the religious origins of proto-socialist doctrines (Saint-Simon, Fourier, Cabet, and so on) in the revivalist Europe of the last century, or the particular affinities between 'actually existing socialism' and Roman Catholicism qua authoritarian religion with a hierarchical structure, a cadre organization and a tightly knit institutional fabric. However, the underlying syntax of collective organization, as revealed here and there by their compulsive behaviour, struck me as less familiar and more pregnant with implications than the morphology of individual behaviour, which an ultimately banal sociological analysis can relate to its socio-historical coordinates.

The dustbins of theory, especially Marxist theory, sometimes contain diamonds. Not that anyone meant to hide them: their public presence is enough to discourage amateurs, and *a fortiori* professional rummagers, from looking too closely. Edgar Allen Poe's police inspector himself could not find the purloined letter because it was in the letter-rack in front of his nose. A wise man once said that you can know the truth by the care it takes to hide itself. But it hides itself best by striving to appear idiotic. Details are important, and the most meaning is sometimes lodged in places that do not merit the attention of experts. Once force of circumstance had made me myopic and almost impartial, certain 'details' of 'scientifically realized socialism' became blinding obvious.

Take *Lenin's Mausoleum* or those of Kemal Ataturk, Ho Chi Minh and Tito. (Tomorrow it will be the turn of Ceausescu and all the rest of them.) The resolutely agnostic mummies kept in them may change in accordance with the imperatives of the moment and the vicissitudes of the line, but the need to preserve a founding father remains constant. Mausolus, Satrap of Caria, born in Asia Minor in the fourth century BC, understands Lenin. For his part, Lenin does not understand Mausolus and would definitely have been horrified at the idea that his Bolshevik comrades should build him a funeral temple. They would have been equally annoyed to discover the religious basis on which Artemisia II, the sister and wife of Mausolus, built the pyramid that was to become one of the seven wonders of the world. The Mausoleum in Red Square will outlive Leninism: mausoleums are built to last (the one in Halicarnassus lasted two thousand years), but *isms* fade away. Can things that pass do without things that span the ages and are at home in all of them? If we look at the common noun rather than the proper name, perhaps we are already on the track of an invariant and necessary relationship between the Many and the originating One, the series and the first term? For a basic political science, there may be less information to be gleaned from embalmed corpses than from the ritual of embalming itself, which allows the souls of living gods to survive their death through the preservation of their bodies. Since this has been a widespread phenomenon throughout the ages, whatever the character of social beliefs or the stage of technical development, there may be some continuity between the electrifying soviets and the Golden Bough of the ancient kingdoms.

Similarly—and this is one more example of prime banality—I eventually discovered a somewhat disturbing profundity in a ready-made expression that my good masters and my common sense had led me to consider inept: the *personality cult*. Obviously, there is no room for such a non-concept in Marxist theory. Yet, concept or no concept, the facts of world history have a stubborn persistence from Nineveh to Pyongyang, from Bucharest to Kinshasa; and if Marxist theory could not care, the cult has shown a ferocious capacity for caring even less about theory. What must be the nature of political authority if it constantly arouses personification? What must the supreme leader of a country be to his subordinates if he is capable of becoming a Dionysus or a Hercules—divine yesterday, a genius today? By focusing on the perfectly contingent personality of an individual, one helps to conceal the fact that the problem of problems does not actually lie with 'Stalin' (or Mao, Ceausescu or Kim Il Sung) but with the 'cult', and to dissolve an anthropological constant into political circumstances. One rarely solves problems by refusing to pose them. Rhetorical denunciation of *the cult of leading personalities* has not led to its *political disappearance* either in the world in general or in the socialist world in particular. (Things do not seem to have changed much since the Twentieth Congress, unless they have moved backwards.) During those Chinese–Russian skirmishes across the Amur River that caused so much ink to be spilled, what shook me most was a two-syllable word that did not have the good fortune to attract the attention of any commentator. In their communiqués, both communist parties simultaneously and solemnly called for the defence of the '*sacred* territory of the fatherland'. One more grain of sand in the conceptual machine for my fellow observers to brush away with irritation! True, it was at a time when one of the most fantastic religious manias of the twentieth century—Maoism—was being theorized in Paris by hard-headed thinkers, professors of philosophy included, as the highest stage of historical rationality. One day, when listening to Radio Peking's Spanish-language service on a transistor in Bolivia, I heard about the odyssey of an old Tanzanian peasant who walked three hundred kilometres to the capital so that she could touch the portrait of the Great Helmsman and 'supreme guide of the world proletariat' in the Consulate of the People's Republic of China. The newsreader added that the old woman died of exhaustion the next day, her heart still radiant with joy. The story was presented to 'comrades and friends all over the world' not as a parable but as a real and exemplary fact.

Iconoclasts only destroy the holy images they can replace. The story of the peasant woman, and much worse besides, happened in the year 1970. Yet nothing seemed to disturb the true believers in the best schools in France, who now think they are square with their past Stalinism or Maoism because they have discovered such eminent figures as God, Raymond Aron, the President of the United States or Bob Marley. I wrote this book to try to understand why the newsreader, the peasant woman and the professors are always right, each in their own way, and to discover the logic that lies behind our day-to-day unreason. In that sense, these memoirs are an expression of loyalty to two or three little questions that have been sticking in my throat for ten or fifteen years. If I have refused to choke them down regardless, it is because I fear having to cough them up again undigested. And if, as this Critique hopes to show, political time is a time that never passes, at least I will have discovered why history stammers and learned not to take its hiccoughs for the apocalypse. Or my own spittle for holy water.

Just as the wealth of societies in which the capitalist mode of production prevails appears as an immense collection of commodities, the infancy of societies in which 'the transition to socialism' prevails appears as an immense collection of ceremonies. Ceremony is the typical commodity of 'actually existing socialism' (like it or not, overabundance of ceremony compensates for commodity shortages). And, to parody the *incipit* of *Capital* once more, 'our investigation therefore begins with the analysis of a ceremony'. We shall not start with the obvious fact that, by the same logic which leads from the subversion of the existing state to the construction of practically unsinkable states, revolutions begin as festivals and end as ceremonies or ritualized festivals. (Our conclusion should not be 'what's the point of a revolution?' but 'what's the point of ceremonies?'). Long before I flung myself into the comparative history of religions, I had seen with my own eyes that societies in which 'scientific atheism' is erected into a State doctrine secrete religiosity from their every pore. Now, this may seem an unfortunate verb, as it suggests something dirty. Yet secretion is an official activity or even a regulatory neurosis in which these social formations (the original models, of course, not the imported socialism of Eastern Europe) invest much more than points of honour and every effort, namely their very soul. In the heartlands of 'real socialism', collective life expresses and exhausts itself in the repetitive enthusiasm of endless popular processions, military parades, cortèges, anniversaries, inaugurations, closures, festivals, congresses, tributes, funerals, visits, meetings, galas, exhibitions, receptions, speeches, oath-taking ceremonies, presentations of medals, flags, trophies, diplomas, pennants and so on. The organization of ceremonies is the prime function of the authorities: not a technical but a specifically political function, as if protocol, that obsession and substance of collective life, were not simply an administrative service among others but the immediate and substantial expression of State power. Since civil society is *de facto* absorbed into the Party-State, social existence is not merely

organized but petrified in the solemnity of civic liturgy, whose spectacles are the very substance of the day's news (press, radio, television, posters, etc). The ornamental becomes the basic fabric,
decorum becomes the substance of the drama.

The term 'religion' is, as is well known, excluded from communist vocabulary on the grounds of impiety, but that same
vocabulary is far from reluctant to let 'ceremonies' take charge or
to welcome the 'grandiose' side of mass demonstrations. Unable to
conceal its hierolatry or the great age of its hierarchs, the communist movement sets great store by *hierarchical* customs and
principles. (Hierarchy comes from the Greek *hieros,* sacred, a term
which first appears in Homer, about 900 BC.) To speak of religiosity in connection with a cell or branch meeting may sound like a pro-
vocation or plain nonsense to a party official ('Heard it all before:
Monneret and Silone', and so on). As if it takes the word to produce the thing! As if the ubiquity of the thing does not presuppose
the *absence* of the word! For more than a thousand years the City-
Church of Classical Greece and the Empire or Republic of ancient
Rome fused political and religious life without ever employing the
term 'religion'. Indeed, there is no such term in Greek, and the
Latin *religio* (which only acquired its present acceptation in the
time of Lucretius and Cicero) may be least inaccurately rendered as
'the gods and ceremonies'. If we also recall that ancient Greece and
Rome had no orthodoxy, dogma or clergy, we can all agree that the
canons of public (or, if one prefers, republican) observances have
become more rather than less strict over the years.

The staggering anachronism of our 'new societies' has never
made me want to sneer. It is a very ambivalent phenomenon,
presenting what is both best and worst. Its ugly, almost touching
aspects may raise a smile: the 'provincial' atmosphere of socialist
capitals, the outdated customs and clothes, the slightly comical
starchiness of everyday life. The barbaric side, which the West
prefers to stress, can be truly frightening: the autocratic brutality,
the dead souls in the offices, the adoration of the Leader. In order
to apply Spinoza's motto, 'neither mockery nor tears but understanding', to the other half of the world, we must rid ourselves of
the clinging weight of clichés. The most blinding, of course, is that
overworked concept of 'terror' which conceals a permanent and
much more frightening characteristic of 'real socialism', namely

boredom. We have already seen 'socialist societies' without Gulags: we can see them now and we will see more and more of them in the future. The real question is whether we shall witness the emergence of socialist societies in which people are not bored. While we wait for a serious study of the roots and methods of social boredom—which I take to be the cornerstone of any socialist anthropology—we can begin by overcoming the screen-notion of 'totalitarianism'. It has been said that this is a source of confusion, since it brackets together societies with opposing 'class contents'. In my view, however, it is confusing precisely because it does make distinctions. It is not that the botany of institutions does not include a peculiar species characterized by a tightly interlocking Party-State-Society. But that is the only content that could be attributed to the foil-like category of 'totalitarianism', which is better left to 'political science', as the medieval study of modern forms of sovereignty is known. The 'totalitarian' schema is not really serviceable in the quest for the postulater of political existence: it conceals the permanence of functions beneath the variety of organs, positing a fundamental difference between two forms of social existence and thereby masking their common conditions of possibility. *Totalitarianism* serves much the same function in the arsenal of our political science as *fanaticism* did in that of the Enlightenment or *totemism* in primitive anthropology: it is both an excuse for misrecognition and a rite to ward off evil. It allows the constellations in question to be considered as forms of deviance external to the natural order or foreign to our sane normality. They are savages, we are civilized; they are fanatical, we are tolerant; they are sick, we are normal; they are totalitarian, we are democratic; they are dangerous, we are inoffensive. Although advances in knowledge have overcome compartmentalization in virtually every other field, the barriers erected by a somnolent reason still stand firm in our political habitat. In the human sciences, extreme situations have proved to be a productive source of knowledge. The roots of things are found in their extremes. Eastern socialism takes us to the outer edge of the political universe, to the point where memory becomes unbearable and explodes.

'If we wish to study men, we must look at things that are close to us; but if we wish to study man, we must look further afield. In order to discover properties, we must first observe differences.' (*Essay on the Origin of Languages*, Chapter VIII) Like everyone else, I had learned the motto of Jean-Jacques Rousseau, the founder of the human sciences. I had looked and travelled further afield, a closer perspective on both my own circumstances and on the permanent elements that outlive all circumstantial variations. Observation of the differences between established forms of political domination gave me an insight into the identity of domination that cuts across latitudes and eras, frontiers and constitutions. In his *Discourse on the Origins of Inequality*, Rousseau had to fall back upon the theoretical fiction of a 'pure state of nature' which 'no longer exists, may never have existed and probably never will exist'. But although he chose to set facts aside, he did not disdain to use such investigative material as was available: savages. The Caribs and Hottentots were not *the* savage, but they were close enough to the real thing, their variation from the degree zero of civilization being sufficiently small to give a semblance of reality to the fiction of origins. For the purposes of investigating the norms and forms of political incorporation, we may ascribe to *homo socialisticus* the role played by *homo sylvestris* in Rousseau's investigation into the foundations of civil society. The difference, not at all negligible, is that the former actually exists. We can see him living and reproducing, so that we do not need to rely on the tales of Cook or Bougainville to find out what he looks like. Where better than in hyperinstitutionalized regimes can we perceive the general mechanisms of the institution? We could not hope to find a better demonstration of the exchange of *security against dependence*—that crossroads where the political basis of the pact of religious fidelity intersects the religious basis of the pact of political obligation. It is there in front of our very noses, as large as life. *Do ut des* between man and the divinity already presided over the ancient sacrifice. The law of give and take now governs the friendly agreement reached between State–Party and social individual: 'Do your military service, take part in my ceremonies and keep your nose out of my business. In return I will ensure that you have security of employment and health care, that you are able to walk the streets, and that provision is made for your own future and that of your children. Let me govern as I wish up here, and I will let you manage as you see fit down there. High politics for me, high productivity for you.' When it is not imposed from abroad, everyone readily signs the contract without a murmur. Our primary social contract has taken up residence in the Natural History Museum, where marble societies are kept safely under glass.

The hypertrophy, not only of the values of hierarchy, authority, discipline, centralization, security etc., but also of their respective organs (the 'security organs' for example) does not disfigure their respective functions. On the contrary, it makes them more clearly visible: disfigurement is a form of divulgation. Doubtless 'real socialism' is amenable to exhaustive and self-sufficient description as a system of interaction in which each feature conditions the next with no apparent reciprocity (economic planning and forms of social communication, for instance). But whilst the notion of the *whole* is pertinent here, it is inseparable from the more general notion of a function which, by 'creating the organ', precedes and outlives it. Such is the immodesty of these 'backward' forms of political organization that they openly display what other forms conceal, tone down or dilute. By liberating the things that are repressed under pale disguises in our 'advanced' Western societies, they give the chemists of political matter, who are only too inclined to work *in vitro* in libraries, an unparalleled opportunity to test their working hypotheses *in vivo* in the great book of the world.

Although he was unable to solve it, Rousseau realized that the only real problem is that of transition—in his case, from 'man wandering through the forest, with no industry, no home and no contacts with anyone' to a rational being united by free contract to a political body. It is not difficult to juxtapose descriptions of the two states: the real problem is to grasp how one is precipitated into the other. Nor is it difficult to transcribe the internal logic of a structure, even if the specific relations that bind the elements together never appear to the naked eye. The hardest task is to reconstruct the logic of the operations governing the transition from one structure to another. In this respect, political anthropology appears to enjoy privileges that cultural anthropology is forced to seek in the most remote corners of the globe and in observations characterized by a highly ambiguous precariousness. Political time dawns anew each day before our very eyes: the agents of the institution are their own ethnographers. Our archive documents are all over the morning papers; our research material accumulates on the walls, the small screen and the newsstands. The whole world ought to be our laboratory. But the Third World is in the forefront of research, as it is only there that we can see unities breaking up and separate things coming together. Nations are appearing, territories are being mapped out and 'social systems' are being tested in places where, only ten years ago, there was nothing but sand and grass. That, in a word, is where the birth of the political can be caught. And birth is the only thing we are concerned with.

We know what Chaos is, or we think we do. We also know what the Cosmos is, or we think we do. But what do we know about the transformation of the one into the other. From Anaximander's flash of lightning to yesterday's big bang, from Ionian cosmogonies to astrophysics, the answers have gained in credibility but the logical nature of the question has not basically changed: how does matter go from one state of existence to another, from gaseous nebulae to stars, from new stars to planetary systems? *Mutatis mutandis*, the kernel of the problem is still the transition from disorder to order, from the 'unorganized' to 'organization'. At first sight, it seems both logically and chronologically symmetrical with the question that haunted the eighteenth century. Instead of looking for the ideal dividing line that separates the civilized from the natural, the degenerate from the primary, we have to reconstitute the reverse process. We have to invert the short cut: the canonic experience, both emotional and theoretical, is no longer to be sought in the appearance of a Guyaki Indian in a clearing or in the stammering of a 'savage child' brought up by chimpanzees. But an equally intense feeling of shock ought to come over us when, in the space of a few weeks, we see a new state born virtually *ex nihilo* (and not simply reconstructed) in a land that has been ravaged by civil war, anarchy and the aftermath of an earthquake; or, on a smaller scale, when we see a scattered handful of guerrillas meet at the foot of a forest waterfall and improvise a central camp with its distribution of tasks, its command structure, guard posts, passwords, and so on. The crystallization of a primitive armed force, resistance made flesh, the formation of an organized nucleus in naked survival conditions—these are no symbol or metaphor, but our 'thing itself'.

The concept of the political lies within the birth of the political, the secret of such things within the thing itself. 'The Birth of the Clinic' (Michel Foucault) was made possible by the epistemological integration of death into medical experiments. The odds are that the birth of a positive political science will take the opposite path. It will replace the motto 'Open up a few corpses' with 'Look at some embryonic states'. Anatomic pathology expected dissection to allow the visualization of the invisible, the observational structuring of illness. We may ask similar things of the institutionalization of subversion, where the hidden mechanisms of order come to the surface. The collective inverts the critical poles. Death is the lyrical core of the individual, the site where he discovers that he is irreplaceable, the site that makes him a poet and makes him sing. Birth is the lyrical core of collectives: it makes them experience that singularity whose evocation will rouse a crowd and put a song on its lips. There is a logic to this lyrical distribution. It is therefore in our interests to tear ourselves away from the seductions of paradisiac anarchy, from those finely glistening mirages of 'societies against the State' about which so much is now heard. Political reality will find its concept not in the ethnographic object, but in the *transition* from hot to cold, at the junction of ethnology and history. Just this side of Eden, where the dream breaks up.

As soon as one takes the pains (and it *is* painful at first) to see the famous 'construction of a new society' as the reconstruction of society full stop, the progressive odysseys of the Third World turn out to be so many edifying returns to their origins. The workshops of genesis, where the structures of collective existence are forged and where the genesis of structures lets slip the structures of political genesis, ring with talk of 'the birth of a nation', 'the construction of the country' and 'the birth pangs of the state'. In the outposts of the sacred, on the ill-defined and perpetually threatened frontiers that divide chaos from order, contemporary revolutions explore the collective past and re-enact the birth of the collective (*Inter faeces et orinas nascimur*). The Young Guard relieves the retiring old guard, the red guards relieve the white guards. In their turn, they adopt the same images, behaviour and mottoes, sometimes quite literally. But the liberal Frenchman, 'well brought up' in times of peace and plenty, takes offence at the unconditional oath on the banners in Havana: 'Comandante, whatever you wish, wherever you wish, whenever you wish.' He is probably unaware of the fact that even a Cartesian under fire does not escape the sacred fire—witness the famous Gaullist in London in 1943 who proclaimed, 'Whatever you wish, General! Whatever you wish, oh France!' At that time 'the awesome and warlike face of France' rose above 'political struggles'. Fatherlands may rise and fall, but war is a law unto itself. It always has been and always will be, and none can condemn the laws of collective survival. Our young cynic is surprised at the pious fervour of the *compañeros* celebrating their '26 July', forgetting that other comrades of a different Liberation display much the same fervour at Mont Valérien* on 18 June each year. In the history of peoples, dawns are cruel and sunsets are naturally modest. In France, the blood that founded the lawful state has dried into articles of law, clotted on the panelling; the blood spilt at the Bastille and in September has disappeared beneath the Aubusson carpets of the palaces of the Republic, even though—or just because—it cemented the foundations of all the Republics, from the First to the Fifth, not excluding the Fourth. Our Fourteenth of July points back to the emotional communion on the Champs de Mars, not to the storming of the Bastille. Our ceremonies to commemorate the liberation of France invoke Leclerc and the FFI†, not firing-squads and women with shaven heads. Heaven forbid! Having communed, sung and cut off heads for centuries as they built themselves up in massacre after massacre, our advanced societies can now afford the luxury of feeling sick at the sight of these backward hordes of greens, blacks and reds communing, singing and shooting people all over the place.

A digression through the so-called periphery is the quickest way for the so-called centre to trace the link between its present state and the conditions that gave rise to it. Realizing that the exotic is what is closest to us, Rousseau was reduced to despair because the state of nature had disappeared beyond human grasp. If, he argued, we are to judge our present state and form an accurate no-

---

* Mont Valérien: fortress on the outskirts of Paris frequently used for executions during the Nazi occupation. June 18: anniversary of De Gaulle's first broadcast to the population of occupied France in 1940. Trs. note.

† FFI: Forces Françaises de l'Intérieur: name given to all armed resistance forces. Trs. note.

tion of natural law, we ought at least to know man as he emerged naked from the hands of the divinity. But nature has been lost; progress has destroyed it. We will have to find nature in and by ourselves, relying on our inner sense of self. The true ethnographer is therefore the philosopher who can discover the primitive side of man without even leaving his room. If, on the other hand, we take seriously the commonplace idea that movement through space involves a journey in time—a stroll in Los Angeles opens up the twenty-first century, whereas a village in Ethiopia takes me back to the tenth century AD—it becomes apparent that a political anthropolgist can only exercise his trade if he goes into exile. Indeed, he can only do it properly by becoming something of an adventurer, or at least by going on 'adventure tours'. He takes his doctorate by making revolution—or rather, since there are not many successful revolutions in the space of a generation, by *not* making revolution. Militancy is his foundation course. After that, he has to go home and turn in his party card in order to able to work on his field notes. You cannot understand the 'party phenomenon' and take part in it at the same time. The worst thing then is not so much to have one's *licentia docendi* taken away just when one finally has something to teach, nor to have one's grant (salary, budget or credits) withdrawn and the doors of the institution slammed in one's face. People are quite right to point out that, from an academic point of view, I wasted my time playing truant. But they are wrong when they say that a political vagabond is a hopeless profligate when it comes to political science. For it hardly seems possible to deny the wild character of so many works that are considered scientific within the corporation, or the rigorous impracticability (or remoteness from praxis) of the political fantasies so fashionable among our intellectual avant-gardes. That is the surest sign of their theoretical frivolity, since in the end a theory that cannot be translated into practice is not a theory but a phantasmagoria. I am foolish enough to believe that if there is any weight at all in this text, and if it can stand the test of actual practice, I owe it to my travels to the 'state of nature' side of collective existence.

The greatest political surprise of the twentieth century, which has already seen the most astonishing technical and social upheavals ever known to mankind, will ultimately be the discovery that there

has been no surprise after all. We are still flabbergasted at the fact
that we were so little affected. Those who keep records no doubt
owe it to themselves to say 'Things can never be the same again' at
the end of each decade. It is a fitting sentence fit for a journalist or
politician. But on the day of reckoning, at the end of a life or a century, reality forces us to murmur: 'After all that, nothing has
changed.' An expression fit, perhaps, for a writer of memoirs or a
historian. After what? After the Revolution. The Holocaust. The
Resistance. The Twentieth Congress. May '68. The last elections.
Etc. A leitmotif for autobiographies, balance-sheets, eye-witness
accounts, memoirs, running through all generations, all camps and
in all directions. 'We dreamed that it would be different. We practically killed ourselves trying to change things and then, bang, we
found ourselves back at square one and had to start all over again.'
It is as though we were constantly having to cut the same Gordian
knots, constantly having to relate to a shameful past we had
abolished as 'unthinkable'; as though some diabolical compulsion
to repeat took a delight in mocking all our 'never agains'. One
could compile an anthology of surprise outcomes and unexpected
returns. The latest example, taken from yesterday's paper, comes
from the pen of a Communist militant (Paris 1980): 'We are
witnessing the return of something we thought impossible: the personality cult.' A list of all the impossible things we have seen return
would make for sorry reading. Breaks made on paper have remained on paper. But in the real world, even at the superficial level of
the atlas; we expected to see breaks in the confrontations and
alliances between states, and yet national undercurrents and hidden
ethnic and cultural continuities have prevailed. The empty wisdom
of Ecclesiastes may sometimes puff up the Joseph Prudhommes*
of geopolitics, but the fact remains that such historical viscosity
points to a rational paradox: the problem today is not one of difference but of permanence. Our past theoretical solutions offered
themselves to the future as solutions of continuity, and continuity
is doing very well at the moment, thank you very much. The idea
that there is 'a *fundamental* difference between bourgeois politics

---

* Joseph Prudhomme: character created by Henri Monnier (1805–1877), a
mediocre, self-satisfied petty bourgeois much given to sententiously banal pro-
nouncements. Trs. note.

and proletarian politics', that basic thesis of Marxism, has had to be shelved along with the doctoral theses. Marxism may well have inaugurated 'a new practice of philosophy' (Althusser), but it has never been translated into a new practice of politics. Historical materialism may well have replaced the classic concept of man 'with a concept of a different sort, not a different concept' (Lucien Sève), but it has certainly not replaced the old practices of power with practices of a different sort. Philosophers may well be able to have a serious discussion on whether there was a break with the Hegelian past, but historians cannot seriously discuss whether there was a break in the government of men 'after the socialist revolution'. After all, if the philosophical revolution of Marx and Lenin had taken the politics of Marxist-Leninists into a 'new world', word would surely have got around by now. The gap between the conceptual inversions and the real repetitions is too great, too stubborn, to be seen in orthodox Marxist terms as the effect of unfortunate mistakes or temporary incongruencies between theory and practice that will gradually be ironed out as socio-economic backwardness, and leadership errors or deviations disappear. On the other hand, the gap is too familiar and displays too many similarities with states of society and history that are widely separated in time, space and doctrinal inspiration for it to be seen, in the manner of bourgeois orthodoxy, as the effect of the perversions and aberrations of a calamitous theory. Even though their justifications may occasionally be justified, both these antithetical apologia avoid the central question of the relationship between theoretical reason and political reason. What, we must ask ourselves, differentiates the space of action from the space of thought? In any case, if we were to make Marxist theory take the responsibility for its unkept promises, we would remain within the circle of *imputation* ('blame Marx'). Such impiety is still too pious, as it avoids a much more embarrassing question: what about the differential? It is one thing to put forward the argument—in laughter or in sadness—that Marxists who claim to be exceptions to the rule are no freer from the vicious circle than are adepts of pan-Turkism, Shi'ism, Calvinism or any other ideology. It is quite another to examine the content of the rules themselves; and still another to replace the second procedure with the first, waving a legal document in the air as if it were a scientific discovery. It might be more profitable to look at the basis of the continuity, so that the despair of our era becomes a cause for exultation. There is a rational joy in investigating why there can be no more surprises, an emotional joy in freeing ourselves once and for all from the servitude of waiting to be surprised, the most frustrating kind of waiting in the world. And there is a political *confidence*, in that 'pleasure arisen from the idea of a past or future thing of which the cause of doubt is overborne' (Spinoza). Such pleasure is neither an absolution of the soul nor a restful perfection, but the process whereby 'a man passes from a less to a greater perfection', the *act* whereby we increase our potential for action by lessening our illusions of power (or our margins of uncertainty). The blockages in our history then serve to unblock our understanding of it, rather than simply fuelling our resentment. Applied progressivism/freewheeling 'archaism'? It is a good opportunity to rid political science of its last evolutionist overtones. The old parade of *survivals* turns on itself, because the residues die harder than we thought they would. In 1920, it was possible to imagine that the kernel of 'scientific humanism' was finally going to break its straitjacket of naivety, just as the young Soviet Union would slough off the old skin of Holy Russia and all its peasant mysticism. The scars now show that it was a mistaken belief. When Lenin was buried in 1924, many villagers came to Moscow's Red Square carrying ikons of Lenin instead of the Virgin.[2] But ikons have not disappeared with industrialization, and images of Lenin are now industrially produced. The theory of revolution could itself account for the fact that 'survivals' turned into 'reactivations'; or that *after* a 'socialist revolution' in the state (or after a 'cultural' revolution in a great 'socialist' state), ideology and false consciousness, leadership and veneration, lumpen elements, juvenile deliquency, alcoholics, jealous husbands, mandarins, mummies and 'rotten elements' are still to be found here and there. But the fact that there are as many (if not more) of them than ever before is a qualitative leap in growth which the theory of qualitative leaps cannot explain without breaking out of its own limits.

Bascially, what became inaudible as time went by was the old Enlightenment couplet, the lullaby of human belief: '*Du passé nous ferons table rase*, but not in one clean sweep; wait for a while, things will clear up, just be patient.' We have lost patience and given up hope, and that might lead to an improved understanding. It is quite true that those who 'guide mankind on its march towards communism' have 'speeded up the passage of time', but probably not in the sense they expected (always assuming that there is some consistency of sense or direction, a before and an after, a below and an above, in this particular kind of space). Seen from the perspective of governmental procedures, it is obvious to all that the so-called socialist modernization of very old Empires is much closer to feudalism than to capitalism. (Is it not said that children take after their grandparents more than their parents?) Nepotism, dynastic impulses, court phenomena, allegiances and vasseldom, the division of the state into fiefs, clans and gangs, palace revolutions, heresy trials, Florentine-style ambushes and executions—these features 'belong' to the fourteenth century in the West. A more precise anatomical section would probably reveal a delicate range of 'anachronisms', synchronized and virtually synthesized under our very noses. I have already mentioned the bottom end of the range: the pompous 'Third Republic' style, the mania for statues and museums, the ceremonialitis, the 'national poet', the patriocentrism, the gerontocracy, the academicism and the offical heroes. There is also a grander side, it is true. In dreams and occasionally in reality, we can see the transparent harmony of the ancient City revealing itself in a stadium or a square (egos merge into a living ethical community, self merges with other, individuals merge into the concrete universal: Periclean Athens as seen by Hegel). Then there is another dark, stagnant era, the moment of the great monarchies of the East, complete with the worship of a deified leader who has gone mad with loneliness in the middle of a desert of sand, laws and luxury: the Persia of the Great King as seen by Herodotus. Who knows, this babel of historical times might put us on the right track. The pomp of state socialism is simply a time machine, perhaps the only apparatus that dares to let political machines speak their shameful aim: to suppress time, to squeeze it into rituals, to freeze it for ever, to abolish all events. The score can no longer be kept in the classic confrontation between old and new, between barbarism and civilization. The combination of the abacus or wooden plough and the sputnik or atomic reactor—which so struck Isaac Deutscher in post-Stalinist Russia—refers to a still elementary hiatus in which one can move from one to the other without changing lines. However, there may well be a more radical hiatus between the acceleration of technical-industrial time and the immobility of political time. The visual symbol of that contrast would be concentric circles of nuclear reactors around a heart of stone: an Egyptian sarcophagus beneath a red marble pyramid. Official materialism had to take that form to put the edge of eternity within our reach. Eternity razes all historical societies, but it pops up where one least expects it, in the one place it denies itself the right to exist. Being a rational animal, I am grateful to 'socialist' societies—those painful symptoms—for having shown me, albeit in outline and at a distance, the atemporality of political sacrifice. In that kingdom, where man dominates man, time, sir, has nothing to do with anything. Dare I add a further premonition, which I owe to the mass lack of interest in politics that prevails in most bureaucratic societies (the only societies in the world where the ordinary citizen does not even know the meaning of the expression 'talking politics'): the apolitical finality of 'political life'?

In 1971, when I was half way through these reflections, I would probably not have formulated them in this way. My ruminations had given me an A, a way of transposing current events on to my stave. I would never stop humming the main tunes as a means of self-defence, but I did not yet have a score. When I left prison I knew the scale, but I felt a strong desire to close my exercise books.

All good things come to an end, and few prisoners stay in jail for life. It is always more difficult to leave prison than it is to go inside, even if you do use the front door. (*La vie mode d'emploi* had not yet been published*.) So I found myself out on the street, knowing too much, I dare put it that way, to allow myself the luxury of a 'developed political consciousness,' yet not enough to see the contradiction involved in that expression or to admit that a political consciousness in the strong sense is really something of a squared circle. Only too happy to find a pressing need for political mobilizations on the outside, I flung myself into 'immediate practical interests' and stayed put in Latin America for a while (Chile, Cuba, Argentina). Drawing a careful distinction between the rules I lived by and the search for truth, I kept public life and methodic

---

* Novel by Georges Perec, Paris 1978. Trs. note

doubt as far apart as possible and devoted my analytic efforts to the simple task of producing critical accounts of present or past practices with which I was directly or indirectly acquainted.[3] 'So that I might not remain irresolute in my actions, while my reason compelled me to suspend my judgement, and that I might not be prevented thenceforward in the greatest possible felicity, I formed a provisional code of morals'.[4] Marx's theory would be my 'provisional code of morals': 'an imperfect ethic, which a person may follow provisionally so long as he does not know any better'. I had no cause for complaint, and nor did anyone else. Quite apart from the minor comforts afforded by Cartesian conformism ('Regulating my conduct ... according to the most moderate opinions, and the farthest removed from extremes, which should happen to be adopted in practice with the general consent of the most judicious of those among whom I might be living'), those who turn their back on this method of analysing possible homes all too often end up with worse results than those who know how to use it at their own risk. There is no reason to suppose that the shack you have chosen to live in while your house is rebuilt according to carefully drawn up plans ('rejecting all propositions that were in the least doubtful') might not eventually become a modest but essential part of the completed whole ('which, presupposing an entire knowledge of the other sciences, is the last degree of wisdom').

When I returned to the fold—one more ghost among the learned shades of my home country—I again started waiting to be surprised, on my home ground this time. That was about 1973. Waiting had cost me nothing. For I had been expecting a newsflash from France that would galvanize Europe and stagger the world.

Many different times overlap in the present of an individual, as in that of a society. Paradoxically, the time of the actual event, with its rapid oscillations, leaves you less breathless than the heavier, slower time of waiting. Events that one imagines to be imminent serve as a vanishing point for collective hopes and as a target for individual projects; they play a decisive part in the real factors of practical history, where what does not happen is often more determinant than what has actually happened, where a whole chain of events can depend upon a missing link. We live our existence in the future anterior: we orientate ourselves in the present (thereby giving it its orientation) in relation to things we imagine we can bring into existence in the future. The existence of living beings is made up of disappointed hopes and frustrated plans as well as of joys and disasters that have actually occurred. That is why fiction is the only accurate form of biography, and why the history of an epoch has to be written in terms of its utopias as much as its discoveries. Shorn of its poetry, its prose remains a dead letter.

Keynes has accustomed us to the idea that economic agents make decisions on the basis of probable anticipations and expectations rather than tangible material evidence. The same applies a fortiori to political action. The only problem is that history is always written by those who do not make it: they have the last and the easiest word. History is forged strategically but explained casually, and the balance-sheets are enough to make anyone weep. There is no reciprocity of perspective between those for whom 'history' means the doubts they have to clear up *hic et nunc* by making calculations in the dark, and the survivors who come along and state that that irreversible, closed 'epoch' was such that it could not be anything else. The posthumous jury of great minds is blinded by its own hindsight. From the heights of their vantage-point they add up facts and figures, never realizing that these results are negative quantities or remainders that have to be subtracted from the sum total of all the actions that were conceivable in a given time and place, never realizing that they have to take into account every possible hope that people entertained before subsequent events demonstrated that it was merely a hope. And so the actors of history take into the grave that secret image of the future which made them live and act in the present. Take the twenties, for example: the German Revolution and, more generally, the revolutionary upsurge on the borders of backward Russia in the aftermath of the First World War vanish like a dream. But without that non-event, the attitude of the Bolsheviks immediately after the October Revolution, and Lenin's choices in particular, become incomprehensible. Or again, the sixties: the Andean *cordillera* is about to become the Sierra Maestra of Latin America. By 1970 it is obvious that that is not the case. Yet without the psychological ubiquity of that non-event, the overall direction taken by the Castroist revolution becomes incomprehensible. All that is real is rational? But what really happened is not the whole of reality. It is not even certain that it has the lead part in the play. The sum total of what was possible and what was imagined may make what actually happened a mere remainder. So we may leave it to historians of the next millenium to show that nothing could have happened in France in the nineteen-seventies AD except a straightforward repetition of the past. Even if we were not personally involved in political games, which are also dramas, or in political dramas, which are also games (usually on television), we were still busy waiting, still enveloped by the spectacle, and time still passed. That is why your philosopher had nothing to say for ten years: a case of the wait-and-sees.

Although I turned to literature, for want of anything better, I was not idle. Convinced of my impunity (given that Billancourt was going to win, to hell with its despair*), I went back to my old note-books. My obsession was still to confront what is unrealizable in theory with what is inadmissible in political practice. Having noted the inability of Marxist theory to explain the ABC of the history made in its name, I was still struggling to give the former some insight into the latter. My skylight, my chosen viewpoint was once again the permanence of the nation; and it was by reflecting on that that I was finally weaned.[5] The nation, that meeting-point between nature made history and history made nature, gave me a perspective on the major absence in our political thinking. This obsessive black box reveals the blank left beneath the heading 'nature' by the 'science of history' and the blank left under the heading 'history' by contemporary philosophies of nature. Georges Haupt, whose advice was always valuable, gave me all the material to study this embarrassing 'national question' from the perspective of historical materialism (well, the Christians did have their 'social question'—we all have our problems). It seemed that, for want of a key, Marxism was reduced to tinkering with the lock as the conjuncture permitted. Historicist thinking can, at best, reflect a given set of existing national conditions, but it cannot reflect the conditions of existence of the national phenomenon. Despite the timid breakthroughs of Austro-Marxism and Gramsci—and far be it from me to underestimate the excellent précis made by Stalin—the energy of nationalism leaves the apparatuses of 'scientific

---

* Allusion to the phrase 'Il ne faut pas désésperer Billancourt', often incorrectly attributed to Sartre. A free translation might be: 'Say nothing that will upset the workers at Ford's Dagenham.' Trs. note.

socialism' looking very sheepish.[6] But by capturing it, channelling it and drifting with it, they succeeded in spreading half-way across the world in the space of fifty years. Socialism itself, however, has lost every time it has clashed with nationalism, and it will go on doing so. Ultimately, the one thing Marxism has been unable to think is actually existing socialism. It is well known that revolutions are neither the realization of pre-existing systems nor the application of some model for the reorganization of society, but the products of an objective process (the class struggle) which theory merely receives and reflects in a general form. Marx was always careful to draw a distinction between his theoretical elaborations and his doctrinal forecasts, and that he expressly refused to speak on behalf of history or to answer questions he thought premature. History has spoken since then, however, and it is her answers that we have to decode. The code Marx bequeathed is not adequate to the task. (Given that the basic thesis of materialism is that any message exhausts all possible codes, it would not even be materialist to deny its inadequacy.) The nation is Marxism's sore point. The abcess is weeping all over the place, and they will not be able to disinfect it until it is lanced.

We can only know what we transform, Brecht used to say, but it is also true that we can only transform what we really know. Thinking after Marx means, first and foremost, thinking Marx through to the end. Perhaps I am looking gloomily back, just trotting out things that have been said over and over again. But judging from what happened when people suddenly grew sick of Marx and rejected him out of hand, that is the lesser of two evils. Ostentatious mourning keeps children in the shade of their dead feather, while the clamour of triumph—'We've got him, we've killed him.'—can cover all kinds of headlong flights. And so from '74 to '78 I made another painful effort (the shortage of books in prison makes you a glutton for reading, but an overabundant supply does tend to put you off) to grapple with the Opus, but not in order to set up as an exegete. Fleeing the verdant pastures of infantile glosses (all those mirror-games between text and commentary, things said badly and things left unsaid, discourse and rectification of discourse), I continued the journey to the end of our night. Theory should go into exile, I told myself; it should disappear into the objective world where it can no longer recognize itself. Then it will prove one of two things: either that it can grow up, or that it deserves to die. Dead thought which remains external to life cannot even think of its own death.

In the short term, it seemed to me—and it still does—that the first duty of a socialist is to account for existing society and not to draw up yet another 'project for a society'. An individual can think up as many projects—or even bills (*projets de loi*)—as he likes: societies know only *processes*, governed in the last instance by laws which are the expression not of the people's will but of a constant relationship between several series of phenomena which programmes ignore at their peril. If it is true that the 'critique of bourgeois society' took on a practical character after October 1917, all our fine phrases about 'the new political culture' will be hot air until the critique of that critique has been taken to its logical conclusion and we have produced a philosophical interpretation of that political transformation.

In rational investigation, meeting-places are always the least frequented. Turning-points are strategic positions, but they are also rather uncomfortable. Presumably this is why in-between places always look like non-places, and why go-betweens who try to stick together the fragments of what is said and done look like displaced non-persons constantly looking for somewhere to sit down. Philosophers see them as journalists and send them to the reporters; while journalists see them as speculative minds and send them to the academics. The sociologists tell them that 'metaphysics is over there', the metaphysicians that 'sociology is downstairs'. Militants accuse them of pedantry; pedants criticize them for their militancy. In short it was something of a gamble to try to place critical Marxism and positive Marxism, western theory and eastern practice, in such a position that they could reflect upon each other—not least because they are unaware of each other's physical existence. No one has yet seen an adept of the symptomatic reading of the *Grundrisse* queueing up outside the Red Square mausoleum or found a pilgrim of Leninism who knew the difference between early and late Marx or the definition of an epistemological break. Each half of the great body of Marxism acts and thinks as though the other half did not exist (except perhaps as its stooge). The vanguards of the West will say that any organized meeting is *anachronistic* ('such anachronisms are no concern of ours')—poor things, they don't know what's in store for them. For their part, the big battalions of the East will say that it is *non-specific* ('On what grounds can you claim that the truth of truths is just any old problematic?')—poor things, they've forgotten that that is where their Holy Scriptures came from, from a philosophical critique of philosophical texts.

Such a project means that we cannot resign ourselves to the overwhelming divorce between militant practice and theoretical analysis. Inside what was once the international labour movement, the divorce was consummated long ago (with a few Italian exceptions) and has had the effect of transforming the leaders into 'pure' politicians or opportunists, and the thinkers into 'pure' theoreticians or schizophrenics. The counterpoint between the two has become the well-known duet: 'Don't bother about my politics. Don't bother about my theory.' It is an artificial quarrel, based on agreement that a politician can do nothing but harm in the field of ideas, and a theoretician nothing but harm in the field of politics. The two sides collude by turning their backs on each another, one outdoing itself in pragmatism in order to protect itself from the other's dogmatism, and vice versa. It is known as a *division of labour*.

The pedagogy of proof governing our reflections will, on occasion, force us to break down the wall between actuality and hypothesis. Making the concept react to an outside environment is, in my eyes, a basic prerequisite of rigour, even if it does lay us open to the jeers of militants and the silence of pontiffs. The political world shuns objective elucidation of its practices as an academic exercise, while the academic world rejects as 'political' any testing of its statements against the real. One buries people first and talks about them afterwards (no theses can be written on living writers in French universities), the other kills men and ideas without any funeral orations. One relies on trial by fire, the other on casting out the nines. These 'sorties' into the profane milieu are not excursions into frivolity, but incursions into our object, towards what I see as the solid core of political anachronism: the day's news.

The tranquillizing properties of the mutual scorn that the chemists of the real and the field-workers feel for one another should not be underestimated. The human race is not short of reasons for wanting to avoid disturbing questions, and people 'on the left' have more than others. Compared with his immediate predecessors (*homo faber* and *homo sapiens*), *homo socialisticus* has a serious constitutional defect: he is cut in half. A man who does not think what he says will have nothing to do with a man who does not say what he thinks. He sometimes makes a point of honour of this inner reduplication, where his good conscience merges with his bad. The irreverent add that *homo socialisticus* has become a painful fossil whose honour depends on making himself unhappy, even though the age of masochism is over. The mockers are wrong, however; for if in the world of the left, serenity is the prerogative of only two classes of individual, these two together account for the entire population. What, until very recently, did the old nation of internationalists look like? On the one hand, there were good-hearted people without the slightest knowledge of Marxist theory, and on the other there were capable minds who turned to Marxism without the slightest political experience. The former are not necessarily imbeciles—far from it. If you look at the gallery of great French intellectuals attracted to Communism in the first half of the century (Barbusse, Gide, Nizan, Sartre, and so on), it is obvious that they were mainly motivated by political sentimentality: the rationalizations came later, like an optional extra. Nor were the second group necessarily fops or Benedictines: men like Politzer and Gabriel Péri, for instance, paid dearly for their personal commitment.* A distinction should be made between political *culture* and *experience*: although the two are not quite mutually exclusive, you often find one without the other. It is also perfectly possible to be a man of *conviction* without having any *knowledge* of political matters, or a man of science or reflection without having the corresponding convictions. (These distinctions, which may seem pointless when everything is peaceful, are thrown into startling relief when the going gets rough. As a rule the men of conviction then turn out better than the men of culture: they can be relied upon to make fewer silly mistakes.)

People of such different temperaments—not categories, because there is nothing socio-occupational about them—are not at all fond

---

* Georges Politzer, Gabriel Péri: PCF militants executed by the Gestapo in 1942 and 1941 respectively. Trs. note.

of one another's company. I have had the good fortune—or perhaps misfortune, perhaps even both—to have spent certain periods of my life among 'militants' and others with 'intellectuals' and to have moved from one to the other without any transition. Had it not been for such incoherent juxpositions of closed universes, which have so often coloured my feelings and behaviour, I would probably never have been so worried about whether there is anything coherent in political existence.

The essay whose theme I have just outlined, and which I called *The Essence of Marxism* in homage to Feuerbach and his *Essence of Christianity*, never went beyond the manuscript stage. (The results will appear later in condensed form.) I saw it as the first part of a *Critique of Theoretical Unreason*, an equally Feuerbachian title that I rejected in favour of the positive (and not theoreticist) title *Critique of Political Reason*. Behind the apparent joke—everyone knows that politics drives people mad, stupid and insane—there was a basic wager in the choice I made: mania implies discourse; faith implies a concept. But the rationalist assumption that there is a reason for every unreason presupposes a certain method of research. Let me go through it word by word. *Critique*: a logical and not an evaluative term, designating the study of the conditions of possibility of a given order of phenomenon, namely the forms and categories within which it can be experienced. *Reason*: a system of describable laws presiding over the development of an experience. *Political*: a specific field of reality delineated by the formation and disintegration of large (and non-natural) human groups. Obviously, political in that sense is distinct from 'state', and the private/public opposition is not pertinent here. The idea of the state as an institutional reality distinct from society appears during the Renaissance; the absolute monarchies give it its concrete structures and it is legally formalized in modern bourgeois societies. Chronologically, the political sphere appears before the state sphere (and may also outlive it). In the space of social experience, it includes the state but extends to any collective territory traversed by relations between leaders and followers (Church, Party, Movement, Group, etc.). Hence *Critique of Political Reason*: the study of the condition of existence and functioning of stable human groups.

If the specific object of the discipline of politics is the social relations of domination, as distinct from the social relations of exploitation that formed the raw material of Marxist economic science, we can see why a study of socialist reality leads spontaneously to a general reflection on politics. Social practices, and the practices of 'actually existing socialism' in particular, are imperfect experiments in that they do not take place within an aseptic environment or a closed circuit; the generalized state of war with the national or international 'class enemy' considerably distorts the hypothesis. Still, never in the course of the history of societies has the singularity of the phenomena of power been so clearly isolated. Experimentation presupposes at least some possibility of modifying the variables at will in order to determine their correlations. Although we shall not posit an inverse ratio between the magnitude of the exploitation factors and the magnitude of the domination factors, the scientific merit and contribution of the 'transitions to socialism' is that, by modifying the variables of economic exploitation, they allow a relative invariable to be openly identified: the relations of (political) domination of one group of men over another.

I have no regrets that I missed the boat by failing to hand my copy in on time. Wearing the label 'Marxist' in the dismal post–'68 period was a matter of elementary dignity, like wearing a yellow star. It is probably unusual to live through such a cruel discrepancy between the things we thought and the things we fought for, between rigour and urgency, research and resistance, as the discrepancy we have experienced in recent years. Thinking against oneself is a common enough fate. But that was not enough. You had to be out of step, even if it meant going against your own investigations. What else could one do when the massed choirs of the defrocked were singing *misereres* on the majority platforms of the moment? The sight of so much peremptory inconsistency rushing to the rescue of a panic-stricken fashionable society confirmed my view that work to (social) order is the best way for a philosopher to nip his little truth in the bud. For it is in the nature of the true to frustrate demand and to give answers that are not to the point. When you saw so many people happy to have escaped a nightmare they never even entered, generally behaving as martyrs of an odyssey begun in a classroom, continued in an editorial office and ended in a salon, you began to think that a little suffering might be necessary in order to think a little. The price of words is an or gastronomic, for example) is presented after the event, but intellectuals demand an advance. It's the old old story: the slightest argument costs you so much misery, so many inner deaths for a single idea, so many tears for a book on philosophy. Thinking can never be happy, and the most you can hope for is an eventual happiness in thought.

1971–1980: periods of overheated intellectual life shun the uphill development of the concept. They twist the first available raw material into line with the dominant interests of the moment, blowing with the wind and the air-waves of radio and television. 'Settling accounts with one's erstwhile philosophical consciousness' is one thing, settling into the mood of the moment is another. Actually, however, they were too similar not to demand an excess of abstentionism. (Any attempt to put the phenomena of politics into theoretical perspective implies a challenge to a certain progressive 'common sense'.) Now that 'common sense' again has the wind in its sails, a critique of common sense is permissible because it is bound to go against the current. Fear ebbs and hope returns. A liking for the off-beat aside, it is to be hoped that philosophy may for a moment escape the disjunctive logic of conflict (annexation or exclusion, recuperation or anathema, here or there)—that wretched binary logic of one and naught which underlies the success of public-service thought. In that respect, the mass departure of home spun intellectuals from the forum must be reckoned a good omen. The general climate of political indifference ('realism and lucidity') gives a new value to reflections on political difference, which now pays too little interest to hold the attention of small-time speculators or big spenders. When nothing is at stake, no one bets. Make way for the rules of the game and let us dissect them without passion or prejudice. But since no one has the power to live without passions, that might be better phrased as 'without passing off our passions as judgements'.

I would rather have postponed the task of setting the record straight—not out of any militant scruples, but because of my professional ethics. (You have to take so many precautions and cross-check things so often.) However, my essays on the intellectual function gave rise to so many unfortunate misunderstandings. I will not discuss the gracious compliments I received from the 'popular press'. Its vocation is not to understand works but to promote or destroy names according to the position they occupy on the imaginary chessboard of the existing relationship of social forces (each square being a brand image). It is therefore not exceeding its limits when it goes in for *ad hominem* insults. I am always delighted and even somewhat flattered at being insulted from those quarters. But when serious critics honestly mistook my intentions in *Le Pouvoir intellectuel en France* and *Le Scribe,** I was convinced that I had done my job badly by presenting the applications before the principles and the scholia before the axioms. As I saw it, my study of the city intellectual was simply a means of approaching the internal logic of collectivities. My ambition was not to contribute to the sociology of intellectuals, still less to add one more strand to the political history of the French intellectual, but to use both those things to open up the paradoxes of the social. To be more accurate, I treated the vagaries of the intellectual corps as variables in order to trace the invariability of a function. Thus I used a restricted lexicon of events (the highs and lows of intellectual power) as a way into the syntax of large groups, into the system of hierarchical relations within which any organized political whole is produced. Basically *Le Pouvoir intellectuel* posed the question: what can symbolic activity be if it has effects on the materiality of social relations in a secular republic like ours? As to *Le Scribe*, it was asking: what can society be it if has always had an organic need for a body of men to indicate meaning? A lively and sometimes polemical tone, together with an excessive contraction of ideas and facts, drowned my attempts at algebra beneath a rather derisory froth of interference which eventually faded into the platitudes of moralism. Granted, the boy-scout style ('It is time to clean up the Republic of Letters!' and 'Shame on the parasites of human misery!') may have a certain claim to nobility in France, but it is of very limited theoretical interest. Apart from Marc Beigdeber, Michel Serres was virtually the only one to detect the nugget contained within *Le Scribe*, to take the trouble to see that the notion of *social incompleteness* might be a useful step forward off the beaten track. That hypothesis (which to my knowledge has never been explored)

---

* *Le Pouvoir intellectuel en France*, Paris 1979: Tr. D. Macey, *Teachers, Writers, Celebrities*, Verso, London 1981; *Le Scribe*, Paris 1980. Trs. note.

lies at the origins of the present work, and I shall seek to develop its meaning and implications.

Before going on to a general *mediology*, of which it can already be said that it will no more be a theory of the mass media than psychoanalysis is the science of slips of the tongue, it was necessary to grasp the first link in the chain by discovering what distinguishes a disorganized collection from an organized whole or society. Such a method does not merely offer the selfish advantage or reducing the gap between what I find it interesting to say and what I have so far seen fit to say about it: it also provides the first definitions for a study of mediation.

Observers of modern societies have yet to discover a society without an 'ideology'. The word was invented and made public in 1801 by M Destut, Comte de Tracy, a French philosopher. There is no reason to think that the nature of human societies changed at the turn of the eighteenth century, any more than did the anatomical structure of *homo sapiens*. And as words do not create things, we can all agree that the social function fulfilled by 'ideology' was not born at the same time as the word. All the evidence suggests that the great historical religions once fulfilled the same function as the great ideologies of the modern era and satisfied the same generic needs. As Bergson pointed out in *The Two Sources of Religion and Morality*, ethnographers have yet to discover a 'society without a religion'.

If we put to one side the classic disputes on the first manifestations of the sacred and include magic and animism in a field that is basically homologous with religious life, the philosopher's formula is still scientifically acceptable. There is no question of challenging the need for a differential typology of diverse systems of belief, even though the subjective naivety of the phenomenological opposition between ideological 'conviction' and religious 'faith' seems no more pertinent than the evolutionist naivety of the sociological opposition that assimilates 'religion' to traditional, homogeneous societies and 'ideology' to modern, conflict-ridden societies. If we have the right to a scale of observation that spans the semantic and historical singularity of the terms we are proposing, if, that is, we can think in broad but not loose terms, it seems that our guiding hypothesis always requires us to take a step backwards. However, what might be seen as a chronological regression is actually a logical progression, in terms of comprehension as well as extension. Given that political practice can only exist 'in and under an ideology' (Althusser), knowledge of the political order is to be sought not within the political itself, but within ideology. By the same token, knowledge of the ideological order is to be sought within the religious order. Knowledge of the religious is not intrinsic—unless one accepts a tautology as an explanation, as do the various 'phenomenologies of religion'. It is to be found in social physics (in the strong sense of the old positivist name for what is now called sociology). Every organic ideology gives the world a meaning, and every human group finds that the world is to a greater or lesser extent meaningful. But cohesion between groups does not exist because the world has a meaning; the world has a meaning because there has to be cohesion within groups. Groups must find the means to become cohesive on pain of extinction. Initially, it need only be an ordering of space and time: the spatial organization of a habitat and the symbolization of astronomical time. A minimal coherence: a territory related to a centre and a history referred to an origin. The cosmos does not need living groups to go on existing, but human groups need cosmological markers to continue their existence. Means of meaning, means of survival. The general question for political anthropologies—namely, the conditions of possibility for group survival—immediately takes us on to the ground of religious anthropology. 'Practical' is not, as Marx thought, the opposite of 'religious', for the mysteries of religion translate the mysteries of human practice. Erecting practice into a shibboleth can ultimately become an excuse for theoretical laziness and its by-product: obscurantism. If practice represents (as in the *Theses on Feuerbach*) the 'rational solution to all mysteries which lead theory to mysticism', we cannot go on as though the solution that we constantly evoke were not in itself highly problematic. Otherwise, through a kind of inverted mysticism, we would be displacing the mystery towards its all-purpose solution.

My initial conclusions may be briefly summarized.

Basic political relations are not explicable in terms of themselves or the manifest forms they assume, but nor can they be explained by the material conditions of life. Not only are they irreducible to the mere projection of an economic base; they cannot be deduced from it either. In other words, politics is not 'concentrated economics' (Lenin). Observation of modern societies shows that the structures of political behaviour are not radically modified when one mode of production is replaced by another, and that they are independent of the degree of development of the productive forces. These structures impose themselves on societies and, if need be, against them, not as fantasies but as modes of behaviour. Despite its historical brevity, the 'socialist' experiment is in that respect conclusive. 'Actually existing socialism' has realized in its practice everything that its theory forbade it to realize or even imagined impossible. It has at all times, though in varying degree, renewed religious forms of social existence which were thought to have been excluded by the new relations of production. This goes to show that at the root of the social, there exists an uncontrolled and apparently 'irrational' force which defies logical norms and programmatic aims. This force, whose effects escape plans and the express wishes of individuals, is usually either conjured away by the traditional study of political institutions or, when it is taken into account, assimilated to some kind of mystical spell which forces the 'politologists' to emigrate to 'wonderland'. The 'share' of dreams, magic or pretence is then evoked as some irreducible and discouraging, residue. But that is to forget that reason cannot be given a 'share', and that local descriptions are possible because the world can be described at every level and from every angle. No one has the authority to transfer the poverty of a discipline on to its object or to transform the provisional and factual limitations of knowledge into an insurmountable barrier to the very possibility of knowledge. In official political science, the last occult science to be approved by the state and to be taught in state institutions, some high priest comes along every year and pronounces inexplicable the things he is unable to explain. As if reality were at fault and not his explanation! That science has 'obviously failed to come to terms with politics'[7] is an inescapable fact, but it does not follow that politics is by definition impervious to rational investigation, merely that it is in the best interests of the investigator to find other tools. The classical political science of regimes and institutions has shown itself to be as powerless before the internal logic of politics as the old psychology of the faculties of the soul was in the face of the realities of mental life.

The conscious mind is no more the essence of the mental life of individuals than political institutions and representations are the essence of the political life of collectivities. It is not the consciousness of men that determines their political existence, but their social existence, which determines their consciousness, is itself subject to a logical system of constraining material relations. That logic persists through the different philosophical, juridical and institutional forms corresponding to each type of economic infrastructure, because it is fundamentally different to those forms. Men do not produce such relations by 'freely associating' with one another; they are produced by those relations, which generate their associations. Just like individuals, but in a different way, organized human groups have a specific unconscious, of which religions and their ideological substitutes are the most obvious symptoms, and which we will term the *political unconscious*. This unconscious is not psychological in nature and is not based upon archetypal representations; still less is it spiritual or initiatory (despite the unfortunate homonymy with Jung's collective unconscious). It is not determined by free-floating symbolic forms but by fixed forms of material organization, the symbolic forms being merely reproductions or traces of these. The study of this political unconscious—or the science of social dreams, if you prefer—is not part of the sciences of the mind but part of the natural sciences (which obviously include the sciences of the mind). It presupposes a reversal of theoretical perspective, or an inversion of centres of interest, which will simultaneously render the residual constitutive and the irrational rational.

Religions and ideology thus appear as truly organizational practices, and not as representative or symbolic practices. Ideologico-religious material may initially be handled in the same way as dream material, as providing a lexical inventory of themes. A thematic of this nature could rightly claim to be exhaustive (or to be a complete enumeration of the themes, which are not infinite in number) in so far as the grammar of the collective revolves around a stable logical core corresponding to innate schemata of organization which, like the transcendental schemata of pure reason, subsume the endless multiplicity of social events and are 'filled in' by successive historical eras. The conditions for the formation and stability of human aggregates (the study of which is the specific object of political theory) thus display a formal coherence that is amenable to description, even though (or because) they have an organic material base qua integral parts of the logic of the living.

If these theses are not totally without foundation, it follows that, like the individual unconscious, the group unconscious has no history; or, in other words, that the essence of human political history is not historical. Cultural anthropology finally accepted that men have always *thought* as well as they do now. So why not accept that they have always *acted* as well—or as badly, it makes no difference—as they do now? (The clinical metaphor here reveals itself to be unsuitable or utopian: ideological formations can be decoded as symptoms, but symptoms of a normality for which the notion of a cure is meaningless.)

At least two temporal stages corresponding to distinct logical orders should therefore be distinguished in human history: one corresponding to relations between man and things and the other to relations between men. Natually the two are imbricated, as relations between men always take certain things as their object and relations between man and things are always mediated by another man: this indefinitely repeated mediation is the shuttle that weaves the fabric of social struggles. But the actual unity between the two orders can only be understood if a preliminary categorical distinction is made between their modes of existence. That is why the first category of relations is of the open cumulative type ('technical and scientific progress') and the second repetitive and finite ('the stammerings of history').

We are still living with the after-effects of Prometheus's error. The definitive version of that inaugural mishap was given by Protagoras, two-thousand-five-hundred years ago.[8] At the last moment, just when man was about 'to emerge from within the earth into the daylight', Prometheus realized that all the other animals had been well-provided for by Epimetheus, but that man was 'naked, unshod, unbedded and unarmed'. Prometheus rushed off to see what he could steal from the gods. He at first intended to make off with the secret of 'the art of politics, of which the art of war is a part', but he had to abandon that plan as the secret was too well guarded in the citadel of the gods, with terrible sentries at the door.

He therefore made his way to the workshop of Athena and Hephaestus and penetrated it by stealth. The pious imagery of the Promethean spirit of conquest, which the nineteenth century found so intoxicating, misses this detail: in the orignal myth, the theft of fire is a stop-gap measure and Prometheus is the ambiguous hero of a partial success. Having come into possession of the principles of the utilitarian arts, men were technically in a position to survive, but they had to live in scattered groups and were profoundly unhappy. Protagoras goes on: 'They sought therefore to save themselves by coming together and founding fortified cities, but when they gathered in communities, they injured one another for want of political skill, and so scattered again and continued to be devoured'. Seeing this, Zeus took pity on them and sent down Hermes, a jack of all trades, to teach men a respect for others and a sense of justice to make up for an incurable lack. The human race was saved from biological extinction, but Zeus kept for himself politics, the art of living together without injuring one another. Everything in the myth hangs together, and it is still hanging around our necks.

When I say everything, I am above all referring to our present dreams and disappointments. Zeus has gone, but the categorical confusion between the two realms still throws out our calculations and maintains the disappointment principle by beguiling us with unfounded hopes. The repression of the 'true story' of Prometheus perpetuates the illusion that 'new times' are waiting behind the door to the future, whose keys have been entrusted to the American engineer or the Soviet commissar, not to mention those who wear white coats over their leather jackets. It is a form of technocratic naivety to believe that the pursuit and spread of technical progress (railways and now microprocessors) will provide a solution to the political problem. And it is scientistic naivety to imagine that because science, by definition, makes progress, the science of society will lead to social progress and social advances, that the attributes of the process of knowledge will be realized in the object of knowledge itself. Some believers in 'the scientific conception of history' have compounded this methodological error by extrapolating the characteristics of the *material* object to the *political* stakes. We are all familiar with the slogan 'Freedom means telematics plus free elections'. Some might also recall 'Socialism is electrification plus soviet power', and it is time that Russia gave the West more to dream about than Japan does today. But that fabulous arithmetic, so simple in appearance, has not produced the expected results. If we look at it more closely, it becomes evident that the sentence was both highly complex and formally shaky. For the *plus*—the pivot around which it revolves—puts basically different factors into a commutative relation. We can no more hope to add together an octohedron and a saddle horse than we can three megawatts and a fantasy or a technical apparatus and a logical interplay between relations. By stringing together a known factor that could theoretically be mastered and an unknown factor that had not been mastered, the Leninist formula may have been an attempt to match them up and thus to exorcise the opacity of the mechanisms of power. As we now know, the magic did not work. Electricity may well have arrived, but we are still looking for soviet power. Neither electricity nor the soviets are to blame, merely the inconsistent arithmetic.

The theoretical distinction between these two areas of confrontation, one mobile and the other immobile, coincides with and founds the real distinction between a technical object and a religious, mythical or aesthetic object, between two kinds of archive. Only archaeologists are interested in Sumerian swingploughs, but the Epic of Gilgamesh may mean something to us because some of its mythical material still lives within us. Tools allow man to progress, language makes him stagnate. His material productions—tools, machines, automata—constantly open up new worlds, but his symbolic productions just as constantly turn him in upon himself. The break immediately closes on itself, however, while the closure is open to everyone. Thanks to this paradoxical inversion, innovation dates and repetition always appears new. Technical development fades away the further it moves along the 'civilized' vector, whereas the stationary equilibrium of the symbolic brings every era face to face with itself by confronting it with every other era in the spiral time of culture. Tools from fifth-century Attica look unfamiliar to us because we produce ten times more corn per hectare than the metics of Athens, but texts from the fifth century BC still intrigue us because no modern philosopher can say what he wants to say more clearly than Plato. No leader of any medium-size power can state more clearly that Demosthenes what has to be done to frustrate the hegemonic expansion of a neighbouring state that is threatening its independence. No sculptor can outdo Phidias. One type of material is at best *documentary*, the other is *exemplary*. On the one hand we have an accumulation of traces, on the other a constant flow of evidence for a trial that goes on indefinitely. It is legitimate to see this dialectical play between two temporalities as further proof that mankind is playing loser wins. Technical man—the inventor, the explorer, the worker—is a conqueror, but his double, his alter ego and closest enemy—the priest, the militant, the citizen—is a born victim. Man's only victories are those he wins over things, but they do not produce meaning. The fact that, having replaced the horse with the aeroplane, we can travel at 1000km rather than 20km per hour has not brought any more justice into the City or any less constraint into social relations. It has changed the way we see things, but not the 'meaning of life'. The decisive battles which stir our passions and mobilize our dreams and interests are the battles that men fight in every age 'so that men may be free and happy and live in peace'. Yet it can be irrefutably demonstrated that such battles are always lost in advance (not that that detracts from their importance or the need to fight them—*on the contrary*). It is the vocation of the scientist to solve problems (or, as in physics and mathematics, to ask certain unanswerable questions scientifically). What unites the statesman, the artist and the philosopher, however, is the fact that their activities are constitutionally problematic. As Chekhov once put it, in terms of the human condition, the artist's role is to pose questions, not to become involved in solving them. The role of the philosopher is to supply answers to questions that cannot be answered scientifically, and that of the politician is to start projects that can never be realized. In that sense, the territory of politics may be defined as one of practical impasses. If, as Brunschwicg argues, philosophy is the science of problems that have been solved, political philosophy differs from the philosophy of science in that it is a science of insoluble problems. The rock always rolls back down the slope. Human reality was born of the intersection of two legends: Prometheus and Sisyphus. But Sisyphus will always be with us, and that will be his final revenge on Prometheus.

In the Introduction to his *Critique of Political Economy*, Marx asks why it is that the artistic productions of the past can outlive their material base. 'The difficulty', he notes, 'is not that of understanding how Greek art and poetry are associated with certain forms of social development. The difficulty is that they still give us aesthetic pleasure and are in certain respects regarded as a standard and unattainable ideal.' Although the thinker of economic history located the problem, he never developed or resolved it except in the form, so ludicrous in its evolutionist candour, of a gentle nostalgia for the historical childhood of humanity. 'The Greeks were normal children'. What Marx relegated to the outer limits of his theory, to the marginal areas of art history that were of no great importance to him, is in fact a decisive question common to aesthetic, physical and political phenomena alike. Since his presuppositions made him unable to see this peculiarity as the principle of another rule, or as the index of a logically and chronologically different realm, he had no alternative but to register it as an inexplicable exception to his rule. It is very tempting to use Marx's own categories against him and to say that in his age of the steam locomotive and the single-shot chassepot, humanity was still in its historical adolescence and that its attempts to find a guarantee for political emancipation in the intoxication of productivism and technocratism were no more than a juvenile fit of eccentricity. We have since matured sufficiently to realize that in many respects mankind was born fully grown, in full possession of all its mythological, libidinal and political faculties. So we are 'big enough' to show our gratitude to all the forms of theoretical expression of the awkward age of industrial societies, and above all to Marxism. We in our turn can say of those over-gifted adolescents of the past what Marx said of the epic masterpieces of the Ancient World: 'The charm their philosophical works has for us does not conflict with the immature stage of the society in which they originated. On the contrary its charm is a consequence of this and is inseparably linked with the fact that the immature social conditions which gave rise, and which alone could give rise, to this philosophy cannot recur'.[9]

A paleontologist who has made a particular study of technological development and, therefore, of the phenomena of 'breaks' notes that the existence of a territorial and functional framework is a permanent feature of the 'social organism'. It is found at all stages, from the initial threshold of settled agriculture, which implies a sedentary group and the accumulation of food stocks, to the contemporary urbanization of the planet. The volume and scale may, of course, vary, but not the relations between the terms of the 'civilization-barbarism-savagery' framework (Leroi-Gourhan). To take only one example, a small quantity of resources is removed from the total reserve supply (barbarism-savagery) and drained towards a centre where it can be transformed (civilization). The historians of history will say that this is a purely formal invariant, and the historians of science will say that it an unverifiable hypothesis. None can deny, however, that what distinguished political activity from technical and scientific activity was its lack of awareness of innovations or discoveries. We might as well say that 'there are no lessons to be learned from history'. Each moment in the political history of societies is a degree zero: each generation starts from the beginning. It simultaneously invents and repeats: identification hysteria, collective hallucinations, sectarian schizophrenia, defensive paranoia, interpretation mania, and so on. Just as an adolescent learns how to make love without being taught and is still no 'better' at it than his grandparents, so each social era reinvents politics as though it had never existed, and it is still as problematic as ever it was. The affinity of political power with both mythology and eroticism stems of course from the fact that the time of myths and the time of eras share the same structure of repetition. Power maniacs and sex maniacs share the same sterile fascination with sterility. In both cases, and for the same reasons, the poverty of possible invention leads to an obsession. Just as one wants to 'see' what a man and a woman can do with their bodies, precisely because everything imaginable has been done hundreds of millions of times over the last hundred thousand years, so the other wants to 'have a go' come what may, precisely because all possible combinations in the game between power and non-power have already been tried, and because the game is at once over and unfinished. This circle is both disquieting and fascinating and may lead to either vice or virtue. The only necessary aspect of the political circle is its form: the individual can choose the direction and length of his journey. The freedom of historical agents occupies the space that separates the repetition of laughter from the repetition of tears, parody from tragedy. The problematic character of their freedom arises because it is identical with the 'irony of history'. We can do the opposite of what we intended. We can be certain that we are repeating something, but there is no way of knowing in advance what is going to be repeated (whether it will be Napoleon I or Napoleon III, Danton or Caussidière, De Gaulle or Boulanger, Lenin or Pol Pot). It would be dishonest to complain, as someone once did, that the dead weigh like a nightmare on the minds of the living—'tradition' as a spell to summon up the dead of history—without adding that the living have the capacity to choose the ghosts they would like to see in the present.

Whether we like it or not, of course, this conception echoes certain milestones long ago erected on the road to knowledge. In fact it prides itself in not being new. If, by some misfortune, it were completely new, the chances are that it would be completely wrong. For, during the seven thousand years that sedentary men have ruled over others, with assistants to write down the mental reflection of this state of affairs, the law of large numbers and simple common sense suggest that the nature of the ideological, religious or political phenomenon has already been suspected or unravelled time and time again. So the sighs of 'It's all been said before' are quite welcome, as are the shocked references to the Classics and the ritual 'It's just Comte, Bergson, Durkheim, Leroi-Gourhan, Mircea Eliade, etc.' (or, in more sarcastic vein, 'Bossuet, Joseph de Maistre, Maurras'). Politics comes straight from the Bible, and so on. Critical assimilation of the great works of the past is not simply a matter of politeness. It is also a precautionary measure, given that you repeat nothing so readily as the things you know least well. Such studies are by definition interminable, no matter who undertakes them, and it would be more than presumptuous ever to say that you have finished them. Besides, it is always difficult for an author to draw the line between what he realizes he has borrowed and what he thinks he has contributed. Just leave me the right to claim that I have shifted a few lines between well-demarcated fields and traced a few links between familiar notions and others that would benefit from being a little more familiar. Even the half-educated will not fail to produce a flood of objections or jokes in response to this laconic survey. The most obvious ones are to do with methodology: 'How dare an "educated" man still talk about politics in general or about religion as a single category? How can he place such distinctive realities as a queue at the butcher's, a political party and a modern nation-state under the catch-all heading of group?' The aim of this book is to reply to them methodically and in detail.

Basically, the ambition of such an approach is no less extreme than its humility. The one implies the other, and they can both be expressed by a single word: Critique. The essence of any critique may be defined as the rational establishment of discriminatory principles, regardless of whether the distinction to be drawn in between true and false, as in a critique of statements, or between the operational and the inoperative, as in the present critique of procedures. The implications of a Critique of Political Reason are therefore neither positive nor negative: its aim is to grasp the limits inherent in any political undertaking. In that sense, it is in its very nature to frustrate desire and to *curb enthusiasm*. If ideologies exist in order to give us reasons to hope, a rational critique of the notion of ideology will put forward reasons to despair (of the former). But the search for causes is as alien to the choice of ends as it is to the inclinations of the heart—besides, it is abstentionist in tone, neither for nor against. The only tangible result of an investigation into the conditions of possibility (of knowledge or behaviour) is the definite exclusion of certain possibilities. It is to be expressed only in the shape of *You cannot* (to talk like Popper). For example: you cannot rationalize your choice except in terms of an irrational first principle. You cannot conceive of a society that is both viable and open—that is, without a territory. You cannot conceive of a territory that is not delineated. You cannot close a territory—be it ideal or material, symbolic or political—without submitting it to extra-territorial jurisdiction by the very act of circumscribing it. At a more trivial level, you cannot throw yourself into an action without believing in something, and you cannot believe in something without believing in someone. If you claim to be replacing an 'outdated mythology' which is 'obviously bankrupt' with a new set of correct ideas, it is as well to be aware that your ideas cannot spread 'to the masses' without being transformed into their opposite (into myths). You cannot hope that your 'comrades, rally ... the Internationale unites the human race' will some day have an effect. For the idea of a generic group is like that of a circle without a circumference: it presupposes an inside without an outside, a whole without totalization, a position with no opposition. The only International that will unite the human race is the international telephone directory. We could go on for ever with similar occlusions—fragments of a proscriptive rather than prescriptive discourse. It does not stipulate any particular kind of conduct nor offer any positive model. It does not point towards a morality, but to a political *discipline* in the Kantian sense of the word: the determination of the limits placed on the use of a faculty. This discipline is articulated with a *canon* of political reason—a set of a priori principles, one of the first being incompleteness, which restrict the legitimate (possible) use of the aptitude of human groups to act and organize collectively.

This self-limitation by means of a theoretical distinction between what is possible and what is impossible derives from the general form of a 'critique'. Normally, it may be summarized as follows: this is what you can legitimately expect of political activity without being quite predictably disappointed. But a Critique of Political Reason, a system of guaranteed disappointments, is distinguished from the general paradigm by two paradoxical and aggravating features which mean that, by virtue of its object, it is an 'unhappy' critique in two senses.

1. The prime adversary of classical criticism is dogmatism.

The opposition between the two is as complete as that between thesis and antithesis. Every advance made by the former is regarded as a retreat on the part of the latter. The textbooks praise the Kantians for having routed the old speculative metaphysics through a critique of the illegitimate use of the faculty of reason. Current opinion congratulates the Popperians for having demarcated the positive sciences from the new metaphysics (Marxism, psychoanalysis, etc.) through the criterion of falsifiability. The peculiarity of a Critique of Political Reason is that it seeks to demonstrate not the falsity of dogmatism as such but its legitimacy as a condition of the existence of human aggregates. It tests received ideas against reality, not truth: its touchstone is not 'true or false', but 'feasible or not feasible', 'realizable or not realizable'. It thereby establishes the transcendental necessity of illusion if political realities are to be constituted. Classical criticism has performed its task once it has proved the erroneous character of a system of propositions: the illusion is no sooner demonstrated than dispelled, and illusion makes way for truth. The task of political criticism, by contrast, is to establish why no demonstration of logical inconsistency can refute systems of belief. It is meaningless to say that the ideological or religious sphere is part of the sphere of 'non-falsifiable' propositions sheltered from the refutation of experience. The problem is to discover why things that should in theory cease to be (considered legitimate) cannot but continue to be (objects of loyalty). The 'truth' of the non-falsifiable is its efficacity, its capacity to be actively integrated as the principle of collective cohesion. Any theory of political organization that does not seek a consoling function must take the organizational matrix of stable groups, a pre-reflective natural property independent of the mind, as the very matrix of its discipline. 'Nature means the existence of things in so far as they are determined by universal laws.' Just as there are laws of nature which are themselves contingent, politics has its own nature and its own equally contingent laws which can no more be deduced from a pre-existing idea than can living beings. (The concept of the living is within the living being itself.) Nature cannot be put on trial and does not have to excuse itself for anything. The nature of a human group is that which makes it what it is. There are many types of group, but there are not many ways for a stable, organized group to go on existing. Since ultimately, in political matters, 'you do what you can and not what you want', a critique of political reason is in the same position vis à vis its object as a geologist vis à vis a fold in the earth's crust. In that sense it is legitimate to say that the high-point of 'dogmatism' in France is 4,807 metres above sea level, given that no one can found the existence of Mont Blanc in reason. When the metaphysician was asked what should be thought of the view at the foot of the Alps, he cautiously replied: 'Das ist'.

In the social sphere, critical rationalism quite naturally leads to a respectable relativism which may be either offensive or resigned according to time and temperament. The Anglo-Saxon positivist school, for instance, proudly claims to have humbled the 'secular religions' of the twentieth century by confronting them with the project of prudently reformist and knowingly agnostic management. Now, if we were to find that the 'argument from authority' was the a priori condition of possibility of the most minimal exercise of authority, that the absolute enters into societies because of their very limitation and de-finition, that their finite nature itself condemns them to an endless search for an infinite founder; if, in-short, we discovered that the political as such is ultimately religious in nature, we would be in a position to see the renunciation of utopia as the height of utopianism and the weary wisdom of 'positive' scepticism as the shallowest of follies. We may as well say it now: the replacement of 'global world-views' with mere 'social engineering' (Popper) based upon 'fragmentary repair' and 'limited readjustments' may well answer the needs of reason and the heart, but it cannot stand up to an objective examination of the facts of history and the logic of the social. That is unfortunate yet inescapable. We may deplore that the the world continually goes against the advice of enlightened sages and experts, but we can no longer blame the devil, the veil of home-grown or 'imported' ideologies or even the mental illness of perverse trouble-makers (prophets and leaders) if fanatics all over the world persist in ignoring the 'voice of reason' and the most elementary calculation of the comparative social costs of fanaticism and tolerance. Perhaps it is time we asked whether such baneful stubbornness corresponds to some objective law and whether it is the deaf or the preachers (moral, theoretical or both) who are the more insane.

Under these circumstances, there will always be some offspring of a Protestant pastor to wail: 'Hell is politics'. For the various religious universes are distinguished from one another more by infernal rather than by heavenly features. The pathos has to be undercut at once by saying 'Is that all?' even if it does mean spoiling the dramatic effect. 'Hell' is a relatively constant part of human reality, but not all of it: 'politics isn't everything'. Mathematical theorems and musical melodies, for instance, legitimately escape the jurisdiction of the group; and although scientific and artistic activities may be related to political activity by the condition in which they are practised, their principles and results are nevertheless very different. One can identify ideal and real objects that are not at stake (in power games) nor subject to appropriation, just as human relations other than relations of force or domination do exist outside the group. Still in terms of myth, a summary profit-and-loss account would have to conclude that there is a purgatory in both cases: a mean hypothesis with a high statistical probability but a low level of dramatic interest. The latter depends, as we all know, on the scale chosen by the observer: the closer it comes to individual elements, the greater the dramatic value. 'One death is a tragedy. A thousand deaths is a statistic'.

The reader will, I trust, have understood that religious metaphors strike me as quite inappropriate to a rational description of religious phenomena.

2. The second paradox derives directly from the first.

In its philosophical sense—as opposed to current usage—the term 'critique' implies not so much suspicion as the will of a primordial and final optimism. It is exhilarating to see a new 'command' replace the old 'obey'. But what promise is held out by an analysis for which we are not in command of the command function? Man is not the hidden sun of his political system but a satellite in its field of gravitation. A critique would be standing on its head if it attacked as imaginary the comforting thought of a great overseeing regulator (the old master of the game of the world or of language 'games') who distributes prizes from on high. But we are not the masters of the political game—the more we think of ourselves as players, the more we become toys. Critical idealism articulates a cry of political victory in philosophical terms: 'Now it is our turn, we are the legislators of nature.' Kantian criticism: 'We are already the guarantors of the real and the true, but we did not know it.' Logical positivism: 'We will be the guarantors of the real and the true tomorrow, once we have learned to construct our sentences properly.' One gives us liberation in the form of the written word; the other a rallying cry. Each of these critical gestures was spontaneously experienced as a revolution, as a war of reconquest against the Infidels of Knowledge. The aim of a materialist critique, however, is to articulate the end of philosophical triumphalism in political terms. A critique of political reason does not claim to be winning back an object for a subject dishonestly dispossessed of his rights: it sees political practice as a practice without a subject, in which we are constituted as subjects or as actors by the practice itself. Still less will it bring its thing-in-itself before any heavenly court, whether the Court of Theory or the Court of Transcendental Subject. Is that counter-revolution in the Copernican revolution, or involution in the evolution of a petty-bourgeois philosopher? What does it matter if it is ignored, mocked or stigmatized? The only innovation intended is to apply the materialist principle of the primacy of practice over theory to the field of political theory itself, historical materialism included. The aim of this 'hyper-materialist' approach is not to put the theoretical world to rights by handing over power to a newly discovered true theory of politics, but to place all political theory, past and present, under the jurisdiction of existing practices that have been restored to their own logic and reinstated in their own rights. We are not asking realilty to conform to our decrees, but asking our decrees to conform to reality—and theoretical affluence to the reality of its own degeneration into 'ideology'. Questioning the scientific validity of ideologies was one thing—and it has been done. Scientifically establishing the validity of ideologies devoid of scientific value is another—and it remains to be done. What does reality tell us? Simply this: just as 'denunciation' of the State never prevented it from existing or growing stronger (by multiplication in the East and division in the West), no 'exposure' of the Churches, magistratures and theologies underlying the most profane forms of modern collective life has yet resulted in the secularization of the modern world. For since it has not been asked why Churches, magistratures and theologies actually exist, or if they can ever cease to exist, the 'unmasking' operation has simply substituted one faith for another (Father Christmas for the Bogeyman, Père Ubu* for our Holy Father the Pope).

It is still too soon to say whether political science, when it finally sees the light of day, will look like medicine or astronomy (like a technique located at the intersection of several sciences or like a science located at the intersection of several techniques). It is well known that, ever since Ancient Greece, the vocabulary of politics has always owed a lot to the medical arts and that the most austerely positivist leaders have never rejected the halo of the healer. But the point about doctors is that they cure their patients, whereas our party leaders simply administer the illness. It is by no means obvious that they can do anything else. The fantasy of a healthy socie-

---

* Père Ubu: the monstrous tyrant in Alfred Jarry's *Ubu Roi*. Trs. note.

ty, safe from crises and fevers, echoes the idea of a society with no specialized political personnel, in which the State withers of its own accord and leaders return to the plough *proprio motu*. Without even considering whether the dream of a 'normal' society is the height of perversion, let us simply point out that it is a dream. No one can say what a sick or healthy society might be, but we can all tell the difference between a sick man and a healthy man. In political matters, the criteria of 'normality' are provided by observation, while the criteria of the organic are given along with the organism under examination.

The progress of knowledge sometimes advances our awareness of our own ignorance. Similarly, an improved understanding of political phenomena does not guarantee that we will be able to control the phenomena of power, authority or personification, lessen the ascendancy of thaumaturges or reduce the number of rainmakers. It may be that the science of political bodies will be as powerless in the face of its object as the science of heavenly bodies. In that case, there will be a certain aesthetic satisfaction in seeing the similarity between the oldest and the newest of sciences, but, more prosaically, a certain bitterness in seeing that an individual at the peak of knowledge (in order of epistemological difficulty) is no more capable of modifying the group to which he belongs than an astronomer is capable of altering the course of the planets.

Psychoanalysis, originally an offshoot of empirical medicine, has been elevated, or diverted, to the status of a speculative astronomy. Although it is an uneasy compromise between therapy and hermeneutics, it still has some claim as a cure. Defenders of the Freudian heritage plead for an astronomy which, in the cause of neuroses, may serve as a medical function: its detractors attack an astronomy which, like any other magical rite, has curative powers despite itself. Whether the relief found by certain analysands is attributed to the action of truth or to their belief in what sounds like truth, the fact remains that the analyst does sometimes contrive to slip between the stars of his patient's psychical system, indicating their orbits and the dangers of collision and finally teaching him to slip through them too. Forms of individual psychotherapy and even group therapy do exist, but it is unlikely that there will ever be any sociotherapy for societies. The exploration of the political unconscious is a much more thankless task, as it provides no remedies and promises no cure. Indeed, by destroying the illusion of social pathology, it calls on the aberrant to account for the normal, the extreme for the 'golden mean'. Whereas religious alienation increases our capacity for political intervention, psychological alienation diminishes our mental capacities. Religion may be a sickness, but we have to live with it: a cure would kill us. We may take Socrates as our patron saint, but certainly not Aesculapius. Our approach proceeds from the *know thyself* alone, without any additives. Being the pure effect of an ethics of knowledge, it restricts itself to applying the Socratic precept to the *we* (the ego of societies) in order 'to see what happens'. Needless to say, it does not offer its adepts much social recognition; nor does it guarantee them the honours of hemlock.

The first explorers of the individual unconscious were rejected by the medical corporation as *charlatans*. In the militant order, the epithet *reactionary* would seem to serve the same purpose, the contrast with 'progressive' giving this term its meaning. I hold that if words have any sense, it is as inept to talk about *progress* in political behaviour as it would be to talk about progress in human sexual behaviour or in the law of gravity. The living lay wreathes by the remains of their great men (Lenin, Lincoln, De Gaulle, Jaurès); the men of the future will still dream at night because they will have the same drives and compulsions that we have. The speed at which apples fall to the ground will not, even in the distant future, be noticeably altered by the transition from 'state monopoly capitalism' to 'libertarian communism under workers' control'. There is neither reaction nor progress in this line of evolution, only real and unreal things. Roses, for example, are real: the gesture of covering the dead with the living in order to denegate the inorganic says more about the nature of political need than all the electoral programmes of great men buried or cremated. The idea that the political future of mankind can contain nothing more than its past and that, logically, it makes no more sense to talk about a 'political revolution' (leaving aside astronomy) than to say that 'the number five is blue' is unlikely to be thought progressive. By the same criteria, it cannot be called 'reactionary' either. That would be to confuse a conception of politics with a political conception. A Critique of Political Reason can tell me what I cannot do, but not what I must do. It states the impossible, not the desirable (or the detestable). Anyone who looks there for the outline of a 'position', and a fortiori a 'line', risks being profoundly mistaken.

My ideas are not my ideal. My only friends are those who share my ideal and loathe my ideas. It would be an understatement to say that I dislike the conception articulated in this book: I find it repulsive and contemptible. However, it seems to me the only one that conforms to the available data, even though it is in contradiction with my own practical interests. If it is neither useful nor pleasant, can it claim the value of truth? The fact that a theory is unpleasant is probably not enough to make it true, but the predicament in which it lands me suggests that it is not exactly an 'ideology'. In real terms, I have nothing to gain and everything to lose by it. My present knowledge clashes with my convictions and seems to refute them. The knowledge I have gained of the objective natural conditions of political or religious conviction does not, however, prevent me from keeping my convictions intact—including the conviction that theoretical knowledge is not decisive in such matters. If I may be allowed to sound presumptuous (but I have already taken your permission for granted), I would put it like this: 'I am sure that this theory is true and I believe it to be of no consequence. It is in any case incapable of providing anyone with a code of conduct. And I am sure that I am right to think it so.' Let me explain.

The problem can in no sense be inserted into the ritual of 'setting the record straight' (normally at the foot of the page) whereby an ideology declines all responsibility for the 'actions of certain agitators and fanatics' who claim, without justification, to be acting in its name. That little game, inscribed in the programme of the works and days of hegemony, would be neither original nor serious, not least because thought is never the private property of a 'thinker'. It belongs to all those who use it and is no more than the ever open sum of all the uses to which it is put. Nor can the problem be posed in terms of the neutrality of a scientific statement towards its concrete applications (not that the theses that follow have any rightful claim to the dignity of a science). A chemical study of combustible combination can, of course, be used for anything: setting fire to a temple, burning the Reichstag, the Tuilleries, Joan of Arc, yourself or a forest in the south of France. But no one would con-

clude that Lavoisier should be tried as the intellectual accomplice of
Herostratsu, Goering, Louise Michel, Gauchon, Jan Palach or the
last pyromaniac to come along: the good or bad use made of fire
has nothing to do with the unfortunate tax farmer's *Mémoires sur
la chaleur*. Anyone who tries to say not what is good but what is
true, acting as an explorer rather than a dispenser of justice,
deserves neither such excessive honours nor such a bad reputation.
His reply to the apologists of the established order will not be 'I
have no hand in it', but 'I'm nowhere to be found in it, and nor are
you?' The subject of the enunciation is absent from his statements.
He is not claiming the right to contradict himself in advance, but
simply pointing out that he is under no obligation to make his acts
conform to his concepts. The man who commits himself to an action and the man who theorizes the general conditions of action are
not the same. That duality should be cherished dearly, like a secret
weapon.

The real question comes down to this: is it possible to work
backwards from the political to politics, and if so, how? All that
the author of a critique of this kind can say is, 'Yes, in theory it is
possible. How? I have nothing to say about that. It's not my
business.' The practical difficulties of the transition are not a valid
theoretical objection. At best they are the objection of a man of action to theoretical activity itself. In short, it is possible to think that
a classless, stateless society is a logically inconsistent Robinson
Crusoe story, and to believe it crucial to fight for the appearance of
such a society. This will be so even though —or because— it cannot
be 'justified' logically.

This question echoes and amplifies a very pertinent objection
that was addressed to me from the left in connection with *Le
Scribe*. 'Your theoretical model of the scribe as a servant who
relays the power of the Prince—Carpaccio's ambassador—leaves
no room for the revolutionary intellectual. Yet throughout the ages
a certain number of scribes, whatever they were called, have refused to go along with their function, choosing either impotence or an
uneven struggle against the dominant powers in the name of a different set of values. It is such a constant and obvious feature of
history that it has to be seen as a real *social fact*. You don't take
that into account. Given that you define yourself as a scribe, the
definition you give of your trade should logically have prevented

you from writing this or any other book.' I am quite willing to accept the evidence: a communicating animal often prefers to retain the integrity of his message rather than to use the possibilities for optimal communication that the ruling class of the moment puts at his disposal. But that goes without saying. There is nothing heroic, still less abnormal, about the rebel who violates his own norms or refuses to act in accordance with his objective material interests. This man in the street simply illustrates a specific difference: our ability to take the losing side, to play loser wins in our own way. Biologists are agreed that man is 'the species which most rapidly adapts to all environments' (Jacques Ruffié) and that his adaptability finds its expression in culture, the sum of adaptive responses to his environment.[10] But this elasticity also implies the *capacity not to adapt*. Its use is called morality and, depending upon the circumstances and individuals involved, may range from annoyance to real anger, from the sublime to the ridiculous. 'Better to die in your feet than live on your knees': it is not a matter of indifference that the highest motto of moral action was taken up by La Pasionaria at the height of a civil war (in Spain). Of all living species, there is one and one alone for whom life is not the supreme value in all circumstances. Without being the monstrous faculty of the human species, the capacity for sacrifice makes *homo sapiens* the one species of animal open to acts which, 'moral' 'for us' are monstrous from the norm-perspective of living creatures. 'Political animal' could therefore be translated as 'responsible animal'—that is to say, capable of conduct 'idiotic' in both senses of the word: peculiar (to a zoological branch) and absurd (biologically inept).

In the present state of affairs in our hemisphere, one historical sub-species stands out by its exceptional failure to adapt and its unreasonable conduct: the militant for whom 'socialist emancipation' is both a password and a myth around which to mobilize (a sign and an ideal). A line of descent is primarily a memory, a transmission system and a shared language. The line in question, just to mention the marker-posts, began with Babeuf and did not die out with Jaurès. There are of course other families which, at various times, have been the honour and horror of the species (what makes the one possible makes the other inevitable): the Catholic, Muslim, Jewish, Protestant and pacifist families, and so on. But since chance had it that I mingled with the socialist tribe, this has served and will continue to serve as my point of reference and, dare I say it, as my point of insertion. If our only choice is between equally absurd loyalties, that is my loyalty and I will take care not to explain it. Who could explain it? Why did Babeuf choose the guillotine? Why did Blanqui choose life imprisonment? Why did Jaurès sit with his back to the door? Why did Trotsky choose to preach in the desert? Perhaps, I will be told, because he was politically defeated by Stalin. But why did he choose to be beaten instead of asking quarter and, like so many others, siding with the majority? Why did Politzer and Cavaillès choose the firing squad?* And why, even in France today, do exiled militants, men and women alike, leave their children and a comfortable life to face almost certain death in their home country, often not even sure that it will serve any purpose? No one and nothing forces them to acts in this way.

The theoretician able to answer such questions would have access to the mainspring of history, but his solution could not be articulated in theoretical terms without a lapse into indecent terminology. Just as aesthetics begins and ends with the work of art, so does ethics begin and end with action. Action is always singular and discourse is always general. In that sense, Ethic and Logos are like fire and water. A critique of political reason displays pertinence without performance; political practices reveal non-pertinent performances. If it designates something that can be neither subsumed under a yet-to-be-discovered universal (with the help of what Kant calls a reflective judgement) nor deduced from a pre-given universal (by a judgement of determination), an ethical system would destroy itself by taking the form of a critique. When it comes to matters of conduct, the example takes precedence over the law and the exception merges with the rule, thereby making imitation or mechanical reproduction impossible. The supreme example is an action that stands the silent test of illogicality. Act in such a way that the maxim governing your action can never be taken as a universal law! Thus it is true that we can only talk about the non-essential, and that any action improperly termed heroic contains within it a call for theoretical abstention which confronts reason

---

* Jean Cavaillès: professor of psychology and resistance leader, tortured and killed by the Gestapo. Trs. note.

with its own limits. Silence is the hallmark of the ethical, that land of secrecy in which chatter is the worst form of obscenity. Hence, no doubt, the nausea that comes over us whenever we hear a speaker pronouncing on something which, if it existed within himself, would make his speech redundant: that something we call a sense of values.

The reserve imposed on theory points towards discretion or a work of art, or even both. Let us remember that the art that gives meaning to tangible forms has the ability to say something without speaking, and that it is more thought-provoking than any abstract thought. A novel, a film, a poem or a video-tape may in that sense be better equipped to go to the limits of the challenge implicit in an action, that series of desperate actions which, in Braque's phrase, allow us to go on hoping. Film-makers, painters, story-tellers, musicians, all thoses who create unique images without laws or concepts may be in a better position than philosophers to understand men of action—those madmen to whom meaning is entrusted and who, in order to save it, fall one after another, dragged into the abyss that divides reason from political action.

SECTION I
The Logic of Appearance

1

The Function of an Illusion

1. The Value of an Obstacle

Of all the recurrent features that indicate the backwardness of political science, the most virulent is the notion of *ideology*. It is a vague idea that passes for a clear idea, an animist entity for a scientific concept, a speculative ersatz for a datum of observation. Presumably the word would not exercise such a *natural* seduction over our minds and give us such an impression of *immediate* transparence if it were not borne out by the rather ill-defined yet self-evident experience: 'Ideas play a role in the course of history'.

Can we continue to think on an overdraft when the notion we are crediting, precisely because it absorbs the *how* into a pre-given *why*, is the one thing that prevents us from thinking that self-evident reality? As we shall see, the notion is untrustworthy because it obscures that self-evidence: it has the virtue of indicating that information may under certain circumstances, trigger certain types of behaviour, but the vice of making inexplicable the truly decisive problem of symbolic efficacity. Leaving aside all the arguments about priority, the most dangerous product ever elaborated by the chemistry of the intellect is not 'history' but 'ideology'. It masks the reality of history (its habit of trampling our bodies without going through our heads).

'Ideology' may well be an obstacle on the road to knowledge of the political, but we should not leap over it too hastily. Nothing is more precious than an obstacle. 'The problem of scientific knowledge has to be posed in terms of obstacles' (Bachelard). Here as elsewhere, truth is a corrected error or nothing at all. The author of *La Formation de l'esprit scientifique* tells us that 'the revelations of the real are always recurrent' and that 'we can only know by going against a previous body of knowledge, by destroying ill-constructed knowledge'. The very subtitle of the book—*Psychanalyse de la connaissance objective*—should be enough to remind us that the construction of a concept proceeds through analysis of the myth that hampers its formation or through examination of the affective values that cling to it and make it so tenacious. Thinking political reason therefore means that we have to think the most familiar of our counter-thoughts through to the end, plunging into it as though it were a tunnel.

First question : What is the function of the notion of ideology? Who uses it, and how? What role does it play in the representation of contemporary history on the public and scientific stage?

All the fascinating debates about 'ideology' between philosophers, anthropologists, epistemologists and sociologists do not necessarily imply that the object actually exists. You can have excellent debates about nothing. It would not be the first time that a pseudo-object has been eroded within a system of knowledge that is in other ways positive, or even alongside basic discoveries that have been verified. The history of the natural and physical sciences is full of ghosts that were perfectly consistent until they simply vanished at a higher stage of knowledge: for example, the *animal spirits* in Descartes's physiology, *ether* in Newton's mechanics, *phlogiston* in chemistry before Lavoisier or, closer to home, Brown's organic *incitability* in the medical practice of the nineteenth century.[1] The invention, whether a being, a relation or a property, comes to occupy a blank square in the descriptive grid or, to be more accurate, it objectively exploits a subjective inadequacy in knowledge. After all, the human mind performed prodigies of logic and displayed astonishing metaphysical profundity in debating the nature of God, but no one would now advance them as an argument for his existence unless they wished to use theology itself as an accepted proof. What is true of the 'religious sciences' is also true of the social sciences: research is no proof that there is anything to be found (where the researchers are looking for it).

Let us be more specific. Ideology 'exists' as an empirical given that finds its incarnation in commodities, pamphlets and handbooks, in civil servants and education, in buildings and letters of gold, blood or lead—depending upon the time and place. Ideology 'exists' as a speculative theme: there are concepts, definitions and theories of ideology. No one is denying that men have ideas or that every culture displays systems of ideas, arranged in a certain order, which may or may not be transmitted in written form. But, even taken together, those two statements produce neither an analytic tool nor a real object. Astrology exists, complete with rites, treatises, merchants and a practical materiality, and no one denies that there are stars in the sky or that constellations or solid bodies with fixed and stable orbits may be seen in our galaxy. The tangible materiality of the planetary system does lend a definite credibility to horoscopes, astral houses and astral themes. The systems of symbolic representation noted in the history of civilizations has done not a little for the rise of the category of ideology in the firmament of the social sciences (or in the hell of common sense). However, that neither confirms nor invalidates the scientific objectivity of the notions that have been advanced to organize each set of phenomena, regardless of the halo effect. For the sake of rigour, we will have to content ourselves with this simple statement: on the one hand we have a series of observable phenomena like phlegmona, fires, attraction, constellations in the sky and systems that interpret the historico-political world. On the other hand, we have a set of rational apparatuses such as organic incitability, phlogiston, ether, astrology and ideology. True, the latter term is still in use. But the entire history of the sciences argues against such projections of 'primary' experience, and any resemblance, mimetic or metaphoric, between a phenomenon and its description has never been a good omen. Before the living could become an object of science, for instance, it was necessary to cease believing in life as an autonomous realm and an explanatory principle. Why, in theory, should it be so scandalous to challenge the category of 'ideology' in order to elucidate the social efficacity of 'ideas'?

Why the dyptych of market and school? After all, anyone who uses the notion of ideology is, *volens nolens*, playing on two registers at once: on science and ethics. As an artisan of knowledge he is speaking the truth; as a righter of wrongs he is talking justice. The fact that the word has two meanings has done a great deal for its prestige and constantly serves to renew it. In its theoretical acceptation, it is the antonym of adequate knowledge; in its polemical or practical acceptation, it is the antonym of integrity. The ambiguity is itself disturbing. 'For knowledge that wishes to attain objectivity, any trace of value-thinking is a bad sign. A psychoanalysis of objective knowledge has to do more than transmute all values: it must completely rid scientific culture of all values.'[2]

Before essaying a precise appraisal of *ideology*, we would like to be able to draw a careful distinction between its two faces: stigma and concept, deprecation and description. We would like to *neutralize* it by stripping it of its semantic values, so that we may fix it as one thing *or* the other. In order to understand what the word means, however we may have to let it enjoy the bad faith that enables it to be what it is not and not to be what it is. It may be necessary to take this dubious character at its word, even though it functions now as a neutral concept now as a badge of infamy, even though it sometimes denotes a population of discourses and sometimes connotes their critical and moral worthlessness. Without warning or any break in step, it can suddenly change from signifying misrecognition to denouncing malpractice.

2. The Beast and the Process of its Creation

Political sociologists unanimously deplore the 'disastrous confusion' that reigns in the language of politics, above all in the definition of 'ideology' as 'a concept which, being infinitely more politicized than that of culture, threatens to become dogmatic'.[3] 'Science' complains about the concept because it is mobile and frenetic. That ought to be a cause for rejoicing, since, far from being sterile, its mobility is, so to speak, pregnant with its own truth. The concept 'dog' does not bark, so why should political notions be involved in politics? Let us look at them more closely in order to see *how* we become involved in politics. The positive counter-effect of the redundancy is that the collective gives itself away by the manner in which it talks about itself. When it says the word 'ideology', it screams. Not immediately: the pitch rises gradually. It rises in a crescendo as it moves from the qualificative to the substantive and then to the substance.

Now, to *qualify* a proposition as ideological is to disqualify it as, at one extreme, too ethnically, socially or class-specific to have any claim to universal validity; and, at the other extreme, an 'over-metaphysical' product of an illegitimate abstraction, too speculative to have any positivity. But if the proposition in question does not serve the interests of truth, it certainly serves those of the speaker: the reason for putting it forward is not, therefore, to be found in the words themselves. Although suspicion immediately falls on the author, no sentence can be passed at this level because premeditation has not been established. He is suspicious, but not strictly dishonest. We may well be dealing with 'a socially determined illusion'. He must therefore be given the benefit of the doubt.

The theoretical claim that the statements of false consciousness are a form of mystified consciousness then produces material evidence in the shape of a *substantialized object*. The establishment of a corpus reveals more than just deliberate intent: it reveals an attempt at public mystification, a maleficent cause as well as a misrecognition effect. So we leap from the *modus operandi* to the *opus operatum*, and 'ideology'. The word does not have any moral value or pejorative implications when it designates a system of signification that accompanies a historically given set of social practices. If you reconstitute the 'tripartite Indo-European ideology' (Dumezil), the 'funerary ideology of pre-classical Greece' (Colloque d'Ischia) or even 'contemporary Arab ideology' (Laroui), you are a historian, not a judge. You are deciphering signs in order to establish organizational laws, not degrees of responsibility. You may be trying to go beyond appearances by organizing them around a hidden principle, but you are not trying to thwart a strategem or a feint, to break down a disguise or to unmask an enemy agent. But when you begin to take the substantive out of context, using it as a rhetorical weapon, you have implicitly moved from error to guilt, from trying the thought to trying the thinker. And that dubious no-man's-land midway between ethics and logic is the field upon which discourses of imputation manoeuvre.

It goes without saying that when I denounce bad faith in another's discourse, I do so in all good faith. 'Ideology'—a word reserved for my adversary's ideas, for ideas I no longer believe in, but never for those I profess at the moment—is at once an effect and a marker of critical distance. Like the horizon of our lost illusions, ideology dogs our steps as we change our illusions, following us at a safe distance just as superstition dogs the footsteps of the true religion (which always refers to the religion it has replaced as superstition). The marker of superiority bears witness to the fact that we are no longer dupes, or rather that we are sufficiently distanced to see the motives behind the stated aims of the other's discourse—'a discourse made for something and made by something else' (Serres). So a Marxist will talk of 'structuralist ideology' and a structuralist will talk of 'Marxist ideology'. Tit for tat. The implicit suggestion of deceit, which automatically exempts me from the same criticism, always comes in useful.

When an *independent substance*, complete with appetites and aspirations, emerges from a qualified substantive, the 'ideological' misrepresentation of the real becomes a real living being with desires of its own. The personificatiion was originally timid, almost rhetorical. But as 'it is in the nature of ideology to *aspire* to become propaganda' (Gabriel Marcel), it has since become triumphal. The prosopopaea becomes a hallucination, the entity an autonomous power. The essence is hypostatized into an existent which, when divorced from its conditions of existence, rapidly becomes a super-fetish and a superpower: Moloch. We are no longer on profane ground here. The transformation of the tool of demystification into a monstrous mythology takes political discourse back to animism and its authors from the status of a rhetor to that of a sorcerer.

It is at this final stage of speculative abstraction that the fetishized notion of ideology begins to reveal its dual function of exorcism and censorship.

Political dementia revolves around a double helix: the facts and the interpretation of the facts. This stroke of good luck allows us to advance the hypothesis that the casting of contemporary political mechanisms into the outer darkness of ideology stems from an inversion of the political unconscious symptomatic of the darkness into which the political mechanism itself is still plunged. The obscurantism of the magico-religious assumptions that lie beneath this bundle of discourses is not visible to us because the darkness in which we live (when we live together) cannot, by definition, be visible to us: a man who is aware of his own ignorance is no longer ignorant. The *we* projects the negative or fearful forces rejected by its conscious mind into a hypostatized the devil, masked or not. The theme of 'ideology as source of all our woes' thus works as an agent of censorship: it prevents a painful inner reality from gaining access to our system of representation.

To sum up, we know strictly nothing, about the collective, apart from the fact that it does us harm. The cause of the harm escapes us, but our exasperation is growing and the need to find a name for the intolerable is becoming more and more urgent. The natural reflex is to look for a guilty party, and that is enough to find one. Ideology is the scapegoat for all our modern ills. The prosecution speech is a cry for vengeance whose aim is not to *explain* but to relieve. It is both an expression of our collective distress and a protest against it. But since it does not attack the real causes, it can in no way diminish that distress. The phantasy of ideology as a *diabolus ex machina* is as unlikely to free the group from its religious nature as the 'oppressed creature's sighs are to free the creature from its oppression'.

The execution rites obey a juridical logic that is both archaic and (therefore) ever more contemporary.

3. The Figure of the Trial

The phantasy of the *trial* is an archetype common to all these ideodramas. Ideally, history as a whole should be put on trial. In the meantime, cases are prepared and the accused are questioned in an attempt to find their weak points. It will be noted that the figure of judgement is also the prototype of religious ideology: original sin and the last judgement: sin, expiation and redemption. If we look at the philosophical literature on ideology, it is immediately obvious that it plays on two rhetorical registers: on the one hand, philippics and speeches for the prosecution: on the other, imprecations and homilies. A double shiver runs through the court: for the revelation is also an accusation. There is nothing didactic or analytic about it. All these efforts admonish us for our sins and urge us to examine our consciences, something we have not done for far too long. Inspiring shame and not reflection, intimidating rather than convincing, using evocative imagery rather than trying to explain things rationally—these are the marks of sacred discourse. The tone of juridical practice and religious practice is similar and derives from their common essence and their essentialism. It is well known that the institutional separation of the two took a long time to develop in the history of civilization. Condemnation sounds very like damnation. The judge's summing up sounds very like the last judgement.

First observation: the two meanings of 'judgement'—assertion and sentence—correspond ideally to two constant tasks of the makers of discourse. Provisionally, we can identify the *professional imputer*, with his binary code of 'thanks to this/blame so and so' as the practitioner, and the *professional 'explainer'*, with his 'this is governed by a law/I don't know anything about that', as the theoretician. (In that sense, Machiavelli, Montesquieu, Rousseau, Mme de Stael and Marx may be considered theoreticians, even though all are clearly marked by the ideas of their day and by the conception of those ideas they put forward for consideration. They were all therefore regarded with suspicion and kept on the fringes of respectable society. What little their contemporaries understood of their specifically 'theoretical' projects caused a scandal precisely because they themselves were not excessively scandalized by the state of affairs they were trying to understand.) The practitioner and the priest are required to judge (preferably people); the theoretician and the scientist are required to explain (things or existing relations between men and things). The basic vocabulary of the former relies upon the guilty/innocent, accomplice/non-accomplice opposition; that of the latter on the true/false opposition. The former try to establish *rules* of conduct; the latter measurable or tendential *laws*.

Second observation: the rules came before the laws and the priests came before the scientists which is, of course, why professional prosecuters take social precedence over professional explainers. The motto of the historian is, according to Marc Bloch, 'Do not judge. Understand.' The motto of the practitioner is 'Do not understand. Judge' (or unmask, denounce and confound). However, the historian is not by rights involved in politics, whereas the latter is both by rights and by the nature of things. The first motto is tens of thousands of years behind the second. Hence political imputation—which consists of attributing things for which force of circumstance is responsible to entities or individuals (in order to praise them or accuse them)—has its roots in an unconscious that is archaic and therefore both irresistible and recurrent. The juridico-religious institution serves an invaluable social function, being primarily an instinct-like search for satisfaction. Its method is to haul the evil-doer (the Bourgeoisie, the State, Terrorism, etc.) before the Security Court (of the Individual, the Proletariat, Liberalism, etc.) It is much more gratifying and reassuring to call him to account and punish him for his crimes than it is to ask why there are states in general or to investigate the different types of state. The language of responsibility is primary; that of causality secondary. The magic that systematically confuses the two appeared before theology (which began to distinguish them), and theology in turn appeared long before experimental reason.

Third observation: The need for the 'blame' discourse imposes itself as a logical form independent of its empirical content. The spontaneous, magical logic of political judgement has nothing in common with the nature of enunciations. The discourse may appear either right side out, as a denunciatory diatribe, or wrong side out, as a dithyrambic defence plea. (Ecclesiastical tradition distinguishes between the 'constructive' and the 'destructive' apologia, but both species belong to the same genus.) Similarly, the devil can change his spots and turn his coat, the essential point being that he has to remain an essence if justice is to be done. If you want to relieve the evil, find the Evil One. The relief function will create the organ on social demand, in accordance with the most credible content of the hour (the beliefs of the subject or his 'ideological choices). Popular justice accepts both that 'he's a lawyer, so he must be a killer' and that 'he's a Marxist, so he must be a killer' (the proof being that they are both judges with just a few years between them). The important point is not to let the crime go unpunished, to arrest an 'author'. Magic makes idols and then breaks them: it burns what it used to adore. The prestigious syntax of prestidigitation is not a mere dialect; the natural language of political passion transcends the nature of motor passions. The magico-religious frenzy of veneration has the same logical (or illogical) structure as that of hatred. Love and hate are opposites, but they speak the same language.

4. The Logic of Witchchaft

The admonition that something is 'ideological' evinces a formal contradiction between the energy of the expression and the indolence of the demonstration. Discourses against the violence of discourse are extremely violent. The denunciation of dogmatism is itself dogmatic. Nowadays, the collective abominations of history are carried out in the name of ideologies. History is therefore the realization of ideology and ideology is *abominable*. Magic, 'a gigantic variation on the principle of causality', works by ascribing the phenomena under consideration to an apparently similar cause. There must be an evil spirit at the origin of human suffering. The explanatory entity is therefore saddled with the attributes of the things it is called upon the explain. The trouble is that adding up incantatory adjectives can never give a book the ability to ooze, words the ability to bleed or texts the ability to clot.[4] Still less can it *tell* us how symbolic information is able to trigger behaviour (aberrant or otherwise) in the collective.

There were no mysteries in magic, but there are in religion. And that is a considerable step forward. Why? Because magic carries the solution over into the problem (or, if you prefer, the labour camps into the body and even the gaps of Marx's thought[5]), whereas religion carries the problem into the solution so that even if it is not solved scientifically, it is at the least posed intuitively. The incarnation of the Word is a miracle because the Flesh did not exist within the Word—so that we should but cannot understand the problematic side of the operation. Magic comprehends everything in advance because it deals only with reproductions or redundancies; religion formulates the incomprehensible because it deals with metamorphoses, sudden appearances and, in a word, with events.

The Word-made-Flesh or God-made-Man transformation was a conundrum for a thousand years or more. Nowadays the transformation of Ideology into Action is seen as something immediate and self-evident. Although theology was our first political code, much of present-day discourse on political philosophy cannot be translated or decoded in theological terms for the very simple reason that it is pre-theological. When it comes to the interpretation of political phenomena, we have moved from what might be called the religious to the magical stage of causality. We are all agreed that the vocabulary of theology is somewhat comic ('Byzantine—hair-splitting', 'the sex of the angels—a pointless argument', 'the work-ings of the Holy Ghost—a magical cure-all'). The irony is, how-ever, that our everyday language relies upon abstractions which are much less operational than the output of patristics. Compared with the Chalcedonians and the supporters of Orthodoxy (451 and after), the polemics between Marxists and anti-Marxists (1950–2000) will soon begin to look primitive if not naive.

There is nothing inexplicable about the appearance of the simple logic of magic is contemporary discourse, provided that we take two hypotheses into account. They may work on different scales, but they clearly complement each other.

The first hypothesis is that the logical cathexis of nature and society is permuted in the general economy of reason of the two periods in question. Accustomed as we are to bringing analytic ef-fort to bear on the world of objects (physical or otherwise) reserved for mathematical or experimental processes, we become very relax-ed when we are faced with the more familiar ground of collective cultural phenomena. Conversely, the price paid for the intellectual rigour of texts from the late Christian Empire was probably a com-pensatory and equivalent laxity in the processing of data from the external (or natural) world.

The second hypothesis is that we are living through an 'anomic' period. Like prophetic discourse, the witchcraft mentality normally appears when there is a crisis of political and moral authority, when the grids through which we read the world no longer 'mesh' and when previously accepted systems of reference collapse or become eroded. Magical behaviour, including the magical interpretation of behaviour, represents a social constant, but in every society magic has a distinctive history punctuated by phases of decline and recrudescence. It reaches its low point in times of order and max-imum consensus, and its high point in times of calamity, wars and public misfortune. Intellectual production in times of crisis is not critical and even tends to be acritical. In that sense, it is true that all prophets are prophets of doom, for, in normal times, men are quite content with a priest.

There can be no question, then, of turning the logic of inculpa-tion against its authors, for if we take up the cry of 'Blame the witches', we too become witches. The shamanic function corresponds to a social and therefore legitimate need. Some individuals are probably better suited to it than others (not everyone is a born shaman), but whereas the organ is individual, speech is collective (efficacious because credible, credited because audible). Being a spokesman for 'public opinion', the magical operator—regardless of whether he plays the role of an inquisitor or that of a man possessed—reduces the public's anxiety by helping to reduce its psychical blood pressure. That is why he should be called a shaman rather than a sorcerer (whose activities imply a certain illegality or marginality). Even if he is not directly involved in treating the patient, the practitioner is a consultant. He guarantees the homeostasis of the social group, and the group therefore turns to him (to learn from his lips what future awaits the human race, how to avoid the third world war, who is responsible for hunger in the world, which moral values should be embraced, which election candidate will save us from the abyss. Intellectual analysis—formerly theological, now theoretical—cannot respond to this demand because it is by definition less gratifying and reassuring than imprecatory or vengeful convulsions. Ideological exorcism of ideology certainly does not restore the collective to health, but it does succeed in reassuring it. The stop-gap measure of a frenzied trial restores morale—and that is enough to make it legitimate. We use prominent ideologues as anti-depressants.

What is the problem that the pseudo-obviousness of ideology prevents us from posing? What is it about the collective that we do not know yet believe we know when we wave our fetish? What *how* does the ideological *why* prevent us from seeing?

We do not know how an idea becomes a material force or what 'taking hold of the masses' means for an idea. We do not know how saying becomes doing. What is the relationship between a belief and an action? How is a communication transformed into a command, information into execution, the product of an individual brain into a mass movement, an absurd idea into an 'institution' (Church, State, Army, Party)? In short, what does the expression 'the force of ideas' actually mean?

In order to explain a cause-and-effect relation, the Melanesians refer to *mana*, a transmissible, efficacious fluid that the sorcerer alone can manipulate. 'At once a force and a being, it is also an action, a quality and a state ... a noun, adjective and verb' (Marcel Mauss). Our *mana* is called ideology, an intellectualist version of animism. Instead of lending his own powers to inanimate material objects, the subject lends them to mental representations or even typographical signs. No matter if our ideas have iron jaws or feet of clay, they still have an occult force and a mysterious strength that puts their producer in the same position as a sorcerer, witch-doctor, or manitou. Men's history will gravitate around his shamanic capacity to localize the evil in the body of a sick society and to combat bad ideas with the good word of regeneration. The stage of magical thought corresponds to the moment of weaning in the child, when the libido is cathected on to the ego. Animism, be it collective or individual, is always a form of narcissism. The narcissism specific to intellectuals is the animism of ideas. This sheds some light on the theatricality of discourses of imputation and on the author's tendency to imagine himself a hero. He appears before us alone against the Beast, like David against Goliath, at once materially unarmed and spiritually unconquerable. The man who tracks down bad ideas has a vocation as a culture hero. It is a symbolic heroism, but much more dangerous than other forms. For it is in the symbolic universe peopled with demonic tempters and seductive spirits that historical humanity risks its all. The Persian hero portrayed by fifteenth-century painters defeats great white demons; our hero defeats red, black and white demons. But their legendary odysseys are the same. The hero has to enter the maze of signs, to venture into the inner labyrinths of those invisible worlds wherein lurk the causes of human misery.

There is a natural affinity between political man and magical man. This is so not merely because our political practices are both demoniacal and demiurgic, because the man with a knife between his teeth—the Jew Suss or the Imperialist Ogre—is confronted and defeated by the Supreme Guide, the Teacher, the Duce. In such practices, evil spirits and the principle of Good are made flesh and blood. Later, we will see that essentialism is a natural condition of political practices, a pragmatism rather than an idealism. The collective really does have a vocation for sorcery, since it is *par excellence* the world in which *speech acts*, the symbolic becomes practice, and gestures, attitudes and words alter the field of forces. This magical effect of words suggests that the political can be thought in magical terms. For there can be no effects without a trick: *mana,* deng, kramat; spirit, power, god. Divinities are powers, and there is something divine about the powerful who can do such extraordinary things. They are beings who make other beings (and things) move: they are all manitous, possessors of a certain quantum of power or *mana*. As soon as we establish a relationship between cause and effect or force and movement, an Ojibway awakes in all of us. Hubert and Mauss : 'The minimum representation implied by any magical act is the representation of its effect.' But the formula can be inverted: 'Magic is essentially the art of doing,' or, to be more accurate, the art of speaking and thereby making people do things. *The magical illusion results from the projection of the principle of causality into speech itself.*

Magic, religion and ideology are three successive yet indissociable variations on a set theme: 'the power of words'. The magician deals with the sacred in crude form in that he tries to constrain where religion conciliates. He deals with the sacred in unrefined form, considering not so much the person as the power that dwells within him. He works at short range in so far as the causal action requires direct contact or contiguity with its object. Basically, however, magic is still the first theory of human practice, inescapable and all the more compulsive for being so archaic. Religion cannot do without the processes of magic, although it is not reducible to it. Biblical prophecy quite clearly bears the marks of Eastern magic in that it produces the things it foretells (Numbers XXXII, 19, Isaiah LV 10, etc.). Monopolizing all the *mana* then in the air, the Judaeo-Christian god took ideological causality to its logical conclusion: his word created the world, no less. 'God said let there be light and there was light'—a marvellous prototype of the self-fulfilling prophecy. In such a statement, conception and will merge into one, as do exemplary cause and motor cause, understanding and life, ideal model and power of expansion. As in the Philonian Word (*sermo* and *ratio*), the incantatory formula—this is an order—and the impersonal principle of power—this is a source —are combined. *Spiritus* and *virtus*.

5. Recourse to Method

As we move up the scale of the sciences, the researchers become more nervous and uncertain. The epistemological precariousness of the social sciences is neither shameful nor abnormal. It is the expression of an objective methodological difficulty.

In political matters, the unavoidably polemical tone of scientific commentary can and must be applied to basics.

Although there is no hierarchical order in the sciences, or at least none that is unanimously accepted, it is not a matter of dispute that the sciences appeared in chronological order. At first sight, knowledge seems to move from the simple to the complex. The exact sciences, which moved from number to space, from inert to organized matter, therefore appeared before the social sciences, in which discoveries again follow a certain order. The object 'man' was in turn constituted as a living being (Darwin), a working being (Marx), a speaking being (Saussure) and a desiring being (Freud). But man as a being of obligation cannot yet be said to have acquired an analogous status.

In my view, the explanation for this delay lies in the rule that the scientific cathexis of objects is inversely proportional to man's affective involvement in the object. Thus, the collective is at the very end of the line of least resistance taken by the progress of knowledge, not merely because of its high degree of complexity (a high number of variables, difficulties in quantification), but also because of the intense anxiety it arouses. I accept that anxiety is the first encyclopedic criterion in the behavioural sciences. 'The order in which human ideas about various segments of reality achieve scientific status is broadly determined by the extent to which man is involved in the various sets of phenomena. As the anxiety aroused by a phenomenon becomes less and less capable of observing it correctly, thinking about it objectively or elaborating adequate methods to understand, control and predict it.'[6] Perhaps our psychical resistance to the idea that objective knowledge of the collective is possible derives from another final twist of anxiety, namely, disenchantment. We would like to preserve a last refuge for spells and curses, a last hiding-place for the sorcerer who has been driven from everywhere else. In other words, we refuse to be dispossessed of our last 'possession'. Whatever the value of this hypothesis, it obviously costs us less to be objective about economic phenomena (labour-values) than about so-called ideological phenomena (belief-values), even though the second set does seem to provide the researcher with as much raw data as the first. For the researcher is more involved in the laws that constitute the *we* than in the confiscation of surplus-value within the *we*. Domination is more compromising than exploitation. It is not surprising that 'political economy' is already a discipline while 'political science' is still a squabble. The one superimposes projects on its objects; the other contrasts projects with other projects.

A second criterion for classification of the sciences, derived directly from the first, might be the degree of physical risk inherent, in any given period, in one or another form of investigation. Such an ordering might then provide the basis for a historical encyclopedia 'from below', taking the scientists' *habeas corpus* as a standard without any reference to external metaphysics or arborescent metaphors. According to that criterion, the line of least anxiety would coincide with the line of least politicization, and the law of diminishing returns of knowledge with the increasing panic of the scientists. Its chronological indices would be the successive stages in the gradual retreat of established authorities before advancing discoveries in the course of establishment. In the priestly formations of the West (once Catholic and now Communist), the stages and degrees of freedom in academic research form a scale of encyclopedic discrimination operating *in vivo*. (The gradual emancipation of the various Institutes of the Academy of Science in the Soviet Union has concentrated into a mere forty years a process that the history of societies has spread over three thousand years.) To save time, we might say that mathematicians have been left in peace since Thales and physicists since Galileo. Only thirty years ago biologists risked their reputations, their posts and even their lives (the Lysenko affair). For a long time, the psychoanalysts were excommunicated (in France by a Party bull in 1949), but now they have the right to mutter on the sidelines (Tbilisi). The science of the collective—history, sociology, politics—is still tightly controlled by the authorities. In the social sciences, the two extremes of certainty and uncertainty produce the same scientific neutralization. In the West, opinions may be exchanged adinfinitum, on a free market, because ultimately their value is the same, next to nothing. In the East, research is planned by a theory in which all possible results are already present in condensed form. Obviously, the chances of positive knowledge are not equal in these contrasting realms of 'each to his truth' and 'one truth for all'. In one it is empirically neutralized through undecidability at the level of public reception; in the other it is dogmatically neutralized by the criterion of what has already been decided, research being nipped in the bud and blocked at the stage of a private show. The two realms are not, then symmetrical: the very principle of bureaucratic 'collectivism' anathematizes the accumulation of theory about the collective, just as Catholicism once left the science of religion without a possible object.

Psychical counter-transference explains emotional disturbances of discourse, and social counter-pressure (e.g., the desire for influence) explains the play of preferences and prejudices. Project and projection are the stuff of my object, and they put me on the spot. Given that I am working at a very high temperature, that is inevitable. The reason for scientific anxiety is the 'overlap between the observer and the object of study'. There are some excellent reasons for political censorship. It makes the researcher take risks since, in these matters, research makes the censors themselves takes risks. Any project for an investigation into the phenomena of belief will be challenged by society at the moral level because it can have physical effects on any individual society and on society as a whole. I am not asking for any guarantees. It is right to keep an eye on yourself, just as it is right to get annoyed.

What actually is the distinction between a so-called 'ideological' statement (or the anti-ideological variant) and a statement that is accepted as scientific? What is the difference between the logical universe of the refutable and the logical universe of the symbolic? How are we to explain the constant difference in tone, the 'excitement' of one and the 'serenity' of the other? In terms of the very different relationship between the spoken word and the object upon which it is pronounced.

Physical and natural reality is independent of our representations of it, but the social reality in which we live can be modified by the representations we make of it. (Despite appearances, clinical reality belongs within the first category, for although diseases do not exist independently of diagnostic grids, a displacement or modification of the tools of analysis does not result in a modification of the pathological mechanisms.) The statements of an astronomer, a geographer and a botanist are related in that the objects of their statements will not be modified by them. 'We are quite free to refer to a given fraction of the waters that cover the globe as the North Sea, but that in no way affects the objectivity of the said sea' (Frege). If the astronomer makes a mistake in his hypotheses and the botanist gets his classifications wrong, the planets will go on revolving and petunias will still have the same number of petals. The mathematical object enjoys a more ambiguous or less independent status, but once it has been posited by the mind it takes on an equally irreversible objectivity. Those who undertake research in the exact and natural sciences therefore enjoy a comfortable margin of freedom. They may be contradicted, but the object of their hypotheses is not at risk. Refutability is a guarantee of irresponsibility. Paradoxically, a 'scientist' has greater freedom of (scientific) movement than a sociologist or a philosopher.

The world of meaning, where statements and their referents are inseparable, is not symmetrical with the world of science. The 'ideological' statement is constructed in such a way that, although capable of modifying experience, it cannot be contradicted by it. If a marabout tells an African villager that his house is haunted, nothing can prove that it is not haunted, but the villager will modify his behaviour as a result. If a teacher tells his pupils, or a lecturer his audience, that the history of the world has a meaning and is moving towards socialism or, conversely, that socialism is a regressive movement that will take the world back to slavery, nothing can definitely prove the opposite. But it is probable that the future actions or reactions of the audience to their socio-political environment will be modified, if only to a very small extent.

This parallel leads us to a first approximation: the 'ideas' involved in 'ideology' are undemonstrable yet decisive ideas; they help to modify the state of things. The fact that they are hollow (and not amenable to empirical tests) does not stop them being serious (they carry weight and change things). All 'efficacious' ideas should therefore be included in (what may provisionally be called) the ideological sphere. The ability of an idea to stir the masses, to modify the balance of a field of forces or to induce one or another form of behaviour is independent of its truth-value; it is a function of its mode of transmission (which is technically and historically determined) and of the type of cathexis or loyalty it attracts. Although the two factors interact and can only be separated in abstract terms, we shall leave the mode of transmission to *mediology*, concentrating here on the mechanisms, nature and implications of belonging to a collective.

A vacuous idea which has effects is a serious idea; a serious idea that has no effects is vacuous. In this area, the criterion is material gravity. Value comes from the effect, not the object. To put it slightly differently, Political Reason takes as its object the effect of ideas that are devoid of objectivity, and the object of the Critique is the conditions of the effectiveness of an idea or ideology. Our rationalism is therefore cynical by nature, judging anything to be of interest so long as it works. Your myths are therefore of interest to me: the Gospel and *Mein Kampf*, Hitler and St Paul. A Critique of Political Reason cannot say 'Serious applicants only'. It takes seriously the things that a scientific critique rejects as baseless: for example, St Paul's eminently dubious idea that the conversion of the Jews is a sign of the Apocalypse. Such nonsense deserves the most serious theoretical attention, if only because the Crusaders who made their way to the Holy Land believed it and put the inhabitants of many a Central European ghetto to the sword so that they would not be late for their appointment with the Heavenly Jerusalem.

'Ideology': a paralysed discourse whose gravity results from its eccentric orbit. Languages which neither begin nor end with themselves are paradoxical: they are the effects of an absent cause and, in turn, have effects outside language. They work at a distance. In order to explain Bossuet's funeral orations or Voltaire's assorted pieces, one has to relate them to the coordinates of the context, of the *hors texte* ('outside the text'). The search for the meaning of their discourse requires us to exile ourselves from it. However, these discursive events are not so much *flatus vocis*, since there came a point in the eighteenth century when men who once thought like Bossuet 'suddenly' began to think like Voltaire. That was an 'ideological' mutation of some consequence, precisely because its consequences were not of the 'ideological' order. Men who thought like Bossuet would never have thought of storming the Bastille.

The Great Fear of 1789 was nothing but a false rumour. Yet the burned chateaux were real enough, and that is why Political Reason is more concerned with false rumours that with theoretical truths that do not spread.

At the level of biology, which, in complexity and historical development, comes immediately before politics, the philosophers are still visibly on edge, even though the objectivity of its results is not affected by the variety of faiths they profess. The discoveries of genetics continue to be vulgarized in militant (that is, polemical) fashion. A discovery concerning the rules of militancy—a discovery at the next level of anxiety—is unlikely to languish in boredom (though every effort would be made to that end). It would have to postulate a theory of polemical practices that is not in itself polemical. If we are to minimize the excitement, we must remain steadfast to our supreme motto, 'It is so!', rejecting both *reductionism* and *evolutionism*.

1) There can be no Tribunal of Reason or Court of Justice; no dais, no tribunal, no verdict. We are not going to judge these monstrosities in the name of a norm. Believe the belief, let it speak, let the polemical demon talk, listen to the confidences of magical spontaneity. We are simply thinking the ideological realm from within, at its own level of consistency, taking it as a plenitude and a positivity (and not as a residue or an ersatz). We are simply respecting the autonomy of ideological production, just as the historian of science begins by respecting the autonomy of scientists, by reasserting that day is not the truth of night or vice versa. The facts denoted by the notion of ideology cannot be broken down, dissolved or reduced to the constituent elements that make up its truth. Astrology, for instance, is not an inferior or substitute form of astronomy. They are not in competition: one has an objective, the other an object. They do not occupy the same ground because they do not answer the same questions. Astrology has the eminently respectable aim of soothing men's anxiety by giving *each of them* an answer to the question, 'What will happen to me tomorrow?' No astronomical discovery has ever put an end to systems of astrological interpretation (and none will ever do so). For new positive knowledge of the heavenly bodies is not on their agenda: they are designed to soothe anxiety (about men's origins or their future). Similarly, astrophysics is in no way concerned with the peculiarity of individual destinies (neither for nor against, but elsewhere).

In refusing to pronounce a normative discourse (correct/incorrect, good/bad) on normative discourses, we have to deny ourselves the narcissistic comforts of correctness, direction and rectitude. We have no wrongs to right and nothing to unmask. Ideologues have no need of watchful tutors to teach them their lessons: for the most part, they are far from being in an imaginary relationship to their practice and know more about its meaning than we do. Just as political theory has to learn from the political sense shown by the practitioners, any theory of ideology must first learn from the ideologues, abstracting and ignoring the political content of their function in the way that a Critique of Pure Reason ignores the empirical content of knowledge. Both *Mein Kampf* and the *Prison Notebooks* are grist to the mill of a Critique of Political Reason. And it will not be horrified to find that Gramsci and Hitler stumbled over the black box almost simultaneously (the former in an abstract, second-degree form, the latter as a practitioner, in biographical form). Speaking of the Nazi leader, Trevor-Roper warns us against deducing the 'moral baseness of an individual from the inferiority of his intellect'.[7] *Mein Kampf* (Vol. I, 1925, Vol. II, 1927) includes two chapters entitled 'Ideology (*Weltanschauung*) and Party' and 'Ideology and Organization'. The fact that the twin functions of *programmatiker* (who establishes the aims) and *politiker* (who realizes them) are united in one person means that Hitler is an ideologue like any other, perfectly aware of the general question that faces any ideologue worthy of the name: 'What conditions of force must an idea satisfy in order to become a force?' (Althusser). It is well known that the author of *Mein Kampf* was convinced that 'The problem of the future of the German nation is the problem of the destruction of Marxism. As I see it, the disastrous German policy of alliances is the result of that doctrine's subversive work'.[8] That was one thesis of Nazi ideology, not peculiar to it alone. But an ideology is not simply a montage of theses, and you do not destroy doctrines with other doctrines. Nazi ideology would never have been able to subvert German Marxism's work of subversion if it had remained at the programmatic stage, if it had not become an organized force or carried out its ideological programme. Hitler the *programmatiker*: 'No ideology, no matter how correct or how useful it is for mankind has any practical significance for the shaping of the life of a people unless its principles have become the banner of a movement in struggle. The *conversion* of a general ideal representation corresponding to an ideology into a clearly defined political community based upon faith and will is vital, for the possibility of the triumph of the idea depends upon the success of that conversion'.[9] As an epistemological rule, respect for the work of the ideologues—who, unlike scientists, rarely do good work—is equivalent to an order to abstain (theoretically). An internal critique of political *originality* catapults us beyond Good and Evil before we even get to the opposition between noble and ignoble. Such a critique is neither haughty nor despairing, simply arid and resigned to the worst.

2) Rejection of reductionism implies rejection of evolutionism. The refusal to condemn errors in the name of Truth is one and the same as a refusal to dismiss the past in the name of the present. We are not within the order of the true, precisely because we are not within history. Truth alone has a history. Let me explain.

The rules for the formation of a true, correctly formulated statement are subject to constant mutations, whether in the form of evolution (Claude Bernard) or of successive revolutions (Thomas Kuhn). A scientific statement is only meaningful in and through its field of historical determination. This may range from the implicit formal play which unifies all the formation rules of an age of truth under a single *episteme* (Foucault) to a practico-cultural framework defined by the state of the available apparatuses (Canguilhem). It is much more than an aleatory context: it is a necessary logical condition. The true exists only where evolution is possible: 'Scientific means capable of nothing but progress' (René Thom). That is why a science experiences epistemological 'breaks' or points of no return beyond which the science can no longer speak as it once did. Such 'breaks' do not provide grounds for a simple division between science and ideology, and it is up to the history of science to reconstitute their complex interweavings through, for example, the various 'scientific ideologies'.

The notion of ideology retains all its legitimacy in the field of knowledge, but the practico-social 'ideologies' which Political Reason has to deal with are radically different from 'scientific ideologies' such as atomism, transformism or vitalism in that they appear within a recurrent history whose every moment is, quite legitimately, the abode of the origin. Scientific ideologies are open to the sanction of truth. They are refutable and refuted discourses which become historically outdated and disappear as science progresses. The prehistory of a science does not outlive it, but there is no before and after in a collective illusion; there is no prospect of its ever reaching a point at which it can go back on its own decisions. Gall's phrenology was once a science and is now no more than a curiosity: its devaluation is definitive and irreversible. Religious doctrines, on the other hand, may experience eclipses or revivals as a result of historical competition, but their intrinsic value is not destroyed by the appearance of a later truth. The teachings of Christ did not invalidate the earlier teachings of Buddha, and nor were they invalidated by the subsequent teachings of Mohammed. The rise of the sciences over the last fifteen hundred years has not prevented mankind from remaining loyal to those three doctrines, amongst others. A scientific ideology is open to a 'I'm sorry to disillusion you, but bumps on the skull don't mean anything. Let me tell you why'. But a so-called practico-social ideology (even when it claims to be 'scientific') is basically impervious to corrections such as 'Don't be fooled. The Prophet was a hysteric. Allah never told him anything. I can prove it'. Such impertinence is not pertinent here. Both phrenology and the Koran belong to the realm of non-science. But the former is the product of discourse and the latter a product of society. One derives from a logical order of judgement—in which errors are possible. The other derives from the practical order of behaviour—where erring ways are all we have. Error is individual. Erring ways (always in the plural) are collective. Erring ways cannot be refuted, either on the grounds of experience or on rational grounds. To *mend* them, you have to *fight* them.

Someone once defined the history of science as the museum of the errors of human reason. One might, if one wished to be equally malicious, define the history of belief as the black museum of human history. But one would have to make it clear from the outset that the only people who visit the museum of errors are historians, a rather peculiar category of maniacs, whereas the museum of horrors is always open to the public. Everyone feels quite at home there. Once you have overcome a theoretical error, you never make the same mistake again. But we always go back to the same collective beliefs because we never get over them. Retrospectives therefore have a quite different status. In so far as it is a process of improvement, the history of science is internal to science but external to scientific research. In so far as it is a process of repetition, the history of ideologies is external to 'ideology' but internal to political research. In one, knowing means forgetting, in the other remembering. The synchronic history of beliefs is both the memory of the present of belief and the laboratory for a physics of belief. The 'archaic myths' which Fontenelle saw as the shameful history of mental errors are still with us (just see if you can find any shame in the mosque on Friday, the synagogue on Saturday, in church on Sunday or in the papers any day of the week). What is more, it is in that past that we have to find the keys to our understanding of the present. These different histories move in opposite directions. In theoretical reason, 'after' sheds light on 'before'. In political reason, it is the other way around. Whereas the history of science seeks its truth in teleology, the history of beliefs seeks its truth in genealogy.

Evolutionism is not, then, to be rejected so much as inverted (which does not involve accepting its idealist assumption of a linear and homogeneous time, a notion that is to the history of society what the pure intellectual space in which sovereign reason unfolds is to the history of ideas). According to Claude Bernard, 'chronological anteriority means logical inferiority'. Were it not for the false analogy, one might also say that 'ideological anteriority means logical superiority'. It is a fact that human groups organized themselves (life, death) in the name and with the help of religious conceptions of the world (with or without a personal god) long before they organized themselves (living, killing, dying) in the name and with the help of 'scientific' conceptions of the world (with or without objective validity). Historically, theocracies came before ideocracies; discursively, religious vocabulary appeared before that of 'ideologies'. But primitive does not signify primary. The most complex forms of the 'life of the mind' include the principle whereby its more rudimentary forms may be understood. However, the order of succession is not a transition from elementary to elaborate. In the domain of symbolic formations, the Hegelian postulate that 'the most ancient philosophies are the most abstract, the least developed, the least rich and the least profound' seems to be anything but self-evident. It seems, rather, that the primary forms conserve and contain subsequent forms, and that the beginning embraces everything that will come after it. The anatomy of religion is the key to the anatomy of 'ideology; Yet religion does not ape 'ideology'—quite the reverse. We have already seen the magical degradations and regressions to which the conceptual apparatus of Christian theology has been subjected by the most current forms of our 'modern' political thought.

2

The Past of an Illusion

1. The Origin of the Word

The formation of the concept began with the theft of a word. Nothing unusual about that. In the history of science, recuperation is the rule rather than the exception. Lamarck took the notion of 'environment' from Newtonian physics and applied it to biology; Darwin borrowed 'natural selection' from Malthus, who borrowed it from stockbreeding and horticulture; Durkheim took division of labour from physiology, which borrowed it from Adam Smith. Perhaps without realizing it, Marx robbed Destutt de Tracy (1754–1836). The reversal of meaning, however, is more important than the act of misappropriation. Not only is the word's application displaced from a *method* of study to an *object* of study; its very content is inverted. 'The science of ideas' (a critical and laudatory category) is transformed into an emblem of the 'ideas of anti-science'—a polemical and pejorative category. It is widely accepted that all the best concepts are derived from the scientific use of notions that were originally 'ideological'. But in this case the formal process is inverted. Concepts, like children, belong to those who can give them the best upbringing. The Marxist appropriation of the concept is an accepted and irrefutable fact, although the improvement in its upbringing is more debatable. At this point, a terminological joke might raise a smile: in the mother-theory, the word comes to designate the inversion of the historical real on the screen of consciousness ... thanks to an inversion of its real historical meaning. This minor case of mistaken identity may be seen as the mirror-image of a future colossal misunderstanding.

'Ideology': the neologism was baptized in the fount of the Institut National in August 1798 when the third of the *Mémoires sur la faculté de pensée* was published after a public reading on 2 Floreal, Year IV.[1] On 27 May 1799, Destutt uses the word in the title of a paper read to the Institute: 'Dissertation on certain questions of ideology, containing a new proof that we owe our knowledge of the body to the sensation of resistance and that, prior to that knowledge, no act of judgement is possible because it is impossible to distinguish between simultaneous sensations.' Then in 1801, Courcier publishes *Idéologie proprement dit*, the first part of his master-work, *Eléments d'idéologie* (sic). Next came *Grammaire générale* (1803) and a *Logique* (1805) 'because the science of ideas includes the science of their expression and deduction' (*Introduction*, p.5). Then the fifth and final part, *Traité de la volonté et de ses effets* (1815).

We will not retrace the history of the ideologues for its own sake. Picavet divides them into three generations, but only the second (Cabanis, Daunou, Destutt) seems to have any serious claim to the title (although Destutt preferred to describe himself as an 'ideologist'). We will simply note that many of them were doctors, orientalists, physicists, chemists, naturalists—in short, practising scientists (Volney, Cabanis, Pinel)—and that their aim was to raise 'the moral and political sciences to the level of the physical and natural sciences'.[2] But they had the misfortune, or the courage, to take an active part in the political life of their day as organizers, legislators and pedagogues. In this way, they handed down the basis of our modern scientific and educational system (creating the Institute's second section, the Académie des Sciences Morales et Politiques, and founding the Ecoles Centrales, the Ecoles Normales and the Polytechnique) and earned themselves the worst of all posthumous destinies. They did find a few descendants in Saint-Simon, Comte and Taine, (not forgetting Schopenhauer), but on the whole it was Napoleon who won. Their academic successors followed to the letter the instructions whispered by their grand-master Fontanes: 'Be positive ... monarchical; no metaphysical ... ideological nonsense!'

Being spiritual descendants of the Encyclopedists, disciples of Condillac, self-confessed materialists and free-thinkers, positivists *avant la lettre*, practical thinkers with a leaning towards experimentation and 'application', the ideologues had nothing but scorn for metaphysical, or what we, brainwashed by the Emperor, would call 'ideological', nonsense. They were nothing if not positive thinkers, and Destutt exhorted his readers to follow their example: 'My dear young friends, do not put your trust in poets and philosophers whose reason follows their imagination and not the facts'. He modestly points out that his neologism 'designates the work that has to be done and not the science that will result from it'; and, that unlike 'metaphysics', which deals with the nature of things, and psychology, 'a word meaning the science of the soul' which 'seems to assume a knowledge of that being that you surely cannot flatter yourself with possessing', ideology 'makes no assumptions about anything doubtful or unknown and does not suggest any idea of causality'.[3] He uses the neutral generic term 'ideology' to designate 'this science of the generation of ideas' which will derive from the analysis of sensation. The positivity of ideology is to place it in the forefront of the natural sciences, along with physiology as opposed to theology.

Destutt was a liberal aristocrat, a delegate to the Estates General, an infantry colonel, a survivor of the last tumbrils, an active Thermidorian during the Directory and the Consolate and, like many of his friends, a republican even during the Empire. Napoleon saw these moderate, anti-Jacobin free-thinkers as the seeds of a dangerous opposition. He was not content with forcing them out of the Tribunat*, suppressing the teaching of the political and moral sciences and finally banning their journal *La Décade philosophique* (1807). The man who invented government by public opinion did all he could to make them look like mere imbeciles, thereby introducing the ideological annihilation of the ideologues. Good sycophant that he was, Chateaubriand started the chorus of official scorn with his *Génie du Christianisme*, and it was taken up by the massed choirs of Catholic and monarchist reaction. With the help of Royer-Collard and Victor Cousin—and Sainte Beuve as a flanker—state spiritualism consigned the heirs of the finest French materialism to nearly half a century of oblivion, branding them with the mark that Napoleon, their worst enemy, had designed for them: dreamer, metaphysician, phrase-monger. And so ideology became established as 'an abstraction without any real foundation

---

* Tribunat: Body set up in Year VIII, responsible for denating bills before they were passed to the legislature. Trs. note.

or practical results'. Despite his philosophical affinities with the reprobates, even Littré defines ideology and related terms in the words of its enemies and fails to mention the inventor of the word.

Stendhal, the one ideologue recognized by posterity, stood firm against this tide of ingratitude. Winner of the first prize for mathematics at Grenoble's Ecole Centrale, cashiered soldier and aspiring philosopher, he 'derousseauized' himself by persistently studying the works of the founder of the Ecoles Centrales; so much so that he thought of himself as a sort of amateur ideologist, an unworthy disciple of the master. *De l'Amour* (1822) is sub-titled 'an essay in ideology'—hence its analytic and descriptive coldness, and hence, too, the total failure of this 'physiology of love' (a dozen or so readers in ten years). Stendhal constantly refers to Destutt's *Idéologie* as the source of his passion for the *natural* against the artificial and affected, his hatred of verbiage and abstract declamations (everything that would, in 1980, be called ideological), and his abrasive, slightly cynical tartness.[4] In 1806, for instance, he writes: 'For a year now, this man has had the greatest and most salutary influence on me.'[5] And in his *Souvenirs d'égotisme*: 'In 1817 M le Comte de Tracy, the man whose writings I most admire, the only man to have revolutionized my thinking, came to see me in the Hôtel d'Italie on the place Favart. I have never been so surprised in my life. For twelve years I have been an admirer of this man, who will be famous one day.'[6]

Unfortunately, his prognosis was wrong: the fame of the invention eclipsed that of the inventor. The 'ideology' project was an ally of the French Revolution: it was born with it and grew up with it. But those who executed the will of the Revolution handed the corpse of ideology over to its adversaries, the mystics and the romantics. When he exhumed it and stood it on its head like some philosophical form of poetry, the Young Marx signed its second death certificate. And so the 'reactionary propaganda' of the day duped yet one more member of the revolutionary camp. 'Calumniate as you may, something will remain.' True, Marx did quote and even discuss Destutt, albeit with a certain condescension: the name appears in the Paris Notebooks, the *Grundrisse* and several passages in *Capital*, but Marx evidently never looked at the *Idéologie proprement dit*, as he mentions only the 1826 *Traité de la volonté et de ses effets* (Parts IV and V of the *Eléments*) and Destutt's last work, the *Traité d'économie politique* (1823). As further proof of this case of mistaken identity, it will be noted that although our Count and Peer of France is mentioned in *The German Ideology*, fleetingly yet favourably, he is quoted against Stirner as an analyst of property rather than the father of ideology.[7] In fact, Destutt's early works were out of print in the years 1844–48, when an obscure German immigrant in the rue Vaneau was elaborating the 'scientific' concept of ideology *ad vitam aeternam*. It may be that he was too busy with more serious matters to look at the literary work of one Henri Beyle (Stendhal), a dilettante ideologue and brilliant political analyst who died of apoplexy in 1842.

2. Marx's Elaboration

If we wish to retrace ideology's trajectory (axes and crossroads) in the development of Marxism, we will have to be fairly schematic, not out of any wish to make a difficult question somewhat lighter, but because the trajectory itself is astonishingly schematic, because the simplicity exists in the texts themselves. There is a straight line between 1842 and 1893, between Marx's first letters to Ruge and the last missives Engels sent to Conrad Schmidt and Franz Mehring in an attempt to 'correct' or complicate the 'simple' materialist notion of the 'historical efficacity' of ideologies. We have to listen to that simplicity without any ill will; to heed what is said, repeated and explained, without adding anything or making symptomatic readings. It is not illegitimate to suppose that Engels, the co-author of *The German Ideology*, was better informed than we are about the intentions and expectations of the 'Marxist' verdict. He gives his own detailed account in the admirably logical narrative, half-biography and half-epic, known as *Ludwig Feuerbach and the End of Classical German Philosophy* (1888). In it, Engels explains why the very act of writing *The German Ideology* forty years earlier was sufficient for their 'main purpose: self-clarification'. His summary account will allow us to achieve our purpose: to clarify the genesis of an illusion. It is all there: genealogy, gestation, birth-certificate. We might well recognize the brilliance of the overall schema; savour the extreme psychological finesse of the Young Marx's analyses, not only of the speculators of his day but of the ageless mechanisms of speculative idealism; and remind ourselves that young dogs should at least show some respect when they carry out autopsies on dead lions. But in the end, when we weigh it all up, none of that will prevent us from surrendering to the sad thought: 'So it was as stupid as all that.'

Let us begin with the framework. The modern notion of ideology emerges against the background of a historically dated settling of scores, as an incidental cost in a theoretical task, as a gauntlet thrown down by Marx and Engels in Brussels in 1845 as they began 'to work out in common the opposition of our view to the ideological conception' and 'to settle accounts with our erstwhile philosophical conscience', in other words with Hegel and his successors. The notion was not produced for its own sake, with reference to a still unfamiliar object or as a result of 'disinterested' conceptual work. It filled a gap in a jigsaw puzzle which, neither invented nor remodelled by Marx, came ready-made and ready-cut from Hegel. When the mysticism of the absolute idea is stood on its head, the logic of the idea is liberated as absolute mystification. No new object appears in its place: an old subject changes position and a cause becomes an effect. Hegel's dialectical method turns a somersault, and ideology follows as a mere sequel. 'According to Hegel, dialectics is the self-development of the concept.'[8] According to Marx, dialectics will be the self-development of the real as an idea, the developed concept of the real. Heaven becomes earth and vice versa. The refrain of forward-rolls and head-over-heels may be outrageously naive, but the founding fathers kept it as their motto from first to last. Marx 1845: 'The ideologists turn everything upside down (clerics, jurists, politicians, moralists).' Let us knock them off their pedestals, and the truth about everything will become accessible to us. 'In Hegel the dialectic is standing on its head, but if you simply put it back on its feet, its physiognomy becomes perfectly reasonable.'*. That is an argument, not a metaphor. Marx never changed his view right up to the *Afterword*

---

* This is a literal translation of Roy's version of the test. The standard English translation reads: 'With him it is standing on its head. It must be turned right side up again if you would discover the rational kernel within the mystical shell.' For a discussion of the significance of the differing versions see Louis Althusser, 'Contradiction and Overdetermination', in *For Marx*, London 1969, p. 89 note 2. Trs. note.

to the second German edition of *Capital* (1873): 'My dialectical method is in its foundations not only different from the Hegelian, but exactly opposite to it. For Hegel, the process of thinking, which he even transforms into an independent subject under the name of the "Idea", is the creator of the real world, and the real world is only the external appearance of the Idea. With me, the reverse is true: the ideal is nothing but the material world reflected in the mind of man and translated into the forms of thought.' Engels in his old age: 'This ideological perversion had to be done away with. We comprehended the concepts in our heads once more material-istically—as images of real things—instead of regarding real things as images of this or that stage of the absolute concept.'[9] The exact opposite, as we have already said, is the same thing turned upside down. Its physiology is different, but its anatomy is the same. The elementary cell of an ideological tissue is always the 'idea' as 'form of consciousness', 'mental abstraction' or 'product of thought' ('what men say', 'the way they imagine or represent themselves'). The materialist point of view follows the Hegelian lead. Rarely has so little scientific imagination been seen at the cradle of a 'new' science, or so much continuity in the middle of an epistemological 'break'. The Marxist revolution in and on the field known as ideology derives from an enlightened conservatism.

Above all, it derives from a strictly speculative hierarchy. We should note that, from the start, the planet of ideology appears in the gravitational field of knowledge, as the negative correlate of the *adequatio rei et intellectus*. Ideology draws its function and status from a primordial relationship with true knowledge—or theory. Its initial oppositional position forces it into a one-way street. As soon as it is crystallized, ideology branches off towards epistemology, not praxiology. Marx approaches the 'world of ideas' not as a historian, ethnologist or anthropologist, but as a philosopher. Ideology therefore indicates a lower degree of knowledge rather than a form of behaviour; a manifestation of a lack of scientific culture rather than a cultural phenomenon to be observed scien-tifically; an indignity rather than a reality. In that respect we may still be paying the price for the chronological split between Marx the mature historian, expert in grasping the interfaces of the im-aginary and the efficacious (as in *The Eighteenth Brumaire*), and the young critical theorist whose professional ethics made him devote himself to tracking down the unnoticed errors of the human mind. Since conceptual systems are more portable than descriptive nuances, it is, of course, the model of the epistemologist that has come down to us and not the example of the journalist. (However, there is so much more theoretical wealth in his concrete observations that in the abstract synthesis.) For the manufacturer of ideology as a catch-all category, the principle of the wrong explanation immediately supplants the social fact that has to be explained, just as the trap to be foiled by reason supplants the play of unreason in things.

A historian who has to reconstruct the internal logic of the *Conquista*, for example, comes up against the *fact* that the huge Aztec Empire, one of the most developed civilizations in the world, was militarily defeated by one hundred and eighteen Spanish soldiers and ten horses. He therefore has to take seriously the theological representations of the ancient Mexicans, and he will not have done with Quetzalcoatl simply by inscribing him in the register of false consciousness. It so happened that, in the Aztec cosmological calendar, the year 1519 coincided with the date upon which the ancient Toltec god was due to return—an unfortunate contingency which cannot be reduced to a non-truth. The fact that Cortes represented Quetzalcoatl, and the Spanish horsemen living gods, had a *decisive* practical effect: no historian can simply *reject* it as an abstract conception, a false perception or a mystification. It is only in its infancy that science rejects appearances in order to understand the world. In its maturity it tends to free appearances from the essence-complex by, for example, reconstituting the specific logic of tangible qualities (raw/cooked, sweet/sour, treble/bass, etc.). Besides, 'if the appearance and the essence of things coincided, science would be superfluous' (Marx). Ideology speaks of appearances, science reconstructs essences by doubting appearances. Such is the theoretical challenge inherent in any project of truth as *aletheia*, as the tearing away of the veil of illusion, the reduction of the illusions of sense-experience. Unfortunately, the dissipation of appearances as the criterion of truth does not entail the dissipation of appearances as a non-critical reality. Rejection is not the same as abolition.

According to Marx, almost all ideology can be reduced to either 'an erroneous conception' of human history or a 'complete abstraction' from it. Beneath this reduction of ideology to conceptual error and hence to virtual non-existence (in the light of the 'concrete reality of history'), there lies the canonical hierarchy from *episteme* to *doxa* that is indexed to a fixed scale of being and appearance. The Marxist epistemological project rests upon the assumption of an ontological hierarchy of objects of knowledge, in which driving force replaces *being* and forms of consciousness, *appearance*. Error has no specific being: it is inadequate to being, something that indicates the shameful place of the lack. Ideology, then, is conceived as lack, privation, failure, insufficiency. The instance of inconsistency cannot itself be an object of science, as it is the one instance that science will reveal to be a false object: a subject-effect with no objectivity of its own, a complement (of the object) or a supplement (of the soul), a qualitative reject of science. It is charming, smiling, agreeable; halo, aura, aureola; flavour, aroma, bouquet; opium. But it does not cure anything, cannot be eaten and gives no light. It is insubstantial and therefore inefficacious. Science separates essence from appearance and identifies the former as truth, the exclusive site of efficacity. Marxist 'effiscience' precludes in principle that the false should have any efficacy. The Leninist slogan—Marx's theory is all-powerful because it is true—is homogeneous with the Socratic maxim that no one is knowingly evil.

The image is the tangible form of non-being. Second bifurcation: the gnoseology of vision; ideology as simulacrum, shadow, mirage. We are still in Plato's cave. The imaginary is not a specific mode of formation of the real; it is deformed reality. Not a mode of production, but a bad reproduction. Ideological images are to theoretical concepts what dioptrics (the study of the phenomena of refraction) is to optics and what anaclastics (an old name for the study of broken or deflected rays) is to the study of reflected rays. 'If in all ideology men and their relations appear upside-down as in a *camera obscura*, this phenomenon arises just as much from their historical life-process as the inversion of objects does from their physical life-process.' What is recorded on the photographic plate can be neither more nor less than what was in the subject of the photo, and ideology is simply a poor negative image of the real. Photography is a somewhat undignified diversionary art, rather like painting in Pascal. It is pointless to repeat things that already exist, and such vanity anyway has harmful effects. For the quite specular spectacle of the forms of representation of the real betrays the system of socio-economic forces that are projected upside-down in the ideological diorama. Forms of social consciousness are therefore redundant as well as unfaithful. Ideology is a stand-in, a reproduction at once inconsistent and upside-down. Yet one more reason to distrust it.

This 'scientific' conception of ideology compounds two forms of naivety: 'thingism' and idealism. It is naively empiricist in that it sees the image not as an act but as a thing, (or something inferior): as the passive recording of an external reality. In Marx, as in Plato, consciousness cannot create its own objects: it receives them, in more or less degraded form, from the outside world. Corresponding to the thing-image without human imagination is a fantastic without fantasy, idols without magic. Ideological imagination is a flat land of shadows, gesticulating against a backdrop of passive retinas. In *The German Ideology*, the spectacle of the inverted real represents a sort of *mimesis* without *catharsis*, a joyless fancy-dress parade, an Apollonian vision with no Dionysiac values, the oneiric aberrations of a society that never knows the functional discharge of tragic release. Sooner or later, the aesthetic of reproduction pure and simple fades before the obvious futility of artificial panoramas. Even the most rigorous interpreters of Marx and Engels do occasionally let slip a general feeling of 'What's the point?' when they rule out 'a distinct theory of the transformational efficacity of the ideological sphere'. Since it is merely the 'dominant material relations seen in the form of ideas', ideology cannot have any specific existence or efficacity. 'Marx says that the dominant ideology is a reflection of the practices of class domination. It expresses material relations: it is not a specific function operating in the unconscious element.'[10]

In addition to the 'thingism' of the image of reproduction, this conception contains a highly idealist and classically frivolous notion of consciousness as a gaze. So often it tends to reduce ideological error to socially determined eye-trouble: confused vision, hallucination, mirage. The implication is that there is an inert relation of exteriority: the real-to-be-reflected is simply juxtaposed to a reflexive consciousness, the accuracy of whose image varies according to the class 'optic' or the prism of interest. Hence the non-essential and instrumental character of the link between individuals and their ideology: change the lenses in your spectacles (i.e., your class position) and you will see things as they really are. Somewhere in the distance, far beyond our myopic fumblings, lies the idea of an objective world as a thing-in-itself that will become accessible when our gaze coincides with each and every object in that world—*adequatio rei et visus*, the panoptic ideal of the Absolute Gaze (in classless society). To be more precise, it hangs over us like a normative ideal. It will be noted that the three assumptions involved in ideology as 'way of seeing' (sublimated in the expression *Weltanschauung*) provide the empirical support for a banal idealism. Their credibility stems from the fact that they express one of the most frequent illusions of common sense. It is reproduced whenever anyone phantasizes about the universal substitution of real data of experience for the construct. 'Nowadays, ideology is not simply a magnifying glass: it is also a distorting mirror that produces all kinds of aberration—chromatic not moral.'[11] In other words, we would act with discernment if it were not for our shortsightedness. On the day when mankind is finally able to see things as they really are, there will be no more evil deeds on earth. In the meantime, our diopters 'produce' our misdeeds. No one would be evil if they did not have to wear glasses. Marxism is Platonism without Eros, the old patron saint of scientists. Theoretical souls have no wings, but they have to see (*theorein*) the truth ... without passion and without desire. They exist between appearance and pure reality, with no help from the analogical myth.

The amazing paradox (obviously both joke and tragedy) is that a philosophy in which there is simply no room for (a serious theory of) the imaginary has been left to fetishize the notion of ideology.[12] For a century now, the task of thinking symbolic efficacity has fallen to a philosophy which equates unreal with symbolic (even if it is a dimension of the real). The 'subjective' element of collective practice is apprehended within a thematic that leaves no room for the subjective and gives it no reason to exist. We have already noted that there is no 'psychology' in Marx. Chronologically, that is not surprising: the experimental science of that name was barely in its infancy when *Capital* was completed. That gap in the doctrine has been filled with such temporary replacements as Politzer's concrete psychology and Sève's theory of personality (to restrict the discussion to France). However, it is not exactly surprising that these projects—despite their merits—never went beyond the programmatic stage. There is indeed room in Marx for a subject, but not for subjectivity as an 'abstract' mode of being or 'concrete' lived experience. If we ignore a few passing comments on talent, passion or taste in the early texts, the psychological subject is an unwanted third party in a problematic with two terms. When Marx talks about the subject, he speaks either as a philosopher or as an economist. In the first case, the subject is an anthropological category invoked to answer the question: 'What is man?' There follows a discussion about his essence (the human essence is not to be found in man in general, in the abstract individual subject, but in the concrete social individual, and so on). In the second case, the subject is a social characteristic invoked to answer the question: 'In what form do the elements of the structure appear?' (In the form of subjects, he replies; such and such a capitalist, for example, is simply the personification of economic relations.) Otherwise, subjectivity is a modality of existence without any specific basis or function, except when it is placed between the classic categories of 'need' and 'will' as a point of transition between the real movements.[13] Given that 'consciousness is a social product', psychology can only attain its object by becoming a historical sociology, the study of the concrete conditions that produce consciousness-as-object. If the latter is ever to become the object of a specific science, it will be as a physical correlate of the physical world, a thing reflecting things, a stimulus-response. In that sense, Pavlov's neurophysiology of the higher nervous system really is an extension of the Marxist problematic (in its turn related to the tradition of classical subjective naturalism, for which the psyche is a natural being). The psyche does not constitute a specific milieu: it is an organ identified with consciousness. The subject cannot therefore have any function in the production of images, in fabulation or in the production of nothingness: these are merely distorted images of the real. *The German Ideology*: 'Consciousness (*Bewusstsein*) can never be anything other than conscious being (*das bewusste Sein*), and the being of men is their real life-process.'[14] It follows that the notion of psychical reality is a nonsense, a *contradictio in terminis*. Either it is real and, in the last analysis, material, or it is mental and therefore unreal. A dynamic of imagination might ultimately be acceptable (although the term never appears in Marx) but not a dynamic image as such: if an imaginary representation develops a certain energy, it must have found it in the non-imaginative reservoir of driving forces or productive forces. Taken literally, Marx's theory can admit of no driving hallucination: it has to be one or the other. From the point of view of the theory of the subject, the Marxist problematic can only come to terms with collective practice through the filling of a 'psychical' gap and a 'collective psyche' gap, in that order of difficulty. If there is no (room for) the psychology of the individual as biographical drama, there is a fortiori no place for a psychology of the collective as historical drama. If there is strictly no activity on the part of consciousness, it is quite impossible to recognize the existence of unconscious activity or to see the unconscious as an activity principle.

A Marxist would of course argue that such a way of approaching the subject immediately reveals the hand of an 'ideologist'. There can be no other name for someone who remains at the moment of the subject, as if it were something other than what it is: an interlude, a moment. The true dynamic of social movement does not cut 'conscious being' out of the circuit: it shunts it by means of a switch known as class consciousness. There is no point in looking for the principle behind the movement of ideas in the realm of ideas, for the driving force behind thought is not internal to thought itself. Alain Badiou: 'Thought in itself is not a source of anything. Thought is powerless. The massive energies of history move through it and move it. That is what the ideologist fails to recognize, and when it is spontaneously forgotten, *false consciousness* appears.'[15] The ideological illusion consists of attributing autonomy to 'thoughts as ... independent entities, developing independently and subject only to their own laws' (Engels, *Ludwig Feuerbach*). Ideology borrows its energies from the class energies that run through it. Thus, sixteenth-century Protestant ideology borrowed its energy from the rise of a new bourgeoisie in Northern Europe at a time when merchants' capital was in the ascendancy. Anyone who lingers in the realm of ideas (thought, the brain, etc.) instead of passing through it to the material conditions of existence is an ideologist. Failure to respect the no-parking sign is like taking the wood for the trees. Originally and theoretically, the Marxist critique of ideology is not meant to be a form of moral suspicion or personal accusation, still less an extension of counter-espionage to the terrain of ideas. It is an accusation of scientific incompetence and failure to recognize the real cause. 'That thematerial life-conditions of the persons inside whose head this thought process goes on in the last instance determine the course of this process remains of necessity *unknown* to these persons, for otherwise there would be an end to all ideology.' The man who transmits forces believes he is strong, not because he overestimates his strength or the force of his ideas, but because he does not know where the true forces lie. The mystifier is the first to be mystified. If the intermediary can, in all good faith, believe he is a producer (because he makes social ideas productive), this is because of a structural gap in practical activity between distant content and immediate form, hidden motor and apparent motives, real and imaginary. In a word, neither Moses, St Paul nor Mohammed *produced* anything that cannot be attributed to something already in existence; they were also there, and it simply passed through them. They were neither motors nor promoters, but simply conveyors and transformers.

'Ideology is a process accomplished by the so-called thinker consciously, it is true, but with a false consciousness. The real motive forces impelling him remain unknown to him; otherwise it would simply not be an ideological process. Hence, he imagines false merely apparent or motive forces. Because it is a process of thought he derives its form as well as its content from pure thought, either his own or that of his predecessors. He works with mere thought material, accepting it without examination as the product of thought, and does not investigate further for a more remote source independent of thought; indeed this is a matter of course to him, because, as all action is *mediated* by thought, it appears to him to be ultimately *based* upon thought' (Engels, letter to F. Mehring, 14 July 1893).

According to the canonical texts—and it seems only fair to recall them—the only theoretical answer to the question, 'Where does the power of ideologies come from?' would appear to be 'From everywhere except ideologies'. But it would also seem that, in the eyes of a Marxist, that is the ideological question par excellence, the supreme mystification.

3

The Anatomy of an Illusion

1. A Fatal Preclassification: Forms and Forces

Ideology is like totemism and hysteria in that its value is completely dependent upon a certain segmentation of reality. 'Once we are persuaded that one can arbitrarily isolate certain phenomena and group them together as diagnostic signs of an illness, or of an objective institution, the symptoms themselves vanish or appear refractory to unifying interpretations.'[1] But unlike hysteria, which, as a diagnostic category, did not survive Freud's critique of Charcot, and unlike totemism, which, as an autonomous system, did not really stand up to Frazer's ethnographic criticisms, the instance of ideology has outlived its utility as an analytic instrument. Indeed, in detaching itself from the *episteme* with which it was connected, the hypothesis has been blown up into a habit. Of course, anything that helps us to classify a certain number of phenomena is the product of a classificatory judgement, governing a certain analytic organization of the social field and establishing the limits between the real and the non-real. Like any critical theory whose vocation is to distinguish between true and false, Marxism has bequeathed us a certain definition of social reality. Just as all social periods are convinced that their favourite ideas bring them face to face with the real itself, all social theories see themselves as theories of social reality. But it is never the reality. The singularity of any historical period, social system or theoretical conception may be defined in terms of the things it agrees are real and the things it agrees to exclude from the real as illusory, imaginary or secondary. This prior decision, never problematized because it is from there that the problematic proceeds, postulates itself as the transcendental element that cannot be questioned within the given system of thought. In Marx the decision is indicated as early as *The German Ideology*, although it is never actually explained. It takes the form of a categorical distinction between 'material behaviour or activities' and the 'representations of consciousness', 'existing conditions' and 'the idea'. It is the bases of this key division that have to be questioned, beginning with the central line of demarcation that separates infrastructure and superstructure as if they were two opposite and superimposed regions of the world.

The classification may rightly be called a prejudice in so far as Marx received it ready made from an imaginary cosmology of Hegelian origin. It was imposed upon him just as he was beginning to oppose Hegel: 'In direct contrast to German philosophy, which descends from heaven to earth, here it is a matter of ascending from earth to heaven.' The metaphor itself is fairly loose, but it has rigorous effects and immediately poses two problems. *First question*: up to what point do we keep our feet on the ground, and at what point do we find ourselves in the clouds? In other words, how do we establish the boundaries between heaven and earth in a historical process? *Second question*: assuming that 'heaven' and 'earth' exist, how do we move from one element to the other? And once the principles for the ascent have been established, in what terms do we outline the principles for the descent? Now, when I said that the problems were 'immediately' posed, the term naturally had a logical rather than chronological value. Before that could happen, the Marxist system of positioning had itself to be problematized. It is now possible to do so theoretically because a century of historical experience has taken it upon itself to problematize the proposed solutions (without malice, but not without a certain mischievousness).

Anyone who goes to live with Marx moves into a fine stone-built house with two main storeys and two basements (or 'instances').

We have all learned how to analyse a mode of production, either at school or from the manuals. Take the developed schema of Heaven/Earth, where the solid lines indicate ascent or 'determination in the last instance' and the dotted lines descent or 'reciprocal action'.

HEAVEN or ideology	forms of consciousness (religion, morality, philosophy, science)
	juridical relations (state, political constitution, law)
EARTH or material base	social relations of production (social classes)
	state of development of the productive forces

And so the little orphan, Ideology, finds a home in the house of history. But in order to have, not a roof over his head, but a floor under his feet, he had to leave the world of living men. It is not much of a bargain to exchange a function for a position. 'What is the point of finding a home if you lose your biology?' Or, rather than be brushed off, he might put it this way: 'I mean what Lenin called the active side of the thing, what he said you often have to look for in idealism rather than materialism.'

Let us look more closely. Using the intuitive form of an architectural image, the system of instances articulates and conceals a thematic pre-division rather than a subdivision, putting a set of good terms on the Earth side and a series of bad terms on the Heaven side.

– Reproduction	Representations	Subjective	Error	Ideology	Visible	Conscious Being
+ Production	Existing Conditions	Objective	Truth	Science	Invisible	Social Being

All combinations are possible for your greater intellectual entertainment: the pairs can be constructed diagonally and there are no restrictions on number, but the Heaven line will always be marked with a minus and the base line with a plus. The opposition between concepts scarcely conceals the opposition between affects: history advances on the wrong side—Marx did not know how right he was—but the system implies that nothing good can be expected from the top line (even if it is not the line of evil) and that all social progress comes from below. The instances crystallize implicit and homogeneous hierarchies, superimposing a scale of coefficients (in the order of causality), a scale of values (epistemological and/or moral) and a graduated scale of consistency (from essence to appearance). We may discuss whether the structure of the instances brings together an axiology and an ontology, but not the fact that this topography merges with a mechanics of forces and movements. We are given no choice between thinking ideology in terms of a system of places and thinking it in terms of a system of forces: the two are inseparable. Since the Marxist schema provides for both a structural theory of instances and a dialectical theory of contradictions, one would try in vain to draw a distinction between the two.

Below: forces. Above: forms. Visible forms may hold the stage, but forces determines the meaning and rhythm of the play. The forces set the forms in motion; the effective work of the motor (economic class struggle) moves the shapes of politics and ideology. The arrows of motor causality go from motor to motive, and the grid of instances, levels or stages has to be situated in the non-reversible vectorial space of determination. The vertical directionality of the place of the social formation sheds light upon the unilinear irreversibility of the time of the social formation, which always moves in the same direction. Regression from the stage of socialism to the stage of capitalism is therefore unthinkable because it does not conform to the essence of social development. In theory it is unthinkable, and in reality it can be punished in the name of theory. The possibility (recently advanced by Godelier) that the hierarchy of functions may be distinguished from the hierarchy of institutions does not seem enough to alter the nature of a law which is inscribed *in nuce* in the Marxist theory of levels.

This spatial schema, which is by definition static, may include a principle that explains the dynamics of historical societies, but the distinction it makes between a forceless system of forces entails that the dynamic itself is inexplicable. Finally, the biggest problem facing the Marxist problematic is to unite elements it has itself arbitrarily made alien to each another: the 'real life-process' and 'ideological echoes or reflections'. It is not surprising that Marx left behind his little spatio-mechanical machine when he made his concrete political analyses. It would not have been much help. As for Engels, the executor of Marx's will, he had the formidable task of repairing the all too obvious damage that a theory had done itself and of doing so in theoretical form (in, that is, *practical*, portable and cheap form). Hence the last-minute tinkering with 'reciprocal action' and 'relative autonomy' (letters to Conrad Schmidt, Mehring, etc.). If we look closely at these notions, we will see that they cannot but oscillate between the trivial and the unthinkable. They are trivial for any analysis that is not forewarned of a sequence of historical facts, and they are unthinkable in the framework of the original explanatory system.

The very vocabulary of *The German Ideology* reveals the Marxist syntax of real and imaginary. Again, they are placed opposite each other, on different sides of the line. More precisely, all *behaviour* and *activity* belongs to the Earth pole and everything that takes the form of a form (the language of politics, laws, morality, metaphysics, etc.) is packed off without prior consultation into the unproductive, essentially *reproductive*, files of ideological representation. In Heaven, no one and nothing works. It is the world of the *re-* of justification : representation, reproduction, repetition. *Post festum*, when all the bets have been placed. The real exists prior to its representation, just as the economic content exist prior to its forms. Second in the hierarchy of beings, secondary in the hierarchy of reasons, ideology is accepted (somewhat late in the day) as a minor partner in reciprocal action that never actually inaugurates anything. It is an eternal late comer in a society where the workmen of the real get up early. Like the red light, it comes a long way behind the locomotive. Half-speculary, half-theatrical, it can never recover from its consoling faint. A lie is the opposite of truth, just as beauty is the opposite of ugliness, and ideology can never be anything more than a mask stuck on to periods that are too ugly to look their real poverty in the face. It is exactly as if Marxist philosophy, preoccupied with correcting the index of refraction inherent in the dominant ideas, had become trapped in a hall of mirrors, duped by the reflected image; exactly as if its obsession with the *re-* (Heaven as the place where Earth is reflected) had prevented it from ever seeing the *pro-* force of images: projection, proposition, production of a reality in and by the imaginary.

From an operational point of view, a distributive model that transforms a methodological demarcation into a real separation or even a de facto disjunction (either here *or* there) functions as a divisive logic or, if you prefer, as a schizoid model. Such a logic forgets that the men who reproduce themselves in their group and the group for themselves in accordance with certain 'ideas' are one and the same as those who produce surplus-value for their exploiters. They have only one anthropological identity card. Throughout the history of three or four Internationals, Marxist economism has granted only a 'secondary' importance to the primary structures of social vitality (ethnic groups, nations, languages, religions). When a segmentation becomes a break and ideology a practice, schizophrenia becomes very expensive. The 'imaginary' does not reappear in 'real history' in the way that the false reappears in the true. It returns like a boomerang.

2. The Double Fault

From a purely critical point of view, the instances model calls for two comments. Firstly, we have to look at a certain paradigm of causality. Secondly, we have to look at the process whereby thought is made the negative correlate of the body and placed under house arrest in the mind (or in conscious being as the negative correlate of real being). The first comment will focus on what might be termed a technical obsolesence; the second on a logical definition of the object.

a) The Technical Objection

Like the rest of his century, and at the same rhythm, Marx thinks in terms of motors. Class struggle is the motor of history, a universal force to be applied at any point whose system produces every movement in class societies. To adopt the periodization proposed by Michel Serres, this is a first-generation, vectorial-type motor.[2]

Marx's pre-transformational and pre-cybernetic paradigm of motion is two (scientific) revolutions behind the times. It is, if you like, the paradigm of Lagrange and Laplace. But then, immediately afterwards, came Carnot and Maxwell. Let us be quite clear: the scientific good sense of an era depends not upon the chronology of discoveries, but upon the much more gradual evolution of the criteria of thought. The history of science can show that chance enters the rational field in 1713 with Bernouilli's *Ars conjactendi* and that the basic idea of thermodynamics was put forward by Sadi Carnot in 1824 in his *Réflexions sur la puissance motrice du feu*. But it was in the middle of the century, when Marx's explanatory model *has already been set up*, that the classical paradigms really began to be shaken by the challenge to the rationalist mechanics derived from Newton.[3] The unity of physics as a coherent vision of matter was shattered by the discovery that not all material phenomena are mechanical—first in Fourier's *Théorie analytique de la chaleur*, then in Clausius's kinetic theory of gases, and finally in electro-magnetic theory. Classical mechanics, for instance, is based upon the twin principles of the law of inertia (any body subjected to the action of a single force will move constantly in a straight line), which is the basis of statics, and the law of the equivalence of action and reaction, which is the basis of dynamics. The latter both posits and assumes the conservation of the mass or quantity of matter. It cannot account for 'the increasing tendency not to use force or the reduced possibility of using energy' revealed by the so-called second Carnot–Clausius principle (which Engels attacks as erroneous in his *Dialectics of Nature*). The truly disturbing hypothesis that nature may be different from matter (understood not as a philosophical category but as a historically determined scientific concept) and that the difference may directly concern human history is ignored right until the end out of loyalty to the canonical principles of the theory. When the foundations of the new scientific conception of history were being laid (1842–48), the same tranquil order of universal gravitation reigned both in heaven and on earth. It is a stable material system, both predictable and constant: the cause is of the same order, scale and nature as the effect; the movement of bodies obeys the same principle as their equilibrium; the points of a system are homogeneous with the system of forces that set it in motion, displace it and within which it moves; the local can be deduced from the pre-existing and legislative global.

Marx and Engels conceptualized history within the framework of classical mechanics, according to which Statics ('the science of the equilibrium of force') and Dynamics ('the science of accelerating or decelerating forces') are governed by the same general principles of the *lever, composition of forces* and *potential velocities*. The famous model of the parallelogram of forces, which Engels and Plekhanov used to explain the effect of individual actions in the social field, is itself borrowed from Statics. Real forces, forces of inertia—the vocabulary still haunts the analysis of relations, advances and retreats of forces whereby we apprehend concrete historical situations (the vocabulary is still used by *L'Humanité* and the 'Report on World Forces' published in the Congress reports). The doctrine is reproduced in identical terms—as we shall see, that is the point of doctrines. The trouble is that the language and syntax of our knowledge have changed since then. More specifically, our knowledge of movement (of internal changes of state and not merely motion in space) no longer takes its descriptive model from the linear schemata of mechanics but from more powerful and sophisticated models that are more adequate to the sophisticated complexity of the social. When Engels (or Badiou) examines the efficacity of a heresy, say the sixteenth-century Protestant heresy, he spontaneously borrows the language of rationalist mechanics. 'The schism in religious ideology is an expression of the pressure of real class relations',[4] where 'is an expression of ' means both 'symbolizes' and 'transmits'. The real forces apply pressure downstream and produce movement upstream. Social movement may not be simple, rectilinear, or direct, but it is assumed to have an intensity analogous to the force of bourgeois ascendancy (the notion of the quantity of movement). Causality is linear or vectoral in that it consists of segments of a straight line between before and after, upstream and downstream. It is also mechanical in that it assumes a proportionality of scale between the movement's before and after, between downsteam and upstream, between cause and effect. If human masses marched behind the Protestant banner in sixteenth-century Germany, they were forced to do so by massive economic forces. It takes something massive to move the masses. There is a dangerous homonymy between (popular) 'masses' and 'mass' (the constant relationship between the forces applied to a body and the corresponding accelerators). Although an excellent historian of the sixteenth century, Engels used an explanatory model which, no doubt unconsciously, owed a great deal to a reading of social development in terms of a grid of forces and movement, one that is still with us and cannot be transcended in its own framework. But in the physical order itself, the orders have since been permutated and the explanatory principles have become much more sophisticated. It is no longer a mystery that, in certain circumstances, a snap of the fingers can make all the difference, and an acute angle can lead to a major change in direction. Whether our descriptive model refers to ordering by noise or to decision-making by quantum of information, there is no longer any necessary analogy or similarity between the quantity of productive energy and the quantity of forces set in motion. The naive distributional model of heaven and earth, heavy and light, motor and moved, serves to hinder rather than assist any explanation.

Without wishing to extrapolate or to generalize on the basis of these new paradigms, one may reasonably point out that over the last century content and form have been inverted in a number of categories and notions. Marx thought within an ordered world, stable and at rest, in which the revolutionary had its place as a predictable and necessary link at the end of a chain of homogeneous causes and effects. Far from being a break with that order, the revolution was its validation and manifestation. A homogeneous nature without anomalies, which could be exhaustively described by a finite set of general laws, gave rise to a single-thread history, the same all over the earth. In like manner, 'the natural laws of the movements of a society' gave rise to 'the economic law of motion of modern society' (1867 Preface to *Capital*).

Since the birth of this 'science of history', the nature of the natural object has been altered, and the physical sciences along with it. By the end of the nineteenth century, systems in which energy can be transformed had appeared alongside those reversible and conservative structures of classical dynamics that relate to a totally predictable and ultimately tautological world. As Maxwell points out in his account of an experiment with gun-cotton, the transformation of energy occurs when 'the system has reached a certain configuration, to attain which requires an expenditure of work, which in certain cases may be infinitesimally small, and in general bears no proportion to the energy developed in consequence thereof. For example, the rock loosened by frost and balanced on a singular point of the mountainside, the little spark which kindles the great forest, the little word that sets the world fighting, the little scruple that prevents a man from doing his will, the little spore which blights all the potatoes, the little gemmule which makes us philosophers or idiots. Every existence above a certain rank has its singular points: the higher the rank, the more of them. At these points, influences whose physical magnitude is too small to be taken into account by a finite being may produce results of the greatest importance. All great results produced by human endeavour depend on taking advantage of these singular states when they occur.'[5] Things formerly rejected by analytic mechanics are now accepted as legitimate objects for our understanding of the real. If sciences which were deliberately ignored by yesterday's omniscience now exist, how can a method of historical knowledge born in the first half of the nineteenth century still be valid when the logical matrix of its method has long since been challenged? Is the science of history the one science that is not questioned by or concerned with the history of science? The answer to that question will not come from the science of history: the facts themselves will answer it.

b) The Topographical Objection

The mechanics of determination and interaction show that Marxism is a product of its time. The criticisms to be made of it derive from history and our historical understanding. In that sense, there is no need to shift our ground. If, on the other hand, we begin to ask ourselves about the nature of *ideo*, we expose ourselves to a more draconian exile.

Imagine, just for a moment, that heaven is empty. We need not puzzle our brains about how to rebuild bridges between what dwells in heaven and what lives on earth. Earth is heaven to itself. Instead of asking ourselves why ideas act upon things or how forms of social consciousness interact with material social relations, we should start by asking whether the relation between a 'thought' and a given system of forces is itself given with the production of that thought or the production of a singular force; whether the home of thought is not ultimately earth rather than heaven; whether the 'idea's' mode of existence makes it an immediately material activity. To put it more simply, the Marxist tradition has not found a satisfactory solution to the problem of ideology because it was a false problem (one not posed in the terms proposed).

It is not a matter of displacing the definition of ideology from the speculary/speculative field to the practical/political field, but of modifying the *internal* determinations of the field. Ideology does not, as we once thought, exist within the sphere of ideas. The spontaneous localization of ideology in that sphere is something that rationalist ideology has handed down, via Marx, to Marxists and anti-Marxists alike. It is that pre-conceptual framework that must now be examined. The root of the error lies in the pre-reflexive reflex which made Marx spontaneously link religions with ideologies *as mental representations rather than organizational processes*.

Thought no more takes place in men's heads than language depends upon typographical characters. Ideology's simultaneous tasks of representing the world and organizing men are two sides of the same coin. In other words, thought is not a subjective determination. It has *the objective materiality of an organizational process*. Men think with their feet. And if you want to know what and how they think, you have to look at the ground they stand on and the people they stand beside. (Hence the vanity of placebos like 'Get that idea out of your head', when it is your feet that decide.) Just as a revolutionary doctrine comes into being by bringing its practical supports into being, so the formation of a religious doctrine is identical with the formation of the hierarchical community of the faithful. The process whereby the group is constituted is neither external nor posterior to the constitution of thought; it is its very body, exoteric but not extrinsic. There is no such thing as a more or less systematized set of representations to which a more or less organizational structure is subsequently added from outside. Similarly, the 'operationalization' of an ideology is never 'neutral' or indifferent: the contents of thought are externalized in the forms of organization which make them possible and which they themselves make necessary. (To conceive of the working class as the agent of universal emancipation, for example, is to turn a historical model of the factory, with its centralization, its verticality and its division of labour, into an organizational model for the bearers of that thought.) The manner in which an ideology reveals itself to the world reveals what it is made of and what it was made for. What is at a given moment in history called the 'collapse of certainties' is explicable in terms of the crumbling of structures of belonging inherited from an earlier moment. In the advanced industrial countries of the West there is not, over here, a 'crisis of Marxism' and , over there, a resultant crisis in the political and trade-union organization of the Communist movement. The ideology is in crisis to the extent that the modes of organization, transmission and preservation of its underlying 'idea' have become technologically and economically obsolete in our part of the world.

There can be no living ideology that is not incorporated in some way. For any ideology stipulates, in its very concept, a certain process of incorporation 'upstream', just as it creates a certain type of corporatism downstream. The truth of Christian dogma is to be found not between the lines of the Gospel but in the organizational structures of Christianity. The truth of Marxist-Leninist doctrine is to be found not in manuals of the same name or the appropriate texts (those closest to the source) but in Communist structures of organization. The ideology and the organizational structures simultaneously engendered and constructed each another, but the workings of the latter determined the nature of the organ known as 'ideology'. To say that thought as such is not a practical operator is to ignore the fact that thought does not exist as such. Any operation in thought refers to a transmission mechanism which structures it *from within* and and from which it cannot be dissociated. Its operation cannot be conceived in terms of an opposition between a pure form and a material system of forces. There is nothing real about such a juxtaposition or segmentation. Marxism began by eliminating the concrete relations between the terms and then demonstrated that an abstract ideality cannot displace real forces. But it forgot that the relation between a form of thought and a field of forces is itself mediated by a thought-group which acts as the practical subject of an intervention into and upon the surrounding forces. One might as well posit the existence of an *esprit de corps*

without a corps. Any understanding of the facts of thought certainly presupposes that we reject belief in the magical virtues of
thought (as an autonomous force), but it must also begin with a
historical cartography of the groups as they organize themselves in
one thought or another. Goodbye topic, hello topography.

The Marxist elaboration of ideology quite fittingly derives from
a critique of religion, the main reagent being Feuerbach's *Essence
of Christianity*. The primacy of religion is logically justified: 'The
criticism of religion is the prerequisite of all criticism' (Marx,
1844). 'The first ideologists, *priests*' (Marx, 1845). No objection to
that. On the contrary, it seems to me that if the materialist dialectic
had put more emphasis on the connection, if it had thought more
about that primordial link and gone back to its initial premises, its
mature form may have produced more practical results in the field
of symbolic efficacity. To be radical is to go to the root of things,
but Marx walked very softly in his critique of religion, so softly that
he stopped half way. Having tried to grasp the spirit of religion independently of the body of the church—forgetting that ecclesiology
is the key to Christian theology and not the other way around— he
missed the point quite radically. The ideological illusion is the illusion of those who believe ideology to be an illusion. The Young
Marx analysed religion as a system of fallacious 'reflections' and its
'social power' as the effect of the alienation of the individual
unhappy consciousness, but he never saw it as a structure of communal belonging, at once political and ethical. He ignored the
organizational level—'the people of God'—and concentrated upon
the sublime representations of God. He therefore failed to understand the positive reality of religious joys (practising or militant),
reducing it to the 'halo' of that 'vale of tears'. His critique of the
religious illusion made him forget the confessional reality of *the
religious institution*. By concentrating on religion as a system of
formal representations, he failed to see it as an organized collective
force.[6] Given these premises, it comes as no surprise that the same
man could give the European proletariat orders for a historical mission without providing the political means to carry it out. Even
though the real title of *The Communist Manifesto* is *The Manifesto
of the Communist Party*, Marx, who had already theorized the
spirit of Christianity independently of the Christian Church, went

ahead and theorized communism without touching upon the nature of a Communist Party (he always reduces it to the social class). Historical materialism does not allow us to conceptualize the difficult dialectic between movement and institution: the implications of the incorporation of a spirit and the need for a body if a spirit is to be born. As a result, the institution did not take long to betray the movement. It was left to Lenin, Marx's St Paul, to elaborate a practical theory of the body (the party) and to give the spirit of communism its definitive incarnation. The Flesh speaks the truth of the Word, not vice versa.

The spirit of religious ideology still cocks a snook at naive rationalism because the latter has failed to come up with any theory of bodies. If it were simply a matter of images in mirrors or ideas in our heads, the disappearance of the reflected objects would lead to the disappearance of the reflections. Unlike the thinker of the *Aufklärung*, Marx did not expect a speculative critique of superstitions to dispel the illusions of social awareness. 'The abolition of religion as the *illusory* happiness of the people is the demand for their *real* happiness. To call upon them to give up their illusions about their condition is to *call on them to give up a condition that requires illusions*.'[7] But if religion was simply the 'inverted awareness of the world' and a world turned upside down, one would legitimately expect it to vanish once the world was turned right side up (the end to man's exploitation of man plus free compulsory education). But, far from being tarnished, the old 'haloes' still shine brightly. The 'ideological' effect outlives its presumed cause not because it is supernatural but because presumption was wrong. The tenacity of the religious illusion in social practice is not in contradiction with the principle of determinism: it simply means that theory has to get its determinism right. It is obvious that in this respect, the spontaneous exercise of ideology is ahead of the 'scientific theory' of the said ideology. It is up to the practice of illusion to answer the question of its own objective truth—a question that might be formulated as follows: why is it that a social situation always requires illusion? If we put it that way, we will remain faithful to the teachings of materialism: 'Man must prove the truth, that is, the reality and power, the this-sidedness of his thinking in practice. The dispute over the reality or non-reality of thinking that is isolated from practice is a purely scholastic question.' (Marx, *Second Thesis on Feuerbach*)

3. The Cost of an Illusion

The history of an illusion is not an illusory history. For a century now, the theoretical fiction has been playing an active role in our midst, and that activity now allows us to take our leave of a model which turns ideology into a *cosa mentale*. That is how Leonardo the engineer saw painting; serious things took place elsewhere and in other ways. The very idea that social ideologies reside in men's thought has had material results outside thought on the lives of millions of men. The word ideology has produced millions of failed (dead or murderous) revolutionaries—those who thought human beliefs could be termed 'ideology'. There is, of course, no problem with the word. But its implicit theoretical basis has long given Marxists the illusion that they knew what they were talking about when they spoke of 'ideology'—namely, that they were talking about an illusion. We· must not give in to what Paulhan, in a memorable phrase, once called the myth of the power of words, 'Novalis said that the word liberty produced millions of revolutionaries. And no doubt it did: all those for whom liberty was the opposite of a word.'[8] The influence of abstractions usually derives from the weight of the historical realities they bring with them: Justice, Democracy, Liberty, Revolution. Here, it is the other way around. The perverse effects of ideology derive from the lightness it suggests, from the airy fluid it evokes. Gaining ground is one thing; winning hearts and minds is another. Marxist theory tends only too often to confuse the two operations, reducing the complex to the simple and time to space. It tends to calculate relations of force (between classes, countries or 'camps') and to 'forget' that forms of culture, themselves forms of struggle, develop a force which, if not quantifiable, is qualitatively irresistible. We have to put an end to the massacre by hollowing out the sign and fleshing out its referent. 'Words pass unseen where there is power; where words appear there is no more power.'[9] It is our intention to show that there is only an empty word where we thought there was a concept, opacity where there was a false transparence, an unknown where there was a certainty.

'It is in the nature of the mind to remain a slave to the things it neglects, not to the things it considers' (Berl). The expulsion of the troubled zones of the collective from the family circle did not put the family at risk—quite the contrary. There was no room for the sacred or for war in the mental universe of the Marxist labour movement in Europe. In 1914, however, that movement rallied as one man to the Sacred Union and the imperialist war. Marxist economic sociology gave at least a minor role to the military function, but so-called Marxist societies are noted for their military strength rather than their economic successes. The masses' answer to 'It is the masses who make history' was to idolize one individual on a scale never before seen in ancient or modern History. As for the role of ideology in our conceptual machine, our century has come up with its own chance mishaps. Sarajevo, Berlin, Buenos Aires, Algiers, Peking, Kabul, Warsaw—the list is still incomplete and still open.

SECTION II
The Physics of Belief

1

A Logic without a Logos

1. The Failure of Therapy

Let us begin with the diagnostic observation that the potions have not worked. Specialists have torn all the ideological systems to shreds, laid bare all the shameful messianisms and exposed all the nonsense to pitiless ridicule—yet 'ideology' buries its philosophical gravediggers one after the other. Orpheus could charm wild beasts and Joshua brought down the walls of Jericho with music. In legend, magical procedures do work. In the political life of societies, they appear to be less productive: the beasts still prowl the forum, and the most solidly based indictments against '*the seekers after God*' do not seem to have slackened the hold of nonsense or to have significantly diminished the charms of the evil seducers. No sooner has one exhausted beast been dragged out of the public arena than another appears, teeth bared. In the meantime, today's demystifiers replace yesterday's on the victory rostrum. Tomorrow, they will be mystified too. In short, it is as if the oft-repeated cry of 'Down with ideologies!' still needed to be answered by the call 'How do we get rid of them?' and corresponding results. Good theories are no cure for harmful ideologies. Perhaps we are all neurotic. But surely not ideopathic? The clinical picture of mankind, considered as a political patient, does not show any significant improvement.

When it comes to 'ideology', the most lucid minds always disappoint us and themselves, because there is no solution of continuity between the 'scientific' definition of ideology and the common nonsense of the animist definition. Althusser: ideology is 'a system (with its own logic and rigour) of representations (images, myths, ideas or concepts, depending on the case) endowed with a historical existence and role within a given society'. The dictionary: *Ideology* noun, f. System of ideas, philosophy of the world and of life. 'Revolution is primarily a matter of politics and ideology' (Camus). *Ideologue* noun, m. One who believes in the power of ideas. 'Hegel justified all the ideologue's work by reference to reality' (Camus).

We should be wary of placing the beginning and the end of a ter-minological journey on the same level (or of lumping together an authentic philosopher and a specialist in general—and generally wrong—ideas). But those who criticize Marxist ideology do seem to adopt, completely but unwittingly, its definition of ideology. The difference is that a consistent Marxist like Althusser is aware that the ideological imaginary is coextensive with the existence of social relations (including communist social relations), whereas an unwit-ting Marxist like Camus imagines that he can hasten the end of ideologies by stigmatizing fallacious 'systems of ideas'. 'The Rebel' is certainly a victim, but a victim of what the Assimil method would call a 'false friend'. The orphans of God have come to a sad end: having taken up the noble position of resistance fighters—against ignoble attempts to persecute the human race ideologically—the noble sons find themselves victims of a pun, persecuted by a homonym. Is it not time to put phonetics in its place? Should we not ask ourselves whether ideology really does 'happen' in ideas, whether is not just a wasted effort to file conclusions against the master thinkers? In other words, what if we could make religions disappear by getting rid of the theologians?

Let us break the mirror. When ideologists think 'ideologies' they show a definite tendency to think their own situation. And that really is the worst possible way to reflect upon the genesis and tex-ture of their favourite target. There are three reasons for their blindness.

First handicap. Like it or not, anyone who works professionally with ideas is still a man of letters. Images make us think, but we think with words not images. 'Graphic' and 'symbolic' are not synonymous. Convinced by verbal obstacles and professional habits that an ideology is made of words in the same way that a wall is made of bricks, the man of letters goes to look for ideology in the most improbable (and probably impossible) places: in books and libraries. He thinks it is a 'big deal' to deal with texts, with the *corpus delicti* itself.

Second handicap. A studious man is by trade a solitary man, and it is true that you cannot think in a crowd. Neither the *I* of the littérateur nor the transcendental or reflexive *I* of the philosophers is predisposed towards thinking the productions of a *we*. The thinker, whose task it is to interpret the *written word* and to comment upon *authors*, is not in a good position to grasp the element of physical communion in a moral conviction or, more generally, to understand or accept that the operations whereby a *we* is constituted are not of the order of thought, even though that order is not in itself unthinkable. Reflective men are not specialists in the pre-reflexive. The unthought is as familiar to thinkers as painting to a blind man or the collective to solitary men.

Third handicap. A man of ideas is a man of the head. It is true that we do not think with our hearts (although we can speak from the heart as easily as we can speak through the nose). But does that dispense us from thinking of the heart as 'the seat of ideologies' (in the sense that the head is said to be the seat of thought)? Is it not the case that—as even their victims admit—ideologies set hearts beating and heads spinning for all who come under their spell. Open up your heart and you will be in the heart of the subject. Open up this Russian doll of a word, where anger, courage, memory, love and generosity nestle inside each other, and you will find what stirs—and therefore sets in motion—both the individual and the collective. 'At the level of popular awareness, the home of emotions that can swell into a Crusade ...' (Alphandéry-Dupont). A man without emotions would not be a man without qualities; but he would be without ideology, a lethargic and almost cadaverous man. How can you survive when your heart 'stops'?

What is felt takes precedence over what is represented. Superficially, an ideology may look like a jigsaw puzzle, but appearances are deceptive. All judgements about public opinion are permissible, provided that they first recognize its materiality for what it is: a product of discourse. 'I describe thinking as discourse, and judgement as a statement expressed' (Plato, *Theaitetos*, 190). But what has since Marx been known as 'ideology' is not a product of discourse. It is primarily a product of sensibility and, as such, ante-predicative. A critique of ideology should concentrate not on 'the shaky ground of certainties', but on the epistemological plinth from whence the authorized critique of certainties and their vacillation is normally pronounced. Ultimately, the history of ideologies is closer to the history of mentalities than to that of doctrines, and the concept of ideology is not to be found within an analysis of the learned productions of bodies of professional thinkers simply because a conception of the world is not essentially conceptual. The political unconscious (of which, as we shall see, ideology is merely a symptom) cultivates anonymity. It shuns authors' names and their *bons mots*. It prefers the image to the sign. The raw material for our investigation is to be found in architecture, painting, photography, the cinema and posters. It is easier to unveil and decode a historical ideology by looking at its imagery than at its phraseology. (Similarly, the history of sensibility owes more to the iconography of a period than to its memorialists.) The visible tip of the iceberg—the printed surfaces—is a speculary lure. Second-degree and secondary rationalizations may serve the historian as a stop-gap when there is a shortage of more elementary and therefore more revealing raw material (as in the period of the Crusades, very poor in imagery). But the a priori inclusion of the object 'ideology' in a juxtaposition of discursive formations obscures the fact that for every theologian there are ten thousand believers and, what is more important, that theologians exist because the faithful exist and not vice versa. The faculties of theology produced the Christian people: they were set up to satisfy a need (*fides quaerens intellectum*), but they did not create it. The faith's lay people (*laos*) were there before the act of faith was legislated and will be there after it has gone, should that ever happen. In practical terms, no one goes to mass because they have read St Thomas or even St Matthew; no one becomes a Communist because they have read Marx or Lenin, and no one becomes a Pétainiste because they have read Drieu, Sorel or De Man. The road of practice leads in the opposite direction: from commitment to rationalization, from loyalty to motives for loyalty. All the reflexive syntheses—superstructures that are readily identifiable because they are stacked on the shelves like portable parallelepipeds—prevent us from seeing the trees, soil and roots of our 'ideologies'.

2. Belief: Sickness or Symptom?

It is a banality to say that the humus is religious, but the triviality of a statement is no argument against its validity. The minimal, objective and, so to speak, material definition of any 'global world-view' that finds adherents on a mass scale is the classic definition put forward by Durkheim: 'Religion is not merely a system of ideas; it is primarily a system of forces ... The main characteristic of religion is the dynamogenic effect it has on consciousness.'[1] The field of socially efficacious ideas: 'ideology'. We have already seen that 'ways of thinking' differ from table manners or ways of dressing (even though they do form a continuity with them) in that they are not simply society-effects but have have effects on society, notably on so-called political developments. Politics, as we all know, is a matter of opinion. Discursive facts can therefore have effects that are anything but discursive, provided that—and this is a *sine qua non*—they are accepted as being true (or correct). An idea achieves political dignity by virtue of its lyrical capacity, which is formally and materially independent of its logical capacity. Our field is political behaviour (where faith rules) and not norms (where law rules). The leader of a certain little group understood this only too well. Meeting a leper on his travels, he said: 'Stand and go on your way; your faith has cured you' (Luke XVII, 19); and, meeting a blind man, he said: 'Go: your faith has cured you' (Mark X, 52). The leper walked away, cured, and the blind man's sight was restored. Those who want to cure men of their beliefs seem to have forgotten that belief has cured more than one man. Theoretically, they are quite right not to believe in miracles. But political reason has to explain why those who do believe in miracles ultimately profit from them. Why, that is, does belief produce miracles and not vice versa? (Of course, today's paper contains no fewer miracles than the Gospels, and the religious myth takes the banal fiduciary nature of our political behaviour to its higher, allegorical limit.)

Belief may be defined as 'the holding of a thing to be true' (Kant). All idealisms of the subject agree that belief is an act of understanding, a function of the rational being like any other. Kant's Critique, for instance, does not isolate an autonomous faculty of belief as distinct from the faculty of understanding.

From the perspective of reason, 'I believe' is a lower degree of 'I know'. In that sense, it is a modality of judgement ('I judge that this proposition is such that I can hold it to be true'). When a reasoning subject finds himself faced with an object and there is no symmetry between the subjective and the objective, he has to 'believe' in the sense of stating more about the object than he actually knows. The author of the *Critique of Pure Reason* makes a distinction between *conviction* and *persuasion*. Conviction may be distinguished from persuasion by the possibility of communication to every man, whereas persuasion is valid for the individual alone. Opinion is the lowest degree of belief: it is insufficient both objectively and subjectively. Belief is subjectively sufficient, but it is recognized as being objectively insufficient. Knowledge alone can provide logical rather than ethical certainties. The practical point of view is not logical (though practical reason does exist) in that it gives rise to insufficient judgements. It is the realm of faith. 'Pragmatic faith': that of the doctor who believes he can diagnose one disease rather than another. 'Doctrinal faith': that of the orthodox believer—'I would not hesitate to stake my all on its truth'.[2] 'Moral faith': that of the man who in his existence obeys 'moral maxims, the renunciation of which would render me hateful in my own eyes'.[3]

From the point of view of pure reason, the subjective phenomena of belief are marginal and subsidiary. (Kant devotes six pages to them at the end of five hundred pages of the *Critique*.) Opinion, conviction, faith, and so on, are central to political reason. No one claims to have mathematical opinions—for that particular science displays a priori and necessary truths whose universality is self-evident to any rational being—but everyone has political opinions. The time-honoured phrase 'politics is a matter of opinion' is perfectly justified. (Even though 'public opinion' is a fiction without an objective basis, the very fact that we believe in its existence makes it an objective political reality, revealed, for instance, in the result of an opinion poll.) It is well known that 'M Teste had no opinions',* and that he was not 'involved in politics'. (The M Testes of this world are not those who 'make history.') The problem is that, like his eminently lucid creator, he did not understand

---

* M. Teste: character created by Valéry symbolizing intellectual impotence. Trs. note.

the political behaviour of his fellow citizens. Valéry, who was 'astionished' by proselytism and thought it shameful 'to want others to agree with us', was a contemporary of Hitler, Stalin and Pétain; not only did he suspend his judgement and thereby do nothing to stop (or help) those madmen from taking power; he was never able to explain the whys and where fores of Stalinism, Hitlerism or Pétainism. Non-believers are solitary men. They lay down the law in their rooms at home, but as soon as they go out into the streets, one of two things happens. Either they become believers (against their will) or they give way to the believers. Sceptics have the ability to respect the law without really believing in it, but not to pass laws in the City or to convince others that they should abandon their beliefs.

We will not dwell upon the endless complex play between knowledge and conviction, as their effects in the history of various scientific systems and in the day-to-day experience of spontaneous consciousness are plain for all to see. (Scientists believe in the value of science, non-believers in incredulity, and so on.) Nor will we dwell upon the semantic distinctions to which the verb 'believe' can (and must) give rise. (Believing it will be fine tomorrow is not the same as believing in Father Christmas, and the belief that justice will eventually reign on earth is not the same as the belief in the ressurection of the body on the day of the Last Judgement.) For the moment, our main priority is to abstract the order of belief from the horizon of knowledge by placing ourselves on this side of the critical dichotomy between belief and knowledge. It is a very recent dichotomy in the history of knowledge which derives from a prior decision—a philosophical *thesis* in the strict sense of the word. We simply have to show that the logic of the collective has nothing to do with the criteria of cognition. Belief is not a lower form of knowledge, mania is not an error of judgement and no one decides not to believe. Questions concerning the validity or legitimacy of collective beliefs simply do not mean anything. Belief is an a priori form of sociability (or political existence) and, as such, it does not have to justify its existence. A collective belief may put forward argued proofs, but ultimately it does not depend upon the proofs it can or cannot put forward for itself. The universe of collective behaviour has its own logic, which exists at a different level and in a different register to that of logical representations (to which, as in Descartes, the infinite will of the subject decides to acquiesce or not to acquiesce by exercising its free will). It also speaks a different language. Devotees of *Minerve ou de la sagesse*, who believe that 'the truth is the one thing you must never believe' and that 'what one believes is never true' (Alain), simply do not have access to that universe. For the fact that there are beliefs in every society does not correspond to a sovereign judgement from on high: it has to be accounted for. Political science—if, of course, the political can be the object of a science—will be a science of non-science. For the things that cannot be founded 'in reason'—opinion, belief, faith—are the very things that found political authority. In order to explain political authority, we must first explain those opinions which are regarded as authoritative. (Mediology will make its contribution by examining the technical system that produces the opinions or public discourses specific to each period in a given society.)

The referral or conveyance of things from one realm to another—from the logic of action to the logic of knowledge—can give rise to all sorts of apologia-effects, both negative and positive, in which the adversaries and partisans of a given belief excel. Pascal's argument plays skillfully on ambiguity. You can be sure you are not mistaken if you say that 'I only believe in stories for which those who witnessed them would die'—that really is how collective loyalty functions (martyrs produce proselytes). But it does not follow that there is any basis to the stories in question: martyrs do not prove they are true. Conversely, no one would die in order to 'bear witness' to the validity of a geometrical theorem; but are we to conclude that the theorem is therefore inconsistent? The political-power argument is double-edged, and Renan's answer to Pascal is sardonic, though not without a certain sadness. 'Men only become martyrs for things they are not sure about. They die for opinions and not for certainties, for what they believe and not for what they know. When it is a matter of beliefs, the greatest sign and the most convincing proof is to die for them.'[4] Although unanimity has never been a criterion in the scientific order (or, at the most, a negative criterion), it is the very basis of the political (or religious) order. The apologetic vice involves its conversion into a logical argument. The proud motto of the apologist for the Catholic Church is *quod semper quod ubique, quod ab omnibus*, and for a long time its universal distribution was invoked as proof of its infallibility. On those grounds, however, magic is 'truer' than the 'true religion'.

The only universal and necessary statement about belief is that the act of believing is universal and necessary wherever a human group is gathered together on a piece of land. Truth is sufficient unto itself. Since the collective is by its very nature insufficient, it stands in need of an external guarantor. This social fact has to be treated as if it were a thing: there is no human group that does not have values, mottoes or aims, even (or especially) when its only ideal is force and when it prides itself on navigating by guesswork. Belief implies division and division implies belief. The subject of the-act-of-believing is a plural subject (the faithful, the flock, the militants, the brothers). The subjective cause of the so-called judgement can only come into play in intersubjective form. Social intersubjectivity—I believe because the other believes, I believe without really believing because everyone else believes, and so on—is not equivalent to logical objectivity. As we shall see, however, the aberration of fraternal fervour and collective exultation does correspond to a rational function. Social psychology does not enjoy a good reputation among adepts of 'the scientific theory of history': it describes effects without providing explanations. Yet the effects are found in practical history, in those house-of-cards or snowball effects of collective adhesions and disaffiliations which characterize the rise and fall of great historical 'ideologies'.

3. The Thing in its Practical State: Location

It is the destiny—banal and temporary as it may be—of a project for a transcendental critique to express itself in the forms and words of the very thing it claims to transcend. Despite our theoretical objections and for want of anything better (or for want of conceptual imagination), we will therefore continue to use the signpost *ideology* as a readily accessible marker. We will try to describe the thing itself, as it works and as it appears in normal experience (leaving aside the theoretical validity of the category). The fact is that, in the history of societies, 'world-views' have arisen, been deployed and been identified by name. How are they to be defined?

When a social ideology is fully active, it is fully natural because it fully informs the culture of the social group. It is obvious because it goes without saying. It does of course speak somewhere—in the sacred texts or official canon that give authority to the articles of faith or the 'scientific foundation'. It seems to me that the link between what is said and what is done, between the object of belief and the practice of the believers, can be defined as a *collective preconscious schematism*. Let me explain, word by word.

Schematism: a link between a representation and an action. In the vocabulary of critical philosophy, it defines the general procedure of the imagination in procuring an image for a concept. A schema is more than an image and less than a concept. It provides a bridge between the Kantian categories of reason and the phenomena given to intuition. It is a third term homogeneous with the other two and pivotal to the entire logic of truth, as it provides the conditions for its effectuation. Our analytic of efficacy touches here upon an analogous zone which is mysterious yet decisive (*verbi gracia* for a communist, for if socialist society or the class struggle were simply concepts or images, they would not be motors). The faculty of acting raises the same questions as the faculty of understanding: what is the link between sensuous lived experience and the ideal finality of the action, between the concept and the image? What is the link that articulates one with the other and causes belief, knowledge and action to circulate within one other?

Schema is preferable to *representation*, which is too speculative and specular a term. Being a mental projection (anticipatory or extensive) of a practical operation, the schema gives the inert 'ideology' its dynamism and restores it to its true role as a trigger for acts which conform to the values posited by the ideology). No system for interpreting the world exists in a pure state: even the most abstract exist as dramaturgies before they become hermeneutics. To use a metaphor from cards, any articulated symbolic formation brings together an intelligible hand and a game of practical interventions, but the hand is subordinate to the game. The one thing that Islam, Christianity and Communism have in common is their ability to provide a synthetic recapitulation of what I need to know about the world and of what I have to do in the world. Ideology tells me my origin in order to point out my destination, revealing what forces me onwards only to show where I am heading. It is an anticipatory system flanked by a sub-system of interpretation and a sub-set of intervention; an expectation ordered *into* an action *by* information.

Collective: an ideology is not an individual production but a collective identity's means of expression. Qua product of belief, it is in its concept a product of society, as is the religious ritual, but not the magical act (if we agree with Durkheim's rejection of Marcel Mauss's argument that 'the possession of a magical technique never brings men together in a group'). Modern ideology is so similar to the religious phenomenon because it so closely controls individual mental cathexis. The markers of the schematism, which ensures the internal unity of a set of conduct and the conduct of a set, are social manners, primarily ways of eating, producing, loving, praying, housing, walking, speaking, dressing, and so on. The function of demarcation is integration and cohesion: if it did not act as a totalizing agent within a space, it would not be able to perpetuate the historical identity of the group.[5]

Preconscious: the term *unconscious* will be reserved for the set of organizational processes which ensure, over and beyond any particular symbolic system, the psychical survival of the group. The preconscious is closer to the official *we* of a community (like the official ego or an individual). Although it is not present in the group's field of consciousness, it can in theory and does in fact gain access to it (in the thematic form of an exposition or a doctrinal teaching). There is no repression or censorship (characteristics of the unconscious in the true sense of the word) but at most embarrassment, boredom or surprise. Formalization of the theoretical presuppositions of his belief may provoke *reticence* in a political actor, but not (as a general rule) *resistance*. Access to verbalization or even conceptualization is not indispensable, but neither is it blocked. The preconscious character of the political schematism is thus radically different from Durkheim's collective consciousness, if we take that to mean the great impersonal reason in which the sociologist of *Les Formes élémentaires de la vie religieuse* saw not only the incarnation of necessity and logical universality, but also the moral kingdom of ends. His method of relating to society the highest forms of human mentality (reason, morality) betrays an admirable civic piety worthy of a great and good republican; but its experimental guarantors leave something to be desired. 'Collective ideation' is a passion curtailed, and it is in collective passion that the political unconscious finds its liberation.

The schematism is therefore polemical by nature. Given that *we* can only be identified in opposition to *them* (the others), political polarity and political identity are inseparable. In the order of the collective, the abandoning of polemical practice is equivalent (an impossible equivalent) to suicide. Born of and from a defensive reaction, a community can only survive by counter-attacking. Its whole reason for existence is to repeat or mime its birth certificate in order to perpetuate itself as a state or to reproduce its identity (See Book II, Section II, Chapter 20). The political fertility of the polemical unthought (*impensé*) is the opposite of the scientific sterility of polemical exercises. In the history of an individual understanding, as in the history of science, an obsession with antagonisms extinguishes understanding, leads to repetition and blocks the discovery of rational solutions to problems. In collective formations, on the other hand (cultures, civilizations or nations as well as confessions, parties or movements), conflict awakens or reawakens the processes of we–identification, mobilizing its energies and crystallizing into an 'ideology', a reactualization of its origins in a continuous and ideal plane of general mobilization. The function of a collective is to posit itself, not to conceptualize itself. It only accepts thought as a means of re-posing itself and reinforcing its distinctive features. The function of ideological positioning is scarcely restful, however, and the preservation of the *we* is a bellicose affair. It is highly probable that historically dominant symbolic formations find their expression in schemata of world reconquest, in which the haunting phantasy of self-fragmentation is inverted in trials of strength up to the final victory. The Antichrist and the spirit of the crusades, the intrusion of evangelical missions and Islamic fundamentalism, imperialist rollback and proletarian internationalism—these are two sides of the same coin, and that is why they are on opposite sides.

A working ideology is a tribute to the historical correlation between the state of emergency and the state of the group. An effervescent group responds to an external threat by crystallizing. It becomes coherent in order to satisfy the demands of the transition to a psychical war economy. The reappearance of the we/they tension forces the community into a doubly regressive mental space characterized by the good/bad, clean/dirty opposition of infantile affectivity and by the sacred/profane, inside/outside opposition that typifies the religious reaction to a threat. The polemical dimension of group affectivity adds to the affective dimension of polemic. To sum up: just as *spirit*, *power* and *communication* are consubstantial in magic–religious thought, and just as *matter*, *energy* and *data* are co-terminous in modern physics, the dynamics of practical ideas (that is, social beliefs) bind together *affectivity*, *efficacity* and *community*. These last three categories are usually thought of as being distinct and belonging to different disciplines, but when brought into contact with one another, they spark off the electrical charge of an ideality: the ideology-effect. It is not possible to think any one in isolation from its complements ('charisma' being a typical product of their conjunction). None of them can gain access to existence unless it transforms itself into its complements. In the absence of three-dimensional space, we can at least play with perspective by becoming a painter, a photographer or a film-maker. Unfortunately, the spoken chain binds us to a flat linear succession in which, given that the whole cannot exist in its parts, any moment of the description may become inconsistent. As everyone cannot make films, we may be forgiven for dealing separately (abstractly) with each of these three critical blind spots of political reasoning.

The Affective Command

It was not, they say, a fish that discovered H_2O. We are bathed in the affective element: it underlies, colours and imbues the 'representative' aspect of our political motivations. 'Ideological' rationality codes as 'ideas' (expresses and conceals) an organized set of sympathies and antipathies, attractions and repulsions, but only their hidden coherence can be described as a motor. We suffer from a cruelly deficient knowledge of affectivity. Until that gap is filled or at least camouflaged, political science will remain in an infancy marked by intellectualism. The group is a sultry passion, and our poor knowledge of individual passions—those minor incitements to crime—helps to explain why we are still in the dark about the collective. If the specialists in political science had prefaced their countless theories of the state, workers' control and the future spaces of sovereignty with a study of grief, hatred or happiness (that of militants or believers), we would be in a better position to understand it.

We have to break out of this vicious circle of objectivist reductionism and protest-centred subjectivism, in which everyone uses his neighbour's naivety to justify his own. 'When a science refuses to recognize the vitality of the zones it excludes', writes Jacqueline Mer, 'the improvisations of a disappointed and vindictive subjectivity find a home in its gaps.'[1] Its phantasies and stammerings justify a return to the wooden language of academicism, just as some people's abstract internationalism turns into an abstract nationalism. It is a miserable process: intellectualism creates a desert and fanaticism promptly puts up the welcoming but empty tents of 'understanding', 'intuition' and 'transcendence'—not that they have ever been known to help elucidate the object of the cult.

It is precisely because we do not give reason its due that we fail to give fire, dreams or mysteries their due by capitulating to the apparent (though patent) irrationality of the facts of sensibility. If the physical world is describable in local terms, it is necessarily describable in its entirety—psyche included—and if the world can be described, so can chaos.

Is intellectualism the lesser of two evils? Definitely. Given that we have to have leaders in the City, better a leader than a *Duce* or a 'conductor'. Given that we have to go to school, better a bad pedagogue than a good mystagogue. Given that we have to make ourselves understood within the group, better an imperfect explanation than an imperious ecstasy or no explanation at all. Similarly, intellectualism—a term designating a 'doctrine according to which everything that exists is, in theory, reducible to intellectual elements, to ideas' (Lalande) but which we will use in the more general sense of a normative attitude which 'considers that, whilst active and affective phenomena are irreducible, they are of secondary value' (ibid)—might be seen as an inevitable side-effect of scientific work. A linguist has pointed out that the tendency towards intellectualism is present in the very fact of apprehending a language from the point of view of the listening subject rather than from that of the speaking subject, as an instrument for decoding rather than as a means of expression and action.[2] It should also be pointed out that the people who talk about ideologies are not the people who live them: they take as their object of analysis remote or defunct symbolic formations whose very remoteness is probably necessary for formalization. However, the distance that makes things visible inevitably distorts our vision. It forces us to reduce the efficacious to the visible and to look for the efficacity of the system within representational elements internal to the system of representation.

When it comes to affectivity, I obviously have no particular explanation to put forward. But I would still stress the importance of opening the debate—simply by looking at the facts—and the danger of declaring the discussion closed before it has even begun. We will therefore look at the evidence, since it is so obvious, and then examine the exemplary theoretical attitude of Lévi-Strauss. More than anything else, this 'Kantianism without a transcendental subject' allows us to see the/price that contemporary anthropology has had to pay for the Kantian assumption of an irreducible duality between sensibility and understanding.

Fear of ridicule is not the smallest epistemological obstacle in the human sciences. When we go to a meeting or a congress, we do not blush deep down at asking a party official, leader or 'intellectual' to move us, even to move us to tears. It is an accepted fact that an 'ideological' intervention, achieves its aim when it strikes a chord within us. But it would seem incongruous to ask the same party official to evoke the chords of his own preconscious: such inner emotions do not belong within the context of an exposition of motives. It might be argued that whereas the market in moving speeches is open, the discourse of emotion is private. However, there is still the phase difference between the motives and motivations of political behaviour, and it is not just due to modesty the high costs of literary expression. We are talking about a cultural taboo which forces us to seek the truth of a public performance by watching the actors through the key-hole; to look through the wrong end of the telescope if we wish to see ideology life-size. For ideology is inscribed not in an official register or in arguments, but in confidences. The original mode of existence of belief disappears when beliefs are expressed; it appears in the wings of history with a small *h*. There is potentially more science in the memoirs, stories and autobiographies of political actors than in all the dissertations of political science graduates.

Rational loyalties are governed by affectivity, and the foregrounding of the system is an a posteriori systematization of primary emotions.[3] Christianity is a personal religion, national-socialism a manic mythology, and Marxism-Leninism a scientific ideology: there is no comparison between them. But no one is converted to these formations through deduction, inference or reasoned argument. It is in a tumult of primal scenes that a world-view is born, announces itself and imposes itself upon the individual. It is expressed in images that are charged with affects, colours, insignia and tones. Primary relations with the family, with the country, the landscape or early companions, do much more than announce the adult commitment: they seem to rehearse its leitmotifs. Affectivity does not enclose the individual within his ego; its function is to open things up, to knit the first stitches that link the individual with his environment. An ideology is a constellation of dynamic affects in so far as it connects an individual with a field of social forces.

We must rid ourselves of the trilogy of the faculties (sensibility, will, understanding) and all the other remnants of scholasticism. We must overcome time-honoured dichotomies and disjunctions: fact or myth; belief or knowledge; notion or passion; phantasy or ideal; perception or hallucination. The lived experience of ideology forces open terminological grills of and breaks down the barrier between the pleasure principle and the reality principle. A social passion is a reawakened idea as well as an obscure idea. A symbolic statement becomes a force by taking on a human face. A logical dynamic is a logical eroticism. We 'espouse a cause' when it becomes a motor cause, and it becomes a motor cause, when we prove our love by 'espousing' it. Fortunately, cliches are less prudish than theoretical classifications and our reach-me-down sarcasm.

'He's a sentimentalist!' 'A dreamer!' 'A poet!' Being an abdication of the real, imagination makes us forget that an image is a nascent action. The art of stimulating and the art of simulating. If you look at Christianity and the idea of the Crusade, industrial Europe and the idea of social revolution, the colonial Third World and the idea of national liberation, it becomes clear that the idea existed as an exciting image before it existed as an idea. Long before it is articulated in a historical analysis, a revolutionary idea inculcates itself into us as a narrative apprenticeship, a subjective narrative. The fiction is called history and its realization is known as pleasure. We act in such a way that history confirms the truth of the fiction. The revolutionary event is a clumsy answer to the unspoken aspiration for a narration that is at once dramatic and pleasurable. To act dramatically is to act in such a way that our lives become as beautiful as a film. An ideology is an anticipation of satisfaction—which is why its operations are controlled by myths. Every social advance on the part of the imaginary expresses a rise in practical demand, although, as we shall see later, the inflation of images can lead to a deflation of the collective imaginary and thence to a radical drop in practical demand ('post-modern' force-feeding). Similarly, if the mystification-myth is described too well, the convocation-myth also disappears in a final twist of non-realism.[4]

In present-day political science, Barthes (or Valéry) seems to have killed Sorel (or Caillois). 'Semiology has taught us that the

task of the myth is to give a natural justification to historical intention, to make contingency appear eternal. This is the exact approach of bourgeois ideology.' And why not ideology as such? The
point is that the myth both mystifies and mobilizes, and that it
could not do either if it did not do both. Light is shed upon its contradictory status by the equally contradictory structure of collective
action, which makes the evacuation of the contingent real (the
myth as mystification) the precondition for the transformation of
that same real (the myth as convocation). The modern idea of
Revolution, for instance, is a myth in that it posits the Revolution
as an essence transcending contingency and all historical determination; yet this regulatory myth operates as a focus for real
forces that is able to mock historically determined revolutionary
movements from a distant vanishing-point. Barthes fails to see the
internal unity of the mythical contradiction because he surrep-
titiously, perhaps unconsciously, adopts the opposition between
the image of the world and the reality of the world, and hence between nature and history. All that he can see in the myth is
'depoliticized speech'; he does not realize that, in practice, a
political project can only establish itself in depoliticized form, or
that nature haunts history from within rather than running along
outside it. There is no need to choose between *singing about things*
and *acting upon things*, for the one implies the other and a human
group incapable of singing is no longer able to act. Sing, chant,
depict, keep time, strike up a song. (Epinal began to produce images just as the French nation was beginning to transform Europe
through the revolution and the Napoleonic Wars. Patriotic sounds
ring out wherever a fatherland has been established; and once the
young people of a young country know two or three lines of the *Internationale* by heart, they no longer go into the streets just to burn
a few cars for fun.)

Barthes's *Mythologies*, for all their marvellous descriptions, still
rely upon the assumption (then Marxist in origin) that ideology is
predestined to be the antonym of the real. The real as a promise of
apocalypse—the last-minute revelation of a constantly elusive 'asei-
ty'—secretly governs his jubilant theoretical devaluation of the
myth as unfaithful reproduction or temporary impotence. He sees
it as a slip in the rendering of a real posited as the normative
horizon of what will one day be an accurate discourse. That

discourse will be revealed on the same day of the Revolution. It constitutes 'what we must seek: a reconciliation between reality and men, description and explanation, object and knowledge'.[5]

'All will contains passion'—Nietzsche.[6] All passions contain a driving image: inside every conquerer there is a man suffering from hallucinations. It is a fact of history that, long before the Conquistadors, the discoverers of *terra firma* (Columbus, for example) set off in search of adventure with nothing more than the legendary geographies of Antiquity and various myths culled from the depths of the medieval mentality. Similarly, as Pierre Gascar puts it: 'The discoveries of the nineteenth century would not have been accomplished so easily if they had not given rise to more dreams than calculations in Europe.'[7] And when a militant (Communist) looks back at his life, inscribing it within the history of his group as the century nears its end, what does he call his realist biography if not '*Et nos rêves camarades*' (Our dreams, comrades)? Not 'Our strategies!', 'Our resolutions!', 'Our scientific theory!' It is not the calculation of possibilities, the number of members or the sum of true statements that makes comrades: it is shared dreams. A reminder of the dreams sounds forth both as a rallying call and as a call to order, because the dream is both the daily bread of communion and the supreme finality of collective behaviour. The interpellation takes the group as its witness, on the strength of dreams taken as *witnesses* of actions past and future (invariant markers which measure variations). It is because there is a Communist dream that there is a Communist *we* and therefore an organized Communist practice.

You can write good books with bad feelings, but you will never make a science out of sentiments, good or bad. Not being scientific objects, they are not entitled to enter the scientific field—or so says structural ethnology, the most respectable social science in modern France. States of sadness, joy, love, hatred, hope, anxiety, pride, etc. can be described, depicted or retraced, but not explained. 'As affectivity is the most obscure side of man,' writes Lévi-Strauss, 'people have always been tempted to resort to it, forgetting that what is refractory to explanation is ipso facto unsuitable for use in explanation. A datum is not primary because it is incomprehensible: this characteristic indicates solely that an explanation, if it exists, must be sought on another level.'[8]

We will have to spend some time on this argument: not only because it is the 'majority' view among French anthropologists of today; but because its concrete target and starting-point is a conception of the religious that we too have used as a springboard.

So we will not ignore *Totemism* because in its critique of immediate enemies like Malinowski and the early Radcliffe-Brown—whose interpretation is, according to Lévi-Strauss, 'naturalistic, utilitarian and affective'-it presents a remarkable synthesis of a certain conception of social analysis. It goes so far as to dismiss Freud on the grounds that he explains social constraints, whether positive or negative, 'as the effects of impulses or emotions which appear again and again, with the same characteristics, and during the course of centuries and millenia, in different individuals'.[9] Durkheim, too, 'derives social phenomena from affectivity', and his theory of totemism 'starts with an urge and ends with a recourse to sentiment'. 'Durkheim's theory of the collective origin of the sacred rests upon a *petitio principii*.'[10]

Let us try to understand the inner strengths of Lévi-Strauss's polemic against the Founding Fathers. He accuses them of a damning logical inconsistency expressed in two forms of faulty reasoning: an inadequacy and a contradiction.

1. *The Inadequacy*. The institution cannot be explained in terms of instinct because the general cannot explain the particular. Tendency and need are specific properties of a uniform character, but we are dealing with an irreducible plurality of customs and institutions. If culture is interpreted in terms of nature, or anthropology subordinated to considerations of general psycho-biology, then it becomes impossible to explain concretely different forms of cultural phenomena. It's the old refrain: 'Valéry may well be a petty-bourgeois intellectual, but not all petty-bourgeois intellectuals are Valéry.' What, I ask, does that tell us about Valéry as an individual? If magic corresponds to a need to reduce man's basic anxiety, all magical rituals should be the same. But since they differ according to the time and culture, we have to reconstitute the mechanisms of the transition from 'a confused and disordered emotion' to 'acts marked by the most rigorous precision and divided into a number of distinct categories'.

2. *The Contradiction*. Explanations in terms of affectivity lead to a logical tautology. In Durkheim's conception of religion as social

and society as religious, does the social experience of the sacred explain the sacred experience of society, or is it the other way round? Lévi-Strauss sees this complementarity as a *petitio principii,* but amore kindly reading would regard it as a happy 'reciprocity of perspectives' implying a break with the mechanical model of causality.

One could wax ironic about whether a final explanation of all observable social divisions in terms of a basic structural principle like the 'unity of opposites' is any better than its predecessors when it comes to simple unifications. The opposition between ying and yang, day/night, male/female, summer/winter does not, a priori, seem any richer or less summary an explanatory principle than need or the feeling of insecurity. But such a critique of formalism is itself formalist. The basis of Lévi-Strauss's argument calls for two sets of comments. The first general remarks apply at the level of logical principles. The second, more specific remarks are situated within the logic in question.

First comment. It is always dangerous to segment being in accordance with the norms of knowledge and to measure the objectivity of phenomena in terms of a given stage in the development of knowledge. 'I can't explain that, so I don't want too take it into account.' One would think that epistemology governed ontology, and that the objections of epistemology were valid as expulsion decrees in ontology! If objective knowledge has postulated from the start that anything inexplicable does not exist, it would not have discovered much about the laws of nature. By stating that psychical phenomena have no voice or even no place within the social sciences, on the ground that their mechanisms are not clearly known to us, we reduce psychology to the status of a decidedly minor aspect of a more or less incantatory technique. We thereby condemn ourselves to remain in ignorance about concrete social practices.

Second comment. If, as it would seem, we have to follow Leibniz, let us go the whole way. Michel Serres once joyfully declared that 'for twenty years now, we have all been neo-Leibnizians' because 'the human sciences have made a whole series of happy discoveries which no one would have dared to dream of'. *Processing by subsets, foregrounding of elements, recognition of simple and general operations, the construction of models, demonstration of invariants, combinatory algebra*—these are six fundamental gestures which 'structural anthropology', having quite legitimately borrowed from linguistics and phonology, might have used to better effect.[11] But in the case of Lévi-Strauss, does Descartes not get in the way of Leibniz? Is he not a scientist scandalized by his philosophical past, an inconsistent structuralist forced, despite himself, to turn back half way because of his old Cartesian puritanism? Is the *mathesis universalis* not intellectually blocked by a prior decision to separate body and mind?[12] For Leibniz, there was no fundamental difference between knowledge through sentiment and knowledge through ideas ('Any sentiment is a confused perception of a truth'), the opposition between the two being valid only for a lower intelligence incapable of perceiving the intermediary degree. In Cartesian structuralism, however, no infinite knowledge can put an end to the primal division of the human psyche. Lévi-Strauss always faces a dilemma (*sive ...sive*) between biology and algebra: if it is not the body, it must be the intellect and vice versa.

'Actually, impulses and emotions explain nothing: they are always *results*, either of the power of the body or of the impotence of the mind. In both cases they are consequences, never causes. The latter can be sought only in the organism, which is the exclusive concern of biology, or in the intellect, which is the sole way offered to psychology and anthropology.'[13]

Why should we exclude a priori any intelligible connection between the biological order and the intellectual order, unless we have taken a prior metaphysical decision that there is a rupture between the two? The only universals would then be elementary structural forms or, to put it more accurately, those logical forms would be found in the mechanisms of thought and not in those of affectivity. But what if the same combination structured the facts of sensibility? Such a supposition is all the more plausible in that structural anthropology sees *association by contrariety* as the basic invariant of that logic of distinctions and oppositions which is common denominator of the savage and the discursive mind. At first sight, the notion of ambivalence and pairs of opposites in the instinctual system offers a very respectable correlation to a symbolic logic operating with binary oppositions. If we assume that this logic is elementary, are we not certain to find it at every level of human reality? Is it possible that there are two central nervous systems, one for vital and the other for logical functions? Obviously not. The brain that secretes the hormones regulating endocrinal functions also coordinates the logical processing of sense data. The chemical substrata of sleep, pain and perhaps even memory are currently being isolated in laboratories for therapeutic purposes (production of beta-endomorphine). Operational elucidation seems more advanced for the nervous mechanisms of 'affective life' than for those of 'intellectual life', although it is still not clear how for the two can be isolated. Genetic psychology has taught us that, as a general rule, affectivity develops hand in hand with intelligence, and that emotivity increases along with the subject's capacity to carry out abstract operations. The late scientific developments thus bear out Nietzsche's claim: 'Morals are a code for the passions. But the passions themselves are a code for organic functions.' To that extent, Nietzsche was a structuralist *avant la lettre*—and perhaps a more consistent one than the current claimants to the title. At the present stage of our knowledge, there is nothing to prevent us postulating the existence of a code that will reveal an isomorphism between our basic affective reactions and our basic logical operations. The fact that, at least until Freud, affective life had to be expressed in scholastic or incantatory language does not provide any grounds for concluding that there can be no real object corresponding to that language or that 'affective state' is merely another name for a 'vague idea'. Nor does the inanity of medieval theories of combustion provide grounds for believing that fires do not occur: it merely points to the urgency of a scientific explanation for the phenomena of combustion.

Why, then, do we see the rejection of an integrated and unificatory pattern, such as any coherent naturalist materialism would suggest? The underlying reason is the logical relationship that grafts the opposition between the orders of body and mind on to the triple transcendental opposition between animality and humanity, nature and culture, affectivity and intellectuality. If each dyad supports and is supported by the others, a compromise over one would lead to disintegration of the other two. In order to preserve the problematic of a *general transition* from nature to culture, it is necessary to posit, within the individual, a *necessary discontinuity* between the affective and the intellectual in which all available rationality is attributed to the latter. Such at least is my explanation of Lévi-Strauss's failure (or refusal) to understand anything about psychical phenomena. The old religious dichotomy between body and soul—and the system's canonical dichtomoies are merely scientific names for it—seems to have inhibited or blocked investigation into the unity of the world, despite the timid suspicion that there might be an isomorphism between the regions of the subject and the object.

All in all, it is better to be summary than lacunary. Our digression concerning the vanquisher of totemism was in a way necessary, since the formal and material structure of 'ideology' proves *a contrario* that affectivity and intellectuality, animality and humanity, nature and culture do exist on the same plane. Paradoxically, it is 'ideology's' mode of existence that allows the problem posed by a radical break between the above terms to be seen as 'ideological'—given, of course, that there can be no scientific solution to an 'ideological' problem. Ideology is in fact the best witness to the law of association by contrariety, as it could not exist without the unity of opposites. A religion, like a doctrine, incarnates the point of transition from one order to the next, albeit in the form of an endless shuttling backwards and forwards. The transition is never completed; and even if it were, nothing new would ever happen on planet earth. Intellectuality exists in collectives because affectivity exists in and between individuals: the individual accedes to social humanity through his animality. This is not to say that man's relationship with his needs is not mediated by culture. But although such mediation removes the immediacy from the multiple processes through which needs are satisfied, it does not alter the natural character of the organic need itself. The interest of Leibniz even extends to his political commitment and occasional writings. More than any other philosopher of his century, the discoverer of infinitesmal calculus (shortly ahead of Newton) was deeply involved in public affairs. Unlike Spinoza, he did not leave a political 'summa', but his two thousand letters to six hundred correspondents deal with almost all the burning issues of the eighteenth century.

3

The Imperative to Belong

Hypothesis: wherever a *we* gets under way, there is an 'ideology' at work; when it is no longer possible to say *we*, there is no more 'ideology'. The 'power to act' depends upon the state of the group. The difficulty is that our analysis of this vital function is hampered by the superfluous category of 'ideology' and by a lacunary concept of the 'group' that is singularly lacking in precision and dignity. 'Group' was imported in the seventeenth century—somewhat late in the day—from the vocabulary of the fine arts (a set of painted or sculpted figures) into that of literature (a group of living characters). By the end of the nineteenth century it has assumed so many meanings (mathematical group, electrogenic group, group therapy ...) that it finally became meaningless. This extraordinary asymmetry between a superfluous word and the absence of a word goes a long way to explain the obscurity surrounding the mechanisms of belief. The fact that current vocabulary still leaves us with the abstract and strictly useless individual/society couplet, divorced from the concrete mediations between the two, obliges political criticism to work with the words of others until such time as it can forge a language of its own. Politically operational groups have a permanence, a gravity and a strength (in the sense of a strong tendency) which brings them closer to an anthropologist's group than to the diagnostic 'small groups' dear to psychotherapists. However, psychotherapists could still learn a lot from anthropologists—for example, that the barriers should be removed between clinical observation of occasional groups, anthropological observation of natural (or 'primary') groups and political observation of voluntary (or 'secondary') groups. Freud never really worked on the problem of collective formations, but he did at least note their specificity in a famous article written in 1921,[1] shortly after the October Revolution and shortly before the mass counter-revolutions of fascism. The terra incognita (which neither Marx nor Montesquieu approached) is no longer virgin territory. One day, political reason will have to repay its debt to such pioneers of the 'group unconscious' as Pontalis, Didier Anzieu and René Kaës,[2] but for the moment we will simply outline the logic of the positions to be described without going into the interpersonal relations involved in particular group situations.

A group demand on an individual (house arrest, a summons, a call for self-justification) is neither a juridical nor a moral process, although it may borrow the language of law. It is not a categorical imperative or a rule of conduct, but above all a reminder. You are not alone. I was there before you. You exist only through us. The symbolic violence is not like rape, which brings to grips two (or more) people, one active and the other passive, a criminal and a victim. It does not externally impose forms of conduct as a thing-like constraint and, in that sense, it is more than a 'social fact'. It imposes itself from within by awakening a suggestible sub-ego, the latent *ideal-we*. It reminds the subject of the duties he owes himself by reminding him that he does not belong to himself and that his innermost personality is not a personal but a patrimonial possession. It does not say, 'Look around you, look at the family circle'; it says, 'Look at yourself in the mirror and look me in the face'. The group is not concentric: its individual peripheries relate to an ideal centre—its own *imago*. The group both exists beyond the individual and is immanent to him. Phylogenetic priority involves ontogenetic priority. The status of 'group member' is not added to a substantial subject as one property among others: it relates to the very constitution of the subject. A crisis within the group therefore leaves the subject naked, alone and terribly 'vulnerable', and therefore liable to answer the group summons. Fatherland, Church, Party and Family call upon us to remember that they have made us what we are. Our ideologies are our marching orders. In peacetime, ideology keeps out of sight, but danger projects it on to all the walls of the City in the graphic form of the mobilization poster (a symbolic figuration and a fantasmatic realization of the structure of enrolment). 'I want you for the US Army.' The personified group—Uncle Sam in his tall hat or the Proletarian with a star on the peak of his cap—points its finger at each one of us and looks us straight in the eye. The ideological structure is ideologically neutral—which is why, during the First World War, America, Germany, Italy. Hungary and even Bolshevik Russia could, with the help of industrial art, unwittingly invent exactly the same propaganda 'visual aids'. Had not the poster been the projective test of the political unconscious, none of them would have been able to recruit every last unconscious subject capable of bearing arms.[3]

'The interpellation of individuals as subjects' (Althusser) presupposes that the interpellated subject is no longer a subject. It is never as individual subjects that men are recognized as having the status of subjects of action, as having, in other words, the ability to make history. (Even for anarchists, individual action, which is both a point of both honour and doctrine, is the doing of the group.) It is never 'Hey, you there!'—a non-ethnic abstraction with neither cause nor effect—but 'Men and women of France!', 'Comrades!', 'Dear brothers!'. Mobilization works by pinning us to the ground and inscribing us within a primary totality (nation, party, God's people). That is why it is not a *faculty* recognized on private grounds, but a publicly declared *obligation*; and why it is not an *interpellation,* but an immediate *convocation*. To interpellate is to speak brusquely to someone and then to question them. But here the requisition precedes the request, since an 'ideology', be it religious or secular, provides both question and answer. It is designed to make the individual act rather than speak. A group which makes 'representations' to us immediately places us in a position of inferiority, legally liable for mobilization. Such inferiority is not, however, punitive, but elating. We are tacitly called to heroic action or martyrdom, not as suspects required to make a statement. The group memory fills us all with pride. By holding out an ideology, the group offers us protection in the knowledge that we need it. The contract on offer is not with a system of 'true' or 'correct' ideas, but with a fraternity that keeps us warm. The ideas in an ideology function as a promise of belonging precisely *because* the group guarantees them. An ideology is a flag, but you do not rally to a flag in view of its colours. You adopt it because you are incorporated into the army. There is a symbolism of belonging, but the feeling is infinitely more important. 'French Communism functions like a memory, with Marxism its mnemonic.'[4] The group-identity is the ballast that stabilizes the oscillations of doctrine, finding expression even in the surface vocabulary. A writer who has done research on long-term changes in Communist terminology concludes: 'This coherent and relatively stable system has a characteristic core: the group, its values and its permanence. In fact our diachronic section shows that the only major paradigm to remain constant throughout our corpus is that of the Party (PCF + working class + communists). The other lexical groups and the basic propositions into which they are inserted are subject to considerable modification. The combinatory varies constantly, but it continues to revolve around the almost immobile pole of the party.'[5] Thus, we cannot posit: 1) that the ideas of the subject are 'material actions inserted into material practices—governed by material rituals that are themselves defined by the material ideological apparatus from which derive the ideas of that subject'; and (2) that 'the category of the subject is constitutive of all ideology', that 'all ideology has the function (which defines it) of "constituting" concrete individuals as subjects'.[6] For a ritual carries with it an idea of obligation that expresses the pressure of the collective—unless, that is, we superimpose the categories of 'subject' and 'individual'. ('Who is there?' 'Its me.' 'Hello, my friend!' 'Hey, you there!') The same confusion appears in the reduction of Christian religious ideology to a *discourse in the vocative* relating a central unique subject to abstract, fragmented individuals. 'I address myself to you, a human individual called Peter.'[7] But St Paul, the real catalyst of the early Christian community, the organizer par excellence, speaks a collective discourse: 'Now you are Christ's body, and each of you a limb or member of it' (I Corinthians XVII 12–30). Peter became the ideogram of the Church, thanks to a nice play on words, but it was Paul who provided the organigram of the institution. It was the man who placed or replaced the new authority in categories (Man-Woman, Christ-Church, Parent-Children, Masters-Slaves) who discovered the basic symbolic operator.

Burn incense on the altar, cut up your bulls, roast their thighs, join the circle, and the gods of the City will appear to you. Kneel down, move your lips in prayer and you will believe. Buy *L'Humanité*, go flyposting, attend the rally, and you will join the Party. What is common to all these different things is that you do them in a group, not on your own. In classical Greece, a myth was 'something said as well as something done' (J.E. Harrison). Our theoretical narrators strike the rock too, but they do not do so alone. 'The whole of Israel is behind Moses as he taps the rock with his staff. Moses may have doubts, but not Israel. The diviner follows his wand. Behind him is a whole village anxiously searching for water. The state of the individual is always conditional upon the state of society.'[8] The ideological spell works best in rites, feasts or ceremonies, when the social body can exercise its influence most intensely. 'Plunged into the transports of the dance, feverishly agitated, they become as one body with one soul'. In Europe, attendance at a meeting or demonstration does not require one to dance, yet the modern techniques of bringing people together are basically the same as those found in Melanesia or New Guinea, even though they may be less picturesque. The ideal *we* is still the group-man of the monastic orders.

The ideal *we* is a *we* in action: the collective gesture breaks down the opposition between the *ego* and the *ego-ideal*. As Freud rightly says: 'There is always a feeling of triumph when something in the ego coincides with the ego-ideal. And the sense of guilt (as well as the sense of inferiority) can also be understood as an expression of tension between the ego and the ego-ideal.'[9] The reconciliation is jubilatory but not sacrilegious, festive but not transgressive. This feast does not signify the suspension of the rules, but the institution of a different rule, a different order, a different law, in which the mind is governed by the body and all bodies are one. Coalescent is not synonymous with ecstatic: ideological ecstasy can begin with a PE class.

The unbearably extreme effects produced by the group state in all the hot spots of the human adventure should not be allowed to conceal its sober, modest character in everyday life. Sectarian ecstasy is merely its outer limit. But nor should our trivial experience of it in daily life mask the truly radical dispossession it implies. Basically, we are talking not about a *sociological misadventure* but about a historical effect of the *anthropological adventure* which requires man to make a detour through the other before he can become himself. Just as the constitution of the psychological subject requires mediation through the image of the body, so *the constitution of the political subject requires mediation though the image of the group*. The subject appears in the centre through a process of decentring, through the double movement of projection on to the other-than-the-self and identification of the self with the other. To put it another way, individual *alienation* and collective *identity* are one and the same. The collective self is constituted through dispossession of the individual self. Both political investigations and analytic investigations reveal the same inaugural expropriation, one at the level of collective history, the other at the level of individual history.

The emergence of historical 'ideologies' shows the effects of this trans-historical constraint in the positive history of the West. Negatively or *a contrario*, let us look at the *paradox of Protestantism*. Taken to its logical conclusion, reformed religion should have been a religion without a Church. The Christian stands alone before God, without any intermediaries in heaven or on earth: his only worship is the reading and free interpretation of the book and he works for his salvation in his own home. What need has he of churches? Is not the Protestant church to be found in the home of every head of every family? What need does he have of ministers? Is not prayer a dialogue between the creator and his creature? What need does he have of a gathering of the faithful or, as the English say, congregation? No rites and therefore no liturgy. There are, however, contradictions of human nature.[10]

Hauser's comment is extremely telling: reformed ideology should have done without a Church and without hierarchical communal structures. If it failed to do so, this was because of a 'phenomenon of crowd psychology which can be seen in the most primitive peoples, in the darkness of Africa and around the totem poles of the human prairie: the call of the tom-tom and the magic of secret dances'. 'Men have an irresistible need to feel things in common, to pray and sing together, to stand shoulder to shoulder when they proclaim their common faith.'[11] A summary explanation? But the facts are there. Geneva, the Church-City, rises against Rome. It is a school for martyrs, and for executioners (cf. the execution of Servet). Orthodoxy and free thought were in contradiction with one another. However, when dissident evangelism becomes a material force, a Protestant orthodoxy emerges. We will see later that although the Freudian explanation—'man is a horde animal'—is not actually false, it is unable to account for such reversals.

Or let us take the *paradox of Marxism*. According to its first principles, 'scientific socialism' should have been a social movement without 'apparatuses' or institutions ('The Communists do not form a separate party opposed to other working-class parties', etc.). The workers stand alone in the face of history, with no other-form of worship than to read abridged versions of *Capital* and work for the common salvation in the factory. What need do they have of cells? Is not the cell present in every workshop? What need have they of full-time cadres? Is not revolution the inevitable product of the deepening objective contradictions between the increasing socialization of the productive forces and so on? No ceremonies, then, and no supreme saviour, There are, however, contradictions of human nature ...

The coherence between structures of belonging ('below') and systems of ideas ('above'), or between territories and doctrines, does not merely invert 'ideology's' centre of gravity by destroying the very principle of the ideological instance (as a level of reality or a potentially autonomous unreality). It also leads one to wonder about the conditions of possibility of communal cohesion (given that the birth of an ideology is the birth of a community). Where does the *we* come from? From common identification with a superior. 'I put myself in your hands and I humbly thank you,' says the Japanese novice after the master of his order has enigmatically or silently responded to the weekly ceremony of questions (one at a time). That is another trivial experience taken to extremes. Believe: it's good for you; it means we can be together, look at one other, love one another. Being together makes you happy, being cut off makes you unhappy. To be undivided is to be redeemed, to be evicted is to fall from grace (and ill-feeling is a poisonous weed). The individual can only truly find himself when he belongs. But the mediation itself rebounds, as the group is not in full possession of itself either: being united *in* presupposes being united *with* (just as a belief *that* implies a belief *in*). Collectives are declined backwards. The nominative plural comes after the genitive and the dative. A *we* is possible because every *I* proceeds from and gives itself *to*. 'Brothers in Christ', we come together in the Church by uniting with the body of Christ through our obedience to Our Holy Father 'who loves and unites us in the name of God'.[12] This subordination is our strength, since it allows us to enter as a legitimate subject into the play of collective forces which divide up the planet (so as to modify it in our favour, 'we' being God's people). The emergence of distinct collective subjects presupposes the dependence of individuals upon the collective to which they refer and the dependence of the collective upon its founding reference (the other that is common to all or to the ideal of the *we*). I am a member *of* because I believe *in*, and I believe because I am a member. The circle eventually results in 'we the faithful', 'we Jews', 'we Communists', 'we French citizens', 'we the countries of the free world' (provided that the whole world is not free), 'we the fraternal members of the international socialist community' (international and fraternal provided that we accept that one country in the family, the land of Lenin, is more fraternal than the rest). The organizational premiss of a group is an act of allegiance (or vengeance, which is simply an inverted form of faith). It may in itself be unjustifiable, but its necessity can be seen in the regrouping effect it helps to trigger. No personal convocation without personalized invocation! An idea becomes a material force when it is transformed into a meeting-place, something capable of elevating a collection into a congregation. But that transformation entails that the idea has to disappear behind its bearer, the eponymous hero of the group.

The exoteric form of the necessity for mediation is the personification of the group, a social process which naturally produces affectivity (as does any relationship between individuals). Since grace is the attribute of a social function fulfilled by an individual, the mediating function is not attributed to those who possess a particular personal grace. In other words, charisma designates a relation rather than a property; 'between you and me', not an exceptional ego. 'Any relation or affinity between a personality and a society which plays a part in defending the group identity and conquering its future' may be described as charismatic (Jacqueline Mer). The word does not express an inadequacy but a very specific rationality, that of appearances. In Greek, *charis* means 'service rendered' as well as 'grace'. The charismatic figure is therefore someone who gives his group the pleasure of recognizing itself through him. The ultimate pleasure: seeing oneself as a body in someone else's body. The mediated group is dazzled by the halo of the mediator. A personal halo is a mirror, not a mirage. There is a certain erotic hypnosis in the frenzy of personality cults; a certain inverted, though unwitting, collective narcissism in the fascination of the leader. The boundless, blind, 'fanatical' devotion of those who are faithful to the Holy Father (or to the people or the

Fatherland) bears witness to the fact that the group, engrossed in worshipping itself by worshipping its incarnation, is simply striving to preserve its own ego.[13] The mad heroism of martyrs is the ruse of reason peculiar to group egoism.

An ideology exists wherever there is a territory, and not vice versa. The most rapid way of ideologically demobilizing subjects would be to deterritorialize them, and the fastest way to identify them ideologically would be to locate them symbolically. Application of a strategic rule to daily life: discussing the basis of their ideas, political or otherwise, with your friends and neighbours gets you nowhere, as we all know. But you can put an end to all such pointless arguments by asking just one question: 'Which group do you identify with?' Do you still belong to your group of origin or do you now feel like an outsider? Who is now your supreme judge? Who will in the last instance pronounce upon the value of the necessarily contradictory verdicts reached about you in the various social circles in which you move? Application to the history of ideologies: 'Tell me what possible incorporations you offer your contemporaries and I will tell you what force of attraction you currently exercise over their minds.'

It is said that you cannot please everybody, your father included. But you can always choose your father: he whose word is law. In other words, you cannot at one and the same time be a 'good guy' for your political or Church friends, your office or shopfloor workmates, your neighbours or fellows-villagers, your family and cousins, the popular press, T.V. viewers and western public opinion. You have to choose: in the eyes of which group are you prepared to look like a fool or a bastard. As you will always be a swine for someone or other, it is worth remembering that the essence of a swine is positional rather than individual. The ideological position of an individual in the City derives from an intuitive, though not always unconscious, calculation of the comparative costs of 'looking a swine' in the eyes of various labelling instances.

The famous mystery of the Moscow Trials allows the mysteries of 'ideology' to be cleared up. The astonishing confessions of the accused gave rise to countless interpretations.[14] Then came the eye-witness accounts and documents from the victims themselves.[15]

These show that, despite the terrible reality of what happened, the physical tortures and the promises of eventual mercy are not enough to explain the fact that the Old Bolshevik 'men of steel' were reduced to broken puppets; or that men of extraordinary moral calibre, unbroken by the Gestapo itself, were nevertheless broken after the war (London); or that men under no physical pressure, because their judges were not in power, could be reduced to silence for so long (Tillon). These 'violations of socialist legality', as the charming euphemism has it, are so many applications of the law of ideological composition that cements the group together (although it is the group that provides the cement). The confessions do not reveal an intellectual logic based upon deductive reasoning (what Aron terms 'chain identification'), nor a movement from objective to subjective (I am an oppositionist, opposition within the Party is a betrayal of the Party, therefore I really am a traitor). Rather, the subjective logic of belonging is turned against the objective logic of ideas, and the effect is so crushing because the former rather than the latter is the touchstone of true loyalty. Party reason is secondary to the passion for the Party. It is impossible for a militant to be right and for the Party to be wrong, not because the Party is dogmatically and explicitly posited as infallible, but because the moral integrity of the militant is inseparable from his physical or phantasmic integration into its organization. If the 'organic links' are broken, the individual may well fall apart. Expulsion means self-destruction. Articulation with a fraternity is particularly prone to brotherly attack from behind, to the very argument of fraternity itself. Then it is no longer a matter of voluntarily sacrificing oneself on the altar of the Party or of final devotion to one's beloved leaders, but of toppling into a chaos with no landmarks, meaning or reality. Tillon says that when he suddenly found himself alone, banished from his Party and treated like a leper by his comrades, he felt his mind going. At least in his case, he was fortunate to avoid a physical loss of reality.[16]

In the East, they began by disconnecting the suspect element before they arrested him, creating a void around him by leaving his requests unanswered, cutting his normal lines of communication with comrades (mail, invitations, meetings, telephone calls, etc.). Then he was plunged into the 'cooler' and left to rot without any explanation, subjected to a diet of humiliation, vertigo and anxiety (loss of all mental reference points). When the time came, the detainee was told that he had been expelled from the Party. The investigation began its wearying, repetitive scholastic course, often though not always punctuated by torture. The interrogation is in the best cases, where there was evidence of resistance, the process was carried out in such a way as to make the expelled man ask to rejoin the Party. Unfortunately he could only be readmitted through his own elimination (political, that goes without saying; physical, well, that depends). Given that the Party had its reasons for deciding that he was a traitor, he would be acting as a militant if he 'freely and consciously' endorsed that decision. The only possible way for him to remain a good Communist was to denounce himself as a traitor to Communism (or to listen in silence as someone else did it for him). In short, they asked him to assume the spirit of the Party right to the bitter end—the 'spirit of the Party' being the scientific name for its esprit de corps—and to confirm his status as member in the eyes of the outside world by disqualifying himself from membership. *They* was his own militant consciousness, now become his enemy in the form of his interrogator. If he denied the accusation, he denied himself because it meant denying the group. And he *was* the group. When he was asked to admit that he was a scum and to participate in the elimination of scum, all that was being asked of him was a minimum of the political honesty he had so often shown in the past. What if he went back on his word at the last moment? Being a scrupulous pedagogue, the referent transformed the interrogation into the maieutics of belonging: it was up to the pupil to go into labour and give birth to his truth (i.e., a totally fictitious list of misdeeds), even if it involved a forceps delivery with a great deal of pain. The model prisoner finally donned the cast-off clothing of the enemy of the people (Hitler-Trotskyite or agent of the bourgeoisie, spy or accomplice) because he had grasped the rational kernel of his convictions: my party, right or wrong. What would have been the point of resisting? Whatever he did, the Party would be right. If he consented, he would prove the group right and himself wrong by making a confession. If he stubbornly denied the evidence, he would prove that the group had been right to brand him an outsider. The bravest finally agreed and the vast majority of group members believed them. It was a question, then, not of individual morality but of the (non-mechanistic) mechanics of the collective being knowingly and cynically taken to extremes. In their own way, the Stalinist trials showed that the most an-ethnic of all 'ideologies' was ultimately ethnic in character.

4

Bodies and Apparatuses

A social ideology is the spirit of a social body [*l'esprit d'un corps social*]. All mysteries which force esprits de corps to take the mysterious form of ideology find their rational solution in the nature of social bodies and the understanding of that nature.

What, to begin with, is a body? 'The material part of animate begins', according to one dictionary definition. The opposite, that is, of an ideality or an abstraction (such as *spirit* or *soul*). A body is a *material* being, but its materiality is not that of a thing or artefact.

It is possible to lend an ideology a material and not an ideal existence without necessarily recognizing the organic character of that 'existence'. Such hesitation is a decision in itself. It is Louis Althusser's great merit to have erased Marx's border-line between imaginary and real relations, between speculations and operations. Borrowing Pascal's 'Kneel down, move your lips in prayer and you will believe', he formally notes that there is no ideology except in and through real practices and no practice except in and through an ideology. Putting us in the position of the individual subject, he writes: 'The existence of the ideas of his belief is material in that his ideas are inserted into material practices governed by material rituals that are themselves defined by the material ideological apparatus from which derive the ideas of that subject. 'Being a logician and not a rhetor, Althusser weighs his words and takes care to point out that, from Aristotle onwards, 'matter is discussed in many senses' and that 'the four inscriptions of the adjective "material" in my proposition must be affected by different modalities'. Although he leaves on one side the problem of theorizing differences between the modalities of materiality, he does say that they are 'all rooted in the last instance in "physical" matter'. But matter is either animate or inanimate, organic or simple. The 'state ideological apparatuses'[1] derive from a physics of the inert. Compared with the bitter complexities of social physiology, this simple physics is a physics of the dream. Would to heaven that *homo politicus* did have the same status as *homo faber*; that his organizations were instruments that could be used from the outside and then thrown away; that his ideas were things he could put out of his head as easily as they were put into it. If ideas were simply weighty matters, as the saying has it, their very weight would soon show their lack of gravity. Materially existing 'ideology' is divided from the physics of matter by the same gulf that separates the living from the dead, hot from cold, the individual from the indifferent and spontaneity from calculation—in short, political theory from politics and the logic of ideas from the paralogism of behaviour.

The notion of *body* belongs to the vocabulary of life, while *apparatus* comes from the field of technology. They are therefore both *metaphors*. No one has ever met a state ideological apparatus walking down the street in the morning, complete with flywheels, gears and counterweights (or electric batteries). No one will ever see a social body crawling out of the bushes, complete with limbs, skin and eyes. Obviously not. But we have to choose between speech and silence, not between metaphors and accuracy. Anyone who opts for language condemns himself to speaking about things other than as they are, to using the tropes and figures that fill both popular and scientific language. Probably no metaphor is innocent, because it is always inaccurate and says either more or less than it means. In the same way, every philosophy is 'guilty' in that its faulty or badly constructed language is made of nothing because always taken for granted. Mathematics alone is without sin: it constructs its own symbols and its own means to its ends. It therefore has no meaning, but simply rules of construction. In mathematics, it is possible to speak without knowing what you are talking about. But we have no choice but to define the unspeakable with the words we have to hand—to choose, that is, the lesser of two metaphors.

We will use biology as a starting-point in order to lay bare a mode of existence and functioning without necessarily defining its ontological status or stipulating its organizational structure (a certain relationship between the parts and the whole). Its value will therefore be phenomenological rather than gnoseological (and certainly not normative). By using this approach, we will be able to go beyond the internal interdependence of the components and to identify the three most obvious characteristics of a group (Church, party, fraternity, and so on) organized in and by an 'ideology' (be it 'scientific' or 'religious'): namely, its polemical relations with the external environment, its self-reproductive finality, and its spontaneity, in the strong sense of the word. Translated into everyday language: 1) It can hold its own; 2) You'd wonder what it was for; 3) You can't do anything about it, it's automatic.

1. *It can hold its own*, against corruption and decomposition. As a category, time is external to inanimate matter, but it is a constituent element of the living being. Organisms, self-reproducing mechanisms, work to slow down their universal evolution towards the thermal equivalent of death. The second principle is the law governing the laws of organization, and it can only be understood in the light of the work principle. A living thing may stop living at any moment, and it therefore organizes itself. All organizations are in danger of becoming disorganized, just as all living beings are in danger of dying. The environment nourishes every living system, but it also attacks it. The 'external environment' reproduces states of organic disequilibrium, while the 'internal environment' strives to offset or neutralize them. Neither internal environment nor duration are given along with the programme. No practical ensemble containing an 'ideology' is intelligible outside its diachronic dimension, for it is the home of an irreversible time which eats away at it and against which it has to work. The history of an ideology—even the philosophy of history—can and must be read as the history of the safety procedures it uses to escape from history and to resist its own dissolution. Bichat's old formula—'life is the sum total of functions that resist death'—applies to all living temporal beings (collective as well as individual). A material structure does not need to defend its integrity: all it has to do is exist. Once it has been made, it cannot be unmade. The second principle does not apply to apparatuses (at least not internally). A living creature is an adventure and machines do not have adventures: they simply have accidents.

   A living being is also something which did not have to be born, and which can stop growing. An apparatus knows neither genesis nor growth. It is manufactured and set to work. When its working life is over, it becomes obsolete or defective and is therefore replaced. A theory which locates ideology in a series of distinct apparatuses (the religious ISA, the educational ISA, the political ISA, the family ISA, the juridical ISA, etc.) necessarily takes us back to a logic of states and not transformations, to beings and not relations, to a statics without a prior dynamics. In doing so, it diverts a description of the phenomena of power towards a theory of institutionalized power. The medical equivalent of such a conception of the organization of ideas would be an anatomy without embryology or a morphology without morphogenesis—in other words, an abstraction.[2] Where do these apparatuses come from? How are they formed? How do they survive? Did they fall from the skies, already working and ready-assembled?

Any operational logic of ideologies must include an explanation for the emergence of the institutions within which they are incarnated. For these churches, parties, universities, schools and radio stations all have their histories: they were *founded* one day and gradually organized, while other institutions disappeared. Here, on the other hand, we have apparatuses with no date of birth, no beginnings and no catastrophes. They are states without processes, instances without birth, growth or circumstances; a flat juxtaposition of institutions without any means of distribution or any room to expand. They are a picture with neither grey areas, perspective nor black holes, evoking homogeneous space at a constant temperature which bears no relation to our real space with its multiform variations of climate. The starting-point of any institution, public or private, is a localized bundle of inventions and fluctuations, gambles and dangers. The very singularity of the institution is 'impure'; it is painfully elaborated as a result of a random series of mixtures and borrowings. These factors produce one another across the generations by interbreeding or even by direct descent. Any ideology that exists concretely is (also, but not only) a throw of the dice that has been so successful that it seems to have abolished the chance which gave rise to it. Take Christianity, Islam or Marxism—just to restrict the argument to politico-religious state ideological apparatuses. Christianity, Islam and Marxism are examples of speech turned into action, of words turned into institutions (clerical, state, political, etc.). But the word sprang forth somewhere, here and not there, at this time and not at any other, and then went out to seek its fortune in the big wide world. A trajectory became a long-distance course, which in turn became acavalcade. It was broadcast from a single transmitter (Nazareth, Medina, London). A tiny community became a transmission vector, a regular flow, a cluster of reception and retransmission points, a front and finally a mass of believers or members. These singular adventures have, of course, resulted in the relatively stable material systems known as Christianity, the Islamic community and the international Communist movement, each obeying formal laws of organization that derive from a permanent structure. But there can never be a general, pre-given system of laws that allows us to predict the appearance or disappearance of this or that organized community in a particular socio-historical milieu. In order to grasp their *beginnings*, all we have to know is that the origin of an ideology lies not within a system of statics (of institutions) but within a dynamic (of messages). If we concentrate upon the play of chance and necessity specific to the formation and evolution of living beings, we can also avoid falling into nostalgic determination. But no answer is thereby given to the question of why things that existed did exist and of how things that once existed can exist again. Ideology may well have no history, yet the genesis of the great historical ideologies does contain, in practical form, the theoretical secrets of the transhistorical recurrence known as ideology. In order to determine the nature of the Christian religious ideology which both Marx and Althusser use as a paradigm, reference and illustration (although neither asks why Christianity should be so ubiquitous in his own discourse), we have to study the formation of Christian doctrine. In other words, a theory of ideology which does not allow us to describe the historical incarnation of ideologies is like a logical model of efficacity that can never be put into effect.

2. *You'd wonder what it was for*. A living system is not formed with an end in view: it is its own finality. Nature is said to be intelligent, and we do talk about the body. But nature has nothing to do with it, and spontaneity of such wisdom allows us to say that it fulfils its function but not that it achieves its ends (because it has none). There is something invincibly *stupid* about a living being insofar as it is both fully determined and entirely fortuitous. The real secret is that there is no secret, no hidden meaning, no message to

decode and no purpose to discover. The group is an end unto itself whose only purpose is self-reproduction. The latest genetic discovery—Richard Dawkin's 'selfish gene'—has shown that the vast majority of DNA in cells serves not to code the protein synthesis, but merely to maintain and reproduce the cells in question. Perhaps this should be related to the 'discovery' that there are political organizations whose only real function is to reproduce themselves and not, as they would claim, to convey a message through which the ideas in the party programme could be synthesized. The comparison between DNA and group selfishness is legitimate provided that the image 'selfish' is given no moral value. The status of a molecular arrangement is as alien to considerations of morality as is a parasite, a bacterium or a political party. The pertinence of the question, 'What is a tree for?' is by no means certain, even if it is a fruit tree. The question, 'What is a clock for?' does not arise, simply because the clock was made to answer it. The fact that a village clock may fulfil all manner of aesthetic, social, affective and other roles does not add to its sole function of telling the time. If by 'apparatus' we mean a set of material elements arranged in such a way as to perform a definite task, we can all agree that parties, churches and even nations are not apparatuses. They do have goals, it is true, but the goals they set themselves do not correspond to the reasons that make them move. This type of community obeys a logic other than its manifest logic, and its behaviour obeys a rationality other than that conferred upon it by its members. Perhaps it is a tree that thinks it is a watch.

Apparatuses never surprise you. They do what they have been programmed to do. We write the programme and we can change it in the middle or even switch to a different programme. A user is *outside* the apparatus he uses, the product of a *partes extra partes* assemblage of parts. The thing is not imposed upon him: it is at his disposal. He does not have to adapt to it, merely to use it. If he does not throw it away when he is done with it, he puts it away in a cupboard, a workshop or a shed until he needs it again. The utensil depends upon the user, not vice versa. It can be plugged in, stopped or moved as required. If it breaks down, you can get another one. An apparatus is one of a type and has no individuality. If the model becomes too outdated, too expensive (quality-price ration) or insufficiently productive (ratio between energy consumption and useful work), the industry will launch a new series. It is a nuisance to have to replace it, but not a personal tragedy. Of course, life also goes on after the death of my mother, a schism in my church, or the liquidation of my party. But I will have suffered a major lesion, not a minor blow. Life will be different, and I will no longer be the same person as before. Does life go on now that I am an abandoned child, an excommunicated believer, a banished citizen, an expelled party member? Of course, for the others. But I give up, and we all know that there is more than one way of letting yourself die. What does that mean?

The fact that the Church is a divine institution should be enough to prevent us from seeing it as 'a product of human industry like any other'. Similarly, the biological function of the family seems at first sight to remove it from the technical field, not to mention the affective role of pregnancy that makes it unsuitable for industrial metaphors. A party, on the other hand, looks like a perfectly prosaic and typically artificial object: it is produced by the intelligence and will of men at a specific moment and for a specific purpose. It is 'manufactured' on a specific date and founded in a specific place. It has an administrative structure or 'apparatus', as well as statutes, a programme and instructions for use. But not even a party with a high turnover of members (the kind you join without having to enter holy orders) has the same mode of existence as, say, a car. If I abandon my car on the street corner or even right in the middle of a motorway, I am being irresponsible but not an outright 'scum'. I am committing an offence, even a crime, but not *treason*. I may be regarded as dangerous, but not as a renegade. My friends will still shake me by the hand, even if the fine is a heavy one. And if I am sent to jail, the warders will put me in a cell but leave me to sleep in peace. The political realm is populated by beings that are also things that are also beings: the things known as institutions. It therefore escapes both the prosaic techniques of utility and the cold jurisdiction of the law. Such hybrids move at a higher, radical level, at once more poetic and more ambiguous. They combine the marvellous and the draconian, the charm of living beings and the gravity of things. Living systems regulate and reproduce their organizational closure by making their components work in accordance with their laws. Technical systems are characterized by heteronomous subordination to the technician (manufacturer or user) who programmed them and controls them in accordance with his aims. A computer is my servant, but I am the servant of an organization. I do not 'inform' a living thing; I am ' informed' by it. A *techne* transforms the world around me; a *morphe* surrounds and transforms *me* (and therefore conditions my ability to transform my environment as my 'form' enjoins me to do). I am what I am by virtue of where *I come from* and what *I belong to*. I made this apparatus with my own hands (my society's hands) : it belongs to me. On the other hand, I belong to my community, from which I derive my form and substance. *Apparatuses* and *bodies* are like chalk and cheese. I used, I am useful; I replace, I am replaced.

This inversion of active and passive, component and composite, shows the difference between being *manufactured* and being *formed*, invention and genesis. Individuals do not exist prior to their ideology: it is always given in advance. A living form, concrete from the very outset, fulfils itself through its organs. An inanimate set is a juxtaposition of discrete elements. They are as different as *pan* and *holon* (to use Aristotle's terms), as different as a total and a totality. A living totality is not produced by the addition of elements (a Party is not one member + one member + another, nor is a Church one worshipper + etc.). It exists prior to its parts: it is born *complete* and does not change its nature when I join it. This organic subordination of the part to the whole finds its expression in the subordination of the anatomy of the living creature to its physiology. The mode of functioning of the whole determines the disposition of the parts, not vice versa. Degrees of individual freedom are limited by the needs of the whole into which the elements are incorporated. The part proposes, but the totality disposes.

3. *You can't do anything about it: it's automatic*. The three distinctive properties of living systems are *self*-preservation, *self*-regulation and *self*-reproduction. Scientific investigations into *autonomy* now recognize that it implies *automatism*. A cell is a 'totally automated chemical plant' (François Jacob). 'Automatic' is simply another way of saying *uncontrollable*. The bodies we are talking about may be compared with organisms in that they obey laws of development and survival that are independent of the will and consciousness of their members. A City, an order, a church or

a party preserves, governs and reproduces itself *motu proprio*. The individual is not the *primum movens* of his ideology : he is moved by it. And he is always at the disposal of something which is not at his disposal (or which imposes itself upon him). 'An intelligent man once said that intelligence can kill a bull but cannot lay an egg' (Emmanuel Berl). Similarly, intelligence may ultimately be able to destroy a community, but in no way can it give birth to one. It can blow up the planet, but it cannot create another one. The asymmetry that now exists between the almost unlimited means of military destruction at man's disposal and the available means of reproduction points to the asymmetry between the technological and the political.

A conceptual system can be elaborated or manufactured, but a social ideology cannot be constructed. It is born, grows up and declines, by itself and of its own accord. On the one hand we have production, on the other formation. An 'ideologue' means a place and not a role, a process rather than a procedure. No calculation, no strategy and no will. Above all, no morality. Marx is no more responsible for Marxism than Christ is responsible for Christianity or Mohammed for Islam. An 'ideologue' is no more the origin of the ideology that bears his name than the earth is the centre of the universe or man the masterpiece of the Creator. We are free to invent as many ideas as we like, but we are not free to invent the organic process whereby the idea does or does not become a 'material force', the new idea a new 'ideology' (the organizing principle of a community). Happiness may once have been a new idea, but there are no innovations when it comes to 'ideological' unhappiness. In other words, the notion of the engineer of the human soul is as inept as the idea of planning (political) bodies: there are no ideological decisions and no academic experts on groups. Even genetic manipulation obeys the same constraints as ideological manipulation. You cannot invent a living being. It either invents itself or it is not invented at all, and once it has been discovered, it 'blindly' reproduces itself (in so far as the environment will allow it to do so). The path that leads to inventions has its rules but also its unruly periods, its norms and its anomalies (the latter being inverted images of its norms and rules). There is no pathology in the technical universe: illness is the prerogative of the living. There is no such thing as a monstrous machine, a monstrous instrument or a monstrous apparatus (they are all normal because they follow pre-given norms). But there are such things as monstrous organs without any visible solution of continuity with the domain of the normal. In other words, whereas we can control nature only by obeying its laws, we cannot control the political bond by obeying it: we obey it but think we control it. And the rebel who refuses to control anything, withdrawing or placing himself outside the group (in the Law, the Word, the Concrete, the Individual, Ethics, etc.), in no way alters the rules of the game. He simply leaves it up to others, the leaders, to obey.

Our first conclusion is a rhetorical demand: ways of speaking must not replace ways of thinking. Karl Marx saw Cartesian mechanics (animal-machines) as an expression of the new manufacturing period in capitalism, in which the animal was no longer man's assistant but a mere draught animal, or motive force.[3] The political metaphor is still the best verification of the argument that 'a change in the mode of production leads to a change in the mode of thought'. Living in the age of industrial manufacture and the steam engine, Marx quite naturally thought of the state as a 'machine'. In the age of electricity, we quite naturally think of ideology as an apparatus. There is no taboo against bringing ourselves up to date, so as not to be two or three technological revolutions behind the times. We must be very wary of the halo effects of 'bio-industry', but if we see a rational correspondence between the emergence of a new domain of objects in the human sciences ('mentality', 'culture', 'ideology', 'imaginary', etc.) and the emergence of new experimental objects in the exact sciences, are we necessarily falling into the trap of a logodicean substitute for the theodicies of the past? In this respect, modernity is not a matter of chronology, and Kant's *organization* may well be two jumps ahead of Marx's repressive *machines* and Althusser's state ideological *apparatuses*.

Marxism obviously lacked a coherent theory of the state, largely because it never looked at what supports the magistrates and the police: hearts and minds. You can't do everything at once. When the ideological apparatus was introduced to complement the repressive apparatus, it produced a dyptych of violence and consciousness through which the symmetry was restored. However, one is not in the police in the same way that one is in a Church; a magistrate does not have the same esprit de corps as a member of the Grand Lodge of France. A prison warder fulfils a task, but the guardian of dogma fulfils a vocation. Even when he is on an official assignment, an 'ideologue' is carrying out a mission, not an order. His duty is an obligation as well as a constraint. (Even a zealous policeman is not at the service of a cause: he is carrying out a function. If he is killed in the course of duty, he is a victim of duty cited in the roll of honour—but his promotion is posthumous and purely conventional. In reality, he is the victim of an accident at work.) The two panels of the dyptych are not on the same level. The false symmetry did, of course play a useful role in reducing anxiety. Thus, the ISA theory fulfilled its 'ideological' (or 'religious') function quite admirably: the imaginary charm of the instrument spared us from having to come to terms with the somewhat sordid realities of the organic. It is quite true that domination largely runs on ideology; but if ideology were a question of apparatuses, it would never take anyone in. The use of the technical model is a pre-political way of posing the political problem. One step forwards, two steps back. The mechanistic utopianism which idealizes ideology as an apparatus can be seen in the 'speculary structure' which it constantly attributes to it: a logical structure of reduplication through the (optical) replication and the (material) reproduction of skilled labour-power. That does not free us from the hall of mirrors or from submission to the established order. The same utopianism can be seen in a magical, pre-theological interpretation of the paradigm of the incarnation. We cannot escape the mystery of the incarnation, for it expresses the transformation of the idea into a force in its purest form (the Word made Flesh). But if we reduce the incarnation to a process whereby the 'same' becomes the 'other' by a mirror-like reduplication, we regress from a figurative theory of real transformation to a magical theory of representation.[4] To sum up: there can be no theory of ideology without a theory of incorporation or belonging. 'Ideology' works at the level of men's bodies and it works in the long term. If we have to keep the state ideological apparatuses, heavy masonry should at least replace domestic appliances. The image of machines for washing the dirty linen of exploitation should disappear behind the Cyclopean apparatuses of Mycenae and Chichen Itza.

Our second conclusion takes the form of a prognosis that the energumen is unlikely to be displaced by operational calculus in the near future. It is in the nature of political action to trigger off uncontrollable reactions, primarily because the agent has no self-control. The cold calculation of interests—the basis of the speculative abstraction known as *Realpolitik*—is what politics would be if it were a technique. Political techniques do, of course, exist (ranging from the coup d'etat to propaganda, from clandestine action to opinion-making), but they are subordinated to a primary non-power which works at the level of the bio-energetic. *Energumenos*, a term in Church Latin, comes from the Greek *energes*, active, acting (*energeia*). It originally referred to someone who is possessed by the demon or, in more popular usage, to a fanatic who went too far because he had no sense of proportion. By definition, a political agent lacks self-possession or self-control. His energy reserves are at once too close at hand and too far away, and his energy thermostat is located within the group to which he belongs. The individual political agent does not really incorporate his source of energy. But nor is it really outside him, given that his group is not a tool at his disposal. The group acts in, on and through him (regardless of whether it is a primary community—ethnic group, family, or nation—or an affinity group such as a party, association or religious group). I cannot act upon the group to which I belong without it acting upon me.

It follows that a social science—and a fortiori a science of societies—cannot as such have any directly political effect. The idea of the 'scientific' transformation of a given society implies that the transformers (those who make and carry out the decisions) are in a relation of exteriority with the object 'society' or 'state apparatus', like a physician behind his laser or a mathematician in front of his blackboard. It implies that the social actors are outside themselves, that they can turn themselves inside out like a glove so as to objectivize themselves, thus reduplicating the organizer and the organized in the organ. Politically—that is, practically—speaking, a social structure does not actually have an outside. It can be observed as a subject by ethnographers or sociologists, but they limit themselves to understanding it. What they call 'participation' is simply a process of knowledge designed to improve their understanding of it (or their self-understanding?), not a means of transforming by mutual agreement the society under observation. If manipulation does occur as a side-effect of the presence of out-siders, it is an unintentional (and therefore not strictly political) result. A social organism can be materially subject to the action of an external force (military or natural, aggression or cataclysm), but it can only be politically transformed, altered or reformed by the action of the social subjects it has itself organized, socialized or 'subjected'. There is no way out of this difficulty, unless we take the theoretical escape-route of solving the problem through a refusal to pose it. Ultimately, and despite the ambivalent Greek reference to mechanics and biology, the logic of organization can-not be assimilated to an *organon*—in the sense of 'tool' (rather than the complete body of Aristotle's logic). Whereas in Aristotelean physics, the organs of the body are the instruments of the soul, in organizational terms, individual souls are the instru-ment of the body within which they are inscribed. Interchangeable souls reproduce the identity of a living institution which transcends its 'members'. The vicariousness of functions and the polyvalence of organs, both typical of living organisms, constantly mock me as a member of the sarcastic totalities that want for nothing and no one. When I resign, defect, give up, retire or die, they go on as though nothing had happened, as though I had never existed and no one had missed the morning roll-call. So I was the appendix. They operate on me, it goes on as before, irremovable, in perfect condition. I was simply the artificial prothesis for a limb that will see many others fitted to it. When my party, for instance, decides to do without my collaboration, it is not cutting off an important limb. Everyone is convinced that it will not be lamed, that I will find it more difficult to learn to walk without the Party than the Party will without me.

To sum up: the idea of 'political practice' is an illusion stemming from the extrapolation of technical activity into a non-technical field. In general, *practice* means 'any process of transformation of a given raw material into a determinate product by a determinate human labour using determinate means (of production)', and 'political practice' 'transforms the raw material of social relations into a determinate product (new social relations)' by means of political instruments (Althusser). The movement from the general to the particular leads to a purely formal and speculative definition which 'forgets' that 'political action' is not a species within the genus 'technical activity'. The definition applies the productive schema of 'raw material, instruments of production, finished product' to a domain of behaviour where such distinctions have no meaning. Social relations are not 'produced': the producer ('the masses') is itself the product of the social relations it intends to transform. Practice presupposes that the subject is external to his object, and thereby posits a distinction between means and ends. But the two are inseparable on the ground of politics. Every subject of a political practice is the object of another subject's practice, as well as being acted upon by his own action. Every member of an organization is at once a means and an end for its other members, and the organization itself is both means and end for the members as a whole. *Homo politicus* does not have the same object, the same methods or, therefore, the same definition as *homo faber*.

A technical activity is carried out with a product in view: it has an *external* teleological structure. Production has to be understood in terms of its end or product, which then serves to make another product that is in turn used to fulfil a need or satisfy a demand. The economy, whose technique informs every phase of production, has use-values as its object. The activity of 'steel-making' serves to produce steel, which is then used to make cars that are used for transport (among other things). We have seen that group political activity does not correspond to the criteria of utility, profitability and productivity. It obeys an *internal* teleology, even if it does make a show of its external aims (a programme or a social project).

A political organization may look like an instrument, but it does not function like one. It is a structure of belonging rather than a tool. I do not stand outside it and use it: I experience it from within. That is why this curious means imposes its ends upon me rather than serving my ends. If the machine does occasionally 'get out of control', it is precisely because it is not a machine. Localized and secondary political techniques do exist, but political activity as such is not a technique in the sense of 'a set of definite and transmissible procedures designed to produce certain results that are considered useful'. There is no need to point out the arbitrary or partial nature of utility judgements (what is useful for a worker is not necessarily useful for a clerk and it is certainly not useful for a middle manager in the private sector). Even if a given society were agreed about the results to be produced—a scholastic hypothesis which, if verified, would signify that political activity no longer had any object or rationale—the means used to obtain those results could still not be reduced to normalized procedures, recipes or methods. They would still be *processes* or phenomena with their own internal active principle. Organizational procedures do exist, but an organization is a process. Political strings do exist, but no one can be certain that the person pulling them is not being pulled by them. Who is using whom? Who is manipulating what? The constant ambiguity of such tactical questions points to the ambivalent status of political beings. Technical procedures can be said to be good or bad, depending on whether or not they are adapted to their ends, but political processes are not subject to evaluation in terms of indices of performance. Although an organization is a process whose results may be judged useless, aberrant or perverse, it develops spontaneously and is indifferent to the accusations laid against it. We have already noted that in the eyes of political reason, medical metaphors have never been anything more than metaphors. But for the benefit of those who insist on talking about illness, we can use their language to say that political pathology does recognize incurable ills, the difference between them and incurable illnesses being that they give life to those who suffer from them. So it should come as no surprise that most of them refuse to admit of a cure. Presumably they prefer the illnesses of belief to the unbelief which produces dead souls and causes political bodies to break up.

We might put the point another way, returning to the equally necessary terms of religion. Those critics who complain, say, of the religious deformations in the practice of the PCF are apparently banging their heads against a theoretical wall. They are sufficiently lucid or cynical enough to identify the religious nature of political practices, but not sufficiently so to ask *why* political practices are naturally religious. Yes, we can see the mark of the sacred in our profane practices, but there is no way we can profane the sacred itself.

BOOK TWO
ANALYTIC

SECTION I
The Logic of Organization

1

Incompleteness

The sequence of great historical ideologies, with the world religions at the forefront, displays the fossil imprint left on the symbolic sand by different human groups during their structuration. We began at the end—with the visible. Given that the visible is always explained by the invisible, we now have to go back from the imprint to the movement that made it, from statics to dynamics. *'Ologies'* are explained by *'urgies'*. An 'ideology' is a sociurgy gone cold, a process turned into a result, what is left of a group that has become organized. If ideologies are ways of organizing ourselves in the world and not ways of seeing the world, the key to the logic of ideology is to be found in the logic of organization. The principle that explains beliefs is identical with the principle that generates communities of belief. Our theoretical task relates to the *'urgy'*, to the discovery of a structural invariant in the genesis of groups. If that invariant proves to be a fixed form of social genealogy, it will give us access to the common core of political and religious science, allowing us to reach a point where their common ancestry becomes visible. We know that the religious and the political field were originally one. Only gradually, and quite late in the history of societies, did they acquire their specificity and autonomy through a historically contingent and reversible social division of the labour of social organization. (Benvéniste, for example, tells us that there is no generic Indo-European term for what we understand by religion: when religion is everywhere, it has no name.)

The 'secret' of our collective miseries, of the a priori condition of any political history, past, present or future, may be stated in a few simple, even childish words. If we bear in mind that surplus labour and the unconscious can both be defined in a single sentence (and that, in the physical sciences, the equation for general relativity can be stated in three letters), there is no danger of confusing simplicity with over-simplification. The secret takes the form of a logical law, an extension of Gödel's theorem: *there can be no organized system without closure and no system can be closed by elements internal to that system alone.* Contradictory as it may seem, a field can therefore only be closed by being opened up to an element external to it. No set of elements is relative to itself: if it is, it is no longer a set (and is therefore nothing). The rest follows logically, 'a tale full of sound and fury told by an idiot, signifying nothing.'

It may be objected that the law of incompleteness is merely negative, but it is the nature of all logical certainties to be negative. In no sense does that detract from the fully determined positivty of negative determination.

If it is further pointed out that the law of incompleteness is theoretically poor, being capable of application to anything and everything, we may replay that its generality is a function of its level of abstraction. The law's ability to provide explanations in the field of politics derives from its very abstraction. In so far as it is an abstract structure (in relation to real historical groups), the formal structure of the group, which derives from its incompleteness, can be said to be immutable in form and permanent in effect. It is omnihistorical because transhistorical, a pure transcendental form of organization without which no localized historical organziation is intelligible. The pure form does not exist: it is the condition for thinking the historical development of the form.

But how can a principle be explanatory if it is itself inexplicable? It is true that the proposition cannot be demonstrated, but the theorem should therefore be renamed an *axiom* (a general proposition self-evidently true to all who understand its meaning). The hypothesis of incompleteness, which in this sense is similar to the first principles of geometry, allows political laws of order to be deduced, but it cannot itself be deduced from any other law. We see here the contingency of political necessity which, like a fact of nature, dominates the will of men and thwarts denegation. This is the axiom and I cannot tell you why it is so. Political law has the same status as all natural laws. (Einstein: 'Everything in the world is explicable, apart from the fact that the world is explicable'.)

A model can be said to be not only descriptive but explanatory when, quite apart from its internal coherence, it proves compatible with the available experimental data and allows us to make predictions within the chosen field of observation. It seems to me that these three conditions can be met. The logical model of incompleteness permits us to explain phenomena that previous theories isolated but could not elucidate. It also allows us to take up the challenge of observable political organs (ideal or material), doctrines and even institutions wherein the mutual and recurrent intervention of *lack*, *closure* and *the body* can be seen.

The logic of 'incompleteness' will reveal their internal unity.

1. Closed, Therefore Open

Initially it makes the link between 'heaven' and 'earth' intelligible, as no surface can be demarcated here below unless it has guarantors and referents in the beyond. 'Universal' and 'particular', 'moral values' and 'ethnic reality', absolute and relative, etc.—all these pairs are correlated by a logical function. Closed and open morality are not opposites but are reciprocally related. It will be recalled that Bergson juxtaposed them in *Les Deux sources*, positing a difference of nature and not of degree between the social morality of pressure and the morality of the appeal to the individual. 'Humanity is not the product of the extension of the City.' No, it is by digging beneath the foundations of the City that we find the in-draught produced by its walls. The open does not exist alongside the closed: it is given along with the act of closure itself. Intuitively, this might be expressed by the image of a cone whose base is 'solid' but whose area is 'imaginary'. A group is not a circle, a plane limited by a line every point of which is equidistant from the centre, for the fixed point of the group is not internal to its plane. The centre of a community is a summit—or, as we shall put it, a *basic hole*—which ensures that the radii of adhesion all go in the same direction. Its lateral area is delineated by the convergence of the radii. It is, then, a paradoxical cone: all that can be seen of it is the elipse of the base. The group is produced by a moving, generating line that passes through a fixed point—Leader,

Author or Father—and is based upon the contours of a territory. The whole process is known as an ideology, a religion or a world-view. Conversely, authority is in the hands of the one who traces the line. It follows that there is no opposition between the surveyor and the magician or, as we would now say, between the field-worker and the visionary. Any territorial division presupposes the privilege of extra-territoriality. We find proof of this in the vocabulary of Western Indo-European, where *rex* (king) and *regere* (to draw a line) have a common root. 'This twofold notion is present in the important expression *regere fines*, which designates both a religious act and the primary act of construction. *Regere fines* literally means "drawing frontiers in straight lines". This operation, performed by the high-priest when a temple is constructed, consists of marking out the sacred space on the ground. The magical nature of the operation is obvious. It differentiates the inside from the outside, the realm of the profane from that of the sacred. The line is drawn by the *rex*, he who is invested with the highest powers.'[1] The correlation between the material act of circumscription and the consecration of a particular space—which can also be seen in the root of 'temple' (from the Greek *temno*, to cut out)—has been described again and again by historians of religion and institutions but never, to my knowledge, explained. The point is that horizontal closure logically presupposes a vertical open shaft, that enclosure presupposes a vocation and that 'being reunited in' presupposes 'being united to'. Once it is sealed off, the space is inviolable and no longer belongs to those within it. The logic of the sacred is automatic.

We can now escape from Durkheim's famous vicious circle. He explains the religious in terms of the social and the social in terms of the religious, but he provides no explanation for the link between the two. Durkheim certainly identifies as determinant 'the very special kind of life that appears whenever men are assembled together', but his intuition does not rise above a descriptive level because, unlike Jesus Christ, he fails to identify the cause of the assembly (the *ecclesia* effect). Social experience of the sacred is one thing; sacred experience of a nascent society is another. If we put the two facts together, we shall be on the track of an explanation, without actually finding it. Effervescence does have its poetry, but

geneses also have their structure. In other words, there is logic in poetry. Durkheim records a historical regularity: 'The great ideals upon which civilizations are based have always arisen in effervescent social groups and in effervescent moments of this type.' However, regularity is not itself a rule: it is rule-governed. Durkheimian sociology erects the essentialist redundancy of a condition of existence into an explanation. The incompleteness model, on the other hand, provides a unitary concept of the religious and the social by supplying a logical rule for the simultaneous formation of social stasis and religious ecstasy. It indicates the paradoxical convergence of fixation and e-motion, enclosure and *raptus*. The collective is born outside itself. The transcendence of the social in relation to itself is one and the same as the delimitation of the social as a totality.

Embodiment means enclosure. What distinguishes? The organic is distinguished from the inert by its possession of a skin, membrane, epidermis or cytoplasmic layer—in other words an envelope of tissue that differentiates an internal environment from an external environment. That is a minimal condition. 'An organized object is a whole that defines itself within the strict limits of the contours determined by the internal interdependence of its components. It is therefore independent of its environment, and that independence gives it its individuality.'[2] Territories also have their frontiers. And when the frontiers were vague or confused—before the birth of the nation-state, for instance—the body of the kingdom was incarnated in the body of the king (and touching one meant touching the other). Doctrines, too, have their frontiers and their sensitive organs beneath the envelope of the institution. The biological metaphor does not free politics from the need for accuracy. The organism is never ill at ease with itself. There is no 'biological' bolthole for the 'end of ideologies'. Far from being mutually exclusive, 'ideological motivation' and 'the biological aspect of social organization' imply each another, being linked by a bond that is fundamental and not secondary. For traditional organicism, 'the biological model means the end of ideological preoccupations'. 'According to this model, man exists only within the famework of a whole in which he fulfils a particular function. Organicism is necessarily unable to conceive of theoretical models.'[3] In Tönnies's nebulous *Gemeinschaft*, there is no room for 'ideology', which is synonymous with separation and confrontation. Group-membership, however, is immediate, primary and spontaneous.[4] By grafting yesterday's 'primary group' on to integration into today's consensus, he arrives at the comforting idea that the givenness of 'personal social relations' will soon sweep away the artificiality of 'abstract ideological factors'. What he sees as the beginning of the 'end of politics' is in fact the end of the beginning, the religious renewal of politics. The contemporary rediscovery of the intuitions of social biology apppears to be an emergency exit that frees us from the curse of ideology, but it is in fact the royal road back to ideology.

Anyone who occupies an acre of ground has a home in heaven. Social man's roots are in his head because he thinks with his feet. The antithesis between the 'land of France' and the 'idea of France' has no object. We do not have *on the one hand* a land steeped in memories, deaths and odours and *on the other hand* an abstract, disembodied idea of the Nation. The metaphysics of Above and Below (immanent/transcendent, individual values/universal values, concrete/abstract) has to leave aside the agents of incompleteness. That is why it exists only in books. The lived experience of political reality knows nothing of such oratorical dichotomies, for territorialization takes place in relief and any division of the land presupposes an anchorage (imaginary or symbolic) in heaven. Combining circumscription and projection, the topography of groups is born of the union between two planes: geography *and* history. There is no point in playing off the transcendence of the Law against 'natural communities', given that all natural communities are supernatural. A distinctive *we* presupposes the existence of an *in-itself* beneath the *we* (it may even be the *we* itself).

Our blasé experts in geopolitics are naive in a different sense. For the planar geography of human groups is inconceivable in insolation from the in-depth history of the symbolic projections that established their respective contours. We do not have, on the one hand, territorial givens with stable imperatives such as the inert spatial juxtaposition of rising populations and, on the other hand, arbitrary fluctuations of adhesion and belief. The plane of political consistency springs from the conjunction of the two levels. As a

general rule, the more 'carnal' a group, the more 'spiritual' it is. The nation has more *soul* than class because it has more *body*, but it has less *soul* than the fatherland because it is less *physical*. (Note for the benefit of general staffs who, in trying to stick to the facts, demand that 'strategy must replace ideology'. The theatre of operations is a three-dimensional space, and what they reject as empty words is the very thing that gives the globe its relief and the map its contours, helping or hindering, for example, the advance of an armoured column.)

To organize: to relate beings not initially related to one another; to turn an atomized swarm into a system. This does not happen automatically, without force or arbitrariness. The work of organization is by its very nature 'religious', simultaneously producing an opening and a closure, saturating the 'below' with an absence 'on high'. Presumably, distinct levels of organization corresponding to different degrees of closure do exist in reality. If the expression *'religious community'* is pleonastic (elements cannot 'commune' in an environment that is homogeneous with them), *collectivity* is still looser, *multitude* even more so, and so on. The index of resistance increases along with the group's degree of coalescence, or with the subliminal gap between its actual basis and the void on which it is founded. Until a minimum degree of closure is reached, the vital thermal difference cannot appear; beyond a maximum degree of closure it can only disappear. Those degrees are obviously functions of the milieu and the moment. The fact remains that any social agglomeration postulates the existence of a metasocial element and that the specificity of political work consists of producing a *between us* from the meeting of an *other* and a *we*. To organize, as we have seen, means turning multiplicity into unity. Since whatever unifies a multiplicity of elements is necessarily external to their plane of consistency, the operation cannot be carried out by abstraction (which presupposes continuity) or by subtraction (which presupposes that the elements are on the same level). There must be a break or a discontinuity at some point. Be it real or symbolic, the point of unification must come from elsewhere. If a community is to exist as such, it has to relate to another term, a Mediator. There are no unmediated *sets*: politics is the work of mediation because it is the work of unification. The whole relates to itself only through the figure of the Mediator—its touchstone or sensitive spot which no one can touch without endangering the living integrity of the whole. The real, symbolic, physical or mythical body around which a community unites is sacred to it: Pharaoh, Berith, the Secretary.

It is quite natural that there should be something irrational about groups, for if there were not, there would be no groups. It is positive that there should be something mystical about them, for a demystified society would be a pulverized society. It is natural that there should be an element of the supernatural, that the being of the collective should come to it from on high. We can see why the *Analytic* of a Critique of Political Reason, its logic of truth in Kantian terminology, is inseparable from its *Dialectic* or logic of appearance, the link between the two being incompleteness. The social decentring of the individual—the recognition that an individual's centre of gravity does not lie within himself—is an important link in a chain of truths that is humilating for reason. 'The secret of human behaviour is not to be found in psychology, simply because it is not of the order of psychology' (Politzer). However, the decentring of the social means that the secret is not to be found in historical sociology either. It is not enough to proclaim: 'The human essence is no abstraction inherent in each single individual. In its reality it is the ensemble of social relations' (*Sixth Thesis on Feuerbach*). Social sets have a social essence which transcends class relations and independent of their content (class content, for instance). Indeed, this abstraction is at the origin of the inhumanity of politics. The 'secret' of human behaviour is not to be found in political economy or a new economy of politics, simply because the secret is inhuman and therefore theological. God does not exist, but politically we are condemned to an essentially theological collective existence. If we want to understand anything about our immediate political life, we have to become theologians. This is a fairly unpleasant situation to experience, but a fairly comic situation to observe.

2. Primal Subjection

The first corollary of the axiom of social incompleteness is the *heteronomy* of the political field. Its motto is *omnis potestas ab*

alio, St Paul's *omnis potestas a Deo* being only one variant in which God represents the other squared. Authority escapes men, Bossuet said, because it is sacred. Although the reverse is actually the case (authority seems sacred to men because it escapes them), the apologetic inversion would not have been credible if it had not inverted a logical structure. The group, in fact, escapes itself and only holds together because of the yawning gap that founds it. Just as it would be a biological contradiction for an individual to give birth to himself (integral cloning as biological aporia?), the government of a collective by itself—*verbi gratia* 'of the people by the people'—is a logically contradictory operation ('generalized workers' control' as political aporia). Self-regulation by the many is a *flatus vocis*—at best an ideal regulator of Political Reason derived from a logic of appearance, but more probably a concept without intuition which no historical experience can satisfy. Similarly, no one doubts that an ideal society would be a society without ideas, assuming of course that 'ideal' is the opposite of 'real'. Incompleteness stipulates that a set cannot, by definition, be a substance in the Spinozist sense: something which exists in itself and is conceived by itself. It requires a cause (to engender it) and it is not its own cause. The arbitrary nature of all power derives from this primary hiatus, as does the necessity to legitimize the arbitrary by means of the 'ideological alchemy which transmutes social relations into supernatural relations justified by inscription in the nature of things'[5] But why does this alchemy still work—even in societies where the occult sciences are no longer in business? If the great labour is possible, it is because supernature is inscribed in the very birth of the group—a set of social relations always looks supernatural to the set—and because no group can found itself. As I would be the first to accept, there is nothing at all funny about this. The logical impossibility that a structured social set should contain nothing arbitrary implies that it will always be necessary and even possible to legitimize the arbitrariness of the social structure. In that sense the incompleteness axiom plays into the hands of every ruling class. It is not to blame: 'Truth, drag me where you will, I am ready'.[6] Its only excuse is that it gives some play to the supernatural, as well as to the identity of the social class called upon to legitimize the arbitrary: it may play into the hands of a ruling class now, but it will work against it later. The class struggle comes into play to decide which class will be the alchemist.

However, that does not change the rules of the game as such—the rational necessity for retorts, formulae and other eminently admirable transmutations. Since a group cannot originate within itself, it cannot know itself fully andis vulnerable to all the tricks played by the hiatus between cause and effect. Their discontinuity necessarily kindles and rekindles social theodicies, the divine surprises of the primal closure. Once it was pedigree: Aeneas, son of Venus, Romulus, son of Mars. Now it is capital letters: the Cradle of the Republic, the Fatherland of Socialism, the Bastion of Liberty, and so on.

3. The Power Effect: Substitution/Repetition

We shall therefore speak of an elementary political *syntax*, which has nothing to do with the *morphology* of types of authority (Max Weber), systems of class domination (Karl Marx) or the institutional forms of the State (public law). But the rules presiding over the organization of a collective and the elementary relations connecting the elements of the group with the group itself are determined from above by the formal nature of social sets. Although negative and abstract, this is not an inadequate determination. Incompleteness inevitably triggers the twofold reaction of representation and repetition. In other words, the axiom allows us to put forward two theorems: 1) any social set presupposes an instance of representation; and 2) any social set presupposes an instance of repetition. These statements may appear banal, but their implications are considerable. They determine the function of what is called 'power': it cannot not exist, and it is by definition 'bad'.

1. The primary splitting of the collective body, whose cohesion is the product of dehiscence, prevents it from entering into a direct relation with itself. It was born by being separated from itself (that is, subordinated to a point of extrinsic coherence) and it has to live in separation from itself. Separation on the ordinate means union on the coordinate: institution and substitution are truly synonymous. Hence the 'emanatist structure common to both the ecclesiastical and the political world' (Bourdieu). A non-representative relation, without mediation or dispossession, between, say, a (working) class and its (Communist) party—an ideal coin-

cidence between self and self—will never exist except on the countless sheets of paper which do no harm but have no practical effect.[7] If it wants to justify its existence (and be 'taken seriously' by others and itself), the Party has to re-present the Class. Obligation and delegation are closely linked, as Bergson well knew. But when we set ourselves up as the delegate of a third entity, it is above all ourselves that we oblige. No element within a social set has its necessity within itself, and this infinite succession of successive decentrings is an effect of the group's eccentricity with regard to itself. No element can justify its presence unless it takes the place of another. 'Kings take the place of God', presidents that of the republic, general secretaries that of the working class, and so on. The necessary condition of representativity follows from the fact that no one has actually seen God, the Republic or the Working Class: in a word, the founding absence. The supreme leader is always a stand-in, a substitute, a replacement. As the group is not its own cause, it can only oblige itself by means of institutions which, like the group, are not answerable for themselves. The *auctor* of an act of authority is only *august* (incontestable) because he sets himself up as an *augur* (interpreter of the invisible). The authentic signs of authority are simulacra. Any foundation which claims to have founded itself is fragile and shaky; it has no real foundation. Ecclesiastical legations, with their internal laws (transitivity, asymmetry, non-reversibility, charismatic communication) are just what stable sets need. Being structurally isomorphic, the Church is an expert on the logic of the operations of investiture. Hence the *ministerium regis*—the servant-king—who is a king because he is a servant. Israel demands a king, but it is Jehovah who gives it one through the intermediary of Samuel.[8] Saul is rejected by Jehovah and replaced by David, but David is annointed by Samuel. The anointed, the Messiah and Christ are synonymous. 'The oil with which Christ was anointed, the chreme which gave him his name, has to be considered a great mystery', writes St Augustine.[9] It is in fact the mystery of political power as perpetual mediation. The same rite of investiture (by water, oil or blood) is found from Mexico to Barabadur. Anyone who mounts the throne *motu proprio* is soon deposed. Western royalty is a Germanic import, not a Judaeo-Christian tradition, but if a biological line of descent had been enough, the hereditary monarchs would not have needed to be consecrated. Napoleon took the risk of placing the crown on his own head, but he had to receive it from the hands of Pius VII, who was given his own tiara by the Holy Ghost.

To sum up: since the group takes shape with reference to a constitutive absence, it has to find some way of making its absence visible. Being completed by an invisible Yahweh, Israel requires a Moses it can have, see and believe. The problematic Covenant requires a tangible Ark to bridge the gap between the Other and us and it makes no difference if the Other is the world Proletariat, the Nation, the Grand Master, the Sovereign People or God the Father. If the Mandatory is not represented, the *we* collapses or suffers dilution. The group's inability to appear transparently to itself as a founded totality entails that the *inter* (-mediary,-preter or-cessor) is the kingpin of the whole. The non-immediacy of the set displaces the core of the political enigma on to the figure of Mediation: the Mystery of the Incarnation, Christology, mediology.

2. The mystical body is a lost body. The fact that power is essentially representative means that it is essentially substitutive. Its archaic compulsion stems from its self-interested assumption that what the absence represents was once present: it is easier to regain a paradise lost than to make a new one from scratch. In that sense, the logical principle of the set merges with its chronological beginning, as the splendid ambivalence of the term *arche* (beginning and principle) would suggest. The principles that explain things lie hidden in their beginnings, and creation myths can also function as an aetiology of the present. *Aristoteles dixit*: myths do not point to the *aitiai* (or immediate causes) of actual situations, but to their *archai* (primordial elements) (*Metaphysics*, 12, 1013a). The 'why' therefore becomes an 'after what?', so that the metaphysical question of the physics of sets is replaced by a cosmogenic, theogenic or historical myth that is both more realistic and more figurative. A group necessarily escapes upwards: if it moved downward, it would not be closed. An element from set *b* can close set *a* if and only if *b* is a subset of *a*. The logical 'above' spontaneously takes the form of an inaugural archetype or origin. *In illo tempore* the Republic, the City, the Party or the People of God was forged in the flames. It is a white lie but a useful calculation, for the second principle ensures that there is always slightly more energy before than after-

wards. The process of becoming is lived as an instance—even or especially in a historical society—and an expectation is always a reminder. Our great hope is for a return (sometimes to our origins). We expect the future to restore the vigour of our past. We expect tomorrow's classless society to close the cycle begun by primitive communism. The end of prehistory or the end of history as such—that is the dream, isn't it? Perhaps Mircea Eliade was a little hasty when he posited a continuity between 'traditional man', who is hostile to any attempt at autonomous history, and 'modern man', who is supposed to make himself by making a history that is free from the ballast of 'nostalgia for origins'. Every historian knows that a revolutionary establishment implies a desire to re-establish something and that every revolutionary culture is influenced by 'the reactionary cult of the past'. Marx reproached the French with this in 1870 (letter to César de Paepe), but without it the Parisians would never have 'stormed heaven' a year later, spurred on by the example of their ancestors in 1789 and 1848. Lenin used the Glorious Commune as a major point of reference during the October Revolution, which in its turn served to...etc. The system of temporality which characterizes the collective is not hidden by archaic ontology: on the contrary, it is clearly revealed by it. Historical groups are haunted by a fear of history—much more so than other groups. We will see below why the cancellation of the irreversibility of time, and the denegation of history as productive of anything new, regulate the group's notion of time by an asymptotic ideal of natural time in which things are identical and reproduce themselves *ad infinitum*. Political evolution thirsts after being as opposed to becoming. The historical character as an identification myth, the historical myth as transhistorical reference, the feast as re-creation, the ceremony as periodic regeneration, the anniversary as cyclical return—all these conversions show, by their very banality, that validation through repetition did not disappear with the Great Year of the Stoics, Plato's cosmic catastrophes or Judaeo-Christian apocalypses, even if the revolutionary conflagration marking the end of the general crisis of capitalism has replaced the *ekpurosis* or purifying conflagration signalling the end of the great cosmic year. The primal split condemns the group to seek a suture in a return to the archetypes of its birth, so that its great adventures look like anabatic odysseys (the paradigm still being the 'return to nature'), all the more commendable in that the point of arrival is identical with the point of departure and is by definition out of reach. Political time is not linear; or if it is a line, it has the form of a loop, a volute that is never finished and constantly restarted. The group's basic incompeteness gives its mechanisms endless tasks: innovation or the (re-) construction of completeness is only acceptable for the purposes of re-establishing a former non-existent state. ('M Jacques Lacan's new school wishes to re-establish the truth of psychoanalysis', to quote a recent headline.)

As incompleteness causes damage, repairs have to be carried out. But in completeness itself is irreparable. It tells us to mend the leaks that it constantly causes—an endless torture like Sisyphus's rock. We all have to face the chore of restoring things, but the 'truth of psychoanalysis' still looks rather battered.

4. Failure as Vocation

These theses (or theorems) have to be completed by the scholium that the collective has a vocation for failure. The political is the natural home of failure, and that should not be taken as a lament. Failure is a motor passion, making us work simply because nothing ever works. We fail to close the loop, to complete the cycle of self-reconstitution. The political animal is waiting for Godot. But if we did not believe that the keys to the kingdom were lost, what would there be to look for? The horizon we must reach in order to find our whole truth recedes as we walk towards it. For hundreds of years the second coming of Christ was lived as something imminent by millions of Christians, who had converted so as not to be too late. Next year in Jerusalem. The kingdom of God. The return of the twelfth Iman. The treaty that will guarantee perpetual peace. The leap from the realm of necessity into the realm of freedom.

It is common knowledge that the deadlines set for realizing the objectives of modern ideology are constantly being extended. The date set for the collapse of the imperialist economies, for catching up with the USA or harmonizing the incomes of rural and urban workers, pass without so much as a self-criticism. No one can even remember what significance they once had. The collective has to gamble on prolongations. It always takes longer than expected, but the delay is unimportant so long as we have a forecast. Christians have seen at least ten apocalypses come and go since the crucifixion, each of them announced for a specific date. No sooner was one forgotten than the theological virtue of hope began cathecting the next. The time is at hand... the time has come. The millenarian scenario is inscribed in the genesis of the group and, far from discouraging converts, the failure of messianism gives new impetus to the need to belong. Prophetic failures restore hopes. The same thing that breaks individuals on the wheel makes communities go round.

Why do the hollowest of discourses ring true in the ears of believers, militants and citizens? Because the body of the group is hollow and because the stereotypes send back the typical echo of incompleteness. How can we not be sensitive to it when we are the 'product' of this void? We have already noted that the *coherence* of a political discourse is extrinsic, that it is not self-sufficient, that it depends upon an ever implicit assumption outside the discursive field. (In Stalinist language, for example, 'the USSR is the land of the proletariat and the proletariat is in power there' and it is 'the function of the discourse to repress it'.[10]) The *cohesion* of a political organization is also extrinsic, not self-sufficient, etc.[11] The formal congruence between the organisms and their logical organs makes them not only acceptable but indispensable to each other. The credibility of ideological discourse derives from its reduplication of the ideological nature of the group (the most effective discourse being that of hysteria). But the broadcast is never any more than a return to sender. According to Hegel, only animals are completely innocent. The political animal is born guilty. His name is Joseph K.

2

'Natural Religion'

We will begin with the hypothesis that 'natural religion' is the effect
of a triple structure (formal, vital and material) which is at right
angles to the logical, biological and physical levels.

1) *Logical level* (first structure): a group is a system of relations.
However, relations cannot form a system unless it transcends the
elements it relates to one another. Social incompleteness is an invariant formal requirement, regardless of the eminently variable
forms of transcendence and the characteristics of the 'being' so
posited as supernatural.

2) *Biological level*: a culture is a stabilized living system. The function of the group's self-transcendence (effect of level 1) is the
spatial and temporal stabilization of a particular bio-ethnic identity, the reproduction and maintenance of a living community.

3) *Physical level*: a living collective system is a bound order of
energies whose 'natural' fate would be degradation if the repeater
mechanisms inscribed in the transmission of the organizational
programme specific to each religion did not intervene to reproduce
the gap in its equilibrium and prevent a return to disorder.

The fact that the group 'stands above itself' (level 1) allows a
structure of belonging (level 2) to operate as a relatively stable thermal barrier (level 3).

Obviously, such a schema is merely a suggestion, not an explanation. The three levels are irreducible and nestle inside one another
like Russian dolls. If we make—or mend—too many epistemological breaks, we violate the rule of the independence of the interdependent levels of rationality that has been revealed by current
developments in the sciences.

1. The Universal Group

'History is the study of the things that differentiate human groups from one another' (Lucien Febvre). A critique such as this studies what historically distinct human groups have in common. The obvious question is whether or not it is legitimate to ignore historical differences. The result of a legitimate abstraction is a concept, that of an illegitimate abstraction is an entity. The concept restores the internal unity behind empirical divergences; the entity dissolves diversity into a vague generality. How are we to distinguish a conceptual approach from a confused approach?

From the outset, it has to be made clear that what is meant here by 'group' differs from both the entity of the 'crowd' and the entity of the 'mass', in terms of both content and application. Gustave Le Bon's *Psychologie des foules* afforded sufficiently acute insights to attract the theoretical interest of Freud (and the practical interest of Hitler). But his object lacks contours and definition because, whilst it is true that the individual is swept away by the crowd, the notion of the crowd sweeps away distinctions between units as diverse as a crowd of rioters, a jury, a Church, a parliament, etc. As a rule, the use of the plural is the mark of the entity ('the crowds', 'the masses'). Another characteristic is the presence of affective or moral connotations which are usually pejorative rather than laudatory with regard to psychological philosophies of history (Chakotin's *The Rape of the Masses* or Ortega y Gasset's *Revolt of the Masses*).

'Group' is not being used here to denote a *real social unit* amenable to observation. Our non-descriptive investigation is therefore as alien to psychology as it is to sociology. Nor is 'group' an *empirical concept* defining a class of objects given by intuition. Since it is a fundamental concept or *category* of pure politics— 'pure' in the sense of 'pure understanding'—it must be used in the singular and with absolute neutrality. The axiom of incompleteness defines an *a priori form of human practice*, namely, the law of the formal composition of structured practical groups. In that sense, its field of application immediately excludes non-structured physical aggregates (a crowd in a department store, a queue at a bus stop, etc.) and non-practical logical aggregates (a socio-occupational category, an age group, a sex-structure, etc). The collective begins where a 'collective' is no longer enough.[1]

Incompleteness designates a law of composition and therefore does not apply to assemblies created by juxtaposition. It applies only to the field of *collective formations*. Given that Political Reason deal not with hymenoptera but with the specifically human world of institutions, we can further specify them as *voluntary collective formations*.

The reciprocal relations between collective institutions and lineage or kinship groups (clan, line, family) or territorial groups (tribe, village community, federation, etc.) are a matter of considerable importance. However, it relates to the study of differences and does not concern us here. The ethnographer makes a distinction between the *gens*, a group formed by one or more lines of descent, and the *phratry*, a group made up of several clans, etc. The historian of Classical Greece will show how, at various times, *genos*, *phratry* and *deme* could simultaneously function as ethnic groups, administrative groups, territorial groups, religious groups, and so on. For his part, the sociologist, distinguishes between primary and secondary groups, income and occupational groups, narrow and broad groups, and so forth. A historian of modern France will show how these fluctuating groups concretely overlap in real life. The social psychologist studies the situation of an individual torn between the plurality of groups to which he belongs (family, region, occupation, religion, party, country, etc.).

The imperative need for such empirical studies cannot dispense us from returning to elementary logical principles or the idea of a logic of practice that is orthogonal to all practical history. Far from being in contradiction with the search for a structural invariant, the quest for empirical variations actually makes it possible to discover one. Nor does the project of a political anthropology conflict with the empirical data of political history: indeed, they fertilize each another. But in view of the endless sterile debate over structure and event, it seems desirable to clear up the misunderstanding that lies behind it. In order to do so, we will have to take extreme if not provocative cases.

The nature of the group implies the idea of a natural religion which has no historical existence but whose theatre is human history. The argument that the religious and the social are co-extensive is by no means original. But our explanatory hypothesis may help us to go a little further—further back, that is, perhaps even to our ancestors. If the human group does have a 'superhuman nature', social man qua social must naturally be religious, and the untranscendable nature of group membership must renew the supernatural element in him. The familiar epic of mankind's triumphant march through immobile nature is replaced by the ancient and faded image of nature's march through history or, rather, 'the march of one religion through all religions' (Henri Gouhier).

The hypothesis of natural religion has all the hallmarks of dangerous nonsense. It is the classic bad, nasty idea. Simply stating it implies two postulates: that nature exists and that religion exists.

Now, we all know two things. 1. For a long time, the idea of nature has been not only a stupid idea, but a right-wing idea underpinning worn-out mystifications (such as 'it is natural for there to be rich and poor'). It should, however, be recalled that this was not the case during the Enlightenment. 2. Religion has no universal essence. Particular religions exist, but each has its own categories and they are not reducible to an essence.

The fact that the political unconscious's form of existence is natural religion clashes with the interests of both the conscious mind and politics. It is an insult to historical humanism, which constantly tells us that 'man is the product of his own creation' and that 'the future of man depends upon man'; and an insult to the scientific humanism which teaches us that any analytic focus on a general essence, rather than specific religious experiences, involves a reductionist extrapolation. At a time when historians have themselves given up trying to produce a general history of religions, natural religion is said to be a theoretical monstrosity, a *Janus bifrons* which deserves to be slapped on both sides of its face. On the left because it revives a fatalist doctrine of innate ideas. On the right because it is confusing, and therefore summary and vacuous.

We will take the most serious objection first: 'the labyrinthine complexity of religious questions' (Mircea Eliade, *Traité d'histoire des religions*).

Cellular biology and zoology are not in competition with each other: analysis of the chemical message in the cell's metabolism does not imply that all pluricellular organisms have to be lumped together or that a geneticist cannot tell the difference between an elephant, a pike and a wall-lizard. Phonology, which investigates the laws behind sounds (of which speaking subjects are unaware), does not invalidate comparative linguistics. Although it demonstrates that 'there are many languages but very few phonologicallaws valid for all languages' (Lévi-Strauss), it makes no claim toreplace the analysis of existing states of language. Information theory posits that entropy and information are identical, but not that cybernetics is secondary or redundant. You can be an excellent programmer without using the abstract general formulae of Shannon and Brillouin. All I am trying to suggest for the moment is that 'the scale produces the phenomenon' (Henri Poincaré) and that there is no quarrel between microscopes and elephants. If we keep things in proportion, our extension of Gödel's theorem should not bring us into conflict with the fertile experiments carried out by Kurt Lewin and Moreno on 't-groups' and other restricted groups. A Critique of Political Reason has to be very wary of setting itself up as a rival to group dynamics ('the science of the laws that connect the behaviour of a group with the system of forces acting within it'), even if it does believe that the psychology of interpersonal relations has more to learn from axiomatics than axiomatics has to learn from psychology.

The question of essence, then, is evidently not reducible to a question of scale. We will never get away from the terrain of *morphology* by studying historical forms of religion, regardless of the size of the units of observation (from the all-purpose Melanesian sorcerer to the modern prophecy industry). We can only make the breakthrough to a syntax of the *sacred* by accumulating documentation and generalizing on the basis of recorded phenomena. We know that no two religions are alike and that every religion is a system. Such configurations may display illuminating differences or deceptive similarities. Max Weber showed that we can more clearly grasp the Calvinist system, as a combination of a cult of transcendence and intramundane asceticism, if we look at it through the prism of Buddhism, an opposite combination of a cult of immanence and extramundane mysticism. By pointing out that Greek sovereignty knew nothing of the Roman polarity of *flamen/ Lupercus* and juridical regularity/magical violence, Vernant has taught us to distinguish between the various polytheisms of the Ancient World and not to dissolve Greek Religion (itself an abstract temporal synthesis) into the tri-functional Indo-European model. We have to agree that 'comparison is the business of specialists and the comparativist is primarily a one-religion man'.[2] Natural religion is not total religion: it is neither the integral of all observable religious systems nor the mean difference between them. Comparisons are always odious and cannot provide a lexicon or a grammar. Not only would the collation of all the facts be an endless task, it would simply take us in the wrong direction.

Historicism, the analysis of every phenomenon and every category in its context, is a defence against superficial analogies and a healthy and necessary reaction against the fantastic generalizations of early twentieth-century religious anthropologies masquerading as ethnologies or sociologies. But historicism becomes nominalism when it rejects any leap into the generative order and uses the 'facts' argument to stay with endless descriptions of singularities—an undertaking whose method is contradictory and whose results are tautological. Historicism can be a precaution, but it can also be a form of terrorism. It can serve knowledge, but it can also repress it. We will not go here into the interesting subjective aspect of modern strategies for segmenting the historical field. Suffice it to say that the defence of academic territory (the professorial chair) against the threat of annexation by a neighbour (the abolition of the chair) is obviously less important than the specialist's passionate devotion to his special subject. We will simply note the objective danger that legitimate rejection of false generalizations may become a point of honour from which to reject the work of conceptualization. A further turn of the screw of the ineffable is enough for the specialist's scruples to converge with the hackwriter's haste at the lowest degree of knowledge. One tells me that every cow is a world; the other that all cows are grey in the night of *mana*. But no one tells me how to define a cow or what stops me confusing it with a car or my great-aunt.

That no two invididuals are alike does not erase the specific genetic unity which entails that human offspring have arms and not wings. It might be useful to adopt Johannssen's distinction between *genotype* and *phenotype*. The genome is a purely logical reality that no one has ever seen, even through a microscope. We can only see individuals and phenotypes. 'Genotype' refers to the basic characteristics of the species, 'the ideal range of potential relating to each species', and 'phenotype' to the variable and idiosyncratic expression of that potential in visible individual systems. In linguistics we find a further distinction—perhaps inspired by the former—in the *competence/performance* pair introduced by Chomsky's syntactic theory. Chomsky ignores individual and cultural differences, positing the ideal existence of a universal grammar beneath different languages and states of society. It is invariable and therefore not subject to individual variation. There is a real competence associated with every language ('the speaker's knowledge of his own language'), and that competence governs performance ('the effective use of language in concrete societies'). Beyond individual competence, however, generative grammar posits an ideal or innate competence—corresponding to the notion of an 'ideal speaker' or universal subject—whose mechanisms are in the last instance determined by the neurological structures of the human brain. Perhaps we can pursue the analogy by outlining the hypothesis that every religion and every ideological formation can be read as the performance of a generic competence, and that natural religion is to historical religions what universal grammar is to actual languages: a system capable of generating an infinite number of possible beliefs through a finite set of elements defined by their reciprocal relations and oppositions (formal and substantial universals). This will, of course, remain a hypothesis until such time as the rules of internal transformation have been formulated (rules that allow a single competence to be transformed into different performances). At present, the task is still beyond our capabilities and knowledge, although, given a collective framework and the appropriate resources, there is nothing utopian about its realization.

The universal group does not exist and nor does the universal speaker. Yet all men are born with the ability to speak and all groups constituted with the ability to believe. The faculty of language does not imply that everyone has to speak Volupak or Esperanto. Nor does the faculty of religion signify that there has to be one world religion, but merely that every collective social formation is potentially a religious formation or has the capacity for a particular religion. In other words, the law of its composition implies the creation of a religion, because it is separated from itself. The very definition of the group—in the sense of a pure relational schema—includes its disposition towards the 'sacred', regardless of the forms in which the latter is actually specified or administered. Existing religions are the fossil morphology of a timeless ideal syntax.

A comparative examination of historical religions would probably allow us to isolate a small number of universals in the shape of constant relations and oppositions; or, more accurately, to see the universality of the relation of opposition. As we know, the most profound definition of the sacred is that it is the opposite of the profane—how Roger Caillois was admired for this remarkable discovery! There is also the even more laconic definition of religion as the experience of radical alterity, from which the phenomenologies derived impressive dissuasion-effects. 'Religion is the experience of mystery, and that is the basis of mysticism', adds Rudolf Otto (1860–1937), to whom we owe the sublime definition of the sacred as the Absolute Other. From this perspective, it is true that 'religion can never be fully contained within its rational statements'. But although the statement of incompleteness, the logical genome of groups, does not exhaust the potentially infinite number of religious phenotypes, it does make rational the inexhaustible nature of religious performances by providing, so to speak, the algebraic function for the relation between alterity and the inside/outside polarity (we/non-we), the two lowest common denominators found in the most diverse descriptions of religious experience.

'Natural religion': a universal, innate schema of behaviour derived from the logical structure of the group. Logic merely points out that wherever there is a stable social ensemble, there will be something supersocial to be managed. It is the task of history and sociology to determine the modalities of management. These forms are not without interest—fortunately, Inca, Greek, monarchical, bourgeois and proletarian societies do not manage the supernatural in the same way—but they remain modalities, whose explanatory principle is not to be found within them. Nature is not what remains when cultures are forgotten: it is what history cannot take with it when it passes through a group. We can therefore say of nature what Jaurès said of the fatherland: a little history takes you away from it, but a lot of history brings you back.

The history of religions and the hypothesis of natural religion are no more contradictory or mutually exclusive than are the study of particular grammars and Chomsky's 'generative grammar'. It is only natural that we should find the former more instructive than the latter because, as Chomsky once said, men are more interested in their differences than in the things they have in common. 'The same is probably true of frogs; presumably they are less interested in what makes them all frogs than in what makes it possible to tell one frog from another. They are not very interested in "frogginess".'[3] Incompleteness is never an entertaining hypothesis, and when posited as a ceiling for political creativity, it attracts little spontaneous attention. It allows us great freedom of movement at ground-level (the history of religion is open-ended), but it does not give us the freedom to break through the ceiling. The ability to believe can take effect in an infinite number of beliefs, but the property of satisfying men and women remains fixed and cannot be transcended. It is written into the programme of groups. Incompleteness institutes the sacred as something social, and religion is its institution. In that sense, the expression 'natural religion' is inappropriate if it is taken to mean a determinate system of beliefs. The experience of the sacred is universal and primordial, religion (or 'ideology') being a secondary elaboration. If religion is a product of culture, a way of managing the sacred element in society, it has to have something to manage. This is the 'something external and superior to individuals'—a minimal but universally accepted definition of the sacred—which is obviously not the same thing as the divine. No religion without incompleteness. No group nature without group culture.

2. Historicism as Paralogism

Our historical awareness of the facts of discontinuity is one area in which contemporary research has made undeniable progress, and it should be enough to keep our understanding of the facts of sensibility away from the traps of continuity, homogeneity and universality.[4] After all, Lucien Febvre and his school did rehabilitate feeling as an object of science, even going so far as to posit its primacy ('Is it the dream of a sick man to say and think that psychology is the very basis of valid historical work'?). The only condition, of course, is that we write its *history* and refrain from projecting modern categories on to the lived experience of the past. The psychology of a population depends upon its nutritional level, climatic variations and the effect of the environment, just as the psychology of an individual depends upon the mental equipment that the group makes available to him and which, conversely, establishes the group *within* the individual. If we endow the actors of the past with our emotions, language and arguments—so that we find them in the past and are then amazed that *nil novi sub sole*—we simply fall into the anachronisms which, by design or accident, make historical romances so popular. Religious feeling has a history, as does attachment to life, belief in the immortality of the gods, and so on. 'There can be no question of obstinately determining *de plano* universal ways of feeling, thinking and acting which may not even exist' (Charles Blondel). For his part, and at much the same time, Henri Berr complained: 'We have no history of Death. Of Love. Of Cruelty or of Joy. Scarcely any history of Fear.' The history of feeling (Lucien Febvre's 'great silence') has found such a loud voice that we are tempted to shout it down by asking, 'What is this death whose history you are writing?' What is it that still gives rise to the perfectly recognizable feeling we continue to call joy—and will go on giving rise to it? Why is it that men are still afraid, now that the millenium—the second millenium even—has passed?

Fear has its history and its social geography.[5] This feeling has assumed completely different forms and modes of expression in the history of the West—forms and modes that have become visible and susceptible to description through iconography, literature, lexicology, and so on. But the fear-situation itself is primary and recurrent. It so happens that the 'need for security' is a constituent element of human reality, even if the basic insecurity it expresses is never coded in the same roles. An investigation into the essence of politics has to explain the whys and wherefores of the constitution of human reality, whereas history merely describes it. The essence of politics beings with neurobiology, but it does not end there.

What sort of viviparious mammal is the political animal? Chronologically, the first answer is: the only mammal born with a retarded neural system. The most premature of all mammals is so constructed, anatomically, that it has to seek protection throughout its life—initially from adults. By virtue of this completely natural state of dependence, history is a succession of various offers of religious protection: the *tutelary spirits* of primitive polydemonism, the *protective gods* of polytheism, the *supreme Saviour* and *patron saints* of Christianity. Ultimately Lucien Febvre will be able to establish an astonishing correlation between the rise of the insurance companies and the process of dechristianization from the end of the nineteenth century onwards. But why and against what does the social individual need to be so constantly insured? After all, the fear of the millenium is not the same as the sixteenth century's fear of the plague, the great fear of 1789, the twentieth century's fear of cancer and nuclear war, and so on. What is it that makes fear return ... neither quite the same nor completely different, unstoppable, imperious? What need is satisfied by the uselessness of yesterday's leper-hospital and today's fall-out shelter?

In the beginning was Anxiety. It has its dykes, its cries, its poems and its exorcisms. What if it also had its laws? Maternal love has its history, written in short (secular) phases,[6] and the collective face of Joy has changed from the mystical transports of our ancestors to the militant rejoicings of our brothers. But what does Joy signify? Does the invention of the feeling of childhood mean that the situation of infancy did not exist prior to the sixteenth century or that it existed only among the ruling classes of the West? Has the paternal *imago* ('whose function is to relate the organism to its reality', according to the early Lacan) varied with the role of the father? These impertinent questions seem to ignore the fact that it did not take the history of mentalities to rid historical explanation of the last convulsions of 'human nature'.

The superstition of history rests upon a speculative paralogism that provides a basis for all the variants on theoretical humanism (from historical materialism as 'concrete humanism' to the most banal moral idealism).

The argument that one can prove the existence of God by analysing his essence alone is known as the 'ontological proof' (canonized by St Anselm). The concept of an infinite being is that of a being who includes all the attributes of perfection. Existence is one of those attributes, therefore I cannot think of God without positing his existence. One current tendency within the 'social sciences' has invented a symmetrical argument that we might call 'the logical proof of the non-existence of nature'. There can be no logical representation of nature (as a separate entity), so it follows that nature is a non-being. This argument is a negative version, or inversion, of the theological argument insofar as it *draws conclusions about being from logic*. But just as the concept of a thing does not imply its existence, so its non-concept does not imply its non-existence. The impossibility of conceptualizing nature apart from history does not entail that history can be conceived independently of nature.

The 'human essence'—i.e., a set of biological characteristics common to the whole species and present in each individual—does not exist independently of variations in culture and social development. But it does not follow that the given specificity is a degree zero of historical humanity, from which mankind continually strays in its forward march. In other words, nature exists inside history, and psychobiological individuality is co-extensive with historico-social individuality. The fact that a single primary given cannot logically determine human history does not erase certain natural characteristics which the historian can no more transcend than can the physicist in his laboratory or the militant in his practical activity. Need does not *explain* the processes whereby it is satisfied, but without need there are no such processes. We know perfectly well that there is more to eating than feeding yourself, more to love than reproduction, more to dying than ceasing to exist, and more to clothes than covering the body. No one has yet seen the biological function of nutrition at work. All of man has a history, but history is not the whole of man. There is a history of eating (of table-manners, cutlery, food itself), but there is none of hunger. The history of architecture revolves around the need for shelter, that of clothes around the need to cover the body. The history of love, like that of the family, revolves around the minimal biological triangle. The father-mother constraint upon procreation has absolutely no heuristic value for the historical determination of paternal attitudes, or even for the choice of someone other than the 'natural' father. But it is of crucial significance for the structure of the political order. It makes the ethnographer of kinship systems or the historian of education smile with pity. And it makes us weep with rage when we read political theorists who are too intelligent to think of anything so stupid. Marx was a good father. If his scientific homonym had taken the trouble to think of himself as a father or to reflect upon the historical constraints that derive from the biological need for fathers, our collective destiny over the last century or so might have been less harsh. The worst father is the one who does not realize he is a father.

3. Nature and History: An Inseparable Pair

The various metaphysics of history which the twentieth century is practically experiencing are theoretical gifts from the nineteenth century. It is by no means certain that the metaphysics of nature being elaborated in the late twentieth century will be useful gifts to the twenty-first century, or that they will help it to understand and tolerate its political history.

The European nineteenth century had the 'revelation' that history was a factor in the transformation of nature. The world twentieth century has the 'revelation' that nature is a factor which resists the transformations of history.

The philosophical nineteenth century saw nature as something that lay *behind it*, a yoke to be shaken off, and saw the past as irreversibly fading away. We view nature as something ahead of us: a regulatory ideal or a paradise to be regained. There is an interplay of revival and novelty, nostalgia and expectation, across the centuries.

Marx saw the explosion of the industrial revolution: railways, mechanical looms, telegrams, macadam, steamers, linotype, and products of human labour. Feuerbach—Marx's Ossian—had elaborated a philosophy of nature against Hegel (nature of nature, of Christianity, of man, etc.), and Marxism was elaborated against this philosophy of the natural. Its critique of naturalist materialism is gloriously summed up by the *Theses on Feuerbach*, 'the first document in which is deposited the brilliant germs of the new world outlook' (Engels, 1888). It expresses the pride of an age captivated by industry and convinced that it can overthrow the *ordo rerum*. 'The philosophers have only interpreted the world: the point, however, is to change it' (*Eleventh Thesis on Feuerbach*). The clarion call still rings out wherever political and technological revolutions unleash the development of the productive forces. Theoretical progressivism is still valid in the 'developing countries'.

The dying twentieth century is restoring the paradigm of nature to a place of honour, especially in the advanced countries: bio-physics, ecology, ethnology, anthropology, duration, etc. After the intoxication of historical activism comes the naturalist hangover; after the Promethean fervour, a more modest tone; after historical activism, the cosmological (and political) reaction. The objective causes of this backlash are so blindingly and deafeningly obvious that we can break off these banalities with a common-sense remark. Quite apart from the fact that every 'revelation' often takes on the appearance of an apocalypse by going to extremes (Good and Evil can change places too), it can also have dangerous side-effects like blindness and amnesia.

From a critical point of view, it initially seems that nature is not a thing but *a moment in a contradictory relationship*. And that is how it appears if we look at past paradigms. Nature and Grace (Pascal), State of Nature and Social Contract (Rousseau), Nature and History (Marx), Nature and Life (Bergson). The logical pen-dulum becomes a chronological see-saw. The values of the natural moment alternate, depending upon which side of the relationship is in the ascendancy. The pendulum is the ideal vanishing-point at which all perspective lines meet. A naive metaphysics of nature is answered by its opposite: a naive metaphysics of history, but they are both generated by the movement that separates each term from its correlate. Naturalism is a metaphysics of spontaneity and leads to 'spontaneism' and 'reductionism'. Historicism is a metaphysics of production and leads to 'productivism' and 'voluntarism'.

4. Communist Society, the Highest Stage of Historical Idealism

Marxism has become a superstitious theory of practice, but what Marx produced was anything but a metaphysics. The thinker of labour never thought of history independently of nature. No nature without labour, he tells Feuerbach. But no labour without nature, he reminds the Marxists. 'Labour is the father of material wealth and the earth is its mother', he notes in *Capital*, adopting a phrase from William Petty. In his own lifetime, Marx saw the letter of socialism being deformed by its spirit and he did everything he could to correct that deformation. In a well-known mishap, the Gotha Congress (1875) adopted a socialist programme which began from the principle: 'Labour is the source of all wealth and culture.' Marx grabbed his pen: 'Nature is just as much the source of use-values (and it is surely of such that material wealth consists!) as labour, which itself is only the manifestation of a force of nature, human labour-power.' Quite so: what would become of a worker without calories, industry without sources of energy, processing without raw materials? This ungracious yet sensible comment did-not protect the *Critique of the Gotha Programme* from being censored and filed away by the leaders of the German Workers' Party. The Gotha statement of principle was gratifying because, on paper and in men's heads, it transformed the heroes of industrial labour into keepers of the keys to the wealth and culture of the civilized world.

This absolutism of production did not, however, fall from the skies. What tenacious phantasy did Marx's rational logic arouse in its partisans? Or was the phantasy already present in his logic? How did we end up with this absurdity?

In order to answer such questions, we must now retrace the thread of Marx's argument.

In the contradictory nature/history relationship, labour is the mediating element through which two categories separated by speculative materialism circulate within each another. Labour—and its extension—industry makes the subjective objective, and vice versa. Nature becomes equal to history. 'History itself is a *real* part of *natural* history, or of the transformation of nature into man.' The lever of this transformation is material production. Man is the only natural being for whom nature, beginning with his own nature, is not simply given. Feuerbach failed to grasp this. Although his critique of Hegel was intended to restore concrete man to his rights, to all his sensuous wealth, he saw the sensuous merely as an object and not as an activity. Hence his materialism may be described as speculative. Feuerbach contemplates the human essence in the same way that he contemplates the fruit-trees in his garden, forgetting that the cherry-trees were transplanted there by commerce and cultivated by determinate men, etc. Feuerbach dissolves history into nature because he dissolves social practice into the sensuous object. Essentially, practice means labour, and material labour means the simultaneous transformation of the world and the labourer. 'Man in General' ignores the historical, material conditions of productive labour. Of course man is a product of nature (as is the cherry tree). But nature is a starting-point, a logical presupposition, not a real basis. The science of the concrete history of man is therefore radically different from the natural sciences in that human nature and the development of social production are one and the same. Mankind is historical through and through because it produces both the world and itself. The specific property of man, as compared with other animal species, is that he has technical tools in place of natural properties. Men 'begin to distinguish themselves from animals as soon as they begin to produce their means of subsistence, a step which is conditioned by their physical organization. By producing their means of subsistence, men are indirectly producing their material life.'[7] Or again: 'The production of life, both of one's own in labour and of fresh life in procreation, now appears as a twofold relation: on the one hand as a natural, on the other as a social relation.' When two terms reciprocally condition each another, one is always more reciprocal than the other. In Marx, the dominant term is of course labour–history–man, while nature represents the inert base, the prior condition for production. Economically, it is the raw material that is to be transformed; politically, it is the far-off ethnic origin (the so-called 'natural' primitive community) which has to become more and more remote (division of labour, etc.) if we are ever to find it again in complete form. We will of course eventually come back to our starting-point: the Marxist history of mankind is an *Odyssey*; Ulysses knows from the start that his sufferings will not destroy him and that he will eventually get home. In the meantime, however, the first term in the nature-history pair has a negative value, rather like 'extension' as opposed to 'thought' in Spinoza or, to put it more simply, like the peasant as opposed to the worker in industrial society. The peasant who cultivates the land owes more to the worker who makes history than the worker owes to the peasant (hence the leading role of the Workers Party, even in agrarian societies). Nature is the site of the past, of fragmentation, necessity, even expropriated man: history is the site of transformation, unification, planning, conscious autonomy, even of man's reappropriation of an essence lost in natural exteriority. Nothing produces itself: everything is produced in a perpetual twofold movement of mutual production which unites object and subject. ('The eye has become a *human* eye, just as its object has become a social, *human* object.' But the role of the natural object in this movement is negative: it occupies the position assigned to extension or the body by classical idealism, the difference being that Marx replaces the original synthetic subject with productive social activity and Cartesian individual *consciousness* with collective *praxis*. But he does not revolutionize the logical disposition of the idealist relation. The lack of symmetry is obvious and the final reconciliation of nature with history in communism will owe much more to the humanization of nature than to the naturalization of man. Marxism is an integral humanism. Before he died, Gide told young people that 'the world will be what you make it'. Marxism puts it better and goes further: 'Man will be what he makes himself'. And he will make himself by making the world his own.

Man therefore produces himself as a species—being in history, and this process of self-creation will culminate in the higher state of socialism or communism.

'Communism, as fully developed naturalism, equals humanism, and as fully developed humanism equals naturalism; it is the genuine resolution of the conflict between existence and being, between objectification and self-affirmation, between individual and species. It is the solution of the riddle of history and knows itself to the solution.'[8] When that stage is reached, nothing will be alien to man who, having reappropriated the whole of his nature, will everywhere be able to see himself in a mirror. Nature is reflected in him and he in nature. There will be equality between the origin and the end, the subject and the object, the end of prehistory and the appearance of an *immediately universal* history (which implies the reduction of plurality to unity, of natural national diversity to a world civilization).

In this naive imagery, absolute idealism reached new heights of narcissism. 'Fully developed' humanism reveals that it cannot be 'fully developed' or meet its premises unless it adopts the *supreme-*

ly idealist aim of the fusion of thought and being. Marxism was a
more consistent humanism than most, and it still has one advantage
over its modern ideological juniors (including the subjective
humanism of Sartre's praxis) and related rhetorics (humanisms of
the moral act, à la Camus[9]). It actually brings out the full implications of self-foundation. The Robinson Crusoe fable of Communism is the result of a transference of the ideal of complete
reflexive self-perception from the terrain of speculative consciousness to that of collective history. The impossibility of its logic is
eminently coherent.

The so-called inversion of idealist philosophy in fact marks the
completion of the metaphysical trajectory: the idealist enigma is
resolved in and by history as the history of the reappropriation of
the object by the subject or of the reappropriation of external
necessity by subjective liberty. Marx's revolution consisted of giving a primal theoretical phantasy—*the subject as cause of
itself*—the form of a historical process and a practical modality.
The image of the Man-God came down from the Cosmos and passed into history, where the author of its days will end its days 'when
the practical relations of everyday life between man and man, and
man and nature, generally present themselves to him in a transparent and rational form' (*Capital*). It will take time and it will not
be easy. But it will eventually be possible because communist society is every man's realization of himself through the use of the faculty of self-determination. The natural determinations which now
weigh down upon him from the outside are provisional and can be
removed. 'The veil is not removed from the countenance of the
social life process, i.e., the process of material production, until it
becomes production by freely associated men and stands under
their conscious and planned control. This, however, requires that
society possesses a material foundation, or a series of material conditions of existence, which in their turn are the natural and spontaneous product of a long and tormented historical development.'

Communism could have been the transcendental ideal of Marxist
Reason, in the Kantian sense of an impossible 'sum total of all
possibilities, in so far as it forms the condition of the complete
determination of everything.'[10] But it actually refers to an objective
process divided into two distinct phases of transition (socialism, the
'lower' stage, and communism, the 'higher' stage). This is taken to

mean a real movement which 'abolishes the present state'. By denying that it is a utopia, historical materialism reveals its utopian roots. Any real movement which leads to an abstraction is itself an abstraction. The fact that Marx adopted the oldest slogans of the detested utopian socialists in order to characterize communist society ('To each according to his needs' and 'From each according to his ability') shows that the keystone of the speculative edifice is the inevitable circularity of science and utopia. There is no great methodological divide between the two types of socialism: the infantile and the mature. In terms of the conditions of existence of a political order, Marx's picture of communist society—the universal realization of anarchy—is a square circle. There is no material possibility of its advent because its concept has no logically reality. (This may explain the metamorphoses of the first phase, which shows a definite tendency not to move nearer to the second phase.)

There is, then, a formal and material *given*. Just as the group cannot be its own origin, the productive individual cannot be the subject of his own existence because he does not produce himself. The viviparious mammal is a creature of nature, from *naciscor*, to be born. My birth certificate (M Dupont, son of Mme Dupont, née Durand, and M Dupont, born on such and such a date) states the most overwhelmingly profound and banal truth that can be pronounced on any man: I was made and no one will ever understand why I was made as I am and not in any other way. Man has no foundation. He does not bring himself into being: his being comes to him from outside. Idealism's philosophical task, like religion's social task, can be seen as an attempt at the symbolic cancellation of the intolerable contingency of the natural. Socialism can be seen as an extension into the political order of a naturally human tendency to annul the natural irreducibility of the social relation by and through the exercise of a unitary rational will, as a 'scientific' exorcism of the ontological difference between things that grow and things that are made, between what happens and what is planned, between things that are produced and things that reproduce themselves. The category of *praxis* (or action) is invoked to dissolve the singularity of the concept of *physis* via a sort of amphibological ruse. It is as if making wine and making cement were one and the same operation (wine is not made and cement does not grow); or as if the status of a zoological species or the logical status of a group could be drawn up, approved and registered with the police like the status of an association of individuals (set up under the terms of the 1901 law). Unfortunately, both the nature of things—such as the referential constraints on groups—and the things of nature—such as *homo sapiens*'s single stomach and sexual specialization—escape the control of the bourgeois social contract as easily as that of the proletarian five-year plan. The abstraction of *praxis* is always subverted by *physis*.

Physis is not simply a preliminary to *praxis* (a reserve of energy, technical means of labour, natural labour-power). It conditions the field of practice from within (as a condition of material production). This is why, despite all the legends, political humanism finally gained the upper hand over Marx's historical materialism; or, to be more accurate, why the qualifier, 'historical' outstripped the substantive, 'materialism'.

The natural materiality of social history put historical materialism 'in check'. But the real check has been suffered by idealism. It should therefore bring us back to the foundations of materialism and, in the case of the political order, to the animal base of religion, the natural basis of human practices.

5. The Sanctity of Nature

It is in fact impossible to think or speak of nature without thinking or speaking of religion (and Feuerbach was quite right to attempt a philosophy of both). The radical, logical implications can be seen from the word's etymology. Nature or *physis*, from the Greek *phuo*, to grow, to cause to grow. The multiple meanings of the word 'appear to have spread in different directions from a primitive idea, probably that of the spontaneous development of living beings in determinate ways' (Lalande, 1926). In a word, nature as power, pressure, life force. Now let us turn to Benveniste. He tells us that, whilst a comparative study of Indo-European vocabularies does not provide access to 'a common prehistory of the sacred' (since there is no distinctly religious institution in Indo-European societies), it does reveal, beyond the historical subdivisions, a common root in which the life force is the primary unit of meaning.

In Avestic, the adjective *spenta*, sacred, initially means 'that which increases the number of creatures' or 'that which benefits creatures'. The nearest neighbours of the term mean swelling, growth and strength. 'The character of the holy and the sacred is thus defined by the notion of an exuberant and fertilizing force which is capable of bringing the products of nature to life.'

In the Germanic languages, the German *heilig* can be traced back to the Gothic *Hails*, which expresses the idea of 'health, bodily and mental integrity', as in the greeting, 'Hail!' Anything is sacred which is intact or allows things to remain intact. Integrity and religion are connected.

The Greek *hieros* derives from the Vedic *isirah*, meaning 'a vigorous, lively, ardent being'. Homer uses it to mean the sacred, the strong and the lively.[11] Some new publicist (i.e., philosopher) has probably already put an end to these painstaking reconstructions with a double jingle along the lines of, 'Nature is sacred: hands off. The sacred is natural: it's ours for the taking'. And they certainly did take it, but not always in the same way. We can now see how the desacralization of history leads as though by magic to the resacralization of nature. No matter whether the sacred is supplied by left or right, by history or cosmic energy, the demand for religion (whatever it may be called) appears to be constant. Phenomenologies of the sacred are fond of evoking the 'religious appeal', especially in the presence of unbelievers. Their false linguistic modesty functions as a *petitio principii*. The shade must exist somewhere if men respond to its appeal. Rational anthropologists, from Feuerbach to Freud, obviously prefer the term 'desire' (Feuerbach: 'The gods are the desires of men transmuted into real entities'). From a materialist point of view, *need* would appear to be more appropriate, since 'desire', 'illusion' or even 'collective neurosis' tend to displace the religious towards the shimmering yet shifting sands of psychology. 'Need' is a category in physiology and therefore pins us down to the solid base of the living. Living beings and collective existence can certainly be objects of desire, but there is more to desire than a subjective disposition (propensity or craving). The facts of consciousness—and they are real—certainly include a psychical lived experience, but only because they relate to physiological facts: the biological immaturity and prolonged dependency of the human child (which have no equivalent in other primates), a precocious awareness of a deficit of energy and therefore an awareness of death (observable in a child of seven or eight years, the so-called age of reason). In individual terms, this predisposition towards the sacred derives from a twofold insecurity constitutive of human growth, but the appetite for security which it arouses is both psychical and social because the same precariousness affects, in varying degrees, the complex living system known as an individual and the even more complex Other known as a hierarchical society. That precariousness is bio-physical in nature. The sacred is, then, a material determinant of culture. To be more accurate, it is an effect of the appearance of the nature/culture junction at the very point where animality and humanity meet. It shows that the two orders are connected precisely because they are contradictory. The sacred is a painful and incurable wound in the side of 'civilized' man.

It follows that the eradication of the sacred, whether wild or domesticated, would spell the end of all organized groups, and therefore of man and all existing individuals. It is an impossibility.

If religions were no more than contingent and singular facts of history, rather than the historical encodings of a natural invariant, it would be impossible to explain the extraordinary longevity of their doctrinal corpuses. It may well be possible to explain the birth of the gods, and hence of universal religions, by reference to the fear of lightning, astonishment, immaturity, hallucinations, and so on. Their very permanence, however, suggests that they are in some way necessary. A chance event that goes on and on, or a contingent event that is repeated over a long period, expresses something more than a statistical regularity. The content of mankind's mythologies has not, as we said before, substantially changed since Babylon, Sumer or Jerusalem. Like the archaic mythologies which evidently inspired them, the historical religions have stood the test of symbolic survival (the most recent dating back to the seventh century).

Borrowing the testing/selection process from the model of evolution, we can postulate that the great monotheist religions, which introduced a new bundle of data into the living human environment, would not have been selected, filtered or stored by that environment if the data did not in some way correspond to its internal logic. The transmission of stable religious rites, mysteries and dogmas through variable and changing states of society (in the case of Christianity from the slave mode of production to the capitalist and even the proto-socialist mode) leads one to wonder whether thepermanence of the data might not be due to the fact that they have encoded the structural invariants of the logic of living beings through an isomorphism between natural structures and mythical structures. Far from being empty chimera invented by rogues in order to dupe simple minds, religious mythologies might be clumsy sketches of objective relations which could not at the time be formulated. Ultimately, such a reading suggests a very simple hypothesis of simplicity itself elevated to a principle. Beyond the formal analogy between the savage and the civilized mind, there may be a congruence between the major religious myths and the mechanisms of nature, particularly the basic mechanisms of organized living matter. If this were the case, the languages of myth and science would have not only the same meaning content but the same syntactic form, 'spirit' and 'power' being the first code names for 'data' and 'energy'. Might not the Holy Ghost of the New Testament (the most mysterious of all the persons of the Trinity) owe its metaphorical obscurity to an inadequate knowledge of thermal phenomena? Etymologically, it is the breath of life, *anima*. So perhaps it represents a premonition of the consubstantiality between heat and life—the Holy Ghost as the sperm of God (*sperma tou theou*) and as 'tongues of fire' (a realization that, in Bochelard's words, 'fire is the principle of all seeds'. Could it be that it was invoked simply because of the familiarity of the unknown: 'Come, father of the poor, light of our hearts, warm that which is cold'.

Natural religion is the elementary form of energy conservation in a social totality. It comes as no surprise to see the solar disk of Aton (the one representation of the divine that is accepted from the Sudan to the Euphrates) rising over the first monotheist empire, that of Akhenaton. Nor is there anything surprising about the universality of 'Uranian' cults (fire, light, sky). From Japanese Shintoism to Egypt's Ra (and his son the Pharaoh), from Iran's Mithras to the Indo-European Zeus and the Incas' Inti (the organizing centre of the Empire), not forgetting the Sun King, sun-worship is the most common and the most irresistible of all religious archetypes. The sun-god was and is supreme because he is the first and last source of energy. From the sacrifices on the pyramids to the summer beaches, the warm-blooded biped has always paid his calorific debt to the day star with the obsidian knife or with suntan oil. His reverence is proof of his prudence. The religious animal is a rational animal. The basic intention was right: all life did begin with the sun and all life in the solar system will perish when the sun goes out. The end of history is contained within the beginning of the myth.

We should therefore be saying *credo quia naturale et rationale* rather than *credo quia absurdum*. I would not believe in these legends and gods if they did not, without realizing it, tell me perfectly realistic (and biochemically banal) stories. Is not kerygyma the reading and promotion of the synthesis of molecules? Before we knew it, we had a premonition that 'the time of repetition is that of inertia and death' (Serres) and that the 'sad chains of order' which typify physical world devoid of data had to be broken. The metamorphoses of Zeus or Dinoysus enchanted us because they are in resonance with the metamorphoses of our cells. We trembled with joy at the mysteries of the Incarnation, the Resurrection and Transubstantiation because we saw in them the irreversible time that transforms the living being and destroys the passive iteration of the identity principle. Beneath the church arches, we applauded the rising sap of life as it produced the improbable, and we booed matter because it fell into endless pleonasms. We called life God and death the Devil. And just as a river makes us think of our life flowing away, so an Easter egg makes us dream of a life that will avenge us. There would be no religious emotion if the religious experience did not have a core of rational knowledge, inchoate as it may be. Dogma is a grammar, not only of the state, but of our collective chemical factories. Stammering and mystified, it is nevertheless an unwitting social biology. The things that an era regards as 'supernatural' are those which, lying beyond the knowledge it has been able to acquire of objective mechanisms, will only be made comprehensible by future science. We would be wrong to smile at the idea of *theologia ancilla naturae* or of religion as an anticipated memory of the nature of politics. In terms of substances, modern psycho-pharmacology contains very little that was not present in the old rustic pharmacopia. But the substances and their chemical components have now been identified. The sorcerers and witch-doctors knew all about psychotropics, even if they knew nothing of cerebral neurotransmitters. The old empirical medicine was not mistaken when it recommended belladonna, nightshade or hellibore to treat pain, but it did not understand why the substances derived from the plants had this or that effect on patients. Therapeutic chemistry has subsequently explained their action by identifying and isolating their cellular and molecular basis, whilst the biology of the central nervous system has revealed the anatomical structures that make it possible for drugs in use since time immemorial to have good or bad effects. The royal road of experimental analysis sometimes leads straight back to primitive footpaths.

6. The Prescience of the Collective

Christian mysteries and ancient myths are the propylaea of the unconscious. Our mythology and theology constitute the archaeology of our human sciences. Just as, to use the familiar phrase, 'man thinks in myths', so does the group think in mysteries. Since they do not appear to exist on the same level, the two archives are actually complementary. Greek mythology tends to be an individual theatre, Christian theology a collective mythology. The individual unconscious found its repertoire in the tragedians, but the political unconscious may have to look to the Church Fathers.

As we have seen, ecclesiology explains theology, not vice versa. It should be recalled that the primary function of the elaboration of Christian dogma was to structure the communal links of God's people. Christian doctrine bears the imprint of the hierarchical congregation and was moulded by the constraints of group survival. Greek mythology did not produce Greek politics and the cities of Hellas were not organized on the basis of mythical stories. In contrast, there was a strict and constitutional reciprocity between the early Christian community and the formative stages of Christian thought. The collapse of imperial power structures and the subsequent intellectual confusion gave the bishops *de jure* or *de facto* responsibility for politics and even social reconstruction. This merging of functions largely explains the secret modernity of patristics. Medieval scholasticism means less to us, perhaps because it does not talk about a *we*. The doctors of the Middle Ages wrote and thought in a vacuum, in sheltered academic pockets, pursuing their clerical tasks without a direct political mandate. Committed to understanding things, they did not exercise any command over men. Since, however, many of the Latin and Greek Fathers of the early Christian world (especially the very first ones) were both doctors and pastors, thinkers and shepherds, it is only natural that their theories should unconsciously use the image of the sheep fold. The authors of the Church's authoritative texts held authority in the City, and their jurisdiction was both theological and political, ecclesiastical and civil. The bishops, like St Augustine in his native town of Hippo, were also the supreme judges and magistrates of their diocese. Writing and thinking in terms of living communities, they held responsibility for both bodies and souls. Their doctrine was elaborated as a function of their inseparable pastoral role. The structures of exchange and authority, economics and politics, naturally left their mark upon the intellectual framework of these great 'captains of the Church'.[12]

We may give two examples of theological grammar, one retrospective, the other prospective. The first concerns the science of economics, the second the possibility of a science of politics. Needless to say, the former looks like a solution and the latter does not even seem to have achieved the status of a problem.

Materialist political economy was born in the form of a Christology. How could it have been otherwise? The Marxist theory of commodities, money and capital not only derives from, but is constituted by, a long meditation on the mystery of the incarnation. But Marx adds to the language of patristics by borrowing the concept of transubstantiation from scholastic theology. From the time of Innocent III, this concept had been officially used by the Church to designate the mysterious conversion of bread and wine into the body and blood of Jesus Christ through the consecration of the eucharist. Marx uses it to designate the conversion involved in exchanging, say, a bound Bible for twenty yards of linen.

In the spring of 1844, shortly after his arrival in Paris, Marx begins to study political economy and immediately comes up against money, the mediator. In other words, Christ. 'Mill aptly sums up the essence of the matter in a single concept when he describes money as the medium of exchange.'[13] Marx then analyses how the act of mediation becomes a material thing external to man, in which the cult of the mediator is an end in itself. Marx's reflections on such alienation through mediation lead him to draw this parallel: 'Christ originally represents (1) man before God, (2) God for man and (3) man for man. In the same way money originally represents (1) private property for private property; (2) society for private property; (3) private property for society. But Christ is God alienated and man alienated. God continues to have value only in so far as he represents Christ; man continues to have value only in so far as he represents Christ. Likewise with money.'[14] When in 1857, after a long interruption due to other urgent political and philosophical tasks, Marx decides to begin the work of economic analysis *ab ovo*, it is once more by and through the Christological figure of Mediation that he apprehends the overall dialectic of capital. Arguing that 'the exact development of the concept of capital is necessary, since it is the fundamental concept of modern economics', he then goes on to use a theological metaphor: 'It appears as mediation with itself, as the subject for whom the extremes are merely its moments, whose autonomous presupposition it suspends in order to posit itself, through their suspension, as that which alone is autonomous. Thus, in the religious sphere, Christ, the mediator between God and humanity—a mere instrument of circulation between the two—becomes their unity, God-man, and, as such, becomes more important than God; the saints more important than Christ; the popes more important than the saints.'[15] His comment sums up and corroborates the most trivial results of applied mediology (in the intellectual sphere, for example, the publisher over the author, the journalist over the author, the gossip columnist over the critic, and so on). It is as if all the chains of communication were haunted by the same incoercible metastasis, with the intermediary eclipsing the predecessor upon whom he depends in theory but who depends on him in practice. Paradoxically, the noise takes priority over the message, as we would now say the information theory that proves the paradox right.[16]

Finally, *Capital* (1857). Volume I, Part I, Chapter 1: 'The Commodity'. Again the author plays the fool and rejects the obvious conclusion. The corner-stone of the whole edifice may be read as an analysis of a micro-mystery of incarnation. 'A commodity appears at first sight an extremely obvious, trivial thing. But its analysis brings out that it is a very strange thing, abounding in metaphysical subtleties and theological niceties.'[17] Marx does not turn theologian for the pleasure of it, much less in order to confuse matters—his sole aim is clarification. The commodity is a problem—the word made object—because it is at once a palpable body (use-value) and something impalpable (exchange-value). A useful object has a dual nature: two points of view are possible and the character of labour is twofold. Theology is present in the objective world of values simply because value is *a relationship between something abstract and something concrete* and because accounting for that relationship means *accounting for a metamorphosis* which, for example, transforms twenty yards of cloth into a coat and the coat into a banknote. 'As a use-value, the linen is something palpably different from the coat.... Its existence as value is manifested in its equality with the coat, just as the sheep-like nature of the Christian is shown in his resemblance to the Lamb of God.'[18] In other words, the 'mystical character of the commodity', the cell of the economy, conceals what is at once the most obvious and the most opaque secret of economic science. 'The value-form, whose fully developed shape is the money-form, is very simple and slight in form. Nevertheless, the human mind has sought in vain for more than 2,000 years to get to the bottom of it, while on the other hand there has been at least an approximation to a successful analysis of forms which are much richer in content and more complex. Why? Because the complete body is easier to study than its cells'.[19] It is the commodity-form itself which creates commodity fetishism, the illusion whereby social relations appear to men as relations between things.' In order, therefore, to find an analogy we must take flight into the misty realms of religion.' To reconstitute the genesis of the commodity-form is *ipso facto* to retrace the genesis of the money-form and to resolve the enigma of the possible transformation of a commodity into gold. The analysis of money, which follows that of exchange and commodities, therefore traces the metamorphoses of value: C-M-C and then M-C-M. Finally, labour (average social labour-time) will be baptized the invisible 'substance' of value, just like the Word in the hypostasis of Christ.

Without going into the details of these familiar demonstrations, we will simply note that it is by treating something obvious—the commodity—as a mystery and by using all the metaphors implicit in something apparently simple and self-identical that Marx tracks down the 'secret of capitalist production', namely, the existence of surplus-value as a general form. If Marx had not seen double when he looked at the commodity (a commodity for the mind and its alter ego for the flesh), he would not have discovered the dual nature of labour, which lies at the heart of his critical conception. In that sense, the theological detour was an analytic shortcut, as if the paradoxical logic of God were the logic of the economic nature of things or of the 'natural law which presides over their movement' in the capitalist mode of production.

It was, therefore, by using theological notions that Marx escaped from the 'theological era' of economic analysis. The revelation of the mystery put an end to the old mystification. His use of the 'archaic' notions of fetishism allowed him to see through the modern fetish. Previously, we believed we knew (what the value of a commodity was); henceforth, we know that we believe (in the autonomy of commodities which dance of their own free will).

When it comes to politics, however the fetishism of power appears to be intact. On this terrain, where belief is to apparent organs of power what labour-value is to visible commodities, we believe that we know and we do not know what we believe. In political ideology, the religious illusion is all the more powerful in that it appears natural and not religious. As in economics, nothing can be really explained because everything is obvious. Our political thought is all the more magical and all the less effective in that we do not apply the elementary tools of theology to the elementary facts of political existence.

7. The Holy Ghost of Organization

Basically, religious matters are too serious to be left to professional worshippers, priests and mystics, or, a fortiori, to social psychologists. What is at stake is the practical question of *organization*, which concerns biochemists and branch (or district) secretaries alike. Priests are the first organizers.

Religious ideologies contain the same programme as political ideologies and the institutions which act as supports for the latter (Nations, States, Parties) struggle, not without a certain success, to take over from the former (Churches, Sects), or even to support them in their tasks. Obviously, a revealed religion is better than a 'scientific' ideology at soothing anxiety. Shi'a Islam, like the Catholic Church of old, guarantees that anyone who lays down his life for the prophet will have eternal life and enter into paradise. All Marxism-Leninism can offer its martyred followers is a very honourable mention in the history books (or the Party handbook). Even so, it gets by: in this century, the 'spirit of the Party' has shown an organizational dynamism equal to that displayed by the Holy Ghost in other circumstances. The organs of the degraded religion known as 'politics' are probably intrinsically less suited to the work of organizing and reproducing complex sets. But in good times and bad, they do insure the safety and identity of human groups against the constant drift towards entropy, even if they do not guarantee them immortality. The cost is, of course, high, but for the moment we are not concerned with cost-benefit analysis. Day after day, we thumb through all the victory of social vitality as if we were telling a rosary: they confirm the important thing, that we are holding out. The 'bastions' are under attack? The undivided bloc is crumbling? We decided unanimously. We closed ranks behind X, our first target for shameful machinations. We overcame divergences of opinion, friction, tendencies, harmonized our points of view, weeded out the foreigners, resisted pressure—adulteration, disfiguration, heresy. We maintained our course, the essence of our heritage, the congress line, the spirit of our institutions. In short, we organized the necessary reorganization. Who are we? The Nation, the Church, the Majority, the Party, the Atlantic Pact, the Warsaw Pact, etc. None of all that happened by itself. And if no one had made it happen, neither you, the reader, nor I, the writer, would be here to give thanks to the workers of negentropy or to add our little negentropic stone to the cracked wall of paradise. Without those millions of stones, life would be hell, not purgatory. The will to believe does not hamper the will to live: it anchors it. Fools and sponges have one thing in common: they stick to things, but they stay alive. Only the dead can let themselves become detached, drifting with the current.

'Superstitious' comes from the Latin *superstes*: survivor.

In biology, *selection* has been defined as a 'machine for reversing time', and in history man has been defined as a 'machine for making gods'. The anthropological need for religion appears to be the product of the application of the first proposition to the second. Man is a machine for making time-machines, of which collective organisms are the most important. Historical time, whose unit of account is a thousand years, is an integral part of biological time, which measures in millions of years. *Homo sapiens* belongs to the order of primates and to the class of mammals. Historically speaking, Bergson, to whom we owe the second definition, intervened before Monod, the author of the first definition. But metaphorical as it may be, the first accounts scientifically for the second. Just as mammals appeared before zoologists, who belong to the mammal class, religion emerged before philosophy, metaphysics before physics and the metapolitics of theology before political science. It seems to be the rule that the order of chronological appearance inverts the order of logical progression, just as localized hypotheses that are initially somewhat shaky invert the general laws from which they are subsequently deduced as particular cases.

The appearance of ever more complex living systems on the face of the earth 'reverses' time in that it reverses the second principle which should 'naturally' (statistically) break down the complex into the simple, the higher into the lower and the organized into the amorphous. The subsequent appearance of organized human groups extends this paradoxical movement towards order, which can only reproduce and perfect itself if it actively neutralizes the physical tendency towards disorder. As a result of a long process of empirical verification, paleontology has been able to show that 'in nature, the human group behaves like a living organism' (Leroi-Gourhan). And just as every organism has to resist a physical process of breakdown that will end in its death by using a certain number of procedures inherent in the cybernetics of living things, so every human group has to resort to a certain number of non-natural operations if it is to resist the natural and statistical law that the most probable state of a group ('left to itself') is dispersal increases with the 'passage of time'. We have all taken part in the foundation of a group at least once in our lives—a drama group, a club, a friendly association—and we have therefore all experienced this law. Physical time undoes the things that the living being struggles to build. At every level in the universe, the unification of diverse elements costs energy: it always requires *work*, be it ideal or material, cerebral or physical, sociological or biological. It is well known that political work shows little profit (a lot of expenditure for little result), but you can always tell when a living thing is satisfied because it becomes so joyful. Militant rejoicings and religious transports are two aspects of the same state of grace granted to anyone who overcomes their natural tendency towards entropy. When we unite several hundreds of millions of scattered men from disparate cultures, societies and races into one community (Christianity or Dar-al-Islam) governed by a single Law pronounced by one God, what are we doing if not transforming an atomized swarm with a high probability and a low level of 'data' into the ordered state of a 'political' constitution with a low probability and a high level of 'data'? What are we doing if not extending the characteristically inverse vector of 'the logic of living things' into the social sphere?

Time flies: religion clips its wings. Collectives disintegrate, but religion assures them maximum cohesion through the recondite performance of rites and the reciprocal recognition function of its myths. Individuals are doomed to die: religion's answer is to promise them all immortality (on certain conditions). There can be no established religion without a theology, without, that is, an intellectual system to rationalize faith. But the force that establishes and constitutes religious beliefs is experienced and communicated through affectivity, even though 'religious feelings' express the living creature's elementary bio-physical demand for life without which it would cease to live. At the same time, however, the precariousness of the supply of life is a given fact of experience, and entropy reveals itself to every individual in the extremely banal yet eminently physical form of the fear of dying.

The universality of funeral rites and the Neanderthal origins of burial indicate something more than a concomitance between the symbolic negation of death and the structuring of human groups. They bear witness to the human being's functional adaption to the one project over which there can be no debate: the preservation of the species without loss of its specific characteristics. This vital function implies that all religions (or 'ideologies') are not alike, for otherwise a religion would not preserve the bio-ethnic individuality of the group. Religion is its anthropological fingerprint, a double guarantee of historical permanence and cultural integrity.

There are many religions whose gods are dead, but very few which do not reserve some sort of after-life for their followers. The immortal god of monotheism is like a central mirror in which the anti-death tendencies are reflected, a solar furnace that transforms a bundle of animal reflexes into idealized energy, a collection of physical drives into a symbolic montage. It must have taken a lot of subtlety, conceptual work and theoretical combativity for men, and especially Catholics, to dare to seek integral self-preservation *ad aeternam*! It is thanks to the hypostatic union of two natures (divine and human) in the one person of the Son of God that the corpses of Western atheists are, unless a specific wish to the contrary is expressed, put into coffins and laid in the ground rather than being flung on to the rubbish heap or reduced to ashes. All because the Nicene and Chalcedonian fathers finally rallied to the thesis of *homoiousios*, the consubstantiality of the Flesh and the Word. You do not incinerate a body that has been indirectly blessed by the Holy Ghost and will eventually be resurrected. Which of us would be mad enough to risk appearing at the Last Judgement with a femur missing? It should not be forgotten that Christianity is the only religion that accepts the resurrection of the human personality as a whole, body included. The Christian (or the convert) has two more births than the average mortal: baptism and death. Given the current state of biological science, that is not an advantage to be disdained. The Brahmin's metempsychosis and the Buddhist's reincarnation only affect the soul, an impersonal principle. (If their future rebirth depends upon good or bad behaviour on earth, it cannot be exactly the same individual who is reborn. It is therefore not really the individual who is burned.)

The act of believing is an organizational requirement and, as such, not subject to negotiation. But there is an art to the practical use or activation of our attitudes—hence the interest or even piquancy of the history of religion and 'political life'. We have to take refuge and therefore to believe. Territorial retrenchment is an absolute imperative, but its application must be relative and ever contradictory. In matters of organization, there is no room for dilemmas—a door has to be *either* open *or* shut. But in order to enjoy continued existence, the doors of the organizational enclosure have to be open *and* closed, in accordance with constantly improvised arrangements, temperature variations and pressure differences. Nations, churches and parties blindly zigzag between death by closure (chauvinism, fundamentalism, sectarianism) and death by exposure (internationalism, modernism, opportunism). If there were any other a priori laws in such matters, the world would no longer be as exciting as it is.

3

Counter-evidence

1. Fragments of a Black Box

The mere existence of 'real socialism' is the greatest contribution that practice has ever made to political theory.[1] The realization of scientific socialism as an institutional orthodoxy for one third of mankind and as a group mystique for the rest of the world should allow the human sciences to reach a new 'qualitative threshold'. Previously, there was no real reason to see religion as anything but an infantile disorder that would disappear when political, scientific or technical revolutions gave mankind enough antibiotics to take away its need for the consolations of opium. But the doctor himself turned out to be an opium addict. As it became a concrete, material force, the Marxist critique of religion found itself becoming the 'spirit of the party', a 'state doctrine'. It's like magic. Enter a radical atheism. Exit a world religion. Is the metamorphosis of a 'science' into a religion not enough to place the science of religion at the head of the agenda of the political sciences? It is up to the agents, victims or witnesses of the simultaneous genesis of a new social order and a new social religion to reflect upon the inversion. What was until recently 'the great charismatic movement of modern times' (J. Mer) will at least have served the purpose of ridding religion of monks (or taking ecclesiastical tasks out of the hands of the professional clergy)—and that brings us a step closer to the logic of organization. The soul of a soulless world did not hold Marx's attention for very long; and Lenin, a born organizer, took practically no interest in this 'minor' question that seemed already to have been solved. (A hundred or so pages out of a total output of almost twenty-six thousand suggests a very passing irritation.[2]) Collections of texts entitled 'Lenin on Art', 'Lenin on Literature', 'Lenin on Armed Struggle' and so on circulate throughout the Marxist planet, but there is no breviary of religion. Contempt for the flowers of the chains of human misery is no longer in season now that practical history particularly that of Marxism-Leninism has dispelled the theoretical errors of Marx and Lenin. More than ever before, the criticism of Marxist religion is now the prerequisite of all criticism.

To argue that the precondition has not yet been met would seem bold indeed to any adult who has kept an eye on the bookshop windows over the last twenty or thirty years. Has not everything already been said in London, Vienna, Paris, Rome or Madrid about the various forms of sectarianism, messianism and fideism? So we need to be more specific: any critique of communist religion that limits itself to communism or thinks it can throw political religion out with the communist bathwater is not a rational critique. For although illusion is present here in so far as communism denies being an illusion, it is also present wherever illusion is refused citizenship because men forget that it is the condition of existence of Cities.

Truths that touch upon men's interests and affront their self-regard have always been greeted with stones. If, in a sense, the stones rained down so heavily that the black box disappeared over the horizon and the problem was finally shelved, this was because the parties concerned with the problem of 'a critical theory becoming religion' never really met one another. For the last fifty years the kingdom of interdisciplinarity has been nothing more than the juxtaposition of three tautological discourses: Marxist theoreticians get on with their theory, anti-Marxist ideologists get on with their politics, and sociologists of religion write the sociology of religious movements, all sublimely scornful of their neighbours and blissfully unaware of the agenda.

Regardless of the rights and wrongs of Marxism's claim to the title of 'science of history', for our present purposes the claim itself provides *a contrario* proof that no specific historical practice can be deduced or inferred from a scientific theory of history. The ultimate proof—which dominates and sums up all the rest—is the very existence of the *ism* as a label of authority that truth functions under and through the name of the author. When societies which claim to have developed 'on a scientific basis' declare themselves to be 'guided by the scientific doctrine of Marx and Lenin', we can conclude that the second proposition gives the lie to the first. A scientific discourse is by definition a discourse without a subject, whereas historical materialism can be efficacious within collectives that appeal to its authority only by hypostatizing Marx as subject and Lenin as subject.

In other words, subversion of a critique (through its inversion into dogmatic cement) is not a moral perversion but a specific process which cannot be explained simply through deploring it. Its specificity is that of a separating space (or of the surplus-value that adherence adds to assent) which allows the rational idea of class struggle as the motor of historical events to be transformed into an emotive valency, an affective theme, a melodic motif, a *chanson de geste*, a badge of membership, a rallying cry, a slogan, an eschatological myth, and so on. Such surplus efficacity is of course a scientific loss. Marxologists have every reason to see the drift of orthodox Marxism as a sign that it is moving ever further from Marx's own conceptions and as a further stage in 'the ideologization of Marxism through political success' (Gabel). But the facile definition of Marxism as the sum total of the ways in which Marx's work has been misunderstood can in turn lead to all sorts of misunderstandings. For it avoids the basic question: is this misunderstanding the result of some unfortunate accident, or does it correspond to a logical necessity?

2. A Tragic Blunder

It is well known that the most acid criticisms of Marxist practices are to be found in Marx himself. Marxologists and Marxians delight in writing sarcastic quotations from the theoretician alongside every aberration of a particular authority—quotations on state bureaucracy as a collective Jesuit, on the rhetoric of moralistic sermons, on the market in mysticism and the spirit of sectarianism, and so forth. The texts are there. And so are the acts, a whole lifetime of them.

Having studied early Christianity, the young Marx was, like Engels, aware that the organization of sects is the first historical form of mass organization. They did all they could to calm the frenzy of the proliferating socialist prophets of the 1840s and to turn it to derision. Witness one of Marx's first political acts, his break with Weitling 'the most eminent Communist theoretician in Germany' in the *Manifesto Against Kriege* (Weitling's disciple): 'Faith, more specifically faith in the "holy spirit of community", is the last thing required for the achievement of communism.' Marx denounces the dementia caused by the importation of religious attitudes into political relations: real complexities concealed by mere verbosity, moralism masquerading as political analysis, the conversion of the militant into a cross between a prophet and a conspirator, intolerance leading to fanaticism. ('The enemy of the party is ruthlessly turned into a heretic, transformed from an enemy of the actually existing party of struggle into a sinner against humanity—which only exists in the imagination—who must be punished.') A whole century of the 'party spirit' is taken apart in a few pages (premonitory in the extreme, but without effect). Nor was this an isolated sortie. Marx constantly contrasts his critical work, which helped him to discover 'the natural laws of history', with the activity of crystal-ball gazers. The use of a 'religious' tone is always seen as the surest index of vacuity. After Weitling, it is Proudhon's turn: his oratorical frenzy simply reveals his 'pretentious platitudes' and the 'emptiness of his arguments'. 'He does not seriously criticize socialist sentimentalities, or what he regards as such. Like a holy man, a pope, he excommunicates poor sinners.'[3]

When the old Marx revised the Gotha and Erfurt programmes, he did set the workers parties the task not merely of recognizing freedom of religious conscience but of freeing men from religious consciousness itself. In Europe, religion meant Christianity, and its inevitable withering away would mark the end of prehistory. 'After Christianity, after absolute religion, no other form of religion can arise', prophesied Engels as he mocked Carlyle for his pantheism. He might have excepted the Marxist's relative religion, which would serve its purpose well enough. After all, historical materialism teaches us that nothing is eternal except movement.

The young Marx's investigation into the structure of the religious illusion was as impeccable as Oedipus's investigation into the murder of his father. To be more accurate, when Marx declared in 1844 that 'the criticism of religion has essentially been completed', he was like a doctor who diagnoses cancer, feels that he has done his duty, exclaims *in petto*, 'Don't talk to me about cancer. Now that I know what it is I can get on with something else' ... and then gets cancer. The 'something else' is the scientific analysis of the capitalist mode of production. And so (say, between 1846 and 1850) Marx moves from the criticism of religion to the criticism of economics. Marx the individual takes the plunge—on paper, the epistemological break. But Marxist organizations mark time in prehistory: the theological non-break. The real's revenge on the idea.

Just as Marx declares that the criticism of religion has been completed, politics begins to take off as a religion.

'The criticism of religion ends,' writes our enthusiastic therapist, 'with the doctrine that for man the supreme being is man, and thus with the categorical imperative to overthrow all conditions in which man is a debased, enslaved, neglected and contemptible being' (*Deutsch-Französische Jahrbücher*, 1844). A doctrine can do away with another doctrine, but not with an objective field of gravity. Marx's 'categorical imperative' has no more become part of political reality than Kant's has of ethical reality. The best explanation for the necessity of this 'accident' is to be found in the astounding deduction of *On the Jewish Question*: 'Finally it follows that when man proclaims himself an atheist through the mediation of the state—that is, when he proclaims the state an atheist—he still remains under the constraints of religion, because he acknowledges his atheism only deviously, through a medium. Religion is precisely that: the devious acknowledgement of man through an intermediary.'[4] There we have the key terms of the misunderstanding: deviously, medium, mediator. The intermediary is the enemy who prevents society from seeing itself as a whole. Communism will enable it to do so because it will do away with the mediator.

It has often been said that there is no specific theorization of the political field in Marxism. We now know why: *it is replaced by the theorization of the religious field. On the Jewish Question*—a work which is both brilliant and, because it does not realize it, embarrassing—is an authentic theory of political objectivity in concentrated form. The only problem is that it deals with the religious illusion (not only Judaism but, through it, also Catholicism, Protestantism, and so on). Marx was not mistaken as to the nature of his object—which *is* based upon a lack and therefore upon the need to make a detour to find a palliative against separation. He merely chose the wrong object. It was a understanding, tragic in the true sense of the word. When an insight comes so close to being an oversight, the frisson of terror/pity is born.

Let us retrace Marx's argument in the light of what we have learned about the structure of political bodies.

The basis of religion is not to be found in religion itself. Religion is a phenomenon (a manifestation of something else). 'Let us not look for the Jew's secret in his religion: rather let us look for the secret of religion in the real Jew.' Religious perfection is an inverted, coded expression of human imperfection.

Of what is religion the phenomenon? Of secular limitation. 'The existence of religion is the existence of a defect.'[5] 'It has become the expression of the separation of man from his community, from himself and from other men.'

This separation can be summed up in a single word: *Spaltung*, splitting. Bourgeois society is based upon a split between the egotistic individual and the moral person, the consumer and the citizen, civil society and the political state. This condemns man to a double life: he can only reach his full essence through religion, through the medium of God. God is an intermediary between man and man because man cannot relate to himself immediately. The end of this alienation will mark the end of the religious illusion or the beginning of the emancipation of mankind. The state first frees itself from religion, which moves from the sphere of public law to that of private law. This brings political emancipation and is the work of the bourgeois revolution. The state then replaces Christ as the intermediary between man and man's freedom, as the mean term 'to which man transfers all his non-divinity, all his human unconstraint'. At this stage man is still separated from himself, still a prisoner of political religiosity. That is why, in the second and final stage, he has to put an end to the separation between the private and the public sphere, between the concrete individual and the abstract man, in order to do away with the ultimate screen of the state. Human emancipation will then be complete; man will be free of all intermediaries. A society fully emancipated from religion is an undivided, self-adequate whole which has no need to represent itself because it is fully present to itself: the end of internal splitting means the end of external alienation. When that happens, man will finally come home: he will be able to go out into society without ceasing to be a whole man. There is no solution of continuity between the young Marx's criticism of religion and the mature communist theoretician (*Grundrisse*, 1857). Communism will complete the criticism of religion at the very heart of material production, thereby suppressing the mean term. In the communist form of material production, commodity exchange will no longer be 'the medium which allows the singular individual to participate in universal production'. Money will no longer be a necessary mediator between freely associated producers; the state will not be a mediator between classes (classless society). Universality ('of needs, capacities, pleasures, the productive forces of individuals, universality generated in universal exchange') will be *real*, not *formal*, a *lived* experience and not something which exists in *thought* alone. The essence of man—a philosophical abstraction—will be restored to concrete individuals.

Transfer the mechanisms of religious alienation into the political field and you will find the incompleteness effect. Marx used religion as a sacred parable for the sacred element in the political, both as an analytic instrument and as a screen for his non-analysis of politics. It absolved him from looking directly at the collective. His evasion led to an evolutionist dissolution of the structure, and a mystical sublimation of the nature, of the object. The inspection of the field is retrospective from the outset: Marx describes alienation in the future anterior because his standpoint is already that of reconciliation. What he says is real enough, but he is speaking as a utopian (utopia as an instrument of discovery). It is as the critical lucidity of his gaze had to be softened by a mystical point of view. The religious illusion appears as a historicist metaphor for an insurmountable anthropological constraint: the detour or *Umweg* as the real basis for the workings of the sacred in society (which, translated into empirical or political form, can take the form of the project, the return, the leader, the spokesman, etc.). Marxism puts up with a lot from modern lay sectarians, but so did Judaism from the young Marx. To each his own scapegoat. In the nineteenth century, political guilt was transferred to the fetish of 'religion'; in the twentieth it is transferred to the fetish of 'ideology'. Every epoch projects its lack on to a 'bad object', believing that the lack will end when the bad object is expelled. Every political epoch has the Godot it deserves.

Marx concludes: 'Only when man has recognized and organized his *forces propres* as social forces, so that social force is no longer separated from him in the form of *political* force, only then will human emancipation be completed'.[6] We can add our own modest codicil as a conclusion to the conclusion: 'And that is why emancipation will never be realized.' For man cannot organize himself socially without his organization becoming *ipso facto* separated from him. Of course, a political body which could incorporate its own foundations would produce coincidence between self and self and, therefore, transparence. But incompleteness nips that perfect adequacy in the bud. Marx's grandiose wish that social man should finally be his own centre of gravity simply ignores the law of political gravity, and therein lies the pathetic grandeur of his failed project for a Copernican revolution. In his own words, 'One does not get an inch nearer the problem by a thousandfold combination of the word people with the word state'. Any organized social body subject to the gravitational field of incompleteness is born, lives and dies alienated from itself. We are born exiles in a strange land, even in our own land; we are defined by our exile and exiled by definition. Banishment is the baptism of *homo politicus*. 'History has been resolved into supersition for long enough; now we are resolving superstition into history'—a circular argument which sums up the project of *On the Jewish Question*. If the programme had no effect—if the *we* of the 'we are resolving' failed to inspire the living, acting *we* of emancipation—is it not largely because Marx, until the end of his life (*Critique of the Gotha Programme*), thought of political organization in the typically idealist form of association. His thought is homogeneous with the classical tradition which, in France, goes from Jean-Jacques Rousseau to Sartre, from the problematic of the Contract to that of Praxis, and according to which the political object is constructed from outside by free subjects who choose to alienate their interiority in the *external* world. We can see why Marxists (who in this sense are neither more nor less than latter-day Cartesians) were and still are unable to understand the political world, even their own. They could not grasp what is political in the world—what cannot be reduced to the projection of the economic base at the political level. To save time, we can say that, for Marxists, politics is what remains in a society when you take away the play of economic class interests; the 'residue' usually being explained in terms of the wicked lies of 'ideology' and the stupid inertia of institutions. For an idealism of the subject, the political world constantly evokes the site of an evil that is at once nauseating and inevitable, specious and captivating, enchanting and enchanted, and evil that can be summed up by the old expression 'superstition'. One does not break the spell by thinking of the Party, the State or the Movement in terms of the classic form of *association*—on the contrary, one tends to make it worse. The beautiful image of 'freely associated producers' does not free the producers from subjection to their real associations. No doubt associationism has the advantage of avoiding the (painful) fact that all institutions imply a superstitious belief in the self because an institution is the *product* of superstitious belief in the self as Other, but that nicety does not lead to the dissolution of institutions past, present or future. It simply makes the world of institutional man more opaque and the weight of superstition slightly heavier. The conscious mind of critical Marxism is constantly stupefied by the spectacle of its institutions: 'How can it be possible?' And a blind and incurably superstitious belief in their own institutions becomes the supreme argument for the actors of practical Marxism: 'As individuals we are nothing: the Party is everything'. Militant religion has become the expression of the militant's separation from his community, from himself and from other men. Only when party militants have recognized and organized their *forces propres* as social forces, so that social force is no longer separated from them in the form of a Party, only then will communist emancipation be complete. In other words, the emancipation of communists is the disappearance of the Communist Party.

It is a circular argument. The mystifying round trip from history to superstition and back again, typical of both religion and religious explanations of religion, does not result in the demystification of superstition in history, it leads to historical superstition, a superstition like any other. The project of materialist knowledge was the opposite of that of the speculative jokers who transform secular into religious questions: 'We transform religious into secular questions'. Unfortunately, the object of knowledge is theologically, that is mediately, structured. The members of a free-thinking community—even an *appellation contrôlée* community—cannot establish immediately transparent relations with one another, since these are necessarily mediated by the organization that relates them to one another. Man is not the supreme reality for man—the believer has his supreme reality in his church, the militant in his party, the patriot in his community, the Afghan tribesman in his tribe, the footballer in his team, and so on ad infinitum. Between abstractions like the individual and his generic essence, belonging intervenes both to give and to take away humanity. Ever slipping between man and man as a third and more powerful party, an institution or an individual brings them into one another's presence as members of the same group. No group can achieve self-recognition without making a detour through the untouchable first principle which acts as its touchstone. The circular dialectic of religious spirit as collective product, and of the collective as religious product, finds its ultimate expression in the cruel joke of a Marxist dialectic which reaches completion by suppressing itself in its own circularity.

For a theory of collective practice, the failure of socialism to achieve a radical break (which, given its expectations, means that socialism is a failure) has a heuristic value as crucial as that of the failure of empiricism for a genetic theory of knowledge. Just as it is now accepted that the human mind is not 'an empty bucket' that can be filled by just any sense-experience, the social group has shown that it is not a piece of wax to be moulded by any 'data' from the political imaginary. The matrix is present within the mould and informs those who inform it. 'An empirical study of the genesis of knowledge immediately reveals the inadequacy of the empiricist interpretation of experience' (Piaget). A historical study of the development of political practices immediately reveals the inadequacy of the historicist interpretation of political practice. The stability, regularity and recurrence of the laws of order governing the construction and functioning of groups points to the *universality of the schema of constraint* derived from the axiom of social incompleteness. Do we have to go beyond Piaget's constructivism in our discussion of the political? Perhaps it will one day be necessary to extend to sociogenesis the validity of the inferences made by Chomsky and Jacob in the area of psychogenesis, even though the fact that something is universal does not imply that it is innate.[7] The practical structures of the historical group and the cognitive structures of the subject of knowledge may have one thing in common: namely, that they do not result from learning or from the translation of the properties of the environment. These structures have a prior, ideal existence. They cannot be the effect of external contingent relations, because 'There can be no regulation without structures which exist and are there to be regulated' (F.Jacob). In that sense, the chronological unfolding of history develops preprinted features on the surface of society, in the same way that a bath of chemicals develops an exposed film. Ultimately, it reveals the elementary and universal logic that underlies the mechanisms of congregation, identification and perpetuation of various human groups immersed in time. There is a formal play at work in the disposition of the morphological features of political organisms, but their discriminatory value cannot be denied (otherwise the historians of institutions and the experts in constitutional law would be out of a job). But just as an individual cannot vary outside the limits assigned him by the 'genetic envelope of the species' (J.-P. Changeux), a collective cannot invent anything that is not included in the 'political envelope' of the group.

3. The Revenge of Auguste Comte

An atheist forewarned is an atheist forearmed. Never talk about religion in the imperfect tense or you will be hoisted with your own petard. The 'class enemy' attacks from the front, but the Holy Ghost stabs you in the back. All the misfortunes of the 'men of progress'—those they least expected—came about because they did not take seriously the most ridiculous beliefs of primitive humanity. In the light of incompleteness, the withering away of the religious era announced by Marx and Engels takes on a *vis comica*. It becomes at least as tragi-comic as the 'end of ideology' heralded by the ideologists of post-industrial society. Positivist sociology would be wrong to forget Van der Leeuw's little phrase in his *Phenomenology of Religion*: 'God is a late-comer in the history of religion, and his coming is not indispensable'. The least acute and the most scrupulously empirical of all political sociologies would add that even if he has arrived, it is not the end of the world if he leaves again. We will miss him, but we will get by without him.

Marx loved the ironies of history, yet he failed to see the finest irony of all: his own 'scientific theory' became a world and provided experimental verification of the 'wretched' balderdash of a petty-bourgeois fanatic. Marx had nothing but scorn for the founder of positivism, his elder by one generation, discovered his work comparatively late and paid it little attention. Apart from two allusions to Comte in *Capital*, Marx makes only one or two sarcastic comments.[8] You cannot stare directly at the political sun. And calling it lunatic is one way of looking in the opposite direction.

Tired of being the Aristotle of his century, Auguste Comte set out to become its St Paul. In order to speed up the metabolism of his theory, he put what he called 'the affective classes' (women and the proletariat) in charge of social practice and spent his entire life trying to find the means to socialize his conception of the world. Formerly a secretary to a Messiah (the socialist Saint Simon), alert to and fascinated by anything to do with the communication or public transmission of a conceptual message, he used every means, good and bad, to make himself popular. He wrote letters in an attempt to find a good Mediator-Prince and gave lectures on popular astronomy outside town halls. Constantly disappointed but never tired, this professor was a professional expert on collective faith and wrote countless professions of faith, summaries, appeals and catechisms. His express wish was to produce something hot, but ultimately his political philosophy remained cold. The transubstantiation he expected, begged and even implored (letters to the Tsar, the Grand Vizir, the conservatives, Napoleon III, not forgetting the imprisoned Barbès) never came about, except perhaps in academic form. Ultimately, positivism's only legitimate heir was the old French university. Despite Clemenceau, Jules Ferry, Pedro II and a few others, the *Système de politique positiviste* (which is subtitled *Traité de sociologie instituant la religion de l'Humanité*) has remained a sort of scientific curiosity and the author's bust languishes in the place de la Sorbonne. There was a posthumous vulgate of positivism, designed with pedagogic purposes in mind, but there was never a political vulgarization except in the other side of the Atlantic, in Latin America. The avatars of the *Catéchisme positiviste* left their mark on the history of Mexico (under Diaz's autocratic regime) and even more on that of Brazil (by hastening the advent of the Republic).[9] When the Brazilian nation hoists its colours, it flies the slogan 'Ordem y progreso', whether anyone really notices or not. Positivism was designed to 'grip the masses', but it only gripped exotic elites and its religion of humanity never became a material force on a world scale. Although the encyclopedist may well have taught a pleiad of great minds, he did not move the 'humble' who were so suited for the Master's message because, in their blessed ignorance, they combined the primacy of feeling with a sense of duty.

The humble of the West and elsewhere united not behind the proferred green flag but behind the red flag of a scientist who hated flags. As they did so, they took the name 'the masses'. Being a professional critic of faith, Marx made no particular effort to make himself popular with his contemporaries or with the various temporal and spiritual powers of the day; nor did he make any effort to understand anything about collective *pathos*. The scientist struggled to remain cool througout his life, and yet he generated a considerable amount of social heat. Positivist sociology was addressed to the heart (a word which, according to Comte's disciple Alain, 'reminds us of the link between the power of thought and the structure of the body'), but in the end the hearts and the crowds were moved by a discourse which, mocking at sermons and melodramas alike, was addressed to the intellect alone. For a century and across half the planet, Marxism prevented Comte's project for a new official religion or cult of the Great Being from coming to anything. In a number of places, the temporal and spiritual powers (whose fusion was not recommended by the pope of the rue Monsieur) asserted themselves in the name of a philosopher who never 'thought politics'. In short, the tiara of the High Priest of humanity was retroactively placed on the head of the materialist who found such fantasies amusing and not upon the head of the eminently serious author of *Considérations sur le pouvoir spirituel* (1826). Without realizing or wishing it, Marx succeeded where Comte failed. The fact that Marx's 'scientific theory' bears his name (like a vulgar philosophical or religious doctrine) is a positive sign of political incarnation, whereas the failure of positivism to become Comtism is a damning sign of temporal unpopularity and spiritual inefficacity. But in a way the 'success of' Marxism failed to check-mate positivism, and he who laughs last laughs longest. Comte himself has the last word: 'You only destroy what you can replace.' Posthumous comment from a ghost who was scorned too soon: 'of course, my dear Karl, you have taken my place, but they placed you on my throne. You wanted a revolution whereas I wanted a restoration. Judging by the outcome of your revolution, I think that time has not done me wrong, even though the future did right by you. Basically, everything is going very well—in accordance with my prognosis, not yours.'

The best overall description of the societies that claim to be inspired by Marx's theory is actually to be found in Comte rather than Marx. Their obsession with order (public and private, political and symbolic) would have reduced Marx to tears and delighted Comte. Positivist sociology (order the base, progress the goal) loathed history. Socialist statolatry does its best to ward off the disorders of history and to turn progress into the development of order. A mania for classification, a ubiquitous hierarchical principle, a cult of discipline and respect for authority, gerontocracy, rejection of the a-social (a neologism invented by Comte), an aversion for disruptive dissidence and improvisation, an abhorrence of the disorderly effects of critical individualism—all these distinctive features reveal the subordination of the dynamic to the static, as stipulated by positivist sociology. Comte's dream: a society in which there is no need for politics at the base because political science is at the top of the pyramid (he who has power has knowledge and vice versa). Anyone who wants to understand real capitalism should read *Capital* but anyone who wants to understand real socialism should read the *Catéchisme positiviste*. With their daily commemorative rituals, their fascination with ceremony, the cult of the dead founding-fathers, the priority and excellence of their pedagogy, their resistance to innovation and suspicion of the unexpected, the contemporary 'Marxist-Leninist' societies are much closer to Comte's idyll than to Marx's ideal. They may not have discovered the secret of transhistorical immobility, but their immobilizing techniques do at least ensure them optimal stability, apart from a few localized anomalies on the fringes. Every individual has his or her place and all the places form a system. North Korea, for example, is a taxonomy open to the skies, an encyclopedia metamorphosed into a society.

It is an astonishing paradox: the social revolution that the French conservative detested so much has in a sense brought Comte into government in the name of his living antithesis. Obviously, certain recent developments in the sciences have been rather unkind to Comte's encyclopedic plans: a whole list of disciplines he declared to be heretical, harmful or even impossible are now flourishing (mathematical logic, probability theory, astrophysics, etc.[10]). But perhaps it is time we recognized the validity or at least the consistency of his 'social physics', as well as the dangers of reducing positivism to its philosophical or scientific 'noble physics', as the keepers of the Academic Museum would have us do. (The museum-keepers are the legitimate heirs—the Littré branch and not the Maurras branch—and they have an obvious preference for the *Cours* over the *Catéchisme*). As others have already pointed out, certain of Comte's insights into the logic of the collective are a logical kernal inside a shell of ludicrous or picturesque fancies, whereas in Marx the shell of crucial historical and economic discoveries contains no political kernel at all: there is no room in it for organization. In terms of political reason, Comte is ahead of Marx. There is a Marxist religion, but no Marxist theory of religion. There was no positivist religion (except on paper), but positivism does have a theory of religion. Comte glimpsed the a priori forms of the political efficacity of a symbolic schematism (or 'the material conditions of force which an idea must satisfy if it is to become a material force', as Althusser has it). The social movement did not keep its date with religion—and the church in the rue Payenne is still empty. Marxist theory did keep its date with the social movement, but it failed to see the typically religious forms of the political dynamics created by the encounter. The celebrated 'union of Marxist theory and the labour movement' still looks like an unexplained mystical marriage. In one case, enthusiasm stood up reason; in the other no reason was given for enthusiasm or for its 'irrational' leaps. Positivism: a theory of political practice with no practice. Communism: a political practice with no theory of practice.

It goes without saying that Comte's philosophy was on the wrong track from the very start, thanks to an idealist naivety (the spirit rules and makes social history) made worse by two ingenuous conceptions of the day.

The first, scientism, argues that since natural knowledge of the political is possible, the political object is subject to natural laws. By playing on the ambiguity of a word, it conjures away the arbitary element in laws that are passed, repealed and no longer respected when they no longer deserve respect; or, rather, it conceals that element by confusing them with inexorable laws that link series of phenomena. We are of course free to believe what we like, but we cannot, as a *we*, free ourselves from the obligation to believe in something. A political science, I repeat, can never be more than the science of an art or the knowledge of a non-knowledge.

The second, evolutionism, transposes the familiar metaphor of the three ages—childhood, adolescence, adulthood—into the law of the three states (theological, metaphysical, positive). This optimism is harmless, but the silliness of it is deceptive. It serves a purpose by allowing the men of order to wait quietly in their corner for the progress of humanity to do their work for them. The wisest of the wise can thus devote their time to converting minds rather than subverting the state of things. When teaching replaces strategy in politics, the battle is unequal from the start. In the meantime, no critique of political reason can look, without laughing, at the spread of the rumour 'peace tomorrow', or of false hopes such as the advent of a 'positive' politics.

4

A Little Morality!

If, in the nature–history interface, the producers of history are also the agents of natural reproduction, how are we to tell who is serving whom, the actor or the agent? The fact that both theses can be argued and that there is no way of separating them brings us back to an exposition of the antinomies of political reason. Schopenhauer saw the sexual instinct as a means of making the egotistic search for pleasure serve the reproduction of the species. This can be demonstrated, as can the opposite thesis. Hegel saw the great butchers of men as business executives of the universal genius. Why not? There is no reason why we should not add the *nth* strategy of 'ideology' to the 'ruses' of life and 'reason'. It could be argued that it is good for the progress of societies if the actor is unaware that he is an agent. The illusion that we have no illusions is probably the most productive of all political illusions. After all, who would bother to carve out a narrow path in the darkness if he knew that the dead-end and the way-out would look the same in the broader light of day?

Being neither diabolical nor providential, the religious structure of collective action calls for neither lamentation nor penitence. Far from presupposing any intervention into history on the part of the supernatural, that structure results, as we have seen, from the constitutional adherence of natural being to political being. Nature sticks to history, just as the unconscious sticks to the conscious mind or the past to the future. That 'sticking' is known as politics.

The recurrence of religion merges self and other, origins and ends. An iron hand in a velvet glove. We can find archaism in modernity, prehistory in the final struggle, a Canaque in the cyberneticist, and New Guinea in the heart of New England. It is a matter not of juxtaposition but of an imbrication of orders, under our very noses, so to speak. When will we have the intelligence to be stupid, the intelligence of that profound stupidity which allows the umbilical chords that link men to their tribes—in both the strict and the broad sense—to become tighter, more nourishing and more imperious than ever in the middle of one of the most prodigious 'technical and scientific' revolutions that mankind has experienced since the neolithic revolution. Not to mention the overthrow of an 'outdated' mode of production in one third of the planet. The era of interplanetary travel is also one of national and tribal wars, and the golden age of the three great iron age religions is the age of telematics. The same man who can quite calmly walk on the moon and build microprocessors will also furiously wave his flag and disembowel his neighbour so that he can speak his own language, smell his own smell and worship his gods in his own land. This is the case in the so-called advanced countries, as it is elsewhere. We may be excused for not listing all the collective identities that are currently fighting for their lives across the face of the earth—the list is in the newspapers. The eminent triviality of such tables should not conceal the logical paradoxes they express, if only because historical 'regressions' give the theory of history an opportunity to progress.

There is a paradox in the intervention of registers, diagonal realms and confused classifications. Etymologically, to act is the opposite of to suffer. But in the annals of the collective, great actions are equated with great passions; humanity's great leaps forward look more like crimes of passion than accurate calculations of probability. In critical terms, understanding has priority over sensibility, high over low. The annals show that the more the impetus comes from below, the higher it goes: judicious groups last, emotional ones live. The historical upheavals of a culture give a meaning to frenzies that earn the disapproval of ethics and logic. Social psychology draws a distinction between 'collective consciousness' and the 'individual unconscious', but collective action is like the individual dream and displays its characteristic triple regression: chronological regression towards the past, material regression towards the image, and functional regression towards the unconscious. To speak collectively, then, is not to speak logically ... or illogically. The 'I' of 'I belong therefore I am' is different from the 'I' of 'I think'. Although the latter derives from a metaphysics and not a psychology, it can still speak subjectively. In collective action, however, the 'I' is always an Other, and that is why it can move so easily from theology to psychopathology, from religion to mental alienation, or from ecstasy to collective madness.

It is as exactly as if men's hold over nature were a function of nature's hold over men; as if the respectable conscious decisions that the various ethics of responsibility urge us to make could only be put into effect or translated into real political practice through the mobilization of redoubtable unconscious forces; as if the same logical subjects who, through a combination of science and technique, have made themselves masters of nature could not extend their mastery to their own social history without becoming slaves to a different logic which neither reasons nor allows itself to be mastered. When we do put our will to work, it simply exposes us to the laws of action, to the passion of belonging and alienation in a belief. However, we should not come to the sad conclusion that 'man is a useless passion', but draw the more cheerful conclusion that only a passion can make a man useful. 'Useful for what?' is another question, *his* question.

The aim of a work like this is obviously not to establish aims and values for political practice but to schematize the a priori forms of political practice in general. These forms are antinomic because freedom (of action) and heteronomy (of the actor) are two sides of the same coin, and because it is impossible to undertake a logical political project without becoming an object in two senses—the object of obedience and the object of a credo. In other words, man can constitute himself as a subject in history only in so far as he submits as a subject (*sub-jectum*, thrown under) to a fetishized group and to the lack that knits it together. The interpellation of individuals as subjects by ideology is realized through their subjection to that which constitutes them as subjects. As there can be no effective action without symbolic hypostasis (and its material effects), intervenors are the object of an intervention, adults are infantilized and the emancipated are subjugated by a law of organization which precludes any principle of sovereignty. In collective space, the state of liberty is a function of the state of individual subservience (in the technical sense of a system in which one physical magnitude imposes its variations upon another *without* any reciprocity). None of this should be seen as a manic taste for the paradoxical, but simply as a statement of a contradiction. It is a constraint, not a curse.

Imcompleteness reveals the logic of political action as well as its absurdity. But here the absurd does not destroy meaning—it founds it. Being a barrier against nihilism and a coherent system of encouragement, it does not bring our actions up against a systematic 'What's the point?'. The examination of incompleteness reveals a coherent contradiction, not a coherent impossibility. The conditions of possibility of action are at once perfectly coherent and contradictory.

The principle that there can be no action without belief might be translated as: convince youself that you are going to change the world, for that is the price to be paid if a fragment of human history is to be transformed into a chapter in the natural history of the species. Be innovative, but if you want to innovate, act like your predecessors.

On the eternal militant as the immobile motor of mobile societies:

'The face of the earth will be renewed', writes the prophet in his psalm. 'Change life', echoes the political orator. Neither boast nor devilry. If we could choose not to believe our ears, the poignant novelty of the ancient lullaby would not thrill us so constantly. Our sorcerers sing only what we ask them to sing—their lives depend upon it—and they themselves are simply the fleeting incarnation of an immortal demand (not to die). The legitimate satisfaction we expect from them neither declined nor diminished when it came down from the altar to the political platform.

The social demand for promises outstrips the prophetic supply. But in disappointments, it is the political supply that outstrips demand. And so, a balance is finally achieved between the night before and the morning after, as we struggle along from one crisis of values to the next. No one has yet seen the timeless promise have any effect, but nor has anyone seen a disappointment that does not immediately give way to a new promise. Good Friday is only a day away from Easter Sunday: one bad day of doubts separates the prologue of belief from its epilogue. The tirelessly banal cycle that leads from *The God that Failed* to *The Birth of a Nation*, from the 'collapse of ideologies' to 'spiritual renewal', is as necessary as the carbon cycle, the menstrual cycle or the cycle of the seasons. They all help to maintain life on earth. The latest revolution of this anachronistic merry-go-round hit the intellectual headlines in the sated societies of the Far West: no sooner had the paper effigy of Father Karl been rejected on the grounds that it was archaic and dogmatic than the electronic image of a certain John Paul appeared in the home, sportive and triumphant. Indeed, he is second to none when it comes to archaisms and dogma. If the seat of the Pontifex Maximus is allowed to get too cold, any 'hot' society will go cold by regressing towards its initial state of inertia. Fortunately, although charismatic leaders pass away, charisma is passed on from priest to doctor and vice versa.

Being born sons, biologically destined for a vocation, affiliated to affiliation, what can we do but go on doing our duty as living creatures like everyone else? Answer tomorrow's call in the full knowledge that there can be no rational answer to it. The contradiction cannot be resolved, but that is no reason not to define its terms clearly and to live the 'conflict of faculties' to the bitter end.

There are probably times and places in which the question 'What is to be done?' has no point and only one answer, 'Nothing'. We do not need to be over-dramatic. There are gaps in political history in which individuals can say 'absent' to their groups and simply get on with *being*—well-being or fine phrases—without any concern for the constraints of *doing*. Refusal to believe is not even an ethical luxury, as there can be no ethics when there is no action (*ethos*). Unbelief is the speculative privilege of the spectator of others' actions—an aesthetic coquetry or a maxim for one's old age: this clean-handed abstraction has no hands. When the physical existence or living integrity of the group is not threatened, when it has enough food to survive, political obligation enters a phase of remission, known to the moralist as 'decadence' and to the historian of ideas as 'effervescence'. The two often go together. Lucien Febvre once asked (à propos of Huizinga) whether it might not be possible to divide history into 'periods in which intellectual life predominates and periods with a particularly well-developed affective life'. Perhaps we in Western Europe are enjoying one of those pauses in which intelligence can take precedence over passion, the individual over the collective and lucidity over belief, simply because our loyalties have been established and our national groups consolidated. In such periods, the activity of the mind can quite happily be spread over two registers: derision and mystification on the one hand, and emotional outpourings and sublimity on the other (the beautiful soul has a weakness for well-fed bodies). Either the group is aggressed and reawakens with a start as archaic elements reappear—in which case the group begins to believe in itself again and rapidly finds leaders, taboos and frontiers. Or else it disintegrates as a group, attracted by the force of intertia to the strongest hegemonic pole—in which case the weakness of the group gives birth to countless agnostics and normalizes non-belief. But whichever happens, it soon discovers that 'Neither Marx nor Jesus'* is an optional moral extra strictly for private consumption by higher income groups, with no possible sociological implications or long-term political effects.

Considerable dangers face those outlaws of modernity who, though not interested in stoic ethics or the virtues of chivalry, are still excited by an ideal (no longer a missionary but a militant ideal). But there again, there are always risks. They risk combining Bertolt Brecht with Victor Serge, as if they were convinced that 'the night is long, but dawn is at hand' and at the same time knew quite well that is midnight in this century.† Social humanity was born fully grown, and it is hard to see how or why its rules of conduct should produce innovations. On the contrary, there is something invigorating about the permanence of its ethical basis. So it should come as no surprise that when we look through the gallery of the great miltant figures of the century, we can recognize the agnostic martyr as a combination of the saint, the sage and the hero of yesterday.

'There is', they say,' nothing scientific about militant behaviour.' Indeed. The following critical considerations may provide a supplementary gloss on the historical formation of the 'exemplary militant' as a model for moral identifications. It could be neatly summed up in a metaphor: like any machine, mankind requires a source of heat if it is to use a reservoir and temperature

---

* Allusion to J-F. Revel's essay *Ni Marx ni Jésus. De la second révolution américaine à la seconde révolution mondiale,* Paris 1971.
† Allusion to Victor Serge's novel *S'll est minuit dans le siècle,* Paris 1939. Tr. P. Sedgwick, *Midnight in the Century,* London 1981.

changes to produce acts as it works in history. Man is therefore physically right to ask for more heat from the group, the myth and the leader, from, that is, collective madness. It has a right to fire. But does it give fire its due? The zealous animal should not forget that fires lurk behind the fervour required for the social production of history, and that fever returns along with the fervour. We make a lot of the virtue of zeal, but it comes from a Greek root meaning to boil, to burn. 'Ideological' is just another way of saying calorific (the former being to human history what the latter is to physical nature). But the political animal—the pride and shame of nature—would do itself even more damage by killing all its gods (including atheism) on the vain pretext that they are false gods. Such a sceptical liquidation, which is fortunately impossible, would lead to nothing less than the extinction of the species by destroying both its will to live and its will to act. We are free to see suicide as the highest manifestation of individual dignity, but that eminently moral act presupposes the existence of living, organized groups. Suicide is permissible, even obligatory in certain circumstances, provided that ethnocide and cosmocide have become impossible. Those who make it a point of honour to choose freely the form and moment of their death should do all in their power to remove the threat of the holocaust. That is already the basis for a political line, just in case.

Anyone who today combines two contradictory qualities—a readiness to die for an ideal, and a sense of humour—upsets too many clichés not to lose his reputation. Apart from the other misunderstandings involved, he would have to resign himself to being an imbecile for the half-educated and an infidel for the fanatics. Let us leave the live wires to their serious mindedness and just concentrate on the learned. We can expect two kinds of defensive comment to be made at this point. Take the good student's sermon: fatalism and moralism are as close as the lips and the teeth—the gritted teeth of the stoic for whom impassiveness is the common coinage of resignation. Or the sermon of the worthy doctor in historical materialism: the return to Kant is an old story, a Trojan horse which keeps appearing inside the theoretical walls of the working class. If 'the rediscovery of Kant in Marxism is a constant theme in the history of deviations in the workers' movement', the sight of Epictetus on the skyline is unlikely to improve our position.

The rules of militant arithmetic are well known (regression + deviation = a hackneyed deviation) and no one enjoys wearing a dunce's cap. Besides, the pleasures of classification are too great, too useful in maintaining our respective territories, for us to dare deny it to those who are entitled to it. But we might at least be allowed to point out that the *Metaphysics of Morals* and Epictetus's *Meditations* are poor evidence for this moral trial. We need the Kant of practical reason because our research precludes any possibility that reason can legislate in the City, and still less over free, reasonable subjects. We are not *legislating members* of the City, and our political obligations assume that we are by nature natural and not super-sensuous. We need Epictetus because our conception implies that, far from offering our legs to be broken, we do as much as possible to break our boots over the torturer's head. It can be done, in theory at least. So it must be done. Our logical premises may be similar to those of Stoicism, but they give rise to very different precepts. It is true that 'some things in the world depend upon us and others do not' (Epictetus). Our every action depends upon us, but not its results. For the laws of group survival are not within our control and neither are 'our bodies, our wealth, our reputation or important posts, all the things that we do not make ourselves'.

If maxims mean anything in human action, we should counter the great Phrygian slave's 'Abstain and suffer the results!' with an even more sober maxim: 'Commit yourself and put up with it!'

SECTION II
The Physics of Orthodoxy

1

The Economy of Lack

Incompleteness applies to logic as well as to practice. It therefore governs the administration of discourses as well of Cities. In both cases, political reason discovers that it is not simply the principle of impasse but an impasse itself. For whereas reason *opens*, politics *closes*. The logical difficulty is usually resolved to the detriment of the former term, so that the critical break-in leads to doctrinal closure and the individual break-through to group territory. The paradoxical nature of the orthodox operation might be defined as an exit with no way-out. The paradox, which lies at the origin of both the tragedy and the pathos of the 'history of ideas', is that for a theory to live (as a collective force) it has to be killed (as a theory).

'Orthodoxy against intelligence', that pious cliché of the sermons of wisdom, does not free us from the need to understand orthodoxy or to investigate the historical reality that goes by that name.[1] The word's bad reputation does not prevent the thing springing up from its ashes as large as life.

As every intellectual knows, the frequency of *isms* in any given discourse is a measure of its intellectual indolence: anyone who refuses to argue and works with ready-made categories is not working with concepts. But if we do not go beyond that statement, we beg the question of why *isms* exist and of whether there is any hope of shaking them off.

No enlightenment is to be expected from 'orthodox thought', and the history of free thought, or simply thought itself, can be read as 'a long protest against orthodoxy'. How is it, then, that the Phoenix arises again and again and outlives the protesters?

My thesis is that the formation of stereotypes is itself stereotyped and that the sequence of religious or ideological *isms* conceals a constant process: incorporation through the production of a lack.

Man is made in such a way that only an absence can satisfy him. That is not a literary formula but a logical deduction.

It is not that literature has any quarrel with axiomatics. Any good ballad is an unwitting translation of a formal structure, and it sometimes appears ahead of the structure. Gödel was set to music —a love song at that—long before the logician was born or lyricism could be explained. From the absent princesses of Occitania to the stanzas of *Le Soulier de satin* (Claudel), the clamour of love is a system. Distance fascinates, and every scholar knows that courtly love is proportional to the square of the distance between the lover and the beloved. Even when the lovers are side by side, they can still overcome the disadvantages of being together by placing a sword between them—and there we have a *chanson de geste*. In order to turn love into a religion, it is necessary and sufficient to set a lack to work (initially a lack of partners during the Crusades to the Holy Land). Our love for God, for instance, becomes stronger when he is hidden. We know the advantages that negative theology has derived from the absence of God as supreme guarantee of plenitude. It is because God has neither determinations nor attributes, neither a name nor a face, that he can fill the souls of the faithful and the world around them. Closer to home, we are all familiar with the salutary effect that the invisibility of the leader of the army, party or state has upon his subordinates. Professional acquaintance with politics shows that the art of politics is to a large extent the art of absenting oneself at the right moment. All great captains are familiar with the manoeuvre of disappearing. Even before he put it into practice (remember that May?), General de Gaulle wrote it into his theory of command structures (*Au Fil de l'épée*).

Variations on a major theme: organization around a void as a support for the appeal to authority. When we adhere to the word of the Other, the *doctor* is the figure of absence. In the mode of the constitution of groups, it is *death*. The organizational optimum, of course, is *the death of the doctor*, a necessary condition for the *birth of a doctrine*.

Only delegates (of God, Science, the Plebs, the Proletariat, Justice, France, etc.) who are sent on or entrusted with missions are able to command our full loyalty. He who speaks in order to be believed must speak in the name of the Other. The master says that he cannot master his word, and reception is best when the sender looks like (or lives as though he were) a mere sender, a vessel for a message which he transmits verbatim and has no power to withhold. Anyone who speaks *motu proprio* is a false prophet: true prophets speak against their will. Provided that it speaks from elsewhere, it is of little importance whether the other is the Almighty, the nature of things or the law of social development. A subject reduces others to subjection by subjecting himself to someone greater than himself. In that sense, the ruse of government is unwittingly the ruse of communication. Even a crude summary of the great 'spiritual' messages of our civilization bears out the constant that it is he who does not speak in his own name who bequeathes the patrimony of his name. Christ speaks in the name of the Father, the Pope in the name of the Son and St Paul in the name of Christ, who resides within him. A statement is accepted as true (credible) when the speaker cannot remain silent. He cannot fight it, and nor can we. The power of the message derives from its humility, and the submission of the mediator makes us submit in our turn. Only those who have been called can call others, and he who hears no voices is unable to summon anyone.

Comparing Stoic ethics and Christian doctrine, Bergson made the telling comment that 'the words are almost the same, but they do not produce the same echo because they are not pronounced with the same accent'.[2] Stoicism was a philosophy, Christianity a blazing fire, but their different effects have nothing to do with their respective tones. The teachings of Jesus were oracular and therefore irrefutable. Those of the ancient Stoics were personal and therefore debatable. Jesus, Son of God, born in mysterious circumstances of a father unknown. Zeno of Citium, son of Meneseus, Chrysippus, son of Appolonius, disciple of Cleanthes: the genealogy is human, all too human, lacunary and devoid of mystery. The gap in Jesus's genealogy authorized the leap from school to church, from scholar to prophet. Jesus is not the author of his doctrine, so he can become the doctor par excellence. The message creates links of obligation. The Stoic recommends: Christ commands. And he commands because he obeys.

1. The Function of Teaching

No one can teach innocently (either the laws of nature or the word of God). Educational practice is one of the *hierogenic* practices, in the same way that some substances are carcinogenic. *Historia non facit saltus*. The Leibnizian law of continuity (which, in the hands of Buffon and Bonnet, helped to constitute natural history in the eighteenth century) is not without its uses for a natural history of communication. It states that 'between any two genera, there are always what might be termed intermediate productions which function as so many links or transitional elements'. Just as it is only quite recently that societies have made a clear-cut distinction between gods and men—the original picture being one of uninterrupted circulation between gods incarnate and deified men—so the history of logical transmission does not show us anything approaching the Weberian dyptych of 'professor' *or* 'prophet', 'scientist' *or* 'politician'; but a definite continuum between the different categories of pedagogue, mystagogue and magus, pupil, disciple and follower, leader of a sect, school or party. We make a distinction between the heterogeneous categories of education and initiation, teaching and doctrination, lesson and sermon, logical and mythical. And we agree to respect one and dread the other (or to laugh at it so as to hide our fear).

Similarly, we are all agreed that the *degradation* of theories into doctrine and the *degeneration* of doctrine into religion is to be deplored. Once upon a time there was a primal discourse, an unpolluted source of neutral statements, but then came the vulgarizers, and they produced a vulgate. Salvation lies in cutting through the interference to reach the body of the text, scraping away the rind of authority (for example: 'the return to Marx' = reading *Capital*).

People still invoke 'communication without masters', 'away with all *isms*,' 'let's put an end to in-the-name-of'. But all these commonsense requests fail to make the discursive City bow to the law of the heart. What is being postulated here is an instantaneous appropriation of the entire available cultural stock by the offspring of men, without any need for personal transmission or mediation. In reality, however, the communication of the word of truth, whatever its content, place or moment, is operationally dependent upon a potentially religious hierarchical matrix. Belief is not a lower form of knowledge or a residue: it is co-extensive with the act of transmission.

A body of doctrine is an organized set of 'truths' that are accepted as authoritative. Their authority is incorporated into the transmission of the doctrine. To be more accurate, it is inherent in the relationship linking (*religare*) a plurality of receivers with a single sender who stands above them. Just as *augur*, *author* and *authority* come from the same root (*augere*, to increase the power of existing data), the word *doctrine*, like *doctor*, *doctorate*, *docility*, etc., comes from *docere*, to teach. Both materially and etymologically, the authority of the word is an effect of teaching.[3] In Greek, the same verb means 'to listen' and 'to obey' (*Upakouein*, to listen from below). The value of a doctrinal assertion is not merely qualified by, but indexed to, the identity of its author. ('Verily, I say unto you', 'Aristoteles dixit', 'As Georges Marchais said to Congress'.) A scientific statement, in contrast, is independent of the subject of its enunciation. The sciences, by definition, advance discourse without a subject, but in social reality they are accompanied by teaching subjects because they are the object of teaching. Can the listener always tell the difference between a doctor and a pastor? Anyone who follows a lecture, and a fortiori a seminar, follows a master. In the Gospels, the verb 'to follow' originally denotes attachment to the person of Jesus, and only by extension to his doctrine. (His main activity was not to perform miracles but to teach, rather like Dr Lacan, who is required to impart lessons, not to cure patients.)

In terms of education, the archives of history very closely correspond to those of language. Let us look briefly at them.

Jewish history. God taught Moses the Law and Moses taught it to his people. He was therefore the 'first master of Israel'. Masters and prophets have one thing in common: they have disciples and they call them their 'sons' (Prophets I VIII 10; II, I; III, I etc.). The son creates the father as the disciple creates the master, like a plea or a leitmotif: 'Oh Lord, teach me!' (Psalms 119, 12, 26, ff.). We want teaching; we find it because we have lost what mother nature gave us in a patrilineal society (and if she didn't, then her brother). The paterfamilias, the first teacher, the author of our days, the first authority. *Talmud* means teaching. The Hebrew word for 'son' designates both a kinship relation and a relation of belonging (son of Zion, son of Babylon, etc.). Not an enviable overdetermination, but a primary one.

Greek history. The 'Greek miracle' did not drive the miracle-workers out of the City of logic in the twinkling of an eye. Profane reason takes root in the sacred East, initially through education and then through the great stories.[4] When he was first learning to write, the Hellenist child had to put down, 'Homer is not a man: he is a god.' Quite true, given that Homer was the educator of Greece. Plato himself (no poet-lover) was quite prepared to admit it, and he even granted to Glaucon that we are right to love and honour those who 'regulate their whole life according to him' (*The Republic*, X, 606). At every stage in this culture, private education is always connected, albeit in differing forms, with civic legislation and initiation into the mysteries. It is now recognized that there is no caesura between religious mysteries and logical discourse, natural cosmology and Ionian theogeny in the history of rational Hellenist knowledge.[5] Unlike the sun of reason in the archaic myths, scientific reason did not suddenly appear one fine morning in Ephesus or Miletus in the sixth century BC. 'The Philosopher takes over from the old magician-king' (Vernant), and our first logical treatises are poems (Parmenides). Even without going back to the legendary Presocratics, who were given explicitly divine attributes, we can see that the four great educational centres of the classical age—the Academy, the Lyceum, the Garden and the Stoa—combined conversion, initiation and correction into the act of education. They are 'at once religious and scientific brotherhoods' (Marrou) in which it is difficult to tell the difference between the leader of the school and the leader of the sect. With the passage of time, the development and diffusion of these philosophical tendencies made their resemblance to secular cults even more apparent. It was not a gradual institutionalization of a primordial charisma but a process of adding to the charisma of the dead founding-fathers (Plato, Aristotle, the so-called first-generation Stoics, etc.).

Christian history. 'Evangelical' through and through, it tells the story of a teaching. Like everyone else, Jesus began by founding a school, and the Twelve were initially known as his 'disciples'. Jesus was authorized to teach by his father and, at the end of his life, he made his best pupils preachers, apostles and teachers. 'Go and teach unto all nations!' The construction of the ecclesiastical body is punctuated by the authorized transmission of the *licentia docendi*. The pastoral message is handed down through catechesis and catechism, finally reaching us via our parish priest. The sequence of doctors and the hierarchical genealogy of the Fathers are one and the same.

Socialist history. The pedagogic magistrature classifies Dezamy, Leroux, Cabet, Pecqueur, Saint-Simor, Bazard, Enfantin, Marx, Engels and *tutti quanti* under the same 'sectarian' heading. They are all 'leaders of schools' who dispensed teaching and gathered disciples. Upon what conditions is a disciple possible? The essence and development of the socialist movement, in all its variants, depends upon this critical question (which mediology will have to examine in relation to the modern structures of transmission). The figure of the master caught up with scientific socialism, overtook utopian socialism and also seems to have affected the great scientists who wanted nothing to do with the master or the high-priests who came hard on his heels. Marx may well have mocked at the unlucky Jesuses throughout his life, but the principle of 'no salvation outside the school' affected him much more than it did the Saint Simonians, the Fourierists or the Buchezians. The Marxist Word was pregnant with an *ism* in that it contained a body of teachings; and the scientist's critical discourse began its worldly career with the same process of transmission as its more lunatic competitors. However, these did not have the good or bad luck to spread from being a local body (a school) to a world body (a tendency and then an international movement). The public reception of the information did not at first differentiate between rigorous and 'other' statements and transformed them all into 'doctrines' (with or without the masters' consent). Originally, the Saint Simonians described the group to which they belonged as a school or a faith, drawing no distinction between the two terms. At first, they saw themselves as apostles, quite legitimately in that the members of the sect enjoyed the unusual privilege of never having known their master (rather like the early Christians who wrote the Acts of the Apostles). As for Cabet, one of the first propagators of Communism, author of *Le vrai christianisme* and *Voyage en Icarie*, the first proponent of the thesis that 'education is the basis of everything', his disciples brought him 'offerings' but no gifts. The very idea would have greatly amused Marx. For, being unaware of the rule, 'in the name of the Other', Marx wanted *Capital* to be read by readers who could think for themselves and the rule of capital to be destroyed by actors who acted for themselves. Unfortunately he found more adepts than readers. The adepts became zealots and finally co-religionists.

How could what Lucien Goldmann called 'religious survivals' (he was referring to Jaurès) return so imperiously in the socialist heritage without indicating a common mediological, rather than theological, origin? Jaurès went on contributing to the *Revue de l'enseignement primaire* until his death. If we transform so-called doctrinal *degeneration* into a mode of *generating* the social word as an object of loyalty, we might be able to get back to its origins in education. Historically, the modern school is a product of the catechism class, of the priest's mission to teach children the rudiments of the faith. What was Jaurès's 'afterthought'—revealed with such courage by Henri Guillemin—if not Marx's posthumous purgatory, the *disciple effect*, which Marx denied and Jaurès sublimated? Historical materialism blames the receivers; the disciple effect is returned to sender by the more spiritualist partisans of the humanitarian socialism of Jaurès, who once wrote that 'socialism will be like a great religious revival'. Nonsense or necessity? Both. The reality of a message depends upon the receiver not the sender: reception determines the workings of the message and its operational value. 'Jaurès ... I think we loved him in the same way that the disciples loved Christ', said one of his last surviving comrades. He continued softly: 'I think it really was the same.'[6] Did Jaurès foresee this terrible dilemma? Socialist theory can only be made flesh if it becomes something like a religion, but socialist theory also implies a pitiless critique of all forms of religion. In any case, his successors preferred to hide their faces.

Historical materialism, however, describes itself as a 'discipline', as a branch of objective knowledge. The trouble is that the word also designates the source of the strength of armies, regular orders and political parties: a rule for collective behaviour or a communal order which subject the group to a unified moral leadership (it also recalls the 'discipline' which the monk used to mortify his flesh or the schoolmaster to flog his rascals). The metamorphoses of institutionalized Marxism cannot of course be reduced to the avatars of the magister. But if we look at its origins, we do see demonstrative arguments being accepted as authoritative and we can trace them back to the avatars. It is not the master who is to 'blame', but the school relation which, even if we try to improvise it outside any apparatus of authority, necessarily recreates the institution (and therefore the inequality): a regular division of time (speaking/listening), the establishment of a protected place (platform, home, tribunal, portico), the deliberate production of signs or insignia specific to a group of listeners (in order to face the ever-present threat of group disintegration or fragmentation of the master's words). It is materially impossible to communicate a symbolic trust from one generation to another without constituting an organised body (association, institute, school, party, academy), without delegating sanctions and establishing an internal hierarchy behind external walls. The disciple's critical question thus becomes: 'Upon what conditions is the closure of a discourse possible?' Those conditions, which are as much material (social) as intellectual (or ideological), are not internal to the discourse itself: they derive from the manner of its administration. The middle term of any syllogism that relates knowledge to power is the element which makes a collection of pupils stick together. That element is a factor in collective mobilisation—in fact it is the very reason for its existence. Unfortunately, all academic, military and religious institutions depend upon education or training (primary, religious, military) to which people have to conform as a group. Applied mediology is content to note that our Western societies are becoming more and more 'dissipated' (less studious) and 'unruly' (answering the teacher back), and that an undisciplined society (one in which it is not healthy to be a good disciple) is unlikely to lead to socialism. Not that socialism is a barracks; but it is a school and there is indeed an element of the barracks in the institutional unconscious of the school (think of the formation of the French *lycée*). The dean of a college is always something of a commander; the seminary has elements of the military academy, and a schoolmaster is always something of a moral policeman. One man's barracks is another man's school. If state television brought the barracks into our homes, we would have to choose between the lesser of two evils. Learning to spell may be the ABC of the spirit of orthodoxy, but an illiterate does fall victim to the doctors of the law more easily than someone who can read. The fact remains that the school is now ashamed of itself and that there may be more than a chronological relationship between loss of prestige by the military and teaching functions. Both are corollaries of the shortage of religious vocations which the bishops so regularly bemoan. Montalembert speaking to the Assembly in 1850: 'Two armies are drawn up face to face: the army of good and the army of evil. The army of good consists of forty thousand primary-school teachers.'

Everyday history. You meet a scientist, say an astronomer. Naturally enough, you ask him about his speciality. You have recently read a popular article on the 'solar wind' and you would like to know more about it (not a lot and certainly not everything there is to know). 'Forgive my ignorance', you begin, 'I'm just a layman.' That says it all. Profanity is an all-or-nothing question, not of degrees but of places, not of quality but of quantity. The *profanus* stands outside the temple, outside the consecrated ground.[7] You can be more or less educated, but you are either initiated or you are not and you cannot be simultaneously inside and outside an enclosure. When you are inside the temple or *fanum*, you are said to be *fanaticus*, inspired by the god who lives in the temple dedicated to him. (Divine inspiration means exaltation and is expressed in frenzy—hence the connection between the various meanings of the word.) Curiously, the Greek verb *temno*, to cut, appears again. A disciple is a pupil who is allowed to follow his master into a discipline, just as a master is someone who brings the stranger across the threshold of his teaching and thereby consecrates him as a disciple. The feeling of piety that binds a pupil to a teacher is, in that sense, independent of the content or even the object of the teaching. In theory, the possessors of rational and revealed knowledge should enjoy equal respect, even if the former are not saints and even if the latter are impostors. Scientists do not normally venerate knowledge, even if the biologist Monod does turn it into a moral philosophy known as 'the ethics of knowledge'. It is no secret that the various academic authorities have as little regard for one another as rival soothsayers in Rome. Nor should it be forgotten that to mock academics is an attribute of academics, just as scorn for wealth is a privilege of the wealthy. The wisest of men is always ignorant in someone's eyes, and one man's ignoramus is another man's soothsayer. It is no good slipping between the temples: wherever we go, there are divisions and so many perimeters as to give us a constitutional feeling of exclusion. When the son of a gardener from Loiret, a French Communist who had to leave primary school at thirteen to get a factory job, can write of his family that 'we lived by the people's sacred respect for teachers, books and intellectuals', he is not speaking for himself or his parish, but for everyone.[8] 'Sacred': the whole future of a political militant is contained within that fatal world, but so, by the same criterion, is the timeless politics of mankind.

These juxtaposed histories (a heteroclite collection put together for your edification) call for two comments.

1. The term 'religious' refers not only to an internal modality of discourse but to the mode of relations implied and created by its transmission. The 'religious' is not located downstream in a specific type of statement but upstream in the material conditions of its enunciation. It is to be found not so much in the letter or spirit of a 'theory' as in its transport costs or the effects of its transmission. A religion is a medium rather than a message. The vulgate is related to vulgarization in the same way that a falling body is related to the laws of gravity. The various forms in which knowledge is communicated are borrowed from the transmission of the magistrature. Just as a scientific instrument is a 'reified theorem' (Bachelard), a religious cult is a reified teaching (and an orthodoxy is what remains of a doctrine when the doctor is dead). This mediation of the religious function explains why the transition from didacticism to dogmatism can be made without a passport or customs control; why it is as easy as that reverse transition from mystical vision to hysterical crisis which takes us across the 'uncertain frontier between religious transport and madness' (to use Frazer's modest phrase). In any case, to come back to critical concerns, it is not only or not essentially 'their excessive level of universality' which makes certain theories generate a metaphysics (as Popper claims). It is basically their over-extended level of distribution (through the agency of 'schools' and 'movements of thought').

2. It is not up to the author or speaker to define or challenge the legal limits which objectively distinguish a professor from a prophet, a magister from a magus, a messenger from a messiah, an instruction from an institution, and so on. Such limits are automatically established by *audience effects*. The process whereby an author becomes an authority occurs without his authorization. The decisive opposition between inside and outside, which constitutes Political Reason, is made independently of the partners in the act of communication and, more specifically, of the sender of the information. The most circumspect of teachers can set out to open up a new domain of objective knowledge, carefully leaving it open to an infinite series of controlled reworkings in accordance with the principle that any science is open. But there is nothing to prevent his listeners or readers from closing it or making it their fief, even if it involves expelling the first occupant and paying due respect to his

memory (the erection of a statue makes it easier to build walls). A truth collectively recognised as such tends to become a territory, with doctors for sentries. For a territory left undefended is a territory invaded. Discourse on the origins of inequality between discourses: 'The first man who, having enclosed a text, thought fit to say "This is ours" and found people foolish enough to believe him was the true founder of orthodoxy.'

There are two principles to doctrinal work, which is itself an effect of the political unconscious in the realm of ideas: *circumscription* and *exclusion*. For example, at the beginning of our era (the past being like a magnifying glass for the present), the organization of the Christian story and the territorialization of the Christian community in concentric circles were one and the same, as were the elaboration of the doctrine and the work of sacramentalization. (See Dumezil's definition of the myth as a narrative that is necessarily connected with a determinate ritual.) The more advanced the definition of the dogma, the narrower the hierarchy of those allowed to take part in the sacred mysteries. Thus, according to fourth-century liturgy, penitents, energumen and catechumen were required to leave the church after the homily, as only full members of the church could take part in the eucharist. The organizational function thus operates in the material and symbolic fields through a dual movement of incorporation and exclusion. An organization which could no longer exclude would find it difficult to integrate.

The well-known saying that you cannot avoid being involved in politics also applies to the most obviously apolitical discursive formations to the extent that they are required to take on bodily form. The only exceptions are disembodied thoughts which have neither force nor effect, neither audience nor influence (one thing compensates for the other). The conceptual workers of the social sciences would be wrong to believe themselves immune to the imperatives of the institution (frontier, selection, delegation, hierarchy), for anyone who edifies a theory becomes involved in politics sooner or later, either directly or by proxy. A statement of truth has a vocation for politics because it has a vocation to communicate itself: the Word is by nature expansionist, and it has been so ever since God opened his mouth and said 'Let there be light'. The prototype of the Word is dynamic as well as intelligible: it is not a message without an addressee but a power with effects. The prophet propagates, the inspired expire and the scientist teaches. It is impossible to climb Mount Sinai and come down without tablets in your hand, to conceive something wanting to put it into execution. Incarnation is inscribed in the concept of the Word, just as transmission is in that of the message. Similarly, it is in the nature of the Holy Ghost to communicate itself to those who do not have it, and even today it is still in the nature of the correct idea to make itself known. ('If it's there, there must be some use for it.') The theoretician is therefore destined to start a school, and anyone who starts a school undergoes the critical experience of producing a body, regardless of the specific criteria for incorporation. No body can survive without that esprit de corps known as the spirit of orthodoxy. Such is the price that has to be paid for organizational work in a hostile evironment (and from a historical and organic point of view, 'hostility' and 'environment' are synonymous).

At the educational level, the problem might be put as follows. How can one practise a pedagogy of freedom when pedagogic relations imply subordination? An emancipated school can certainly free reason from religious superstition. But can a school be strictly non-denominational when the acceptance of a reason involves loyalty to the speaker and when loyalty implies belonging (at least to a chapel)? Our republican ancestors: 'A school opened is a prison closed.' The newspapers: 'A school of thought cannot be opened without being closed.' The supporter who watches the drawn match between Light and Dark through his binoculars has to hold on to his seat, so quickly and often do the roles change. (In the Enlightenment, too, the roles of illuminati were constantly changing, from Jacobins to theosophists, Diderot to Cagliostro.) Whenever there is a return match we 'come back to the sticking-point', as one of the few masters who knew what he was doing and why he was doing it used to say every time he had to go through it all again. 'I have produced glue rather than a school', Lacan declared (*J'ai moins fait école que colle*). We at least have the consolation of knowing that he was not the first. No one can think alone, and thinking (in company) always brings bad luck.

When things are not what they should be and the facts make nonsense of the principles, there is a very strong chance that the principles are wrong. Like a political party (of which it is the historical embryo), a school of thought is in principle an elective community formed by those who freely choose to join it. Spiritual conviviality with the master or intellectual conviviality with the professor does, however, imply obligations, above all the obligation to survive. The *ashram* has to outlive the *swami*, the entourage has to become a community.

If it is to perpetuate itself, a community must have an ecclesiastical structure. The transition from unstable to stable, from the precarious to the durable, requires the message to be delineated in a doctrine and time to be governed by rituals. The elaboration of the doctrine perpetuates the message, and the work of sacramentalization actualizes the past. This dual operation prevents the mediator from drifting away and guarantees the stability of the organs of mediation. The message can thus outlive the messiah and the institution its founder, but the price to be paid is the transference of the sacred from the founding subject to the foundation. 'Thou art Peter and upon this rock'—now I can return to heaven, the Jesus Foundation is born. 'The Party is immortal' and I can therefore die tomorrow: the Lenin Foundation is born. Continuity is expensive—for the institution alone holds the sacraments. Salvation is ensured, but there is only one way to be saved: the total School, the total (Catholic) Church, the total Party. 'I have defeated the second principle—but what a state it has left me in!'

Any doctrine (even a 'scientific' one) regulates identities and stabilizes chance. It is thus conservative by nature and function. It is the organ created by the social function of self-preservation. Real subversion can be, and is, ideologically instituted in the shape of the historical institutionalization of any given revolution. There can be no—and there is no—revolutionary ideology, because it is impossible to be both subversive and immortal: you have to choose. The expression 'revolutionary ideology' is either a logical nonsense or a knife without a blade. If it is the former it can only produce dupes; if the latter, it can only produce States. (There is no need to choose between these alternatives: you can be in good faith and on the right side.)

The deviation is present in the line. Since the line goes astray as soon as it is drawn, orthodoxy has to mount a preventive coup d'etat. Orthodoxy is the orthopaedics of cultural entropy. (There are now two stages: rectitude followed by rectification. The right always has the means to right things.)

It leaks, so we mend it: foundation-closure. As it will anyway come apart, making means remaking: installation-restoration, institution-reconstitution. I am about to be betrayed, so I name my heir presumptive, who will in turn name the authorized inter-preters. This assumes, of course, that I the author (or founder) have acquired authority—that is to say, the rare ability to *augment* (*augeo*) the quantitiy of information circulating in the world and to diminish the quantity of entropy. I shall die and return to the world: who will protect my titles from being usurped and my be-quests from being stolen? Here, then, are the rules for capacitation and co-optation. The point is not simply to bequeath a doctrine of truth: our heirs must be able to recognise the false doctors who will soon spring up everywhere. So we may as well dissolve and exclude immediately. 'Otherwise the initials you receive from me will fall into the hands of known forgers' (Lacan). A school is founded by a master and his teachings must be perpetuated throughout the generations. Hence the *diadoche* of investitures, starting with the first scholar (*deus ille, Memmi*) and the succession of *diadascales* at the head of the school–party–sect–state. Just as Plato chose his nephew Speusippus to lead the Academy (and he chose Xenocrates, who was succeeded by Polemon, etc.), so Lacan chose his son-in-law Miller (who will in turn ...). Marx chose Engels to execute his will. Engels chose his personal secretary Kautsky to be his heir, thereby crowning him 'pope of socialism'. Kautsky fought the good fight against Bernstein's revisionism until he too was de-nounced as a renegade (from the Italian *rinigato*, apostate) by Lenin. Lenin demonstrated the law of succession *a contrario*: ill-ness did not leave him enough time to name his best pupil or to sort out his heirs, and so the people inherited a certain Stalin, 'the con-tinuator of Marx and Engels and the associate of Lenin'. The worst of all continuations are those that take place behind continuity's back. If history did contain a moral, it might be summed up as: 'If there are two heirs, choose the lesser of the two.' For there has to be an inheritance, whether you like it or not, my dear masters.

2. The Function of Funerals

The literal meaning of 'to sacrifice' is to make sacred. Execution is the first vital need of a community.

The proposition that 'it takes a vacuum to fill a group' could be translated as: 'Die and leave the rest to us.' Archimedes's slogan, 'Give me a lever and I will lift the world' becomes 'Give me a corpse and I will make a society', beginning, of course, with the society of the dead man's friends. Not that the image of the lever is all that appropriate for the undertakers of organization. A good corpse is more like the generative axis around which a fluid and amorphous mass solidifies into a stable body. Christ dies and faith in the resurrection is immediately born—as is the Christian sect.[9] Lenin dies and Leninism is immediately born—as is the Party-Family.[10] In French, the beginning of a funeral procession is referred to as *la levée du corps*, literally 'the raising of the body.' It is a marvellous expression. It is thanks to its ascentional faculties that death is a factor in organization. It promotes one element in a set to the status of an ordinate, a reference, a 'charge'. Whether it deifies, canonizes or creates a hero, it always introduces value. Every death is a potential apotheosis. The adverb *apo* combines the meanings of separation, distance, completion and return. As a fulcrum, assembly-point and pivot of a perimeter, a corpse ensures that the political and the mystical meet by simultaneously producing circumscription and sublimation and making them coincide. If a hole is made in a set, it is possible to make a subset. Provided that the whole is supported by an absent subject, it is irrelevant whether his death was natural or unnatural. We organize ourselves so as not to have to kill one another, but one person at least has to be killed if the others are to be organized. Incompleteness rivets the closure to the gap, while the legendary murder assures the inviolability of the newly drawn space. Of all the interpretations to which the myth of the origins of Rome has given rise—including those of the Romans themselves—the most laconic is probably the most accurate: *Caeso moneia firma Remo*, 'the boundaries having been consolidated by the death of Remus' (Propertius). Civic and family piety, parricide and infanticide. We can now understand why, far from being contradictory, family spirit and family murder are complementary. Contemporary anthropology has relegated the murder of the father at the hands of a primal horde of jealous brothers to the museum of speculation. Freud got the details wrong, but not the essential point. He thought he had to provide an empirical content for a logical form, as if it took a historical novel to make an operational invariant of collective life credible by making it look like a libidinal conflict. That was his mistake. Modern metapsychology has, so to speak, taken over the moral scenario of mythology (Remus was guilty, Romulus was wrathful) in order to give a human face to the inhuman law that the horizontal axis of relations of reciprocity requires a vertical axis of relations of order to complete it. In other words, any fraternity on earth requires an 'our father who art in heaven', though sending a brother *ad patres* will of course do the trick.

The group's inability to found itself explains why death has such organizational power. Since it is the basis of the group unconscious and the source of group history, death is present in all foundation myths. The myths of the 'sacrifice of the hero' and of the 'exemplary' murder thus have the same rational kernel. In civil states with a stable organization, a birth-certificate is a death-certificate. For whom tolls the master's bell? For the greater glory of his listeners. The cradle of the group is stained with blood. Such is the 'death insurance' required for historical cohesion. Alterity is the guarantee of organicity, and death is the ultimate form of alterity. Anyone who puts someone (himself) to death makes one thing certain: his victim is the Other. And so, if you want to stop the collective élan from falling away, cut off a head. The father of the nation was guillotined in the place de la Concorde.

The mechanism of expiation has become a commonplace for political indictments and evangelical consolidations alike (a Tsarevich sacrificed, a paschal lamb). They say that the scapegoat removes the violence present or latent within the group, and that the ritual sacrifice should be seen as a sort of vacuum-cleaner for Evil. According to this consoling conception, Christianity should have helped—or even did help—Christendom to be sparing of violence. God the Father sent his only Son to make collective expiation once and for all. However, it takes a historical sleight-of-hand to make the thesis theoretically credible. (The Christian religion is not noted for being less 'totalitarian' than its rivals—at least it hasn't been for the last thousand years—because it only goes half way towards the concept of closure and falls into ethnocentric spiritual comfort—the Apostolic Roman faith.) Ritual sacrifice provides no 'solution' because it is the product of a problematic without a beginning or an end. The ancient *numen* is indivisible—the *tremendum*, the *fascinans* and the *augustum* are given and taken away as one. It would be nice if we could have the sovereign glory (*augustum*) on the one hand and the shiver of terror (*tremendum*) on the other. But the very thing that structures sovereign rights inspires sacro-sanct terror: *delimitation*. It would be nice if we could have the religion without the violence. But unfortunately, *sanctus* cannot remove the primordial and constitutional *ambiguity* of *sacer*, which means both cursed and august, horrible and venerable. It is at its most venerable when it is at its most horrible. What terrifies us is not spilled blood but the line that is traced. We can pay our blood debts and turn over a new leaf, but we cannot shirk our collective duty to believe without our collective body breaking up. When we draw frontiers and defend them, we put our territories into debt without agreeing a repayment date. The insolvency upon which all existing societies are based is the principle behind 'political obligation'. It signifies that violence is always present within religion, that barbarism is always present in culture (in the sense of all the means necessary to maintain a stable communal identity).

Death transforms time into space and a biography into a topology of actions and words punctuated by our memories. When another has closed the circle of his life, we can recall a solid volume of humanity, a smooth firm volume which becomes superhuman. The only beings we can ever know completely are the loved ones we have lost. To transform the memory into a cult, it is enough to move in and live with the dead. The movement from cult to religion takes place through the closing of doors from inside. Living people can only fuse together when they a share the same coffin. Putting someone into a coffin makes him taboo. When someone is locked up by death, they automatically become sacro-sanct. In a world of draughts and banging doors, the silence of the grave is more than enviable: it is exquisite. We are indefinable; the dead are characteristic. We are fissured; they are closed. We are vulnerable; they are untouchable. We are mortal; they are no longer mortal. A living fellow creature is a vague, friable totalization that is quite unpredictable. We never know who we are dealing with or what we can rely upon. How far can we commit ourselves, what guarantee is there? Any collective has an organic need for a *guarantor*. The dead are the only ones we can rely upon; they are our only certain values. All beings need values, and the political being needs security. It is not surprising that the 'dead rule the living'. Paradoxically,

the funeral tropism of historical societies (a constant drive expressed in a variety of ways) expresses the unconscious instinct for self-
preservation. We respect the dead because we want to live together,
in peace.

In terms of personal consciousness and personal experience, the
death of a friend is a tragedy: a black day. For the group unconscious, the disappearance of a member is a happy event: white
stones along the roadside, stele, signpost, requiem. For the collective, there is nothing lugubrious about funerals; and not only
because of the material—if not mundane fact—that the cemetery
has become the last meeting-place where we can all enjoy meeting
people we've not seen for years. ('Everyone was there. I even met
so-and-so'.) A death puts the broken pieces of the collective back
together again. The feeling of fulfilment which is so often seen in
the crowd at a funeral—and it can range from comfort to exultation, from discretion to secrecy, depending upon the participants
and the circumstances—is such a constantly striking spectacle that
we have to delve deep into the unconscious to explain it. It is not
unusual for people at a funeral to show a vivacity or ardour for
which there is no equivalent in their everyday life. For a brief moment, the funerals of famous people crystallize the floating unity of
the nearest group, giving it an opportunity to experience its existence as a group and to love itself in the image of the man who is
being taken to his last resting-place. The group rejoices because it
at last exists; the spectacle (service, procession, dais, catafalque,
speeches) is the ultimate expression of the narcissism of the *we*. It
has been said that France excels in the ceremonial side of funerals,
official or otherwise, possibly because the country has—or had—
politics in its blood. A 'good funeral' is a secret triumph.[11]

It is no accident that the last festivals on the international
political scene are the funerals of great heads of state. Their mortal
remains unite the worst of enemies, who can be seen shaking hands
and standing together in condolence at the funeral. For the duration of the ceremony, what unites leaders who are as far apart or as
hostile to one another as it is possible to be is stronger than what
divides them. Common to them all is their struggle against death,
such a laughable enterprise that the crowd of empire-builders and
defenders of law and order inspire a sort of pity. Interludes of this
kind provide some insight into the political unconscious and are

therefore both touching and comic. Important funerals perform a considerable service for the 'international community', allowing it to come into existence for a moment (in somewhat more solid form than the UN General Assembly). This makes intense diplomatic activity possible: unexpected rapprochements, surprise reconciliations, speeded-up, negotiations, etc. Nehru, Churchill, De Gaulle, Tito, Ohira—hardly has the good news come off the teleprinter than major world figures are flashing back that they can be counted on to attend.

Death revitalizes the survivors by making them congregate together. Alejo Carpentier once remarked that 'nothing brings people closer together than the revolutionary ideal'. As a statement, that is irrefutable, but it does raise certain problems. The political conscience of the individual revolutionary expressly forbids him from seeing his own death or that of his comrades as an ideal. But the revolutionary collective's unconscious stipulates that the ideal revolutionary is a dead revolutionary.

Physical death is no more than a raw material, and it is up to the group to elaborate it into an instrument of political production. Death is by definition a force of order, but some forces are not used and some deaths are wasted. A society cannot let its dead die without running the risk of disorder and even death, but symbolic resurrections do not happen automatically. The transition from latent to manifest information is neither immediate nor automatic: the political efficacity of death is a process. If organization were simply *given* to us like a gift from nature or God, politics would no longer have an object and religion would have no function. The individual unconscious works upon memory traces, sense stimuli and residues of daily life; but the elaboration of the lack is the object of political work is to elaborate a lack after death has taken place, so that sacralization is by its very nature retroactive. Organizations are made in the image of Catholic canonizations, according to a posthumous process. Political and psychical work proceed in different directions. In the individual, the work of mourning consists of 'killing the dead' (Lagache). In the group, the work of loss consists of bringing them back to life. In one process, the subject strives to detach himself from what has been his object of attachments; in the other, the subject (the *we*) reattaches itself to an object from which it has become (ever so slightly) detached. The individual tries to forget; the collective tries to feel remorse. By identifying with the lost object, the psychical ego falls into melancholy, but the political *we* becomes exalted. What is pathological in the group is normal in the individual, and vice versa. The individual consoles himself by masking the absence, the group by recreating the void (anniversaries, pilgrimages, exegeses, public commemorations, etc.). For a collective, the long labour of bereavement is designed to reinforce the loss it has experienced through the posthumous construction of a 'spiritual heritage' or even a 'political testament'.

If further proof of the informative capacities of the lack are required, they may be found in the fact that testimony and covenant are synonymous. New Testament, new convenant. The word is a translation of the Greek *diathiki*, which *originally* meant disposition or arrangement. It then came to denote pact or convention and finally took on the significance of testament, a covenant between god and men. This involved an unfolding, not an accumulation, of meaning, the successive dictionary definitions revealing a sequence of spontaneous gestures. Bury someone and prayer comes spontaneously; the funeral oration puts an end to dissension. Just as the line behind the hearse forms a cortege, the funeral director puts an end to the pushing and produces a more orderly crowd. Similarly, but at a different level, commemoration gives rise to a written tradition, a law of succession and then to the dynastic legality of authorized interpreters.

The mythical sequence of psothumous legends obviously inverts the chronological order of the production of order. What the representations of the collective consciousness place at the beginning, the elaborations of the collective unconscious place at the end. The official representation places the founder at the beginning as an ultimate, non-founded term. He sends out a message which leads to the formation of a group responsible for decoding it. As in the history of science, where the true precursors are those who are only later recognized as having come first, so in the history of collectives, the founders are only regarded as such when the foundation is no longer something to be feared. In that sense, the will is executed before the last wishes have have been expressed. We only discover what they are by carrying them out. The work of mourning is a lawyer's work: it consists of writing apocryphal documents and giving them a canonical value after the event. Obligation and delegation are none and the same thing. Anyone who wants to be obeyed (or listened to—the word is the same and the thing almost the same) has to look like the executor of the will of the founder (ofthe Church, party or republic—say, the Fifth Republic). As successions—both apostolic and political—usually occur by accident, *ab intestat*, the heirs have to find a will as best they can. It is well known that the Aramean testator in whose name the Holy Scriptures have governed the life and death of a large part of mankind for the last two thousand years, wrote on only one occasion (and that was in the sand). The New Testament (twenty-seven books in the Greek) is an echo-effect, a posthumous record of hearsay written seventy years after the event. The Messiah vanishes into the divine message, which then vanishes into the echo of the Gospels. It is precisely that cascade of metaphors which gives the scriptural text its authority.

Collective time is always late—that is to say, the institution and its members are always out of step with or outdone by its founder. The time lag is projected on to each civilization's calendar, on to the fixed points which it uses as zeroes for dating things. The Hegira was not long in coming (16 July 622 according to our calendar), but that was because of Mohammed's astonishing success. The Christian era began, so to speak, five hundred years after its beginning, as it was Dionysius Exiquus (who died in Rome in 504) who determined the date of Christ's birth as the eighth day after the Calends of January in the year 753 of the Roman calendar. However, that calculation marks a purely theoretical beginning. The Christian era did not become a historical reality in Christendom until the time of Charlemagne (and in France it does not figure in royal documents until Hugues Capet).

The latency period of political foundations (which is somewhat similar to the 'purgatory of authors' in literature) thus gives a sardonically chronological meaning to the famous 'Since I am their leader, I must follow them'. No founder of any religion pronounced its law during his own lifetime: the law took shape with and through his death; textual codification and political succession intervened together. The foundation stones are laid by those who come afterwards, the authorities are produced by the authorized, and masters are produced by disciples. The 'collection of memoirs' is the first stage in recollection. So there is no need to take sides in the old quarrel between those who, like Cicero, connect *religio* with *legere* (to collect, to assemble) and those who, like Tertullian, opt for *ligare* (to bind). A religion binds us together by connecting us all with an external element (the divinity), but that link presupposes that we collect and shape traces. Originally, *religio* meant a subjective disposition like scruple, concern or meticulousness. The original meaning and derivatives can thus be combined (as in *superstitio*, survival, bearing witness, superiority). The cult of the dead person who unites the survivors begins with the collection of scattered materials in a safe and central place, not least because those who aspire to the succession to power have no time to lose. Numa makes Romulus the divine founder and crowns himself king, but he does so in the name of his predeccesor. When Lenin dies, Stalin immediately decides the issue of succession. He is the first to take the ritual oath (the only binding oaths are those sworn on tombs) and then publishes it in the *Foundations of Leninism* (1924). Here, the work of mourning looks like an instant book and an immediate occupation of the throne. Leninism is nothing more than a gravestone. What was at stake in the erection of the monument was Lenin's inheritance.

Buddhism is the only great historical religion to have done without a doctrine, or, more accurately, the only one whose doctrine has done without writing and whose faith has no orthodoxy. But legend has it that after the death of Buddha, his two best pupils, Ananda and Makakacyapa, felt a need to fix the canonic version of the master's words in the sutra—an orthodox arrangement of the text which is still used today. Less than a hundred years separates the death of Jesus from the writing of the Scriptures, and St Jerome's Vulgate appears three and a half centuries later. From the death of Mohammed to the Koran: twenty years. At that point Uthman, the Third Caliph, establishes a *ne varietur* version in order to preserve the unity of the emergent community. Under the Oumayyades, this becomes the definitive text. Only fifteen years from the death of Marx to the appearance of Marxism. The shorter the gestation period, the shorter the life expectation.

When it comes to doctrine, the other is always our best friend, regardless of the time lag or the tenor of the doctrine. In fact, this is not surprising if we think that alterity is the greatest favour an ego can do itself—and others. Tradition takes it upon itself to increase the transcendence that a master has already transcended by his death—each of the heirs marks his own legitimacy with the seal of the inimitable eminence he must imitate. The collective work of loss and the process whereby the historical group identifies itself are one and the same in that they help the losers to find themselves in He whom they have lost and help all of us to see ourselves as the Other (the commander as his delegate, he pays allegiance as his obligee).

2

The Defence System

The collective causes the human species pain, but it would rather
suffer from the religious than disappear. Social bodies do not have
the same degree of freedom as individual souls: forced to choose
between the disgrace of being and the grace of not being, they opt
for the lesser evil. 'Opt' is not the right word. We are talking about
a *tendency*, closer to a *tropism* than to masochism. And if there
were an element of masochism in hierotropism it would not be
gratuitous. You do not build walls, expel foreign bodies and em-
balm living ideas 'for the pleasure of doing so', even though such
activities may provide a certain (anal) pleasure for their adepts. If
we want to see the collective stop producing 'noise' and start producing information, we simply have to admit that it has no choice
(except between the miseries of life in common and no life at all).

The nature of the *political*—its vital minimum—can be seen
where *politics* is reduced to its simplest expression, when the only
alternative is an unceremonious death. If you want to know what
something consists of, ask yourself what it resists. Organize a
biscuit. A sweater. A cigarette. A bout of hypochondria. A com-
mando. 'Organize' was a password for those deported to the Nazi
camps, a joker of a word which was apparently applied to any
operation that might increase a prisoner's chances of survival.
Other wartime circumstances, less extreme but equally rigorous,
confirm the elementary rule that resistance means regrouping and
that regrouping means reorganizing.[1] The simplest critical experiment ratifies the famous intuition that 'life is the sum total of
functions that resist death' (Bichat), and the political organization
of time is one such function. Homogenization has the goal of
preservation. If you want to stockpile things, you have to build

walls. Immunization involves a filtering process. 'You have to look after yourself.'

The last thing we civilizations want to know is that we are mortal. Born of that denegation, we obsessively maintain it day after day as we struggle against the tendency that leads to a degree zero of difference. Any civilization that lets itself go soon finds itself reduced to 'free' (unbound) molecules, to its initial state of inertia. Listen carefully to our rhetoric, think about the adjectives we use most frequently and you will see that anything that can bind—alliances, charters, oaths, pacts, friendship, memory, doctrines, principles—is immediately qualified by an epithet such as indestructible, indissoluble, unshakeable, inflexible or immortal. They are all negatives turned into positives. They are all denegations of entropy, our public enemy number one. Without realizing it, we know that energy runs out and that physical time is irreversible. Hence there is not a single makeshift time-machine that we have not put together and tested at least a hundred times. Do not be surprised if we seem to be repeating ourselves, for such machines are not in infinite supply. Our language is as poor as our resources. But, basically, we would rather bore you than perish.

Now it is my turn to recapitulate.

In the beginning was anguish: the biological distress of the infant, the mental distress of the adult, the political distress of the group. The prime quality of existence is triggered whether or not there is a signal or a real danger. Anguish itself is scientifically guaranteed (in the last instance by the laws of physical nature), and so we always have a ground even though it is in the nature of anxiety (anxiety nothing) to be groundless. Just as an individual is sure not to be mistaken when he senses something like a void at the end of the road, so a collective has every reason in the world to fear its dissolution because the most probable state of an organization is disorganization. The evolution towards disorder, through the statistical disappearance of individual features, moves from organized to unorganized, complex to simple, improbable to probable. For any system left to itself, 'the future is the direction in which entropy increases'. We have all had the somewhat unhappy privilege of verifying the formulae of Clausius and Boltzmann in trivial form: we have all seen associations, committees, circles, clubs and brotherhoods into which we put a lot of personal energy and communal hope fade away and then disappear in a matter of months. We all know that 'organizational' work has the lowest productivity in the world. Work in general is tiring, but political work more so than most: it produces less for an equal expenditure. The joys of a few moments of productive activity stand out against a backdrop of waste, viscosity and pointlessness. When the balance-sheets are drawn up in individual terms, the sadness definitely outweighs the fervour. If at time t' we find a group structured in the same way as at time t, we can be certain that it is no accident. It is the effect of a constant investment of energy which has been transformed and channelled against the flow of time.

A novelist to whom the names of Carnot and Clausius probably meant nothing once said that 'all life is a process of demolition'. He added: 'The mark of a first-rate intelligence is the ability to concentrate on two contradictory ideas and still go on functioning' (Scott Fitzgerald). It has to be said that, providence and finality apart, living matter is not short on intelligence. And nor is the life of collectives, which are an extension of such matter. Despite its apparent incoherence, the political reason at work in history has, so to speak, become fixated on two contradictory ideas that ought logically to have blocked it: namely, self-preservation and duration. In order to reverse entropy and annul chance, the strategy of tension leads to what are now called conservative structures. At first sight these seem highly unlikely to minimize the production of entropy or to avert the danger that living practical sets will return to the'primal soup' (the multicellular mass of primal chaos). We have here an internal contradiction that requires some consideration.

1. The Inscription Principle

The characteristic dimension of the political order is space. That of the living being is time. These two propositions are connected, but the former derives from the latter. Political reason plays for safety, backing space against time. It gambles on stabilization through spatialization. The demarcation of an ideal or material territory is a defensive reflex-action of self-preservation. The inscription principle which governs the workings of politics exists alongside the antagonistic principle of dissipation ('the second principle') which governs the course of the world. The former exists only in order to block the latter.

Inscription: inscribing oneself somewhere, inside an enclosure. The inscription principle is an economic principle in that it tends to maximize a given difference in temperature and, above all, to maintain it. Rock wall, palisade, earthworks are rudimentary translations of a thermically determined biological drive. The living is the product of a difference that appears in an isothermic environment; or, more concretely, of the establishment of a stable site (HQ or central camp) where a fire can be kept going (as any guerrilla who has lived in the virgin forest will tell you). Having a fire to cook food and to provide warmth is the precondition of all life. *Ignis mutat res*. Before the neolithic age and agrarian sedentarization, inscription was principally a matter of lineage rather than spatialization, although every known nomad group practising a predatory economy—hunting and gathering—has one or more clearly defined territories. Political behaviour, which does not in itself have a history, cannot appear prior to history. In a cold society—one, that is, without writing—the forms of such behaviour are evidently not the same as in societies where the first critical threshold (the neolithic revolution) has been crossed. The inscription principle fixes existence in one place, as it is the place that gives rise to existence. Man regards as sacred anything upon which his life depends. Religion was the first sedative, and building a wall—from whatever material—was the first religious act. Unless it is enclosed, life ebbs away. The enclosure is at once military, political and religious, and it was only late in the day that specific areas of competence became attached to the sacred, the sovereign and the defensive. Originally, the City is where the citadel is and the citadel is where the sanctuary is: on a summit, in the acropolis, in the upper town. The strategic imperatives of defence merge with the logical obligation to have a reference. The group builds (and builds itself) on high ground.

The example of Ancient Greece, where ostracism was equivalent to a death-sentence, shows that a man can only exist if he is inscribed. A man who could not name his City or home port became one of the living dead, a man with no identity whose murder was no crime. By losing his space, he had already ceased to exist. Any inscription is better than none, and although modern man's vague insight into the inscription principle no longer takes a territorial form, it does in its own way perpetuate the ancient curse. We always have to be able to answer the most religious question of all: 'Where are you from?' We are somehow aware that the question of origins refers not to one attribute among others (name and profession) but to the substance. Someone from nowhere is no one. Someone who is going just anywhere is just anyone. It is better to make for Pitchipoi than to become a homeless wanderer living from hand to mouth, wandering like the shades in the underworld and drifting towards death. We are haunted by the fear of dispersal. Be it Trojan, Jewish or Greek, the diaspora symbolizes the negative time in which the community dissolves in the flow of aimless migrations.

Doctrines that last take the form of topographical systems. Every symbolic formation produces spatial systems of varying complexity. Hades, The Elysian Fields and the Styx. The circles of hell and the seventh heaven. On the right hand of God the Father. No salvation outside. The spontaneous vocabulary of political discourse displays a ritual and probably compulsive handling of space: East–West, Left–Right: the Iron Curtain and the wall of freedom. Joining becomes 'entering', 'taking the plunge', 'going into'. Participation involves 'holding one's position', 'closing ranks', 'sticking by (the leadership)'. To leave is to 'break with'. He's one of ours, he's an insider. He's been expelled, he's changed sides. Which side are you on? Which camp do you belong to? What is your position? What line of demarcation do you draw? What line do you follow? The mission of authority is to provide answers to these prototype questions. It has been made responsible for space. The spontaneous geometricalization of human relations spares us the one question we cannot answer: what will become of us tomorrow? The compass is used as a horoscope because extension is the opposite of duration, controllable is the opposite of uncontrollable and reassurance is the opposite of insecurity. Since the organization of time is the basis of culture, the group resorts to the space of ceremony to domesticate the unpredictable and to exorcize the future by commemorating the past. But playing off space against time is to play off repetition against innovation, and so the delineation principle telescopes the death principle and the life instinct. Ideology's insistence that space is everything makes anguish a matter of ground, marks and roots. Its ideal would be a completely 'outside' world, open and laid out in squares with every citizen in their place and a place for every citizen. A perfectly 'ideologized' society (the utopia of the 'total city') would be a continuous performance with no spectators, with only the ticking of a clock to break the silence. The group would put its own eternity on display in a grand exhibition of hierarchically arranged lines and colours. In the meantime, political reason is active wherever the index of a statement's value is the position of the speaker. When 'Where is he speaking from?' is the primordial question, we have entered the realm of the political in which a position is enough to give someone authority. Just as a good covering quotation can legitimize a rather inapt statement by invoking the right name (a shield without which the discourse would become illegitimate, suspect and therefore inaudible), so it is possible to close a debate before it has even opened simply by pointing to the 'bad' place. A proposition becomes an argument, and a summary topography (*topos*) becomes the *ultima ratio* of a dialectic. What is aberrant in theory is the norm in politics. 'It is a fine justice that is bounded by a river. Truth on one side of the Pyrenees, error on the other!'

'Narrow-minded dogmatism' is a pleonasm that belongs to the sphere of unnecessarily disturbing redundancies, along with 'religious communities', 'myths of origin', 'agrarian rites' and 'spiritual families'. No one has ever seen a family without a spirit or a spirit without a family, myths that do not relate to origins or origins that are not mythical, agriculture without rites or rites without agrarian nostalgia, a community without religion or a religion without a community. We are just as unlikely to come across a boundless dogmatism, because the function of dogmatism is to set limits beyond which 'everything is permitted', murder included. Limited vision makes it difficult to understand things; but a failure to carve an ordered space out of chaos would make it even more difficult for human beings to survive.

Instead of blaming 'crazy doctrinairism', let us try to identify the reason for the formation of the spatio-temporal units known as doctrines. It is in part a matter of evolution. However, it is crucial to stress that cultural innovation cannot be conceived in terms of the model of biological mutation, not only because the rhythm of its evolution is much more rapid, but also because the raw material is much more fragile. The difference between a cultural and a genetic patrimony is that the former is recorded in the memory and the latter in the genome. DNA keeps much better records than museum curators and university vice-chancellors. Integrity is even more precarious in the ideosphere than in the biosphere. The genetic helix does not work in our favour, and the structures of politico-cultural organizations do not enjoy the same invariance and self-replication as organic structures. There is no guarantee that what has been acquired will be passed on, and the other side of what we call progress is the permanent possibility of regression. Political defence mechanisms therefore have to compensate for the reversibility of acquired modifications. Unable to rely upon the nucleotide sequence, they improvise with anathemas and expulsions. As cultural time and identity are not given to us by nature, we wrest them violently from nature. In the gap between heredity and heritage, or between the biosphere's self-preservation mechanisms and the ideosphere's potential degradation, the thought-police takes up position in order to reduce the gap. Dogmatism is the child of fear, constantly produced and reproduced by the basic insecurity of cultural time. It is the price that society pays for its sociability, for not being taken over by the 'logic of the living'. Paradoxically, it is because we are responsible for our historical transmission services, without the assistance of any genetic unit, that bodies of cultural functionaries specializing in the maintenance of acquired characteristics and in resistance to erosion have been able to constitute and reconstitute themselves throughout the ages (Schools, Clergy, Parties, Institutes, etc.).

We can locate the difficulty by using metaphors from immunology. Politico-cultural organizations do not have the 'natural defences' that protect physical organisms from functional disorders and outside aggression, but like them they do have surfaces that come into contact with the outside environment. They therefore develop, *motu proprio*, organs to control and regulate that contact. The various cultural totalities that are struggling to survive have, for the most part, incorporated them into their primary corpus. By clinging to their idiosyncrasy, they fight as best they can against the threat of phagocytosis or infection by microbes from competing organizations. The precautions that have to be taken increase as the level of organization rises. No one will dispute the fact that, although doctrinal formations (Islam, Catholicism, psycho-analysis, Marxism, etc.) are irreducible to living cells, they are still complex systems. And the greater the complexity of a system, the more aleatory its stability. Even a minor localized disturbance can have repercussions on the whole, and any shift away from equilibrium is countered by more or less effective corrections, normalizations and rectifications in accordance with the norms of 'right opinion' (*ortho-doxy*). Otherwise the cultural totality in question would merge with its environment and eventually reach the point where it could no longer distinguish between self and non-self: In-difference or Death.

The phenomena of belief (and therefore of power) will remain indecipherable so long as they are not decoded as symptoms of biological *impotence* and logical *incapacity*, if not a combination of the two. The signs of authority displayed by different social groups can be seen as so may SOS calls put out by a mankind that is terrified at the prospect of *having to do more than it can do*. That panic-fear constitutes the political order. In order to come into existence as a constituted body, social humanity has to find a basis that is by definition missing (lack being the essential ground of societies). It has to find a seat, but it is always seated upon a void. Political bodies would not be what they are if they were not hollow. Politics is not the art of creating a void, which is by definition already there. It is the art of making things with the void, while political reason is a system for managing the lack. *Scarcity* is not a contingent and historically dated phenomenon typical of a primitive stage of development but the ultimate category of the economic order, without which all its operations and constraints would be incomprehensible. Similarly, insecurity is the first given of collective existence, just as the feeling of *inadequacy* is the common denominator of social individuals.

A history of impotence would have no difficulty in showing how, chronologically, the institution took over from personal improvisation in the handling of a certain logic of compensation. What is conventionally known as 'the birth of the gods' may contain in allegorical form the same admission of failure that is found in the institutionalization of charisma. Remember Frazer's explanation of the transition from magic to religion. The magicians believed they were powerful (or others believed they were, which comes to the same thing). But they rapidly became aware of the ineffectiveness of their rituals and incantations and discarded, so to speak, their function, letting supernatural beings take responsibility for sunshine and rain and for making the crops grow. These beings were soon personalized and became gods, all the more powerful for being invisible. Power was officially handed over to them because the men who once held it could not (or could no longer) satisfy the demands made by their group. It is possible that a similar handover of power may have contributed to the birth of the state in feudal Europe, an embryonic bureaucracy that was invisible and therefore 'not responsible'. The thaumaturges may not have been unwilling to hand over the power to 'solve problems', if not to 'work miracles', especially since it had been their personal responsibility to 'do the impossible'. In the Third World, charismatic leaders, modern rain-makers, founders of nations and heroes of independence still try to remove the functional vectors as far as possible from their own persons by building or cobbling together one-party states because they can no longer satisfy the demand personally. The leader tells the crowd, 'Go to the Party. It is the Party that gives me my mandate: I simply carry out its decisions'. The discontented masses find a scapegoat at once impersonal and disposable, so that the Leader is able to choose sacrificial victims from a politico-administrative personnel that can be easily replaced (if not so easily taxed). In a sense, the Leader has no choice, and nor does the group which recognizes itself in and through him. He can only retain a certain illusion of power in the eyes of his people by making that admission of political impotence. He can do nothing against the encroaching bureaucracy, which is largely responsible for errors, mistakes and crimes. It does not matter if the admission is sincere or calculated, half and half or neither sincere nor calculated. Necessity is a law unto itself.

2. The State of War

The inscription principle, which cannot logically ground itself, establishes a morphological constant in *the territory*. But as it is the function that explains the structure and not vice versa, forms are always the effect of forces. The territorial configuration is an adaptive response to the constant which actually founds the political: *hostility*. In so far as it is the milieu for resistance against the forces of destruction, dislocation and dissolution, the territory of a doctrine is no less dynamic than that of a City. It results from a perpetual and shifting clash between opposed forces, some working on the organized systems from within, others attacking them from without. We have mentioned the former and we can now look at the latter, bearing in mind that the order of logical exposition inverts the chronological order of factors. (Death is man's 'ultimate enemy', but in both his historical and his personal life, the enemy is the form in which death first appears.) *Degradation* is inscribed in the physics of the living as a tendential law; physical *aggression* is its most striking aspect, its exoteric translation. The threat of destruction, ever nibbling at the thread of time, plunges down on us from the skies. Entropy hurls its thunderbolts: razzias, raids, incursions by nomadic hunters inside the walls of sedentary agrarian communities, barbarian incursions into the midst of the civilized *oikoumene*, savage incursions into the marches of Barbarian Empires.

Doctrines and cities are closed places, but their closure is *preventive*, not *punitive*. It is the first anthropological act of self-defence. A human group is faced with an alternative, not between the destruction of the walls and the cessation of hostilities, but between the armed peace of organization and unconditional surrender (if only for the technical reason that it takes less time to break a truce than to rebuild ramparts). 'Us or them' = 'Kill or be killed'. Let us be quite clear about the order of the factors. It is the armed confrontation that creates the frontline, not the reverse. The besieger creates the ramparts; the clash of arms, the security system. There would be no circumscription if there were no encirclement. The *force majeure* of 'hostilities' creates the major forms of doctrines.

'In the beginning was War.' The demand for security (of people, property and ideas) constitutes political 'need', for the state of war is the horizon of the social and societies can never see beyond it except in terms of the juridical mirages of humanitarian pacifism. Even though popular wisdom always has a treaty for general and complete disarmament ready for us to ratify and sign (and such treaties are no less admirable than the countless Enlightenment projects for universal peace that unfortunately escaped the notice of young Bonaparte). War is a universal and recurrent fact of the history of societies because, despite the infinite diversity of its forms (including war on war), it is inherent in the existence of social groups and actually conditions their constitution and dissolution. In its own terms, it is as important as climatic variations, demographic catastrophes or the food/territory ratio (factors which are in themselves belligenic). To say that this is an ultimate fact—ultimate because primary—does not mean entering into the discourse of eschatology, but simply into that of genealogy. The task is not to announce an apocalypse but to restate a genesis. Given that the aim of the living is to live, war is obviously not the finality of social life. Everyone knows that war is waged so that we can have peace, but also that we cannot have peace without making war.

The political world is a world in which there are always two of us: the enemy and me. The enemy is behind and before me; I come after and against him. There are other universes in which man lives alone and has no neighbours, in which he can thought as an essence, independently of the conditions of existence concretely required for the execution of his tasks. In these he is alone with his bodies or his dreams, with the products of his thought, the artefacts of his laboratory or the givenness of things. Artistic, technical or scientific activity takes place in a smooth homogeneous space which is simultaneously open and closed on itself, whereas political space comes into the world already split by a line of demarcation that constitutes it as political and separates me from my other, my negation. The delineation principle here finds a limitless field of application, for the state of war (limited as it may be) knows no limits. War itself is a principle of delineation. There can be no really open society, no society whose essence or identity (or both) is not to some extent threatened by a neighbouring or more distant society. Enclosure is the basic category of the political world, since the opposition between inside and outside establishes both its identity and its necessity.

The law of duality is a corollary of the split that founds political existence, that original sin for which utopian thought tries to forgive us (but for which remission can only be obtained in thought). It manifests a vertical formal constant that is perpendicular to the various observational sections cut through (organized or unorganized) matter. It is like a column rising up in the middle of a staircase, each of whose 'scientific' landings provides a different view.

Let us now briefly describe it by going down the staircase landing by landing.

(Jacobin) politics: 'What constitutes a republic is the total destruction of everything that is opposed to it' (Saint-Just). Ethology: the division between prey and predators is a fundamental law of the animal world. Ecology: the opposition between two categories of living beings—photo-autotrophes and heterotrophes—lies at the origin of the emergence of complex systems. The heterotrophes feed on photo-autotrophes, which feed on sunlight alone. Physics: 'If a system in which something is happening resists degradation, it is not an isolated system. It must be a privileged sub-system of an isolated system which necessarily includes one or more sub-systems bearing the weight of the degradation of the whole.' Human paleontology: Leroi-Gourhan has demonstrated the 'biological coherence of the "civilization-barbarism-savagery system" and the fact that the material progress of humanity was until our period connected with that system'. 'Like any other living organism, that system includes apparently privileged elements and obscure masses whose role is to supply the small reservoir of energy that allows it, albeit at enormous cost, to reach the next stage.'[2]

If those who are professionally involved in politics—ideologues and politicians—would learn by heart these principles, formulae and axioms whose pertinence is no longer in question (but merely problematic), it would save us all a lot of time and saliva. It would spare us the *moral fiction* which currently appears in two versions: on the right, the *sermon* (freedom and human rights) and, on the left, the *programme* (universal justice and classless society). Such a wish is, of course, quite vain because completely scientist (or objectivist): if it had no subjective moral motivations, the political combat would cease for lack of combatants. It is in fact in the nature of social organizations to want to shake off the yoke of organic nature—and it is that desire which defines them as social and distinguishes our organizations from organisms in general. But a critical approach such as ours, which is under no political obliga-

tion because it is trying to identify the nature of political obligation, will retain the dialectical relation of hostility that traverses the
various floors of nature, animate and inanimate alike, from top to
bottom. If we wanted to find the last instance or ground-floor of
the dialectical principle according to which contradiction is at the
heart of all things (the motor of the movement of things), in the
way that war is the motor of technical progress, we would have to
look for it in this basic infirmity: man cannot produce energy, he
can only transform it. In other words, production means destruction (and a refusal to destroy is a refusal to produce). If I produce
something here, I have destroyed something over there. It follows
that, in our field, collectivity A cannot produce and reproduce
itself as an organized group without disorganizing collectivity B,
without, that is, preventing B from producing and reproducing
itself by destroying A. If, as reality and the composition of forces
require, we replace 'destruction' with 'decrease or decline' and
'production' with 'growth or development', the logic remains the
same. Hence Mars, with his priests and walls.

All doctrines are exclusive because doctrine is a product of exclusion. A doctrinal corpus is hollow: it is produced from the outside,
through the negation of its negations and by reacting against a centrifugal process of fragmentation. According to Tertullian, orthodoxy necessarily gives rise to heresy, but that common-sense
deduction does not correspond to the observable facts. By a profoundly logical paradox, heresy produces orthodoxy, just as blas-
phemy produces anathema. The instance of death appears before
the resistance of life. The forces of dislocation produce and crystallize the forces of cohesion. Orthodoxy is the opposite of heresy,
just as negentropy is the opposite of entropy—logically and
chronologically, it comes first. Translation: an *ism* is a common
front drawn up by a common enemy. Give me a good enemy and I
will give you a good community.

The general phenomenon for which any theory of organization
(and, more generally, any theory of social development) has to account is the systematization of elements outside a system. How do
'ideas' come into politics? Raw material A is transformed into product B. How? Through the intervention of a third-party operator,
in this case the war situation. The transition is not theoretical but
strategic, and the principle of systematization is to be found not in

the nature of the elements present in *A*, but in the action of a critical milieu on a given theoretical raw material. It is not, then, surprising that doctrines flow from the marches, appearing on the effervescent fringes of empires and moving from the frontline to the 'civilized' centre. Doctrines are war machines, built not in a society's schools but in its arsenals. They come from the conversion of schools of thought into arms factories by the state of war (between ethnic groups, nations, religions or classes). The more polemical the notion of the *norm*, the more normative the notions produced by the polemic. Initially, they are regulatory, but they soon become repressive. The military element is the natural milieu for cultural normalization—and the median term in its logic.

The first collective security pact in our culture, namely Hellenism, was born of a rallying cry and a self-preservation reflex: 'Stop the Persians!' Curiously enough, the same cry and the same enemy can be seen in the late Empire as the source of the transformation of a modest Syriac cult, based upon a magma of oriental doctrines of salvation, into a universal religion complete with dogma, clergy and hierarchy. Our central *ism*—Catholicism—is also the product of a military conflict. On a smaller scale, but closer to home, the same phenomenon is visible in the 'birth of Protestantism', in the transformation of an *ecclesiola in Ecclesia* into a Church. The 'counter-reformation' intervenes between the raw material of the Reformation and the finished product of Protestantism. Armed struggle marks the transition from the evangelical spirit to dogmatic decisions, from the young Luther of Christian liberty to the intolerant leader of a state doctrine. The dividing line between Catholics and reformers was traced not with the pen of priests and pastors, but with blood and fire unleashed by princes and rogues. Only twelve years separate the ninety-five theses of the young Augustine monk from the first recorded use of the vulgar term *protestant* (1517–1729), but that period witnessed the massacre of Münzer's peasants and the death of the first Evangelical martyrs in Antwerp. First, there are protests against Charles Quint (Second Diet of Spire). Then a regroupment in order to survive: the Smalkaldic League. Finally, the theological system of the Small and the Large Catechism produced an internally homogeneous and externally refractory whole. Nevertheless, it was still necessary to 'subdue the Anabaptists with corporal punishment'

(Luther), to say nothing of crushing the Nicodemites, the supporters of Zwingli and all sorts of other visionaries. Shortly afterwards, the re-establishment of the Inquisition and the creation of
the Papal Index precipitated the crystallization of Calvinism. Officially converted as early as 1536, Geneva became a sanctuary with
the publication of Calvin's Cathechism (1541) and Ordinances
(1542). Commitment and indoctrination, militarization and institutionalization of evangelical communities everywhere went hand in
hand. Half-way through the century, the reform spirit solidified into the reformed churches. The prophet, the conqueror and the
administrator were all linked. Faith, law and regimentation provide
the parallels between the European Reformation of the sixteenth
century and the world-wide revolution of the twentieth. In both
cases, the first generation makes the breakthrough by being inven-
tive, imaginative and hot-headed. The second generation governs
the bastions by establishing dogmas and drawing lines. An orthodoxy, be it secular or religious, is what is left of a victory when
the war is over.

Doctrinal stublization will remain on the agenda of the 'life of
the mind' so long as political destabilization is still on the agenda of
social life. It is consubstantial with it. Sweep the front doorstep as
long as you like, you will still find *isms* in the gutter, simply because
the Persians are at the gates of the city. Such is their nature and
their vocation. If the Medes did not exist we would have to invent
them. No need: a historical culture is already such an invention.
Any living culture can be defined as the continuous creation of Barbarians.

3. The Constantine Complex

Constantine is the Oedipus of the political unconscious. However, their symmetrical stories are also very different in that one is a
history within history while the other is *the myth of a myth*. There
is a Constantine legend, but Constantine's reign lasted for thirty
years, and there is nothing legendary about that. Paradoxically, the
real base worked to the detriment of the saint of orthodoxy, whose
exemplary history is fairly well known. Not all accounts are
hagiographies.[3] The poetic fiction of Oedipus, on the other hand,
was guaranteed its ubiquity from the start.

Apart from the difference between historical and mythological material, Constantine represents a positive version of Oedipus. Our most pious emperor killed his eldest son and then his wife (in 326), not his father. The double murder did not result in exile, but involved a bloody confirmation of his earlier conversion. For the moment, we can leave this mark of family piety on one side, although it does remind us that the apostles of Christianity had a sense of organization too. (Constantine awarded himself the title of 'The Thirteenth Apostle'.) Constantine built, Oedipus destroyed. The Roman monarch won a kingdom, the king of Thebes lost his. Freud compared the unfolding of Sophocles's tragedy with the process of an individual analysis: the epic of Constantine reveals the process of collective synthesis. Constantine is the symbolic invariant in the synthesis and therefore the incarnation of 'good' government, just as Oedipus is the invariant in the analysis and the incarnation of 'bad' government. The true story of Constantine has the value of a transhistorical myth, containing as it does the concept of the consolidation of political totalities. It is as if everything the Emperor touched became solid (*solidus*, entire, complete). Even money: it is to him that we owe the gold *solidus*, the basis of the first lasting monetary system.

Where better than in the genesis of Orthodoxy to see the emergence of the little orthodoxies that succeeded it? The hard kernel of the political unconscious is displayed in all its glory in Constantine's inauguration of Christianity at the beginning of our era, and all the episodes make sense once we refuse to undo the knot. Render unto Christ what is Christ's—his teaching and his death—and unto Constantine what is Constantine's—the institution of Christianity. And in order to do so, render unto the man all his attributes, military, political and religious. This genesis merges with the history of a city, and the content of orthodoxy coincides exactly with the city perimeter it defines. Constantinople, the advance post of Roman civilization, was planned in 326 and dedicated by Constantine in 330. Constantine was the first sovereign to draw up a doctrine, a barrier and a banner in military formation. Three units in one: the novelty is still there. *In hoc signo vences*. The *labarum* has kept its promise: the Christian West has, in terms of power, had the better of its rival civilizations. 'The queen' of cities deserves to be to the Christian community what Mecca is to the

Muslim community and what Leningrad is to the 'socialist' community: its authentic and most precious holy city. It brought
together the new Rome and the new Jerusalem (like two pieces of
the True Cross) at the point where East and West met and confronted each other. The capital of the Byzantine Empire (*obit*
1453), the most powerful and long-lasting capital ever seen in the
Greek world was built on that spot. A thousand years of stability
on the very edge of the *oikoumene*: that in itself should be of interest to anyone studying the conditions of the formation and
stability of human aggregates. But the stupefying repression of
Byzantium by the conscious mind of our culture, which seems to
cultivate the memory of its official origins simply in order to conceal its real origins, suggests that something much more important
is at stake. Staring at Rome or Jerusalem means that we can avoid
looking at our own image in Constantinople. Could it be that no
one is able to look his destiny in the face with impunity?

Constantine unites in his person the figures of the sovereign, the
warrior and the theologian—figures which modern political
philosophy normally keeps apart. This human synthesis produces
unity at every level. He finds an Empire torn apart by and under the
rule of the Tetrarchy: he puts an end to secession and re-establishes
a monarchy. He finds a Church in fragments, a mosaic of juxtaposed bishoprics: he regroups the dioceses into prefectures, maps out
the provincial synods and gives the emergent ecclesiastical institution an administrative, jurisdictional and disciplinary basis. He
finds Christian doctrine torn apart by the effects of the Arian crisis
and by national differences: he calls the first general assembly of
'nations' (Nicaea) and the first of the Church's ecumenical Councils (325), and personally promotes the first definition of dogma to
have imperative value in the West. It is also at Constantinople that
the Church born of Christ is baptized 'catholikos' or universal.
Well might we talk of a genius for organization, but the case of
Constantine is not simply that of a good administrator. He provides a universally valid proof in that he unveils the secret of producing the universal: namely, the interdependence of the different
levels of organization. It is the unbearable coherence of his totalizing approach that makes the founder of Orthodoxy much more
than the father of 'Byzantine Caesaropapacy' and certainly much
more than the presumptive ancestor of 'modern totalitarianism': he

is the living fulfilment of a basic collective wish. Everyone knows Constantine's dream—the one painted by Piero della Francesca (*In hoc signo vences*). If you want to defeat your rivals Maxentius and Licinius, take the cross as your emblem. But no political leader would dream of modelling himself on Constantine, precisely because he is the paradigm of legitimacy. What has to be repressed here is not merely the fact that our official religion was established by force of arms (the battle of Milvian Bridge) and that the truth of the 'true god' has for seventeen hundred years rested upon what was in the last instance a political decision made by a hesitant warrior-chief. There is also the fact that the political, the religious and the military were originally indivisible and that their conceptual unity, taken to the point of incandescence; has the tangible form of a historical process which gave birth to our modern history.

Although universal, the *Constantine complex* is the nightmare of the West. Rightly so, for it is a nightmare about its own origins. The past retained by the unconscious never quite passes away. Although it has been weakened by almost immediate vulgarization, we cannot refrain from using the term *complex* in its original sense of a set of *operations* with a high organizational (or negentropic) value that are partly or fully repressed by the collective censor. The term is applicable here because there is both *combination* and *compulsion*. Orthodox behaviour is a compulsive tangle of elementary forms of behaviour, borrowed from deceptively distinct or secretly interconnected networks. The Constantine complex derives not from a pathogenic kernel, but from a function that structures working political totalities. There is therefore no hope of eliminating the pathogenic element and regaining our health. Like the Oedipus complex, it personifies the basic schema of a triangular relationship (War, Territory, Dogma) by giving an extreme value to delineation compulsions whose traces can be seen in the most relaxed and least totalitarian collectives. Clinical observation provides very few examples of individuals who really have unwittingly killed their fathers and married their mothers. Historical observation provides very few examples of political leaders who have had the opportunity to reunite an empire, found a capital, establish a state religion, slaughter their family and promulgate the dogma of the Incarnation. In both cases, the norm is to be seen in an exemplary monstrosity: a destiny which sleeps in us all comes to life to tell us: 'You too must have gone through this without actually reaching it, and you will always have to fight against it'. Awareness of the inevitable is liberating: ignorance of it is repressive. Just as 'every human being has to face the struggle to overcome the Oedipus complex', so every emergent political body has to negotiate with the Constantine that sleeps within it on the least unfavourable conditions possible. We are now separated from our truth by a fragile screen of indifference. But, to paraphrase the letter to Fliess, every collective formation, no matter how small, bears within it the seeds of a Constantine the Great. He lives on in its phantasies, and every age is terrified at the fulfilment of its dream-become-reality. The extent of its fear depends upon the degree of repression that separates its infantile state from its present state. We have been walking in circles ever since the founding of Constantinople, which was an *en-cyclo-pedia* in the strict sense of the word. We have here a local history that combines a treatise of the origins of God, a summary of universal history and a precis of the interpretation of dreams. Let us look more closely.

Orthodoxy is initially a place—not just anywhere but a dangerous and therefore fortified place. There is nothing new about the strategic value of straits. Here, we are facing the Persians at just the right distance from the Danube, the most threatened frontier in the Empire under attack from both Goths and Sarmates. Constantine chose the Greek village of Byzantium (Byzos) as the site for his new capital, in preference to Alexandria or Antioch (the greatest city in the Roman East), because it was the ideal position from which to break an encirclement. The city was built facing East like a citadel, so that the barbarians could be denied access to the Bosphorus. (Facing in the same direction was Constantine's famous statue on its porphyry column, the symbol of the city.) The Eastern replica of the Eternal City (senate, praetors, etc.) was more real than the original. The delineation of the second Rome was actually carried out in accordance with the legendary rituals of the founding of the original. A divinely protective space was sanctified: after the *consecratio*, which abolished the profane character of the chosen space, came the *dedicatio* that set the seal on its religious allegiance. The whole process was reflected in the perimeter of orthodoxy—a notion at once sacred and political, and therefore territorial. Initially, the word 'orthodox' was applied to everything inside the walls, because anything that did not belong to Constantinople was alien and therefore 'barbarian'. So there was an opposition between the good side of the Bosphorus and its bad side (the Persian side). Orthodoxy and demarcation go hand in hand, and the orthodox canon itself confirms that doctrine is a fortified place. Although the earliest definition was a purely topographical result of a strategy of geographical divisions, the geography certainly had its strategic importance. Orthodoxy originally designated the territory of Byzantium—the control of a certain administrative territory—but it later came to denote loyalty to the Nicaean faith (a religious metaphor for political loyalty) and, still later, the 'ultimate sign of Roman civilization', the supreme rampart of identity. The combination of faith-king-law welds together the links in a chain of identification: integrity of faith, loyalty to the king and obedience to the law, and thereby transforms heresies into 'crimes against the *res publica*'. 'Imperial legitimacy and orthodoxy are indivisible because the heritage of Rome cannot be divided' (Dagron). Orthodoxy did not produce the Capital: it was the other way around. Constantine *first* traced the outline of the closed space on the ground (with the point of a lance, according to legend) and *then* traced it in the texts. Just as the unity of the Empire was re-established not by movement from the part to the whole but by integration of the parts into a pre-given whole, so the unity of the Catholic faith (assured by the universal legislation emanating solely from the ecumenical councils) was not the syncretic product of successive articles of faith. Although it was elaborated over a long period of history and in the face of numerous vicissitudes, dogmatics is not in itself historical. It is immediately inscribed in space as a closed and already organized form with a variable geometry.

Constantine was God's Vauban. He built concentric fortifications in accordance with a logic of staggered yet static defence: dogma as 'the expression and rampart of the faith', faith as 'the rampart and expression of the Empire', the new city as the shield of the new faith (the *palladium* of Latin civilization). The walls were built before the houses (and they themselves came before the inhabitants). Our great unifier and stabilizer worked with marks and de-finitions. The man had, if we can put it this way, the frontier in his blood. Born on the edge of the Empire, trained for a military career on the *limes*, acquainted with the Breton, Spanish and German borders, he seems to have spent his life keeping watch on every possible covered way—religious, geographical and institutional. The monotheist circumference—put forward in 325 as a thesis at Nicaea—closes the unity of the restored Empire. The paradox is that, for the sphere of imperial sovereignty to be extended and secured, the diffuse and floating sanctity of the late Empire had to be tightened and concentrated as much as possible on the person of Christ.

Legend has it that, after many hesitations and trial marriages with other doctrines of salvation, Constantine converted to Christianity on the eve of (and in preparation for) a difficult battle in 312, the year of Milvian Bridge. Since it was the custom at that time to win *instinctu divinitatis*, it was evidently important not to choose the wrong divinity. However, we know that the conversion did not take place until Constantine was near to death (the banal calculation being that you could arrive in heaven with the fewest possible sins). Although his faith was bolstered by military success, there was nothing mystical about it and he did not offer himself without receiving something in return. According to Zosimos, Constantine was an unprincipled man: our first dogmatist was a straightforward opportunist who rallied to the cause of Christ out of pure self-interest. But no psychological interpretation—true or false—can conceal the political logic of Constantine's choice or the opportuneness of transforming the mystery of the Incarnation into the centre of gravity of collective belief once the definitive 'seizure of power' had been carried out.

Christianity provided the emperor with a guarantee of absence. Like the gods of the Neoplatonists, the Christian god was a hidden god, inaccessible to mere mortals. No one could see the dead Christ, whereas the deified emperors who had until then assured the unity of the Empire were no longer credible because they could be seen, either in the flesh or in images, by all and sundry.[4] It is said that Constantine briefly experimented with the *Sol invictus*—the image of the king of heaven—as a unifying principle. It was further away, but even more visible. The god of the Christians was known as the sun of justice, but had the advantage of being invisible and of warming hearts alone. From Julius Caesar (supreme pontiff during his lifetime and posthumously deified by his adoptive son Augustus) to Diocletian, the tendency to deify the imperial person went hand in hand with the increasing fragility of the Empire's political cohesion. The imperial cult of the state was becoming overblown and ruining the basis of the state. According to Suetonius, no living man had the right to be considered a god; and it is true that, in the early empire, the emperor was 'divine' or 'brilliant' but not actually a god. He was regarded as a descendant of the gods or venerated as the father of the nation—the household god of the great house. However, only the function was worshipped—the apotheosis was personal but posthumous. The cult evolved from the theophanic sovereign to the god incarnate: after the Severine dynasty, for instance, the emperors were openly referred to as gods. This change resulted in the disintegration of the Roman Empire, not only because of the accelerated rotation at the summit, but because of the multiplication of allogenic divinities of all shapes and sizes. Petronius could once remark: 'Our country is so crowded with divinities that it is easier to meet a god than a man.'[5] Thus, after the death of Diocletian, the Empire was divided among seven heirs, all called Augustus and all divine. Which saint to turn to? By devaluing the object of signification, the inflation of the signifiers of the sacred gave religious cults a very low organizational productivity. Political unity was no longer guaranteed by a primal hole. The divorce between the new oriental-style religious mentality (which tended to heighten divine transcendence) and the increasingly immanent legitimacy of the Caesars made the lack of a stabilizing lack patently obvious in the here and now. The fluctuating metapolitical basis of political loyalty entailed that authority could no longer be transmitted in a regular, peaceful manner.

The 'new David's' stroke of genius in this conjuncture was the (intuitive) realization that there can be no personal power because all commanders are lieutenants. By taking the title of Vicar of Christ, the Emperor came down from the altar, but ipso facto the Empire went up to it as a collective body. The real personification of the sacred element in society (*I* am the *we*) has everything to gain from an apparent depersonalization of power (as an individual, I am unimportant; my power belongs to you). By projecting it on to

the Other, Constantine denied himself divinity. He could then
govern or speak in the name of the Other without making people
laugh. His apparent demotion in the divine hierarchy was the key to
the reconstitution of power. What the leader of the terrestrial City
gave to the bride of Christ, the representative of the City of God
received back a hundred times over in terms of political authority.
After Constantine, the Emperor abandoned the title *Imperator
Caesar* in favour of *Dominus noster*. The substitution of *principat*
for *dominat* is anything but a *diminutio capitis*. For majesty is in-
direct: it does not spring from the man but reflects back on him. By
swearing fidelity to Christ, the ideal mediator, Constantine re-
established the fading boundaries between the human and divine
levels and set himself up as the effective mediator: the worship of
the Emperor became the visible expression of the worship of
Christ, and the population of the Empire once more became God's
people. Loyalism was guaranteed (in principle).

The break between Diocletian and Constantine centred not on
the finality of imperial action, but on the *means* to assure the cohesion of a swollen Empire in the face of internal and external centrifugal tensions (barbarian incursions, economic crisis, etc.). The
various heads of state were all more or less aware that the road to
political *renovatio* led through religious *restitutio*. But only Constantine realized that the total state would be a state of lack. Using
the accounting techniques of incompleteness, he concentrated upon
Christ, backed scarcity, created a void around himself ... and won.
Dicoletian and his predecessors backed superlatives (*Jupiter
exsuperantissimus*), flooded the divinity market and achieved nothing. At a time when only an absolute could save relations between
the various parts of the Empire, the pagan emperors did not have
the religious means to achieve their absolutist ends and looked in
vain to a reinforcement of the imperial cult, a revival of old traditions or an accumulation of local cults. Constantine acquired the
means through a process of subtraction. He stripped himself of the
attributes of adoration and bathed in reflected glory. He was no
longer a god, but had divinity lent to him. The emperor opted for
the One God and gave Him responsibility for choosing the emperor
as His delegate on earth. Monotheism traded for monarchy: the
give-and-take of the Edict of Milan. I make the sacred a state issue;

you sanctify my state. In the long run, however, the founder quite logically gained the upper hand over the foundation. The ecclesiastical institution would survive the collapse of the Empire, and Christian imperialism would outlive imperial Christianity.[6]

Constantine thus remedied the diseconomies of scale produced by the indiscriminate addition of foreign gods to the central Pantheon. The bigger the political territory to be covered, the fewer absolutes it needs; and once a certain geographic or demographic threshold is reached, it is more productive to have only one god. Polytheism is a luxury for small-scale republics and modest cities.

The rise of the monotheist imperative spontaneously rationalized the political investment. It is in fact easier to deal with one absentee than with several. Savings in heavenly absence will allow the group to economize on belief (or spending) below. The cost of authority will fall accordingly. Fewer 'holes', fewer 'leaks'. Principle of sufficient reason: when a parish has several saints and wants to last, it eventually dedicates itself to one. Social theodicies (or sociodicies) optimize their performance by having only one god, as can be seen from the polytheist gluts of the Roman Empire, the unviable nature of theoretical triads (Marxism–Leninism–Mao-Tse-tung–Thought) and the purely formal character of dyads (Marxism-Leninism). Soviet society has in fact only one divine founder: Lenin. And the Communist counter-societies finally had to choose a single term of reference. A similar phenomenon of decantation may be seen in the micro-societies that grew on the Christian trunk: sects which tried to socialize God by incorporating him into the daily life of the group proved less viable (or more easily eliminated) than Churches more openly respectful of divine transcendence and more strictly polarized between profane and sacred life. Basically, the act of coming together requires an absolute, but the collectivization of the absolute exhausts the collective. It is less tiring to love one another through a single transcendent principle than it is mutually to worship one another (as, in a sense, the Albigensians, Montanists and Bogomiles tried to do).

The chief still had to secure the source of his authority. The disappearance of the divine king did in fact open up the possibility that a glut of absence might give way to a shortage, that an unbridgeable gulf might open up between men and god, subjects and sovereign. Hence Constantine's insistence that his fellow bishops adopt the mystery of the Incarnation as a dogma. Subsequently, a tendency to deny Christ's divinity posed a serious threat to the stability of institutions. If he was a man like any other, why should anyone obey his representatives? Ultimately, that was what was at stake in Arianism, the most dangerous heresy of the day.

If God (or the Word) exists fully *within* Christ, popular piety may confuse Father and Son or even serve the Father by worshipping the purely imaginary figure of the Son. Arius defended the Father's identity against this idolatrous deviation, stressing that his nature was different to that of the Son and maximizing the 'man' element in Christ in order to restore the 'god' element to its full transcendence. Christ was born at a certain time on a certain day in a certain year. God, the principle behind all life, is uncreated (*agenotos*). God created the Word to exist alongside Him, but 'there was a time when the Word did not exist' and nor, therefore, did the incarnation of the Word. Christ is not an accident, but the divine essence does not flow through him and could ultimately do without him. Arianism accepted the divine powers of Jesus, but not the divine nature of his physical person. However, if the Flesh is external to the Word, it follows that one can remain outside the Flesh of Christ, the Church led by Peter's successor, without thereby betraying one's duty to God. Not by chance did Arius begin his career as a heresiarch by challenging the authority of his bishop. It is impossible to question the nature of the relationship between Christ and God the Father without eventually questioning one's duty to obey the bride of Christ and one's obedience to its leader and all who derive their authority from him. Of these, the most important of all is the Emperor-Bishop.

If, on the one hand, the Church is part of an all-too-human Flesh, it is no longer deified and cannot deify: laymen will no longer render it the honours due. In other words, they will no longer pay their taxes. Why serve the bride of a natural man, even if he was superior? Conversely, if the Church represents a being whose nature is completely divine, what relationship can there be between such a god and his designated servants? Why not relate to him outside the institution? The Church has either too much or too little charisma. The Incarnation had to find a way between Scylla and Charbydis, because both extreme solutions threatened the basis of political authority. Logically enough, the first to be concerned was Constantine, an emperor quite determined to continue his trade.

In order to safeguard the unity of the state (at least for the remainder of his reign), Constantine had at all costs had to reinforce his religious base. As a general rule, the more centralized the State, the more simplicity and homogeneity it requires. Too much emphasis on the dual nature of Christ might weaken the new imperial power by eventually separating spiritual and temporal powers, legitimacy and legality. It was in Constantine's interests to unite in Christ, and so he called all available bishops to Nicaea and told them in no uncertain terms that he expected them to approve a synthetic motion that would ruin the hopes of the Arians. In 325, the Son was declared 'begotten but not created', the truly divine son of a true god. The mystery of the Incarnation became the State Church's first article of faith. The year 325 is an important date: it may even mark the beginning of our era.

Constantine's peace closed a chapter in world history, but it opened the great book of political theology and therefore initiated a long and complex period of violence which cannot be fitted into the peaceful grid of our academic categories. For theological controversy is at once political, national, hermeneutic, military and metaphysical. The debate over the dogma of the Incarnation tore the Christian Orient apart for centuries. The reason why the West was less affected is simply that it was more barbarous. Since the great duel between Arians and Monophysites (who went to the opposite extreme and tried to maximize the divine element in Christ) did not touch the West, Byzantium became the very laboratory of our civilization. This is not surprising if we remember that Christianity is an Eastern religion: it originally spoke Greek, for that was the language of the Hellenistic East, the last refuge of classicism. Nor should it be forgotten that the Western Empire was invaded by Barbarians, whereas there is no break in continuity between the Ancient World and the Middle Ages in the Eastern Empire, which was spared the invasions. Only there was it possible to achieve that singular alloy of logical and terminological rigour and popular passion which characterized these subtle and bloody wars—a world in which everything hinged on the one-letter difference between *homoousios* (Christ's consubstantiality with the Word) and *homoiousious*, (similarity to the Word).

The rival heresies were openly organized into political parties—and Catholic historians of the Church try to thread their way through these confused labyrinths (which specialists still have difficulty in mapping) by using the language of politics: the 'Nicaean party', the 'Arianist far left', or even 'a broad majority coalition against Arianism'. The bishops and the leaders of the various schools in the cantons of emerging Christendom began their electoral campaigns with epistles, but they usually ended them *manu militari*. In the interim, a treatise on dogma could serve as a diplomatic note and an adjective as an ultimatum. The metropolitan crowds waited with bated breath for the results of the successive councils (the question not being whether the left or the right would form the government, but whether substance or similarity would carry the day). Riots, pitched battles, hostage-taking: of course theology was a code for national confrontations, but over a period of three centuries, men were killed in huge numbers for the sake of an iota. Hence the paradox: the structures of the West were debated and decided in the East. It is there that the dramatic kernel of world conquest was conceptualized.

The mystery of the Incarnation is the central fact of our culture. It introduced modernity as the organizing and driving principle of a threefold ascent, scientific, asethetic and political. Negative proof: places untouched by Constantine's dogma developed neither pictorial perspective nor a constant ratio between two sets of phenomena visible to the naked eye, neither history as an epic idea nor history as the epic of an idea. Why did Western space, informed by the Christian religion after Antiquity, become the chosen land and testing-ground for the sciences of nature in the sixteenth century, the plastic arts—painting in the fifteenth century, cinema in the twentieth—and the great philosophies of history in the nineteenth century? In other words, why has the West been able to conquer the planet by making *its* intellectual and material culture *the* world civilization? Whilst there is obviously no simple answer to the question and no single cause for all those developments, any attempt to knock this spread of power off its theological pedestal will sin by naivety (that is, by modernism).

The Christian incarnation is at the origin of our *political faith*. When he agreed to be born and to die for our redemption, the Christian God sanctified profane history by giving it a meaning—one specific meaning. The intelligible world of meaning and the irreversible world of events were superimposed. Belief in this god-as-process assumes that history does not advance in vain, that it has a real origin and destination. A belief in history-as-process presupposes that the transcendent works in the immanent and that the only way to gain access to the transcendent is to pass through the immanent. This is the first condition of possibility of politics as the supreme art, of salvation as political masterpiece. Once the rational logos has come to dwell in the real, we can in our turn grasp the totality of the real by making its hidden rationality our own. This is also the first condition of possibility of history as the supreme science upon which the efficacy of individual salvation depends. If the Word which dwelt in heaven came down to earth to suffer like anyone else, it is the duty of all men on earth to suffer, in full self-awareness, in order to reach heaven. *Homo politicus* is simply another name for *homo viator*, and he is an effect of the imitation of Jesus Christ who was sent to live in the world of men in order to attack it from within. For a long time, it has seemed obvious that there is a single Subject of History (Humanity, the Nation, the Proletariat); a single direction to history (the unilinear succession of modes of production, ages of the human spirit, the stages of technical development); and a single end to history or prehistory (the socialist revolution, the League of Nations, universal respect for human rights). If it is only in the Christianized West that this obviousness has been articulated in the form of a discourse, it is because it expresses the curious theological assumption that one God used his *only son* to make laws for all men. It follows that the flesh of Christ, the Apostolic Church of Rome, has to be unique and catholic (just as, in later stages, a nation in revolution becomes *the* great nation and a 'vanguard' political party becomes *the* Party). The *urbi et orbi* of papal blessings, the unicity of God's Son and the universality of the message are all bound up with one another. If Christ had not been fully and completely God, if he had had, for instance, a younger brother, none of our modern philosophies of history would have been possible (we could neither have dreamed of them without laughing nor lived through them without crying). The very fact that even in our agnostic eyes there can be a relation of biunivocal equivalence between a discourse (logic) and a form of behaviour (politics), or that a political logic can even exist, would have had no impact upon our immediate history ('we demand an explanation') if the bridges between God and sinners, heaven and earth, the Word and the Flesh had been destroyed. The passion for programmes and justifications (strategy and propaganda), which is at once our burden and our pride, can also be traced back through Constantine to St John.

At the time of Constantine's death, it was merely a matter of elucidating a conjunction which contained the major unthought question of our time and was in itself a problem. Christ was like you and me, carnal and corruptible, *and* like no one else (his flesh was the word, immortal and transcendent). The *and* indicates not an addition but a union of two natures, one divine, the other human, in the person of Christ. How did that union come about, in what order and in what proportions? How can two become one?

It may seem surprising that the basic principle behind the certainties of Christianity—namely, the divine nature of Christ—should have given rise to so many doubts and uncertainties. The point is that any decision of principle necessarily has repercussions on the organization of the Church's authority. 'Political divisions slip into the pages of dogmatics. The theological meditation on the Incarnation should therefore be read as a grammar of the State.'[7] The articulation of the dogma accompanied the constitution of the Church as a single and centralized apparatus of authority. The various doctrines that appear in the course of the first seven Councils follow the establishment of the Church's internal structures of order with its pyramid of centres, metropolises and patriarchates. As an integral synthesis, Christian doctrine is an effect of government. And it was the Incarnation that 'set' the pivot of the hierarchial system. The establishment of the dogma of the Incarnation put an end to the shifting interpretations of the gospels and to the fluctuating frontiers of central authority. Anything that might seem irrational in the definition of an article of faith—in this case its very content—becomes coherent when examined in the light of the cohesion it gives to a doctrinal and geographical territory threatened with fragmentation by the vortices of heresy. The heretics on the other hand seem to have wanted to rationalize the Revelation by eliminating one of the terms whose union produces the mystery common to the person of Christ and the nature of governments. Faced with the God-Man, a normally constituted analytic mind familiar with the basic logical principles of identity, non-contradiction, etc. has to tackle a puzzling dilemma. If he is a man, he cannot really be God, and if he is God he cannot really be a man. Alternatively, if Christ has two natures, he must be two people, for how can two become one? By accepting the absurdity as it stood, the mystery became a mystical record of a cybernetic rationality that still resists analysis.

After the Council of Ephesus (431), which failed to reconcile the rival theses, came the Council of Chalcedonia (451), at which Cyril of Alexandria, the Doctor of the Incarnation, provided the miraculous solution. He found a way to reconcile the claims that Christ had either too great or too small a proportion of human nature. His solution prevailed and became doctrine. Since Chalcedonia, the union of two natures in the person of the Son of God has been known as the 'hypostatic union'. The Holy Fathers had already borrowed the notion of hypostasis from the doctrine of Plotinus and the Alexandrians in order to resolve the enigmatic dogma of the Trinity: 'one substance, three persons or hypostases' (Father, Son and Holy Ghost). Fifteen hundred years later, the theologians of the Curia frown at the very mention of Cyril's terminological masterpiece and keep saying that 'we cannot be too careful when it comes to the hypostatic union'. After all, the unity of the organization and leadership of the Catholic Church is at stake. If in 1980, the vast majority of the Christian Churches of the East (Syrian, Uniate, Armenian, Copt, etc.) are still 'separate', it is because they refuse to accept the decisions taken at the Council of 451.

It took, therefore, a long and complex elaboration to bring off the delicate (conceptual) manoeuvre which allows the Eternal to appear in history, the Verb to be born of a Virgin and, more generally, the spirit to be made flesh. A process of exclusion finally led to the right word. The hypostatic union of divine and human nature, which is at the heart of the mystery of the Incarnation, does not designate and will not designate itself a mere union (*enosis*), mixture (*mixis*) or fusion (*krasis*). It is a communication (*antidosis*) between two idioms or two natures. The black box of Christianity is contained within this communication or exchange between two terms, in which each can be transformed into its opposite without losing its own nature. It was very much in the interests of theology, queen of sciences and science of kings, to make it an article of faith inaccessible to natural reason. Touchstones would not be what they are—or not for long—if they were not untouchable. Theoretically unable to elucidate the source of its power over minds and bodies, the Church triumphant makes an impenetrable divine reason responsible for its own claim to be recognized as bearer of the word of God and legislator for the whole world.

The Greek for rudder, as in the ship of state, is *kubernes*. The Greek for to govern is *kubernao*. The modern word *cybernetics* applies to all those theories relating to the processing of information, or to the programmed transformation of a communication into a command, information into execution.

3

Atopia

1. Strategy Versus Utopia

Utopias are basically atopias. No place and therefore no future. The question to be put to them is not 'Yes, but when?', but 'Yes, but where?'. Their inability to answer the second question settles the first. They are ahistorical because they are astrategic. It is typical of all utopian socialisms—Marxism included—that they exclude the factor of war from their plans. All the makers of idylls (and disasters) make the same 'little oversight': they fail to reckon with the enemy. Societies without frontiers can do away with wars from the outset. No neighbours, no wars. Ever since Thomas More, this non-place has taken the canonic form of the *island*. It is the home of a happy, isolated group, but no map-reference is ever given. The reality of the island is a deliberate denegation: no to all possible places. It is no more than a stage-set, where the actors relate only to one another. These kingdoms without kings have the privilege of being at once far away and at the centre of everything, thus combining the advantages of the periphery and the metropolis. This space without polarities or division is therefore non-strategic in that it is at once totally open (no frontiers) and totally closed on itself (no outside)—a cosmic microcosm with no hidden or dark side, in which claustration means plenitude rather than limitation. Owen wanted to utopianize the world, in other words to make it an island. Non-strategic means non-dialectical: the ideal society is never a nation. National messianisms do exist, but utopia denies nationalism by drowning it in an abstract generality. The island is at once a place in the world and the whole world, just as the phalanstery is both the world on a small scale and a small world. The impotence of utopianism lies in this inability to think the universal as a concrete singularity: it dissolves the particular into the universal and can therefore produce nothing more than hollow generalities. Such projects for salvation, which give mankind messages without a bearer, are hollow and therefore universalist messianisms, condemned to endless abstract lamentation of the 'bad' state of the world. Just as a political construction which leaves no room for myth and imagination has to be described as unrealistic, so any self-transparent society which has no outside must be abstract in that it assumes the possibility of colour without space and produces a mystique without mystery.

The *City of the Sun* receives its totalization ready-made. This closed totality, a pure present with no past, is a gift of nature, not the result of historical confrontation. In their immediate existence, the blessed island colonies, phalansteries and Icarias do not have to turn themselves into fortresses because they cannot be besieged. They know no economic blockades—and therefore no shortages (no queues outside the collective shops). No threat of invasion—and therefore no defence forces or military service. No foreigners, no espionage and therefore no counter-espionage. No terrorism and no sabotage: no need for a police force. An undivided society, a festive society. Their geographical isolation crystallizes a state of weightlessness, a social state of grace reached by bathing in the sea and washing away duality—the 'original sin' of politics. No possibility of destabilization, and therefore no need for stabilizers. The status quo is not a transaction between two dynamics but the immobile enjoyment of divine immobility. Pure duration—of the self and by the self. The hell with adversity, adversaries and entropy. This blessed state is known as the eternity of the moment, and the joy of the festival is merely its small change. A seventh heaven and a dream world—who would be mad enough to argue against that?

'I like to be alone,' said Fourier. The political dream is the fulfilment of a universal wish for solitude. The height of pleasure is to be alone in company—hence the joys of the phalanstery. Utopians enjoy themselves and give us pleasure, all at the same time. Which is why all criticism is beside the point. Not surprisingly, the kill-joy rationalist gets a poor reception: he talks about the real, and that is less gratifying than the pleasure principle which social utopias promise in tautologies of varying complexity. The non-political is obviously more pleasurable than the political, and no one would disagree that it is more pleasant to make love in peace than to make war in uniforms, to feast than to work, to commune than to tear each other apart. Political Reason is reduced to silence by Utopia, because there is no refuting a dream. A political utopia has its logic, but utopia is not the product of a logical discourse. The possible/impossible opposition is not pertinent here; it has to give way to the pleasant/unpleasant opposition. Hence the vanity of all rational critiques of utopian constructions: they debit their object with the unreality that forms the basis of their credit. The production of utopias is as vital to political health as oneiric activity is to mental health. In its own terms, it is both legitimate and indispensable. It would be as stupid and sadistic to stop a society dreaming as it would be to stop an individual doing so: the behavioural problems it would cause would very rapidly put the victim's life and personality at risk. Similarly, there is no reason to fear that the utopian vein will run out: utopia has no end because it fulfils a social need, just as a dream fulfils the physiological need to deny social reality by dreaming. Compared with singers of serenades, the Cassandras of positive history suffer from an insufferable handicap: it is impossible not to agree with the commonplaces of pleasure, the only platforms that are open to all. It should, however, be noted that whereas the demand for utopias is a social constant, the market in utopias is subject to historical fluctuations. The production of utopias is cyclical. Roughly speaking, peaceful periods of social development spontaneously produce utopianism and dangerous periods produce orthodoxy. A well-established order can tolerate projects for disorder, but once disorder has been unleashed, it runs for the shelter of order. When no serious threat hangs over spaces that have been made secure, the individual feels a greater need to keep his distance (for example, by setting sail for far-off lands) and the room for manoeuvre increases between the imaginary and the real. But when the danger of real dislocation reappears, the group has to close ranks and reconstitute a territory in which it can survive, come what may: it expels intruders and fills in gaps. The history of society thus alternates between utopian dilation and orthodox contraction, conceptual limitation of ends and material limitation of means of existence: the diastole and systole of the social heart.

The political utopia, with its beautiful dream of a religion without a Church, regularly slips into the slender interegnum that separates a declining Church from one undergoing reconstruction. The need for religion outlives the institution and goes on producing dreams of Atlantis until the next war breaks out and stiffens the new faith into a new law. More describes his island in 1516, Erasmus writes the *Praise of Folly* in 1511 and Rabelais describes Thélème in 1534: before the outbreak of the civil wars. The republican utopias of eighteenth-century France rise from the ashes of the monarchy just before the establishment of the harsh Jacobin Republic, but Bernardin de Saint-Pierre's work cannot survive that of Saint-Just. The development of political praxis always leads to the destruction of island utopias, as if there were a relation between the ink and the blood a historical era is ready to spill for its projects of happiness. Utopia is born in and of peacetime because it cannot think war and flounders in the squalls of civil and world conflict. The major utopian thinkers of the modern world—Fourier, Saint-Simon, Owen, Proudhon, Marx—gave birth to their theoretical wonders in the long peaceful years of the nineteenth century—after the revolutionary and Napoleonic wars and before the great cataclysms. Similarly, the limited but fruitful period of relaxation which the industrial West is now enjoying—forty years of civil and international peace—encourages the singing of lullabies. We are once more living in a period in which it is feasible to embark for Cythera (Illich, Marcuse, Touraine, Morin, etc.). There is no answer to that, unless you simply want to look disgruntled. You cannot demonstrate on paper that a paper-boat can never be seaworthy or ready for war. The only way to prove it irrefutably is to launch the boat. Until then, we can politely resign ourselves to the fact that all theories are equally valid (on paper) and that, in the immediate and in the marketplace, the least practicable find the most practices.

To tell the truth, observation shows that complete historical cycles—that of the Reformation or that of the Revolution, to restrict the argument to 'modern times'—begin with a utopia and end with an orthodoxy. The opposition between the two periods is the basis for the oscillation between orthodoxy and utopia: the antithesis creates the alternation. The creative imagination (of liberty) launches an innovatory disorder and recreative reality (of constraints), channelling and solidifying it into repetitive structures of order. The point of inflexion which separates the ascendant and descendant phases of this cyclical curve is an ever-present imponderable which is always excluded from predictions and principles (originally humanist and more recently socialist): namely, 'the outbreak of hostilities'. A historical cycle usually ends when its inhabitants move from one neurosis to another—as if social humanity were fated to recover from schizophrenia only to plunge into the paranoia of orthodoxy. This toing and froing between two manias, one imaginary, the other real, sometimes produces a certain historical and mental equilibrium. What we call the wisdom of an era or an individual is not a rational pause between two bouts of madness, but an uninterrupted movement between them. Our epoch has the unprecedented privilege of closely observing the chronic alternation between the two major syndromes of political psychopathology. This currently takes the form of the spatial coexistence of two universes: 'East' and 'West'. Might not the most correct of all 'correct positions'—*more teorico*—be to walk the tightrope between the two worlds? Between an introspective escapism that turns its back on war and the all-out defence of a territory which sees enemies everywhere; between erotic phantasies and police phantasies; between the centrifugal autism of marginals and the centripetal autism of the authorities; between the asphyxiation of the meaning of the real by possibilities and the asphyxiation of possibilities by the argument of the real; between the fluid hedonism of ahistorical thought and the thoughtless moralism of solidified history; between too much organization and two little; between a dialectic undone and a dialectic imitated.

The disadvantage of such facile formulae is, of course, that they suggest a sort of golden mean between the devil and the deep blue sea, as if dialectics were the art of the well-tempered synthesis. We all know, however, that it is the art of identifying heterogeneities and positing irreducibles. The difference between political and utopian space is not a matter of degree: they are different *elements*. No bridge and no mediation can link banks that do not belong to the same world, and it is up to the critique of political reason to take stock of that incommensurability. It can in no way compromise with a rhetoric, inherited from the nineteenth century, which contrasts utopianism with realism in the manner of the noble and the ignoble. Victor Hugo once said: 'The dreamer prepares the way for the thinker. The possible is a block of marble which first has to be rough-hewn. The dreamers begin to make the model. This initial work always seems mad. In its early stages, the possible is impossible.' Never trust such politician's formulae: it is no accident that they combine the visionary's certainties and M Prudhomme's platitudes. So the dreamer anticipates the reformer, his only mistake being that he is right too soon. Then comes the thinker, the workman of history, with the statesman hard on his heels. This is a combination of evolutionism and idealism. There is no discontinuity. Ideas make history in dream form and little dreams lead to great deeds. ('Flush out your dreams and you have reality.') No need to worry: it is always *the same* history. Utopia leads logically to industry. No. The lawyer of history has to break both the spell and the continuity. He is no more in a position to reassure than the poet is to disturb. He who has to speak the reality of history has nothing reasonable or sober to say. He tells tales of terror: that utopia and strategy are not like prose and poetry, a single language used in two different ways. They are two different languages which, though they may intersect, can never actually merge. Our lawyer is eminently logical.

The physics of history is not, to put it mildly, on speaking terms with the metaphysics of history elaborated in the last century. Military societies have not been replaced by peaceful industrial societies, as the liberal bourgeoisie said they would be (Benjamin Constant, Jean-Baptiste Say, de Molinari). The international proletariat has not put an end to nations and aggression, not even in its own world, as the socialist thinkers prophesied (Proudhon, Cabet, Marx, Jaurès). Industry does not mean liberty and socialism does not mean peace. The similarity between Marx and Victor Hugo or Jules Verne—and it is not inconsiderable—is that Marx stands on the side of his despised utopian brothers, on the wrong side of modern history. Perhaps the disappointments of our times are born of a meeting that never took place—the meeting between Marx and Clausewitz. Marx never took war seriously (theoretically). Despite the advice of Engels, who was more perspicacious in such matters,

Marx never paid serious theoretical attention to the phenomenon of war. He was born either too early or too late, after the fall of Napoleon (1818), and he died before imperialism tore the world apart (1883). He lived in an age of limited or far-off wars, yet Marxism became a reality in the age of world wars. It therefore became the reality *of* those wars. In short, Marx gave no attention to Mars, while Mars paid considerable attention to Marx. The things you leave unthought always take their revenge on your thought.

As a general rule, the nineteenth century erected a barrier between its two greatest discoveries: history as system and war as system. The twentieth century is still paying the price in a long-standing hostility between the founders of sociology and strategy, between the Institute of Moral and Political Science and the Institute for the Study of National Defence. *Sciences po* and *St Cyr** are two separate academic universes which are not very fond of each other's company. The trouble is that our century is as ignorant as ever of protocol. It has broken all the rules of etiquette and intellectual manners, as if it took a perverse pleasure in constantly contrasting 'military' and 'ideological' at every turn and in every flash-point ... and in damning them both. Utopia: rationalism gone mad. The inevitable rusticity of its phantasies may well have the shimmer of sophistication, but its madness is that of a poeticized logic rather than a logical poetry. The force of the image conceals the superior force of the pure idea, and the communion of hearts is the most banal form of intellectualism to be found in the social field. Intellectual circles have a liking for these secretly or openly hypothetical—deductive constructions à la Fourier or Orwell. For the amorous new world or air-conditioned nightmare is proof of the narcissism of the family circle. Utopian pleasure is solitary and therefore only too likely to become peremptory, domineering and sure of itself. Nothing resists it: nothing is there to stop it. The past is swept away with a stroke of the pen and the event can be deduced from axioms. The optimism of pure reason can alternately or simultaneously make its home in the Café du Commerce, a socialist platform, a discussion club, a technocratic cenacle, or any kind of

---

* St Cyr: France's main military academy. *Sciences po*: slang for *sciences politiques* and for the corresponding academic department.

good or bad place. But it is always haunted by the speculative void into which the 'loftiest of thoughts' usually fall. Philanthropy and strategy are basically incompatible, both emotionally and intellectually, and one day we will have to accept that the inhuman misanthropy of the dialectic is a logic of antagonism. But we will still have to remember that blueprints for universal happiness are the most effective bad-luck charms of all.

The best of all possible worlds is announced in programmes, manifestoes and social projects (whose composition regularly absorbs the best intellectual forces of the progressive parties), but the worst of all possible worlds (worst, because it combines necessity and contingency) is the world of the relationship of forces in which the other world has to be put into effect. That is why the two antithetical worlds get on so badly together in everyday life. In the universe of *that's-the-way-it-is*, political experience always comes up against real constraints that could be neither deduced nor predicted. And yet, the wording of the programme assumes that effects can be deduced from one another, that there is no need to calculate the irreversibility of their cumulative effects or the side-effects of their application: this is the universe of *all-we-have-to-do-is*. Chalk and cheese.

In that sense, the ultimately *strategic* dimension of collective action necessarily precludes the utopian form of the programme. A programme tells us what to do; strategy tells us that we cannot say in advance what we will do because it takes two to play politics. What the adversary does to us (and not even he knows that) will determine what we can do to him (and that will in turn determine the enemy response). Strategy is essentially the 'incessant action of two camps upon each other' (Clausewitz). The conflict situation periodically upsets the best-laid plans in the world by confronting historical agents with a truly disturbing truism: 'You are never alone at home.' The *lex suprema* of war can be summed up as a contradiction between the absolute necessity to carry the decision and the impossibility of making absolute (i.e. sovereign, unilateral) decisions. Since the opposing forces endlessly determine one another in and through their relations, any attempt to resolve the conflict in advance is doomed to failure. If we also recall that attempts to represent decision-making in mathematical form (games theory) are quite inapplicable to historical conflict because they make non-dialectical assumptions, we can see that this logical impossibility has the character of a law. Perhaps it would be more accurate to say that the negative certainty of the principle of strategic indeterminacy allows us to state confidently that the universe of political action is, in the last resort and despite all the barriers, a universe of uncertainty, risk and chance. And therefore of decisions, instants and gambles.

It also allows us to understand the overpowering need for security created in the actors by this space of indetermination. However, no longer turn to the oracle, the haruspex or the augur before going to the battlefield or the forum: we consult the text of the programme (which stipulates, Chapter 3, first paragraph, clause two ...). The need for propitiatory rituals has obviously grown considerably worse—and that illogicality is quite logical. The rules of the political 'game' have not changed since the time of Apollo's oracles, but the stakes in each round have become considerably higher (for specific peoples and for mankind as a whole). More people are involved and they have more weapons. Hence our anxiety at the yawning gap between the rising stakes and the constant uncertainty. But the strategic principle also allows us to understand the insolence of contemporary history in general and revolutionary history in particular. For a century now, we have not made a single step forward. Not a single revolution, socialist or otherwise, has failed to announce itself with a programme; but although they have all been duly elaborated and ratified, not a single programme has had any effect. The trivial observation that the best programmes can have the worst effects, and that the absence of a programme does not prevent the best from happening, cannot relieve the politicians of their responsibility to prove their sense of responsibility, to temper their inability to answer for what they will be doing tomorrow by talking about programmes. Anguish, impotence, distress: these unspoken masters of the collective have given us a fine crop of multi-volume discourses.

The military backdrop to political activity implies that the 'conduct of operations' is a pious euphemism. We all know that a historical agent is influenced by his action as much as it is influenced by him, but that is not the crucial point. The familiar microdialectic of 'becoming caught up in the machinery' is determined from above by an operational schema that exists prior to current operations and whose nature is independent of the actors' will or motives. The strategic principle subsumes all its possible contents (just as categories subsume the concepts of the understanding). If strategy is the 'art of mobilizing one's forces, organizing and arranging one's battles in order to win the war', there can only be one strategic logic. There are certainly no two ways of winning a war: you either impose your will on the enemy or you do not. But in victory as in defeat, it is impossible to change the procedures that a political will must follow if it wants to make another will bend to it. Whatever the balance between two societies, parties or factions, they both have to be as strong as possible and to relate every element of force to the overall relationship of forces. First 'assemble your forces', then 'subordinate them to the necessity of winning'. The law of economy entails that, to adopt Foch's admirable expression, we have to 'deploy our forces systematically'. The law of strategy, to use Clausewitz's canonic phrase, dictates that we have to 'go to extremes'. Neither law can be mastered: they are by definition objective processes. Like it or not, war has its reasons of which reason knows nothing. The rationality of war shapes reason in its own image. A class ideology, for instance, consists of a class's ideas 'erected into a system'—the ideas, that is, of a society which has had to struggle not to have its antagonist's will forced upon it. And as the conflict escalated, the ideas took on the 'doctrine-form'.

As the procedures for the confrontation are obligatory but not infallible, unavoidable but involuntary, *isms* cannot possibly be planned. We know in advance that we need *isms*, because social ideas live by fighting, but we can never be sure which ones will triumph. A doctrine is a military trophy, and every *ism* in our cultural panoply masks the remains of its victims: defeated ideas that cannot get to their feet again. In other words, not everyone can found a religion. No ideological visionary, mediator, leader of a school or sect can get up in the morning and say, 'There will be a testament this evening'. The survival of his thought does not depend upon him, and although *isms* follow and resemble one another, they are not made at will or on an assembly-line. Hence the irony: one begins with a failure and ends up winning; another trumpets its victory and ends up gathering dust on the library shelf.

Of the countless sect-founders swarming on the edges of the first-century Empire, all of which reached Rome 'where all things horrible or shameful in the world collect and find a vogue' (Tacitus, *Annals*, XV 44), Christos of Judaea was probably the most unfortunate. He was crucified like a vulgar subversive and thrown unceremoniously into the common grave. 'On the evening that Jesus died, no one could have predicted the incomparable future that awaited the unfortunate prophet whose expectations had been so cruelly and completely ruined by events.'[1] Of all the authors of socialist systems in the nineteenth century, none failed quite so miserably as Marx in his academic and political expectations. *Das Kapital* had a print-run of one thousand copies. It passed unnoticed, and academic circles contributed no more than two reviews in obscure specialist journals. On the evening that the *Doktor* was buried and once the meagre funeral procession had dispersed—seventeen people according to one historian—no one could have predicted...

2. Flags Versus Science

Our 'singing tomorrows' have no today. It is true that the collective sings—the group state is by nature lyrical; but its songs, hymns and canticles are all martial—group lyricism is by nature polemical. No banners flap in the theoretical void. As soon as one appears on the horizon, we are back to Political Reason, which tears utopias to shreds, including the scientific utopia known as 'the higher phase of communist society'. Look at this *lapsus calami* let slip by that most sarcastic of all destroyers of utopias, the pitiless *Critique of the Gotha Programme*: 'In the highest phase of communist society', writes Marx in this illuminating text, 'after the productive forces have developed with the all-round development of the individual, and all the springs of co-operative wealth flow more abundantly—only then can the narrow horizon of bourgeois right be crossed in its entirety and society *inscribe on its banners*: "From each according to his ability, to each according to his needs".'[2] Let us not discuss here whether the indefinitely renewable character of relative scarcity at the level of the productive forces vitiates the logic of the famous slogan. (It would not be difficult to show that, capacities being *limited* and needs *unlimited*, the only way to relate one to the other is to mediate them through a centre that is able to allocate necessarily inadequate resourses. A centre of power. Call it a state.) We shall focus instead upon the one part of the sentence that seems to be of no importance but which, if applied in context, immediately snaps its rational thread (assuming, of course, that it is self-consistent). Note first that, since 'society' is not a physical person, it has no hands to write with and no brain to choose its words. It is an allegory, someone will say, a mere posopaea. But the rhetoric itself points to the theoretical lacuna. We are already familiar with the effects of the concept of the working class as collective person, as *direct* subject of its own history. According to the letter of the theoretical texts, the Party should have been a mere attribute of the realization of class substance, but in practice, the class substance became a mere attribute of the substance of the Party, the subject of real history. Tomorrow's communist society may play some equally nasty tricks on us. Given that 'society' is an abstraction, as is a physical non-person, delegates will have to be nominated to write on its banners the formulae that are supposed to represent the general will. How are they to be nominated? What electoral criteria will be used? That remains a mystery. As we cannot have a random juxtaposition of banners with different slogans—a republic has only one banner and only one slogan—how are we to choose the right one? An opinion poll? A referendum? A show of hands? Whichever we decide to use, who will ask the questions or choose the options to be put to the vote? That again in a mystery. The absence of any theory of *representation* in Marx is, as we have seen, matched by the absence of a theory of decision-making. Even if that difficulty is removed—a scholastic hypothesis itself—the problem of the banner still remains. Marx would have every excuse for saying that the word is unfortunate, that that was not what he meant. There is nothing in the thought of the great economist that allows us to understand the nature and function of banners, even in the lower phases of social development. What is a banner? An emblem we can rally around. To understand why emblems exist, we have to have a theory of the imaginary and of the subject, or of the imaginary constitution of identity. In order to understand why men rally around banners, we have to have a theory of the group and of entropy—that is, of the bellicose constitution of fixed and inheritable territories. Within the framework of Marxist theory, all we can say about banners is that they are bad omens, provisional and revocable because mankind's divisions are not anthropological (constitutional) but historical. Banners are stigmata from man's prehistory, the final stage of which is marked by the bourgeois formation of nation-states and inter-imperialist battles to win markets as a way of offsetting the constant fall in the rate of profit. The economic theory did not take the trouble to specify whether its model *social formations*—among others, the capitalist mode of production—took a territorial form and were therefore nations. Until that question is settled, the entire battery of concepts connected with 'socio-economic formation' is left floating in a state of international weightlessness that renders them somewhat unsuitable for political use.

Marx never took any interest in banners, but they are very interested in him (and well they might be). Not only does the symbolic of the emblem preside over the subsequent diffusion of his doctrine (Red Flag, Under the Banner of Marxism, Raise high the standard of the proletariat); all the societies which claim to be inspired by a man who had nothing but scorn for symbols are distinguished by their truly mystical love of banners—either in the form of an unprecedented cult of patriotism or in that of an immoderate and visible taste for standards, pennants, banners, insignia, trophies, flags, etc. Theoretical socialism is iconoclastic; actually existing socialism is iconomaniac. The doctrine is naked, but the states are dressed in flags. They have their reasons, but they are reasons of which the doctrine knows nothing. The colour ceremony is rather unfortunate, never having entered the author's mind. Of course, he could not think of everything, but a historical thought that overlooked the nation and war was taking definite risks right from the start. Marxist social formations hoist and fly flags, unfurl and defend their colours and give decorations because they are, first and foremost, national formations tempered in and by war (USSR, Yugoslavia, Vietnam, Cuba, and so on).

Someone is bound to object that the chauvinist rages of real socialism merely illustrate the 'lower phase of communist society'. But if the society of the higher phase still has *its* banners, it must still have a military form. So why is it so superior? It may no longer *be* an army, but at least it still *has* one. So it has all the attributes of a nation-state exercising and defending its sovereignty in the inter-national arena. A banner means a state, even if it is only a coercive apparatus capable, if not of imposing its will on others, at least of putting them into check. Is attack not sometimes the best form of defence? Is there a great difference between counter-attack and ag-gression pure and simple; preventive and offensive war? We could of course politely lead the enemy back to the frontier and wait for the next offensive. But what kind of national defence is that?

Peaceful as this flag-waving communist society may be, it necessarily has frontiers because peace is uncertain and national an-tagonisms have not disappeared. It therefore has to have the material and administrative means to deal with the threat of war: above all, a hierarchical, disciplined and well-equipped force (or at least one that is not worse equipped than its potential adversaries). Clearly this precludes the abolition of the division of labour and the application of Saint-Simon's slogan. For it implies—and, at another level—produces the organization of society. The 'construc-tion of socialism' is one country or in one limited community of countries was a logical if perhaps debatable thesis. The idea of na-tional communism, however, is meaningless if words have any meaning at all. If a communist society is national, it is localized. If it localized, it is encircled by non-communist countries; and if it is encircled it has a state and state secrets, a police force, generals and ration-books. Communism presupposes abundance, but war in-creases shortages. A war economy means controls over shortages, in other words, an inflated bureaucracy. There will always be some-one to argue that by the time communist society has reached its higher phase, the 'revolution' will have been made long ago. Point taken. But that assumes that revolution has to take place 1) *everywhere* and 2) at much the *same time* (otherwise the 'law of the uneven development of contradiction' will take off again and presumably give birth to new antagonistic contradictions between unevenly developed revolutionary processes). All these hypotheses may look scholastic, but the evidence is there in front of our eyes. In the meantime, communist society, the idea of which Marx begins to outline in the *Critique of the Gotha Programme*, will be univer-sal or it will not be. If it is communist, it will no longer need ban-ners. (Its identity has been given once and for all: unshakeable, in-tangible. More than indestructible, it has no possible adversaries.)

The political unconscious here speaks through a slip of the tongue.

3. Frontiers Against Atheists

Religion being the continuation of war by other means, everything we have just said can and should be transposed from 'strategy' to 'theology'. The political order comes into its own by virtue of this transfer: the superimposition of the two registers gives it its specific unity. A classless society would be a society without an army (the Latin *classis* means both an army and a demographic category), and consequently without a Church. No warriors, no sorcerers. *Arma sacra*. Remove war and there will be no more priests, no more Party, no more Doctrine; no more paladium, aegis or armouries. A *polis* without walls is a State of nature, a dream-state whose stability can do without stabilizers. Order without ordering would be unity without synthesis, nature without history. This ideal anarchy would, so to speak, mark the degree-zero of politics. The instrumental abstraction allows us to isolate an independent variable and to locate the correlations between the different factors of order in the variations of concrete history.

Defence is essentially theological, but social existence knows varying degrees of theology. It is a fact of experience that whenever a country, a religion or a party is encircled, the level of sanctity obtaining in that party, church or country rises ipso facto. We are surrounded, therefore we are consecrated. Indeed, this is not surprising, given that it is the circle that produces the sacred (*moenia sacra*, to use another consecrated expression). Woe unto the impious, the libertines, the dissidents; the pacifists, the anti-socials and the anarchists! Encirclement reinforces the feeling of sanctity and therefore the encircled group's self-transcendence. The sanctity of the surrounding environment is the measure of its inner dehiscence. The more the group has to transcend itself, the more tightly it closes its ranks. Naturally enough, it draws up into a square at the foot of the altar because it is the assembly that produces the altar (the sacrosanct effigy of the Marshal, General, Comandante, President, Imam, Secretary, etc.) and not the other way around. The self-consecration of the threatened group increases its capacity for sacrifice and murder (the two always go together). On the register of doctrine, this can be expressed as follows: in every collective formation, the capacity to control and the capacity to exclude vary concomitantly. Theory has it that all wars are religious. Observation confirms that if you make a war inexpiable, you make religion savage. When Mars becomes the sole judge, God becomes judge and executioner. There is no comparison between the thirst of these courts-martial and that of civilian courts. As history advances, the supreme judge digs in.

The collective is by definition regressive. But aggression produces regression within regression, as if the prehistory dormant in history were suddenly to wake up. Not only does it oblige us to leave the island and revert to orthodoxy; we have to go back from orthodoxy to the inquisition, from the Church to the sect. As we retreat, there is a resurgence of latent hierotropism. Logically, the act of systematization renders the system external to itself. Hence psychologically, the ecstasy effect within the sanctuary (transcendence, exaltation, intoxication, etc.) 'We could feel a magnificent and fearful collective sensibility growing with us' (Victor Serge, Moscow, 1919).

The outbreak of hostilities triggers the archaic mechanisms of resistance to dislocation and an irresistible escalation of the sacred. 'It'll turn out badly' means that the wheels of history are about to turn backwards, towards the Constantine complex. War—hot or cold—takes a historical community back to the conditions of its genesis. If we want to unite, the need to reconstruct the altars becomes urgent and the endemicity of dogma becomes epidemic once again. Confrontation irritates the skin, stirs up our defence mechanisms and revives memories *ad majorem Dei gloriam*, that born border-guard. Gods are creatures of the frontier because they are appointed by frontiers. Weakening the definition of a structured group exasperates its need for infinity, and the alliances it then forms recreate a community at once religious and military. 'Tense climate', 'suffocating atmosphere', 'collective hysteria'. Besieged fortresses have never been noted for their rational policies, not that that is surprising given that a policy of unity always plays into the hands of the gods. 'Strengthening a country's defensive capacities' means that ideologies of salvation have to return in force. Theoretical reason tends to consider messianism a 'crime against humanity'. Political reason tends to ask what dangerous missions humanity could have carried out in a hostile environment if it had not believed it had a mission to save the world.

Nothing could be more exemplary than the historical formation of the United States, the promised land of 'spiritual movements'. It is a diagram of the spirituality/insecurity ratio. From the seventeenth to the nineteenth century, the base-areas of new biblical sects moved West with the covered wagons of the pioneers. Priests and pastors stayed in the rear: prophets sprang up on the borders. The great fundamentalist revival of the eighteenth century gained ground on the edges of the colonized areas, while the great renewal of the nineteenth century followed the movements of the scattered and threatened communities of the West, who were only too eager to form solidly organized collectives (to find, that is, divine guarantees against arrows, malnutrition and disasters of all sorts). The terrifying aridity of their environment gave birth to revelations, visions and visitations. Far too resolute to seek salvation in flight, the adventurers found it in the Pentecostal, Methodist, Mormon and Adventist sects. If a graph could be drawn for the level of religious fanaticism, it would fall off as men move away from the frontier—the frontline—and come closer to safer inhabited lands. The hostile environment whips up the need for the absolute, and a new god appears whenever a new land is conquered. Born in the deserts of Sinai, the God of the Bible reappears in Ohio and Missouri and settles with the Mormons in Salt Lake City. Further avatars appear until the last Sioux has surrendered and the last Pacific Coast state has been settled. The hostility of the world and the lack of allies reinvent the Ark of the Covenant. New forms of the Ancient of Days appear. Sectarianism becomes a rudimentary form of first aid for immigrants in search of a home. Religious fundamentalism appears to be connected with periods of political foundation, and the characteristic feature of the dissident sects that spring up during the American long march is their religious anti-rationalism. Some profess obscurantism and all stress the emotive at the expense of the intellectual. Yet one more proof of the retrograde nature of collective epics. The forward march of Christian savagery against native 'savagery' is accompanied by a retreat towards 'savage' modes of organization and forms of belief. In any case, 'pragmatism' is not the opposite of 'fanaticism', and despite a persistent rhetorical tendency to see them as opposites, cowboys do make the best crusaders (not that the crusaders were poor settlers in their day). That is in fact a constant feature of North American psychology. The Bible and the Colt-45 need each other. The alternation between the democratic pastor preaching the good word and the republican pioneer calling for new conquests restores a certain balance. Obviously, in terms of the Eternal Return, the New World has nothing newer to offer than the Old, but the very novelty of the experimental framework makes the constancy of the rule even more significant. The logic of action reproduces the logic of faith. Hence the unity of heroism and fanaticism (as other people's mysticism is known). Zealots make better fighters than Pharisees, but they are not such good Talmudists. That was in the first century AD. The creation of Israel in the twentieth century was not the result of hermeneutic rationalism, and Judaic fundamentalism is growing before our very eyes as the Jewish national feeling of insecurity increases. Zionist colonization of the occupied territories draws its volunteers from the ranks of the most retrograde of the mystic sects—the fanatics of Gush Emoin.

These picturesque and far-off examples serve to bring us closer to home. Droughts, famines, wars and catastrophes constantly remined the collective of its origins. Mormons and witch-hunters are of no interest to specialists in public law, but pioneers are of considerable interest to critical genealogy. For they are the *explorers of the institution* which appears before political institutions, just as the universe of the statute dominates and encloses that of the contract. It is well known that critical epochs and religious crises are interconnected. Periods of historical crisis are the test-beds of rational criticism and manifest the internal unity of political instances of synthesis. The good thing about disorder is that it reveals the laws of order. Men of order and statesmen are past masters at turning their theoretical usefulness to practical advantage, at using crises to restore discipline and wars to restore their own power. (The Roman civil wars of the first century prepared the grounds for Augustan order; and the wars of religion played a similar role for the absolute monarchies of the seventeenth century.) Extremes of destabilization and installation, establishment and overthrow, are therefore crucial 'experiments' for the student of the conditions of stability. His favourite figures are emigrants and emperors, outlaws and founding fathers. The graph of order and disorder registers its statutes—'a set of articles defining a society and governing its activities'—by moving through inflexion points which lay bare, in every sense of the word, the roots of *stabilis*. The war–religion–institution sequence provides a clear exposition of social physics, revealing the normally latent mechanisms of the establishment of order. All these canonical situations have the virtue of showing quite unequivocally the direction in which the vector moves: from dynamics to statics. The 'dynamic of the group' tends towards its stabilization, not vice versa. Just as one emigrates in order to settle elsewhere, travels in order to stop travelling or clears ground in order to harvest, so the outlaw overthrows the founding father in order to become a father in his turn. A political revolution is a movement from 'less state' to 'more state'. Institutions, Parties and Churches change in order to remain the same. *The only concessions that a political being makes to evolution are those which allow it to return it itself*. In the long run, the sedentary man always defeats the nomad, but he is the reason of the nomad's existence. A critique of political reason would be unfaithful to its object if it failed to think dynamics— concepts and events—in terms of the categories of statics.

4. Epicurus Impotens or Mars Against Venus

We therefore have to make a distinction between the science of relations between things (physics) and the science of relations between men (politics). Social physics is an inverted physics: its *ordo rerum* stands *De natura rerum* on its head. Lucretius dedicates his poem on nature to Venus (I 1–28), the goddess of birth and growth. The lyre of politics, on the other hand, remains prisoner to the epic and makes a display of redundancy and rigour. Its primal pact was made not with foam—born Venus but with Mars—who, in this context, is the sacrificer rather than the victim. In this order, it is love that is defeated by the 'eternal wound of war'. The praise of turbulence has no founding virtues for political reason; it may be a conjunctural necessity in practice, but it is not a structural necessity for theory. The need to reject such comfort, not out of masochism but because resistance to turbulence (not only to crowds or riots but to anything that disturbs the lines) is inscribed in the inscription principle itself. The ramparts of the City are not volutes and its frontiers cannot fluctuate: they are there to annul environmental fluctuations and to reduce inclinations and variations to zero. Political institutions exist in order to stabilize chance and to fight fluids with solids, thus minimizing the possibility of disorder. Everything except the reproduction of the gap is a departure from equilibrium, and political reason contradicts the aphorism that 'the world can as a whole be modelled upon vortices' (Michel Serres). It cannot, therefore, find its primary models in fluid mechanics, a discipline which has been seen as 'the birth of physics in Lucretius's text'. A gap or an angle of inclination (clinamen) appears in a laminar flow of atoms in which nothing happens. The spiral is thus born of the tangent, and organization springs from of the vortex. The primitive question of physics—how are things formed?—might therefore be translated and elaborated as: how can turbulence occur in a flow? Through declination. The goddess of love is also the goddess of nature who gives birth to the *foedera naturae* by presiding over the mating of atoms. Venus incarnates the conjunction of the elements, Mars their disjunction. She gives life by bringing things together, he brings death by separating them. She is the principle of good: he is the principle of Evil.

It would be a fortunate mythology of happiness that could explain everything but unhappiness and its reproduction, everything but politics. 'The laws of Venus/nature cannot be deciphered by the children of Mars'—and those of Mars/history cannot be read by the children of Venus. This painful distinction is unlikely to procure us much joy (either politically or epistemologically) in festive periods of effervescence. Fluids are currently in vogue and it is well known that walls have a bad name. We have every reason to prefer the gentle caress of flows to the prickly, concave, metallic universe of politics. But preferring is not the same as understanding: the question is why the world of private happiness cannot do away with or annex the world of public unhappiness. Thoughts of nature abhor the social, but that abhorrence is not an explanation: it has to be explained. As a contribution, we might suggest that the disgust and denegation are provoked by the truly horrible overthrow of the laws of physics by the laws of politics. One world's life principle is another world's death principle. Mars federates by issuing ukases, brings things together by excluding others and builds by destroying. The political universe reveals the dramatic telescoping of birth and death, a short-circuit represented in allegorical form by the myth of 'exemplary murders' and the birth-certificates of cities. The partisans of Eros are quite understandably horrified by the collective, for blood is there a seed and the plague is springtime. Its walls are consecrated in blood. In other words, the collective's hymn to birth is not a prayer to Venus, 'mother of our race, delight of men and gods', but an invocation of Mars. For the collective, a funeral is a genesis and the nurse is always a murderer. To use the language of thermodynamics, in nature the goddess of love stands at the threshold of negentropy, at the exit from entropy, whereas in history that key position is occupied by the god of death and separation. Political 'pockets of order' are the product of violent delimitations (both ideal and material). A mere collection of individuals cannot transform itself into a durable set without building solid walls. These stubborn raw materials, the only ones capable of stemming the 'all is flux' of nature, are not 'given'. In a universal flow of liquids, static elements are expensive. Wars, religion, institutions: such is the price that has to be paid for a little solidity—or for the consolidation of a gap. In physics, the overheads of negentropy are known as hatred, dogma and drabness. An objective knowledge of the natural world became possible when certain objects were posited as existing outside the group, as not being at stake in power struggles: the mathematical object, for example, or the physical atom. 'The Greek miracle'. In our knowledge of things, we are still dependent upon those who, like Epicurus and Lucretius, 'laid down their arms and kicked Mars out of physics' (Michel Serres). But that expulsion made it impossible to gain any understanding of politics, which had thereby been cast into the outer darkness of science. In order to understand politics, we have to comprehend the most stupid god in the Pantheon, the only one whose strong-point is his stupidity. The tenacious complexity of simple military minds has defeated more intelligent beings than Mars. Archimedes, the founder of hydraulics, died alongside so many others defending the walls of his home town, Syracuse. More recently, we have seen how Mars sent Marx *ad patres*, leaving us with the megalith of Marxism. Liquidation via posthumous crystallization. In short, an idiot with a service record like that deserves to be taken seriously, at least by wise people who mean to take care of themselves. In order to do so, they have to understand Mars the intruder without passing judgement on him. They will find no salvation in hydrodynamics, not even a metaphorical salvation.

The philosopher of nature seeks 'to invent liquid history and water ages'.[3] It has already been invented, and it is called the debacle. History does sometimes become liquid—for example, whenever a structured group goes into liquidation. That just goes to show that it is not a dream but the fulfilment of a wish which has, until now, looked like a nightmare. Take the cascade of France in 1940, our most recent 'water age' which put the theories of vortical organization through the grid of social practice. Or are the old soldiers taking liberties with language when they describe the '*flood* of refugees', the 'uninterupted *flow* of the exodus', the '*dilution* of authority'? 'Whole regiments broke up, flung down their arms and were *swept* into the *whirlpool* of confusion'. Venus defeated Mars: panic. No more front, no more commander, no frontiers, no capital. Leaks everywhere. A whole people with their hands in the air on the roads of the exodus. A minimal degree of resistance in the midst of this flood of defeated people would have created an island of firm ground (in the sense of firm *convictions*, a firm *hand*, a firm *hope*, to use a truly political vocabulary). It is possible that the flooding of France, which became half-viscous and half-aqueous, gave a number of French people an intense feeling of liberation and allowed some citizens the opportunity to enjoy personal and intimate pleasures. When the epic goes on vacation, everyone can play truant. National calamities and personal happiness are not always concomitant, but it is true that what makes groups unhappy makes individuals happy, and vice versa. Fluid suits the *ego* in the same way that solidity suits the *we*. Given that a *we* is not a collection of *egos*, a collection of streams and cascades will never produce a political body. The work of the collective has its own element, and it is in the interests of the producer of knowledge to respect its consistency. That is the primary, irreducible stage of any subsequent reduction of the political to non-political explanatory principles (which are biological and, at a higher level of abstraction, physical). Conversely, one favour deserves another, and Political Reason cannot pretend to rule the destinies of things outside its domain. Since it will not tolerate ethical imperialism, the annexation of ethics by political imperialism is all the more fatal. Render unto Epicurus what belongs to the garden and unto Marx what belongs to the Forum.

First of all render unto Epicurus his logical modesty. The master urged his disciples not to become involved in public affairs or scientific research. It was a coherent, even canonical abstention. The founder of the garden held that the dialectic is useless in nature and the political has no specific nature. History cannot have any meaning if (as in the letter to Herodotus) you define time as 'the accident of accidents'. Living in accordance with nature—the sage's ethical ideal—means finding your happiness in the present moment. And given that there are an infinite number of worlds, we lose nothing of importance by withdrawing from the one world on to which chance has thrown us. A quiet life, apart from the world in a present that knows neither past nor present, makes it possible to enjoy perfect happiness—complete self-sufficiency. Anyone who is autarkic has no master: he is *adespotic*. He is also agnostic, believing in neither demons nor heroes because 'the gods take no interest in human affairs'. This ethic of domestic happiness unwittingly ratifies the theory that the constitutional lack of the *we* is the cause of political unhappiness. I can annul death inside myself, but the collective cannot evacuate its content. Haunted by an absence, the collective is always behind or out of step with its origin, its law, its aim, the ulterior, the anterior, and so forth. It can never be self-satisfied: it is essentially hysterical and is doomed to be the plaything of God's fools and fanatics of all sorts, of anyone who acts and speaks in the name of the Other. In the hollow time of the collective, the present is linked with past and future: only the sage can flourish in the *carpe diem*. When the collective becomes anxious, the individual becomes exultant; when the individual collapses, the collective rejoices. Epicurus's philanthropy cannot avoid being misopolitical, and the community of friends were quite right to withdraw from the Agora. They never made any claim to dictate laws to the City from the shelter of the Garden, and in any case it would have been rather late to do so. Epicurus philosophizes in comfort, but he does so after the battle—at a time when the defeated Athens no longer had the right even to mint its own coinage (306 BC). Alexander's *diadochi*, who were then fighting over the Empire, looked after the grain and the Persians, the supply of victuals and the defence of Piraeus. It is always possible not to make war—provided that others do it for you. The ability to choose well—to choose peace—is not given to everyone. However, a reminder of the objective conditions of choice is not a logical argument against choice itself. It simply explains why the return of Epicurus should be a natural slogan for a sluggish *fin-de-siècle* ebb tide, and why it should serve as a rationalization for an involuntary state of civic irresponsiblity. In such circumstances, the non-political option is in itself consistent and logical, not *although* but *because* it leaves the political problem intact. It would only become inconsistent and incorrect if it claimed to be the theoretical solution to a practical problem it does not raise.

Constancy

We have already distinguished two types of temporality in the historical process: technical history, which is cumulative and cannot be programmed, and political history, which can be both programmed and recapitulated. They are as different as the 'obliging mobility of Hermes' and the 'painful immobility of Prometheus'. Only the former deserves the name of history (although it is the most neglected), whereas the second, a stage on which scenarios from the group unconscious are played out, in fact constitutes a non-history (even though it usually claims to be history).[1] The situation is paradoxical in two senses. On the one hand, Hermes the understudy has stolen the leading role from Prometheus, and the palliative of exchange has already given rise to an economic science, while the constituent punishment still awaits its political science. On the other hand, the discipline of history looks for signs of change or discontinuity in the home of immobility.

The conceptual distinction between the different modalities of history obviously does not appear in crude historical reality, the site of the practical synthesis of things that theoretical analysis has to separate out. The two orders of phenomena are not inertly juxtaposed; they actively complement each another. That may sound self-evident, but it can still bring down the whole discursive regime of antitheses that constitutes our normal political diet. Day after day, we see the rival pairs clash: sacred and profane, irrational and rational, archaism and modernity, universal and local. Day after day, they dance their ritual steps. We would now like to suggest that these antithetical factors form *an equation with variable but correlative values*. Association through contrariety determines a logical relation, a general form of contradiction. Anthroplogists use it, we know, both as a marker and as a tool for revealing structures. Theoretical reason in enough to elucidate history as it has been made, society as a given state. But in order to understand the way in which history is made by a controlled play of structurations and destructurations—that is, society as process—Political Reason has to grasp the logical relation in its dynamic aspect, in terms of a general economy of collective energies.

Hypothesis: there is a constant ratio between so-called progressive factors and so-called regressive factors. The history of mankind is written in a double-entry ledger. Whenever its equilibrium is disturbed by technical progress, ethnic factors intervene to re-establish it. Contradictions between the homogenization of the world and the claims of the right to be different, between the intellectual and the affective elements, between the economic imperative and religious need, etc. derive from an automatic compensatory mechanism designed *to maintain a constant relative intensity between 'historical' and 'non-historical' terms*. I would argue that this constancy principle governs the functioning of the social apparatus. We are familiar with the tendency towards equalization in the psychical apparatus. Freud borrowed the notion of the *stability principle* from the physician Fechner; the physiologist Caron, using the term *homeostasis*, subsequently extended it to the processes whereby elements in the blood are recombined. At the level we are discussing, however, the 'wisdom of the body' and 'the laws of nature' may well have less happy results. Identical causes do not have identical effects at different levels of organized matter.

The spontaneous self-regulation of collective identities is no guarantee of stability and harmony. There is nothing providential about it. Firstly, the tendency towards equalization does not operate equally and constantly, but with critical thresholds and sudden reversals (we are at the present moment experiencing such a crisis). Historically, dynamic equilibrium appears as a dynamic of disequilibria that gives free rein to antagonistic and ever less controllable tensions. Secondly, the ethnic factors which restore equilibrium become more and more savage as technological progress advances. The constancy principle applies to ratios between magnitudes, not to the magnitudes themselves. Every new level of equilibrium takes us a step further in the escalation towards extremes. It follows that, once it has reached a certain level, the self-regulation of the collective does not preclude the possibility of involuntary implosion. A constancy principle can thus become a nirvana principle and a process of self-preservation can pass into a desire for extinction. But before going into such metapolitical considerations—which it would be wrong to see as speculations with no observable empirical basis—we will begin by questioning the ground of classic oppositional discourses.

1. The Impossible Divide

Between past and future. North and South. The believer and the atheist. Let's not go through all the commonplaces. The one thing they all have in common, and the only interesting thing about them, is a certain distribution of space and time, a superimposition of legendary geography and chronological common sense.

The past becomes remote. It was emotive and it becomes intellectual. It once believed and it is becoming indifferent. These age-old banalities—which can be either plaintive or cheerful—serve as a backdrop to the most serious research and to the creators of despair. Frazer in the *Golden Bough*: 'For ages the army of spirits, once so near, has been receding further and further away from us, banished by the magic wand of science.' Max Weber tells us how scientific rationally produced a disenchanted world and how the privatization of religion that typifies the advent of bourgeois societies sealed the fate of the prophets.[2] He also reminds us that bureaucratic domination is the legitimate successor to charismatic domination: 'In traditionalist periods, charisma *is* the great revolutionary force.'[3] As we well know, traditions die out and charisma with them. Henri Wallon, the eminent psychologist, saw the evolution of civilization as 'the gradual repression of emotional activity by intellectual activity' or the 'covering up of emotional archaisms by rational systems of representation'. Jean Giono to his disciples in Contadour: 'Purely intellectual speculations are stripping the universe of its sacred mantle.'[4] Michel Serres on those who control the dew: 'The end of agriculture signals (the beginning of) the end of culture. The earth has, since time immemorial, invented religions. All religions are agrarian: they represent the entirety of the peasant's knowledge and pathos. There have been no new religions for centuries, not, as Nietzsche seems to think, because of some imaginary decadence, but because there has been no basic change in our relations with the earth since our last religion.... The point is that the industrial revolution is by its very nature anti-religious: it does away with necessity. Humanity's atheism dates from then and it is irreversible.'[5] The road to the gods has been cut. Humanity's journey from myth to knowledge, from the sacred to the profane, from the cosmic to the political, seems to have been a one-way trip.

The South lies south of the equator and the countryside is not the town. Megapolis covers the northern hemisphere and the gangrene of urbanization (synonymous with politicization, from *polis*, city) tears the individual from the collectives that once nourished him and plunges him into the arid solitude of anonymous crowds. At a planetary level, the dichotomy between eras is spatially projected on to the bipolar opposition between economically poor but social-ly rich countries and the cultural desert of the industrial heartlands. *Folk* versus *urban*, *Gemeinschaft* versus *Gesellschaft*. This dis-course, a banal version of the first, is based upon an obvious and cruel reality. But even in its most extreme forms—bemoaning lost affectivity in an attempt to shake our technical rationality—it starts out from naively rationalist premises.

It is quite true that nature and the supernatural disappear together. But they have nothing to lose by waiting. The corollary of the constancy principle is the 'law of the return'—in every sense of the word. Common sense (*bon sens*) and one-way streets (*sens uni-ques*) notwithstanding, it means that both time and space are eminently reversible. Both 'progressive' enthusiasm and 'reac-tionary' nostalgia can, it should be noted, use the same discourse. Mircea Eliade speaks the same language as Karl Marx—the vocab-ulary is different, but the syntax is the same. In *The Eighteenth Brumaire*, Marx takes it for granted that the transition from the bourgeois to the proletarian revolution will mark the transition from collective magic to scientific rationality. The antediluvian suckers of 1848 'timidly conjure up the spirits of the past' and dress up as Romans to go about their business. They are still duped by a superstitious belief in ancestral ghosts, and they need these illusions 'in order to hide from themselves the limited bourgeois content of their struggles'. Bourgeois revolutions are 'set in sparkling diamonds', each day's spirit being ecstatic, but they vanish 'like a series of optical illusions before the spell of a man whom even his enemies do not claim to be a magician'.[6] It goes without saying that the proletarian revolutions of the future will take place in a permanent atmosphere of self-criticism, that they will have neither dogma nor saviours. They will keep their feet on the ground and remain level-headed. Being lucid and determined, they will bid a cold farewell to the mystical fables of origins. Forlorn hope! Mircea Eliade inverts the same logic, contrasting the archaic ontology of archetypal agricultural societies with the precarious historicism of a modern consciousness that has to create itself without any models to follow. According to this view, history is an irreversible process of secularization, a sort of machine for producing the profane by expelling the sacred. The sacred is man's past. He has to turn his back on his political history, swim against the tide of time so as to discover primitive religious values which socio-economic evolution is bent on destroying.[7] Judging by the facts, there seems to be equally little ground for such despair. Historical consciousness is lined through and through by the a-historical unconscious. Anyone who hopes that political history will eventually be secularized (Marx) forgets that the thread of this age-old everyday history has no history: some ages and cultures are more propitious than others for the collective experience of the sacred, but the sacred itself is ageless. The nostalgia for origins forgets that they are always with us, stubborn and invisible. The political unconscious is a memory with no memories, a fertile past which contains things that can never be destroyed (least of all by a reactivating revolution). Between the past and our present there is a relationship not of chronological anteriority, but of logical priority.

The real question therefore becomes: why is our most archaic past making ever greater inroads into our modernity? Why is it taking us back to something very remote in calendar terms? How can the agrarian South cross the equator and the tropical seas and spread across the electronic North in an explosion of barbaric forms which are as intriguing as they are irresistible? The rhythms of pop music (with primitive percussion drowning out more recent stringed and wind instruments), oriental psychologies at a scientific colloquium at Cordoba, gnosis at Princeton, mystical sects from everywhere and anywhere, communes in the Cévennes, amulets with pictures of pop stars, papal blessings for crowds in a state of trance, collective and individual suicides, the paralogical dementia of terrorist grouplets, organizational fanaticism and wars of religion in the heart of the factories (Ireland, Spain, Belgium, etc.), collective hallucinations and hallucinogens in the home, gurus, grand masters, clairvoyants on the TV and radio, barehanded surgeons bending metal at a distance—the *folk* is taking over from the *urban* and the shamans from the high plateaux of Siberia are now on television. Cheap occultism? Cheap rubbish? No, surface ripples caused by a strong underwater current with far-reaching implication. The term *irrationalism* is appropriate enough, but it is far from adequate. It describes the effect without accounting for the cause.

The effect can be described simply as a 'wave of religiosity', but there is nothing unusual about the reversal of a tendency as such. Dodds, the historian of Hellenism, sees a massive return of irrationalism in the final stages of ancient culture (from 200 BC onwards). For a thousand years, rationalism had been dominant (1300–200 BC), but the final stage represents a return to the most religious initial phase (300–1300 BC). The same author argues that the rationalist trend of seventeenth to early-nineteenth centuries was followed by a new phase of obscurantism that began about 1800.[8] In this perspective, adopted by many scientists who are well aware of the dangers of comparison, human history becomes the theatre of a mechanical or pendulum-like alternation between a day-time and a night-time mentality, of an oscillation between antithetical and incompatible tendencies (Renan). It is possible to go beyond the imagery of ebb and flow, pendulum swings, etc. and postulate a regulatory logic of 'returns' that would rid us of both seasonal swings and mysterious resurgences (resurgence in the sense of the reappearance of ground water or underground rivers)? Historical science (particularly since Lucien Febvre) deplores the anachronisms whereby we project our feelings and ideas on to the past. But why is our present also riddled with anachronisms? What vice is this?

It is exactly as if the strange avatars of African religions seen by Roger Bastide in the cities of contemporary Brazil illustrated a process that could quite legitimately be transposed on to a world scale. Transplanted by the emancipation of the slaves, industrialization and the exodus from the countryside into the *favelas* of Rio de Janeiro, Afro-Brazilian possession cults regress towards forms that are less ritualized, more ecstatic and, in a word, more frenzied than the original models, which are subject to collective norms, almost to a protocol. The destructuration of religious brotherhoods by the sub-proletariat's conditions of existence produces a syncretism which breaks down the group's collective controls and involutes religion into black magic.[9] The *candomble* is transformed into the *macumba*, a wild trance in which the dancer is possessed by Indian divinities who are supposed to be 'fiercer' than the better-behaved African gods. Whereas traditional societies tend to move from a 'wild' to a 'domesticated' form of the sacred, modern societies experience the reverse process. Agrarian rites are violent, but urban rituals are savage. In other words, urban counter-culture is more savage (lawless) than primitive culture. Savagery comes later, not earlier. As the scale changes (from Brazil, 'land of contrasts', to the contradictions of the moment), other changes become obvious, notably in intensity and seriousness. Anomic deculturation releases more than a desire for carnival and frenzied dancing. More radically, it liberates communions and, in the long run, it liberates us from discipline. The loosening of communal links (by the telephone, among other things) multiplies the number of gaps in our groups (and at the same time facilitates individual communication), but the place of the religious cannot remain empty. And so, being unable to repeat or to commemorate, we improvise. As established religions (confessional or otherwise) move out, syncretic substitutes move in. The sacred becomes more diffuse (and is diffused by social breakdown), but not exhausted: it becomes uncontrolled. If it is not channelled, the group energy circulates 'freely': it invents, destroys and imagines. But putting 'imagination in power' does not free the group from the sacred, but desacralizes existing institutions and then usually leads to carnage rather than effusions, to mystical regression rather than bucolic nostalgia, to murder rather than poetry. The outpourings of libertarian spontaneity are the golden legend of our *brave new world*; its black legend is the slaughter of fanatics and terrorists. But it is still the same world of computerized state administration, in which factory labour-time is controlled by automatic time-clocks.

2. The True Meaning of 'Archaism'

The notion of archaism has become the object of an expensive misunderstanding, and the scorn which assimilates it to 'dated', 'obsolete' or 'worn out' presents serious dangers. Let us look at the etymology. In Greek *arche* means not only *beginning* or *starting-point*, but also, inseparably, *commandment* or *authority*. The modern usage of the word tends to separate the two meanings of anteriority and authority, reflecting the fact that modernity has become opaque to modernists. 'That's just archaeology, you're digging into the past, comrade' means 'you are turning your back on the present'. It ought to be taken as a scientific compliment: 'You're getting close to the kernel, you are unearthing the foundations.' But that is small consolation for the sarcasm (putting a brave face on it?), for there is nothing consoling about the reality we discover. 'Archaic': a place in the stratification of determinations, not a point in time. Not the out-dated, but the substratum; not the obsolete but the repressed. It is no accident that many contemporary cultural mysteries can only be penetrated by the X-rays of primitive societies.

We all belong to three or four collectivities. In normal times they coexist through more or less spontaneous or painful compromises. Even within the group, there is a conflict of loyalties. The prior of Taizé, for example, belongs to his order: whom does he obey, his superior or the bishop of Rome? Both, obviously—the authority of one implies that of the other. Which just goes to show that the Church is perfectly healthy, in spite of everything. Peace leads to ecumenism: wars threaten compromises. Luther was originally excommunicated (by Leo X in 1521) for having dual loyalties. Before long, no one was allowed to be something of a Catholic *and* something of an Evangelical: you had to be one *or* the other. In periods

---

* Taizé: Ecumenical religious community in the South of France. Trs. note.

of tension, you have to choose. It is because we have a choice that there is a crisis (*Krinein*, to separate, to decide). Crises are spectral. The anthropological interests of these fleeting X-rays of time is that they reveal the stratification of internal determinations in the visible behaviour of the group by bringing to the surface the oldest, most active strata. The crisis demonstrates that the most modern strata are the most superficial, that they give way and crack under the pressure of the repressed. The more recent of two loyalties is always the more fragile.

Unfortunately, our loyalties are genealogical, and reflexes take precedence over the reflective. It is not a case of 'out of sight, out of mind', but temporal distance does make the heart grow fonder. The group (in general) comes before the individual (who abstracts himself from it a posteriori): its chronological anteriory determines the hold of ideology over individual subjects within the group. But even within phylogenesis itself, the order in which the group appears is an ontogenetic order of political priority. Our personal allegiances provide an outlet for the involuntary memory of the species. The inscription principle is dynamic: having failed to understand it, rationalist (progressive) generosity reads individual inscriptions upside down and imagines that, because they are concentric, the smaller circle is contained within the larger. This spatial view of inscription is morally flattering but morally impotent. Individual morality teaches us that each link depends upon the next, but the test of history proves the contrary to be the case. The Baron de la Brède et de Montesquieu had to spend a long time alone with Plutarch during a lengthy period of civil harmony in Europe before he could afford the luxury of this abstraction: 'If I knew something which was advantageous to me and prejudicial to my family, I would put it out of my mind. If I knew something which was advantageous to my family and prejudicial to my country, I would try to forget it. If I knew something was advantageous to my country and prejudicial to Europe and to the human race, I would regard it as a crime.'[10] That is an honourable remark from an honourable man, but the group instinct would put Europe before the human race, one's country before Europe and one's family before one's country. When the duties of class allegiance are incompatible with those of national allegiance, the former are spontaneously and completely sacrificed to the latter. In 1914, no proletariat in Europe hesitated for a moment when faced with a choice between a general strike and the sacred union: nation was more important than class. When ethnic or confessional loyalties are old and the national formation is recent or separate, religious or tribal obedience will take precedence over national feeling: religion is more important than the nation-state. (An Iraqi Kurd is a Kurd rather than an Iraqi, but a Pole does not have to choose between his nation and his faith—the two are historically interdependent.) In periods of crisis, buried territories always come to the surface. Tendentially, anteriority and preference merge. That should not, of course, be taken as even the ghost of an abstract rule or as some sort of automatism: it is because there is always an element of uncertainty and complexity about the play of allegiances in a concrete situation that action contains 'political', and knowledge contains 'historical', raw material. The facts warn us against divorcing political predictions from cultural (and in the last instance natural) determinants. Progressive generosity has been taken by surprise before now, and universal reason has more than once been repressed. The chronic confrontation between the rights of minorities and the central state is simply a clash between the archaic group's egotism and the egotistic right of the modern group. Given that the smaller primary circle can never be assimilated into the greater secondary circle, and that received cultural intensities can never be assimilated into a definite territorial space, the group's unconscious and the group's official conscious mind can never arrive at anything better than compromise solutions, in other words at non-solutions. The unsatisfactory nature of such transactions is the basis of the value and stability of national compromise formations, regardless of the institutional modalities they choose (confederative, federal, unitary, etc.). Hence the difficulty and the importance of being able to be a Jew in the Soviet Union, an Arab in Israel, a Kabyl (or a M'zabite) in Algeria, a Catholic in Northern Ireland, a Hoa in Vietnam, a Kurd in Iran, a Basque in Spain, a Québécois in Canada, a Corsican in France, and so on.

3. Retrograde Progress

Physically, social humanity gets out of its depth as it becomes industrialized; mentally, it agrarianizes itself so as not to drown completely. Cultural territories effaced by technical progress are reconstituted in the imaginary. When overpopulation, pollution and concentration make a return to the land impossible, we use symbols to cobble together ill-divided allotments: the legendary geography of lands of salvation (model countries), the tangible geography of sectarian communites, the bellicose geography of political affiliations. The compulsion to believe is geophagus. We are frustrated territorial animals—and we satisfy our needs as best we can. Modern ideologies are homelands for the homeless. The demand for 'secondary' homes in the idea compensates for the disappearance of primary frontiers in reality.

Words ending in *ism* make a relatively late and timid appearance in our vocabulary. 'Catholicism' appears in the sixteenth century as a reaction against Protestant dissidence. The first philosophical *isms* appear in the seventeenth century (Thomism, Cartesianism); idealism and materialism date from the eighteenth century. Virtually all the political *isms* in current use stem from the nineteenth century. *Isms* (not all of them nominal) appear to have gained considerable ground since the industrial revolution, but the relation of affiliation implicit in the suffix expresses an immediate genealogical relation which classical languages expressed through inflection (*-ikos* in Greek and *-eus* or *-icus* in Latin) or the use of adverbs or prepositions. Aristotle's disciples were known as the men of the Lyceum, the adepts of Stoicism belonged to the Portico, and so on.

So long as the limits were marked on the ground and in the cadastre, they did not need to be recorded in an index. Thought segments space historically because it is no longer segmented by socio-cultural space. Obediences were ethnic long before they became ethical, and doctrinal inscription itself operated with regions and areas before it turned to *isms*. The West's first schools of thought connected individuals with places by means of the metaphor of an idea; the latest, on the other hand, connect them with an idea by means of the metaphor of a place. Before they became Platonists, the followers of Plato were for three hundred years called after the Academy, an area lined with plane trees near the potters' quarter in Athens. Before Stoicism we had the philosophy of the Portico (the Stoa), where Zeno sat to teach in the shade and to have dialogues in the agora. Before Epicureanism we had the Garden which Epicurus bought in the deme of Melitus. His house was his school; his discipline was his frugal home life. The

Lyceum was considerably less scholastic than Aristoteleanism. Our doctrines now have the thankless task of turning ideas into land and inventing paper territories. Doctrinal, confessional and finally ideological, our territories have really taken off, all the more limited for being air-borne. In the space of a few years we have moved from a topography of speakers to a topology of words, from sites of filiation to commonplaces of affiliation, from the familiar real to family virtues. Nowadays, we have fewer acquaintances and more knowledge, less conviviality and bigger crowds in our few remaining meeting-places. 'Ideology' is what remains when the acropolis has been razed, the walls have been destroyed and the plane trees have been cut down.

As soon as we lose sight of our birth place, the threat of death appears. We no longer know how far we have come because we do not know where we have come from. Our constituency boundaries are vague, and so our appetite for inscription increases. There is a necessary relation between the disappearance of meridians and the increase in the number of certificates of origin. It is quite true that industrialization is anti-religious because it uproots people through rural exodus, immigration, emigration, accelerated social mobility, and so on. That is why, in the industrialized countries, it is prompting moves to relocate workers (regionalization, environmental protection, radio stations, associations, etc.); and why, in agrarian countries subjected to compulsive industrial rape, it is provoking an equally compulsive return to the well-springs of identity that were supposed to have dried up with modernization (the Shah's Iran unleashes Khomeini, to take only one of many examples). Far from diminishing the archaism of mentalities, the modernization of economic structures actually exalts it. America is a promised land for primitivism in all its forms. It is well known that religious sects are most deadly (Jim Jones), racial conflict most fierce and political conflict most ferocious in the most advance, standardized and post-industrialized country in the world. But the cultural minorities are also the most lively, and America has the greatest number of local radio stations in the world.

The song of the nightingale becomes more beautiful; and once we are used to plexiglass archaisms, we become nostalgic for the bush. Our all-too-familiar world-weariness promises us a surplus of enchanters, not a shortage. God recruits by placing small ads in the papers; his alter ego the devil recruits wholesale, especially in countries where mass is said in the vernacular. Parishioners without missals, private meals without ceremony, public ceremonies without a public, calendars without holidays, feast days with no fairs, cohabitation without neighbours, old men without authority, uninitiated adolescents, commemorations with no memory; the wasteland of the North is no longer even missionary country. It is wide open to the messianism that can offer the most (the only remaining question being the choice of a suitable Messiah—and it is up to the professionals to provide the answer to that one). As daily life becomes deritualized and as cultivated land returns to desert, a formidable paleosocial frustration builds up to such an extent that it may one day be reckoned in megatons (assuming that the survivors can count). Our investigation has shown that the need for an absolute both produces and subcontracts a need to relate (need is a physical and mental echo of the logical function of incompleteness). The lonelier the crowd, the more savage its need to believe. Whenever group relations break down, a mystical need for an absolute appears. It is well known that the various contemporary forms of the return to the past are attempts to soothe our anxiety about the future, but the tranquilliser can itself produce a new anxiety attack. 'The sudden appearance of the religious on the political scene' is no illusory headline, but two points need to be clarified. Firstly, it is not an unexpected irruption, but a manifestation of a slow continuous evolution (or the index of a tendential law). Secondly, evolution itself evolves, and there is no reason to suppose that the irruption in question is interrupting it. It may simply be a transitional phase on the road back. Belief in magic is older than belief in personalized gods, but the age of magic corresponds to the stone age.[11]

We have already noted that the chronogram of sovereignty forms is not irreversible, and that it is, for example, possible to revert from the model of the City to that of Royalty. We have seen it happen in our lifetime and our civilization has witnessed it all before. Think of its origins: the Hellenic *polis*, which had few religious values, gave way to the Hellenistic monarchy, in which the *basileus* was deified. The democratization of the magistrature in the classical City presumably did not mean that it was fully secularized: we know that as political life in the Greek cities became more rational and more democratic, closed and hierarchical religious groups appeared on the edge of the Agora—sects, mysteries, theiases, brotherhoods.[12] The fact remains that some progress was made between the twelfth and the seventh centuries BC, with the transition from the archaic palace society of Crete or Mycenae (superhuman kings and no citizens) to the classical agora where magistrates were elected after contradictory debates and public challenges. But between the fourth and the first century BC, the same cultural stage was the backdrop for a general involution, both philosophical and political, as a new wave of mystical irrationalism (from which the Christian sect would emerge) washed away the rational gains of Greek thought. And with it came a concomitant reaction of 'anti-democratic' monarchism. Chronologically, the cult of kings appeared after the civic cults, but logically, the Hellenistic *basileus* is closer to the Mycenaean *anax* than to the Athenian *archonte*. We now know that the long march from the ancient magician or witch-doctor to the divine king was punctuated by a number of halts, reverses and hesitations, but we are right to see it as an interminable and ever recyclable march (recyclable in the strict sense of the word, of course.) Strictly speaking, the 'divine king' belongs to the West's past and we can consider the cycle of the Golden Bough complete.[13] In theory, the elective principle banishes the religious mystery from the sphere of politics (or the command system). But one would have to be very naive to believe that an elected president escapes from the communal link and the sacramental aura of his function simply because he no longer carries a sceptre, a baton or a bough. Quite apart from the ritual protocol of his investiture, inauguration (in the strict sense of asking for the consent of God), consecration, swearing-in, etc., the continued irradiation of the 'image of the President' in the day-to-day life of liberal democracies bears witness to the latent magic of our behaviour, maintained for its effects if not cultivated for its own sake. The legal state (*état de droit*) has not done away with the state of grace (*état de grâce*) in France.

The 'transition to socialism' is not alone in combining economic and social progress with idolatrous regression in the forms of political existence: the socialization of the means of production and the personification of the processes of government are not at all contradictory. As a general rule, gains in economic rationality (planning, mechanization, automation) seem to be offset by equivalent losses in the political order. Even within the capitalist mode of production, technical progress tends to make the reality of power anonymous, both masked by and absorbed into the system of technostructures. But what economics disperses and divides, politics reconcentrates and individualizes. Megamachines and Megaboss go hand in hand. The more complex the state, the more abstract it becomes and the greater is the demand for a concrete incarnation. The bureaucratization of functions is unthinkable without its opposite: the monarchization of an imaginary organ. It is as if the increasing personalization of decision-makers were a palliative for the depersonalization of the real processes of decision-making (commissions of experts, consultative committees, think-tanks); as if the citizen of a disembodied state were reassured by the face of the supreme leader, the ultimate and tangible guarantor of an intangible system. All available social meaning clings to the body of the Leader, and the bureaucratic institution (State or Party or Party-State) clings to the Leader because, without him, it would lose its identity. You do not play around with symbols and when you have one you make it last. The physical monument to the group is therefore artifically kept alive as long as possible, so that after its death it can become what it was during its lifetime: a public monument.

4. The Universal Inverted

Finding a balance between *micro* and *macro* is like finding one between *archeo* and *neo*, and what applies to time also applies to space. Just as past and present have to be grasped as a complex antagonistic logic, within which conflict is a form of collaboration, the unification and fragmentation of social humanity constitute the two sides of a single process. The past does not outlive itself in the form of survival. The regional does not fade away as the national advances, and nor is the national resolved in the final instance of the universal.

When theoretical reason looks at the history of men, it usually does so in order to admire its own reflection. Reason is our higher faculty of synthesis (in Kant, the concepts of the understanding synthesize the data provided by sense perception at the lower level). Its internationally recognized function is to reduce diversity to unity and the tangible to the intangible. For speculative reason, history becomes a mirror for the understanding: a synthesis in action which can be read as the slow reduction of natural (or national) diversities to the final unity of man. The epic was a panoramic translation of the break-down of natural barriers (families, tribes, communities, nations), and from the sixteenth century onwards that process was brutally accelerated by the birth of a world market (universal history begins with Magellan). In the nineteenth century, the last airlock before the world state, the process was completed by industrial manufacturing. Neither the unity of the world nor the human essence are simply given: they are products of time. The rationalization of the course of the world or the awakening of Reason within history go hand in hand and constantly interact with the triple transition from the herd system to the world system, from heteronomy to autonomy, and from anarchy to order ('anarchy in soical production is replaced by conscious planned organization').

Marxist legend has handed down to us the '48 myth of the springtime of the peoples. The notion itself came from further afield, from the philanthropists and the Enlightenment, but the socialist gospel easily fitted between humanitarian pacifism and technological optimism, Victor Hugo and Jules Verne. After all, Proudhon and Comte also saw war between nations as being doomed to extinction by the industrial revolution. All Marx added to the vulgate of the day was an important mediation (but it was still just another mediation): we will move from the 'capitalist world of exploitation and murder' to the 'proletarian world of peace and the unity of peoples' by means of the socialist revolution (final resolution at the 1913 Basle Congress). The abolition of classes will not be a gentle process, but after that final violence, there will be no more national demarcations or antagonisms. Proletarian humanity will unite 'all countries'. There was a real historical basis for such extrapolations. The curtain was being allowed to fall on old feudal Europe, and the multicoloured marquetry of patrimonial States was giving way to homogeneous and economically viable entitities. The arrival of railways and customs unions overcame the parish-pump mentality by assuring the transition from out-dated principalities to vigorous nation-states (both Italian and German unity date from this period). The impetus given to scientific, technical and human productive forces was supposed to extend the curve and assure the transition from national exclusivity to the universal interdependence of nations. With the help of the international division of labour, the bourgeois exploitation of the world market had broken the shackles of the agrarian past. The proletariat would then finish the job, and economic unification would lead to the political unification of civilized humanity. Although Marx was only half-mistaken about the facts, his theory was totally wrong: dialectically, a contradiction shorn of one of its terms is not a half-truth but a complete error.

The totalization of the planet has, of course, occurred in one sense: the world is a single whole, and the interconnection between its parts is becoming more obvious every day. But, by the same criteria, a different tendency has also asserted itself, complementing, resisting and finally reversing the movement towards totalization. How surprising that this has happened primarily in the one movement supposed to hold the keys to all the frontier-posts in the world: the worker's International. It has taken only a century to wear out four Internationals—superb organizations for defeats—and there is little sign that we will ever see a fifth. They all valiantly came to the front of the stage and recited their revolutionary (unifying), rationalist (unitary) and moral (universalist) lines, but the real revolutions took place in the wings or on a completely different stage (the Paris Commune, the October Revolution, the Chinese, Vietnamese and Cuban victories).[14] In little more than a century, the so-called universal class went from 'the workers have no country' (1848) to 'the workers of the world have a country—the Soviet Union' (1928) to 'the workers have as many countries as they have nationalities-each to his own' (1980). It is not easy to be a Quaker these days.

The dreams of Marx and Montesquieu have been shattered, and the unparalleled, though not unlimited, 'savagery' of the twentieth century has destroyed the received idea of 'civilization' (a joint legacy from the previous two centuries). In fact, it is the savagery of limits, (of the limit as a savage act) which has thwarted the idea of civilization as a process of breaking down limits. Yet again, history has not unfolded as it ought to have done and the collective has failed in its duty. If a Marxist is someone who subordinates the interests of their national group to the world socialist revolution, then the real world is not Marxist. What is worse, the Marxist world itself is anti-Marxist: it is one in which Eritreans fight to the death against Marxist Ethiopians: Chinese Marxists fight Russians of the same 'ideological' persuasion, Chinese fight Vietnamese, Romanians fight Bulgarians, and so on. If a humanist puts the interests of humanity above the interests of country, then real humanity is not humanist: we constantly see 'sacred egotisms' cheerfully sacrificing the humanitarian principles of the rights of peoples (and the liberal principles of free trade). Practice takes theory from behind and turns the logical order of its subordinations upside down. For fifty years now, there has not been a single example of a socialist revolutionary movement leading the struggle for national emancipation: nationalism has 'led' socialism in every sense of the word. The liberation of the colonial and semi-colonial countries has not resolved the national question, but has compounded it and raised it to the power of n. The emancipation of the wretched of the earth has not led to the overthrow of existing 'demarcations and antagonisms', because these have been overthrown by the erection of new barriers. The world-wide 'anti-imperialist struggle' is a struggle not between nationalists and internationalists but between small-power and great-power chauvinisms. If that were not the case, there would be no struggle. Similarly, the anti-fascist struggle of World War II did not mobilize the partisans of universal values against the madness of a retrograde ethnocentrism: basically, it set a collection of national allegiances (the allies) against another (relatively isolated) nationalism: Nazi Germany. The motor has the same nature as the things it sets in motion, otherwise there is no (collective) movement. In that sense, intellectual polemic differs from political polemic (a state of war is an X-ray of political polemic). One is a conflict between logical discourses, the other between group energies. And a given quantum of energy will always be destroyed by a greater quantum. In the field of political forces, like can only confront like (one archaism against another, for instance). Otherwise, there can be no real struggle—it is broken by a rupture and a transition to a lower level of efficacity (logical discourse, for instance). In other words, to use the current jargon, the forces of reaction were not outside or over there, but—horror of horrors!—within the forces of progress. Thank god, progress had the strength to fight reaction.

Statement: 'Our poor world is so divided. The division is dynamic and highly unlikely to come to an end in the foreseeable future.' Translation: 'The mirror of reason has been broken.' The Balkan question is no longer restricted to Central Europe: it has spread to the headquarters of the United Nations. The whole universe is being balkanized, and the areopagita of universal consciousness is beginning to look like a mosaic without a pattern (the young micro-states, and there are more and more of them, cannot fail to remind one of the dated buffoonery of the Duchies of Parma and Schleswig-Holstein). Just as the economy is becoming planetary, the political planet is cracking up. On the one hand, an obsessional territorial neurosis, on the other an increasingly fluid flow of commodities and data. A migratory fever and an obsessional crisis. Our village, ever more planetary and ever more patriotic—the two things go together—lives in the age of nationalism, separatism, irredentism and tribalism. Its darker features are known as segregation, racism and xenophobia. In varying degrees and forms, the fragmentation drive primarily threatens the great multinational federal or confederative states. But the oldest 'civilized' and centralized states in Europe do not go unscathed: the UK, Spain, France. The repressed material of international progress ('international', a neologism coined by Bentham in his *Plan for Universal and Perpetual Peace*, entered the public domain in 1831) is everywhere returning, and the discharge of nationalist adrenalin offends all our good manners—not least our intellectual manners. Some say it is scandalous—like the cosmopolitan aesthete who denounces the 'archaeology of roots' in the name of fertile transnational dissidence.[15] Others say it is enigmatic and highly embarrassing—particularly the socialist theoreticians who find it 'devoid of any discernible rational theory' (Eric Hobsbawm).[16] It is quite true that if we rationally exclude the fact of nature a priori, the national fact becomes irrational. But the fact is there, and we still have to say what are we going to do about it. Truth is unitary, error multiple. It is not surprising that the right should profess nationalism—a decadent form of pluralism which presupposes a natural plurality of nations and the exclusivity of one nation at the level of values. Such would be the conclusion of a man of the left who uses the canonic criteria. But, in this context, we are not on the left and it is not our task to pass judgements. Our aim, let me repeat, is to put forward reason, not precepts. We do not have to distinguish between reactionary and non-reactionary by weighing up good and bad. We are concerned with possibilities and impossibilities, with the logic of real operations—beginning with a description of what is happening. With absolutely no elation, we have simply taken note of the twin crisis of socialist internationalism and liberal cosmopolitanism. We ask why they are not operational. Ask a silly question... Because neither of them can count to two. Think of contradictions as twins, or think of the unity of singularity and multiplicity. Nothing is more difficult (and traditionally, nothing has been more problematic in the history of philosophy). How, then, are we to think the unity of will and memory in a political agent who acts in accordance with his group's history and geography? Our memory is geographical and our will historical. Collective efficacity and collective legends are inseparable—which is why the history of a group cannot be divorced from its geography and why our projects and visions cannot be separated from our referential territory. Such is the warped structure of all political temporalities that a group relates to its future in terms of its past. (You do not need to be Jewish to know that, even though the Jewish people exemplifies the contemporaneity of past and present much better than any other in the West.) Our memory is basically not discursive but affective. The motor of real political movements is not intellectual, but it is the responsibility of intellectuals to think and prepare the movement. That chiasmus sums up a lot of misunderstandings and failures. Those who are responsible for thinking are not always in the best position to do so, and rather than reposition themselves they conclude that the axis of the historical movement has been displaced. Theoretically, and taken in themselves, socialist internationalism and liberal cosmopolitanism seem to be spontaneous expressions of intellectualism in the universe of action. From a sociological point of view, they are the prerogative, or even the attribute, of intellectual avant-gardes (political vanguards for internationalism, aesthetic and cultural for cosmopolitanism). The usual mode of action of professional intellectuals in the political arean is voluntarism. They spearhead the rational will, especially when it comes to concrete international solidarity, the only problem being that they leave their memory (the masses) behind them. The divorce between will and memory produces the martyrs and the bankrupts of the social movement: their marriage makes revolutions.

The combination of the economic integration and political dis-integration of the world means that we have to reflect upon the interdependence of two series. The proliferation of political micro-units can be seen as a mere by-product of economic concentration, which topples traditional national ramparts as transnational capitalism gradually wears down the sovereignty of its local interlocutors.[16] Without denying the rational basis of profitability strategies, I tend rather to see it as both a side-effect of a levelling of the economic ground—which leaves the field open to the play of cultural demarcation as an outlet for difference—and a pause in the tendency towards technical uniformity. At one level identity is lost, but at another it is recovered. The imposition of universalism results in a deliberate stress on particularity as an antidote to the homogeneous. The macro-spaces of dispossession lead to a deficit of belonging that is covered by the micro-spaces of sovereignty. Centripetal politics counter-attacks the centrifugal economy, and the transfer of competence to external and uncontrollable decision-making centres provokes a compensatory rise in the cultural appetite for internal sovereignty. How are we to decide if this is an antagonism or a complementarity? The bard of lower Brittany is no enemy of the European technocrat; Celtic mysticism can quite easily have its headquarters in Connecticut. Such uncertainties are no concern of ours. It is up to politics or policy to evaluate the relation between the two and to decide upon the criteria of choice. We simply note that the process of universalization has two aspects: retrenchment and redeployment, contraction and dilation, deculturation and reculturation. The production of the local does not contradict, but is produced by, the global. Standardization of the norms of production and consumption speeds up the differentiation of forms of behaviour and feeling. Every new device for uprooting people liberates the mechanisms through which they sink territorial roots (either symbolically or in reality). Given the present state of our knowledge, this schema is obviously speculative, but it does imply the existence of something like a thermostate, an (as yet) mysterious anthropological regulator which corrects changes in the group's integrity.

The ideal evolution of culture thus corresponds to a well-known rule of aesthetics: a work is all the more universal for being particular. Horizontal communication is optimized by the vertical deepening of the incommunicable. The original reveals the truth of the genre. Far from presupposing the elimination of diversity, the present unification of the world is a product of the multiplication of its units. Cultures have to become differentiated if civilization is to go on becoming universal.

Man retotalizes himself by fragmenting himself. Ultimately, contemporary universalism consists of a 'dialogue between cultures': it presupposes a plural definite article, and therefore requires that the barriers be maintained. An individual would be denied the possibility of entering another culture if there was only one defined place he could leave or enter. Civilization transcends cultures in that it neither asserts nor denies differences but circulates them among historical groups.[17]

The need to defend ourselves against technocratic homogenization forces us into ever more drastic politico-cultural counterattacks. And that is the danger. The quantitative rise in the factors of 'progress' increases the qualitative intensity of regression. The tendency towards stability thus generates a growing instability. The regulatory principle which tends to maintain the group at a constant distance from the surrounding environment is not in fact a mechanical principle (even if it uses a physical model as a metaphor). An 'action' is evidently not equal to a 'reaction': there is an asymmetry between the forces of the one and the many, between the planning of world cultures by the Western growth model and the erection of archaic closures to protect collective personalities. The distance is everywhere growing between inherited meaning and acquired power: that is why the panic associated with loss of meaning results in forced 'catching-up' marches, thick with more or less dangerous and convulsive somersaults. The regulation of collective identities paradoxically appears as a logic of excess.

Is the regulatory principle, then, of a dialectical character? Or does it pressuppose that dialectics is reduced to a mere process of composition? The answer to these questions lies beyond our capacities, but there does seem to be more in the historical process than a ceaseless permutation of places between 'ancient' and 'modern' within a finite system in which invariability is the result of substitution. The overall process is dialectical in its logical principle of the unity of opposites, but it is not dialectical in terms of temporal progression. The reassuring model of thesis–antithesis–synthesis is not applicable to the historical spiral. According to that model, the local archaic moment would be followed by a-modern-world negation, the process being completed by the negation of the negation in the serenely Japanese form of a society in which the robotization of work is tempered by ancestor worship. The synthesis is not in fact homogeneous with the thesis; it is not the *Aufhebung* of the first two stages. At bottom, dialectical reason contains a guarantee of recuperation, whereas historical evolutionism contains something irrecuperable, in the two senses of irremediable and uncontrollable. Social time gives us vertigo: not that of (combinatory) iteration or (dialectical) progress, but of the exponential. On the one hand, we have the curve of 'the release of religious energies', on the other that of 'the domestication of natural energies'. Universalization of subjects = tribalization of subjects. Re-established at every stage of evolution, the old equilibrium produces a new disequilibrium. An equation with inverse but correlative values can see its values increase to zero. Tension rises until the final zero is reached. By then the various hostile tribes will have discovered nuclear fire.

Notes.

Introduction.

1. 'Temps et politique', *Les Temps Modernes*, April 1970. *Journal d'un petit bourgeois pris entre deux feux et quatre murs*, Paris 1975.

2. *Au Pays des Soviets*, Paris 1979, p. 56.

3. *A Critique of Arms*, Harmondsworth 1977; *The Revolution on Trial*, Harmondsworth 1978; *Conversations with Allende: Socialism in Chile*, London 1971; *Che's Guerrilla War*, Harmondsworth 1975.

4. Descartes, *Discourse on Method*, London 1969, Pt. III.

5. Cf. Discussion with Michael Löwy, 'Marxism and the National Question,' *New Left Review* 105, September-October 1977.

6. See Georges Haupt, Michael Löwy, *Les Marxistes et la question nationale* (1848–1914), Paris 1974. In 1913, Stalin published a series of articles on 'The National Question and Social-Democracy'. Lenin expressed his admiration for them to Gorki.

7. Georges Burdeau, *La Politique au pays des merveilles*, Paris 1980, p. 7.

8. Plato, *Protagoras*, Harmondsworth 1956, 320c–322d.

9. It might be possible to deduce an apposite stratification to the temporal strata which, since the work of Fernand Braudel, have customarily been found within large practical sets. At the bottom, the almost motionless history of man in relation to his natural environment, above it the slow rhythms of social groups and, on the surface, the jerky rhythm of events. But the distinction I am suggesting applies only to the middle layer, that of social time, and does not affect geographical or individual time. In that sense, the two systems of chronology are not contradictory (and may even be complementary). In any case, no concrete analysis of a given historical period can procede by deduction (the use of categories). At most, it can infer certain localized results and contrast them with a global conception of social history.

10. Jacques Ruffié, *De la biologie à la culture*, Part Two of *L'Emergence humaine*, Paris 1976.

Book I.

Section I.

Chapter 1: The Function of an Illusion

1. See Georges Canguilhem, 'Une Idéologie médicale exemplaire: le système de Brown', in *Idéologie et rationalité*, Paris 1977.

2. Gaston Bachelard, *Le Formation de l'esprit scientifique*, Paris 1960, p. 65.

3. 'Idéologie' in *Encyclopedia universalis*.

4. Except in the explicitly magical language of a story-teller like Rabelais.

5. 'The fault which later leads to the unparalleled barbarism of Correct Thought and *generates* the labour camps can be found in Marx's theory', Jorge Semprun, *Un beau dimanche*, Paris 1980, p. 149.

6. Georges Devereux, *De l'Angoisse à la méthode*, Paris 1980, p. 25.

7. Eberhard Jakel, *Hitler Idéologue*, Paris 1973.

8. *Mein Kampf*, Munich 1942, p. 171.

9. Ibid., pp. 418 ff.

Chapter 2: The Past of an Illusion

1. See Henri Gouhier's historical introduction to the new edition of the *Eléments*, Paris 1970.

2. The standard works of reference are, in French, Picavet's Thesis (Paris 1891) and, in Italian, Sergio Moravia, *Il Tramonto dell'illuminismo*, Bari 1968. I have only been able to consult the former.

3. 'Mémoire sur la faculté de penser' in *Mémoires de l'Institut National des Sciences et des Arts pour l'An IV de la République* (August 1798), pp. 322–24.

4. 'A treatise on ideology is an insult: do you find I argue badly?', *Histoire de la peinture en Italie*, Book 3, p. 66.

5. 'Journal, 1806', in *Oeuvres Intimes*, Paris 1976, p. 790.

6. Ibid., p. 1410.

7. See the ironic description of Destutt as 'that very distinguished writer, member of the Institut de France and the Philosophical Society of Philadelphia, and certainly a genuine luminary among vulgar economists'. *Capital, Volume Two*, Harmondsworth 1978, p. 564.

8. Engels, *Ludwig Feuerbach and the End of Classical German Philosophy*, in Marx/Engels, *Selected Works*, New York 1968, p. 619.

9. Loc. cit.

10. Alain Badiou, François Balmès, *De l'Idéologie*, Paris 1976, p. 19.

11. Octavio Paz, *Le Débat*, No. 8, Paris 1981.

12. A 'serious theory' implies something very different from a materialist rewriting of the classic status of the imaginary in idealist rationalism: imagination as 'mistress of errors and falsehoods' (Pascal) or 'madwoman in the house' (Malebranche).

13. Cf. Engels's classic distinction between 'the ultimate driving forces of history' and 'the motives of men who act in history'. Or again; 'Everything which sets men in motion must go through their minds; but what form it will take in their minds will depend very much upon the circumstances.' *Ludwig Feuerbach*, p. 624.

14. *The German Ideology*, in Marx/Engels, *Collected Works* V, London 1976, p. 36.

15. Badiou, p. 32.

Chapter 3: The Anatomy of an Illusion

1. Claude Lévi-Strauss, *Totemism*, Harmondsworth 1969, p. 69.

2. Michel Serres, 'Moteurs. Préliminaires aux systèmes généraux', in *La Distribution (Hermès IV)* Paris 1977, pp. 43–65. Serres distinguishes between three main types of motor: successively, the vectorial (physical), the transformational (calorific) and the informational (cybernetic).

3. Sadi Carnot's paper was not discovered until twenty years later and was published by the English physicist Thomson, Lord Kelvin, only in 1850.

4. Badiou, *L'Idéologie*, p. 35.

5. 'Does the progress of Physical Science tend to give any advantage to the opinion of Necessity (or Determinism) over that of the Contingency of Events and the Freedom of the Will?' (1873). Reproduced in Lewis Campbell and William Garnett, *The Life of James Clerk Maxwell*, London 1882, p. 443.

6. Only Engels, who really does not deserve his bad reputation, paid any attention to this aspect, but there was no feed-back on the definition of ideology as the superstructure of the superstructure, as the phenomenal form of juridical and technical forms. Obviously, a theoretician like 'The General', who, as a theoretician, took war seriously, could not avoid taking religion seriously when it came to politics.

7. Marx, 'A Contribution to the Critique of Hegel's Philosophy of Right. Introduction', in *Early Writings*, Harmondsworth 1975, p. 243.

8. Jean Paulhan, *Les Fleurs de Tarbes ou la terreur dans les lettres*, Paris 1941, p. 78.

9. Ibid., p. 94.

Section II.

Chapter 1: A Logic With No Logos

1. 'Le Sentiment religieux à l'heure actuelle', *Archives de sociologie des religions*, No. 27.

2. Kant, *Critique of Pure Reason*, Tr. J.M.D. Meiklejohn, London 1969, p. 468.

3. Ibid., p. 469.

4. Renan, *Nouvelles études d'histoire religieuse*, p. 7.

5. Or, therefore, of transforming a culture, in the sense of a fact of nature, into a political community, as can be seen in the transition from a religious regional minority to a national movement for independence. See, for example, Christian Lalive d'Epinay, Daniel Alexander, 'Les Communistes anabaptistes du Jura', *Archives des sciences sociales des religions*, 49/1. The minority is cemented together by a history not by some infrastructural determination. For the Jurassians, that history is the history of a land, a territory in the sense of a certain reserve of space and time, the production of the 'nature—culture' interface.

Chapter 2: The Affective Command

1. Jacqueline Mer, *Le Parti de M. Thorez ou le bonheur communiste français*, Paris 1977. This concrete analysis would appear to be the decisive modern contribution to any project for a political science. The number of masterpieces of this type produced in any one century can be counted on the fingers of one hand.

2. C. Bailly, *Le Langage et la vie*, cited and discussed in Pierre Bourdieu, *Esquisse d'une théorie de la culture*, Geneva 1972.

3. 'It was at this time (1907–1913) that there took shape within me an image of the world and an ideology that later became the organic basis of my action. No studies could add anything to what I created for myself at that time and I see no reason to change any of it.' *Mein Kampf*, I, p. 20.

4. A striking example of the absurdity of idealist demystification can be found in Valéry, especially in his *Petite lettre sur les mythes*: 'Everything that perishes when a little more precision is introduced is a myth. You can see myths dying and the fauna

of vague things becoming infinitely poorer under the stern gaze of the enlightened thinker, under the multiple and convergent blows of the questions and categoric interrogations which such a thinker uses as his weapons.'

5. Roland Barthes, *Mythologies*, London 1973, p. 142.

6. Nietzsche, *The Will to Power*.

7. Pierre Gascar, Preface to Pierre Mertens, *L'Inde et l'Amérique*, Paris 1969.

8. Lévi-Strauss, p. 140.

9. Loc. cit.

10. Ibid., pp. 141, 142.

11. Michel Serres, 'Estime', in *La Distribution*, p. 277.

12. You can only have good polemics with close relatives. The fact that Lévi-Strauss felt the need to discuss Sartre's approach (in *Critique of Dialectical Reason*) shows that they share the same basic Cartesian assumptions of which Sartre was the last great philosophical representative. Structure versus history is a classic example of the meaningless philosophical quarrel. It is only possible on the basis of shared assumptions, namely, those of ontological dualism.

13. Lévi-Strauss, p. 142.

Chapter 3: The Imperative to Belong

1. 'Group Psychology and the Analysis of the Ego', Standard Edition, XVIII, London 1959.

2. J.-B. Pontalis, *Après Freud*, Paris 1969; Didier Anzieu, *Le Groupe et l'inconscient*, Paris 1975; René Kaës, *L' Appareil psychologique groupal*, Paris 1974.

3. Cf. Max Gallo, *L'Affiche, miroir de l'histoire*, Paris 1973. Reproductions on pp. 186, 187, 213 (Poster: 'What, you haven't volunteered yet?', Lenin Library, Moscow).

4. Jacquline Mer.

5. Dominique Labbé, *Le Discours communiste*, Paris 1977.

6. Louis Althusser, 'Ideology and Ideological State Apparatuses', in *Lenin and Philosophy and Other Essays*, London 1971, pp. 158, 160.

7. Ibid., p. 165.

8. Marcel Mauss, *Esquisse d'une théorie générale de la magie*, p. 124.

9. Freud, *Group Psychology*, p. 131.

10. Henri Hauser, *La Naissance du protestantisme*, Paris 1940, p. 94.

11. Ibid., pp. 94, 95.

12. Freud, *Group Psychology*, p. 94: 'There is no doubt that the link which unites individuals with Christ is also the cause of the link which unites them with one another.'

13. There is no documentary record of the 'incomparable' charisma of John Paul II prior to his elevation to the Vatican. The charisma of Colonel Charles de Gaulle, Maurice Thorez, Djugashvili (a Georgian) and Mao Tse-tung (a librarian) does not seem to have appeared prior to the formation of their respective reference groups.

14. Raymond Aron tries to classify them and then proposes his own interpretation in *Démocratie et totalitarisme*, Paris 1965. Cf. Arthur Koestler, *Darkness at Noon*, Harmondsworth 1981; Maurice Merleau-Ponty, *Humanisme et terreur*, Paris 1947; François Fejtö, *La Tragédie hongroise*, Paris 1956.

15. The most important are Artur London, *On Trial*, London 1968; Charles Tillon, *Un Procès de Moscou à Paris*, Paris 1978; and, more recently, Fizbin's *Que les bouches s'ouvrent*.

16. The terrible cruelty of the methods used is not enough to explain why resolute men who had stared death in the face on several occasions so often broke down

under interrogation and made such monstrous accusations against themselves. The real reason is that they had been brutally torn away from the soil in which they had grown up. The prisoner was like a plant that has been torn up, exposed to wind and rain and deprived of food, water and sunlight. His ideals were destroyed. He was not faced with his class enemies. The entire Soviet people was against him.... He had nothing left to cling to. He was thrown into an abyss without knowing why. Why? Why?' Chablakin, cited in Medvedev, *Le Stalinisme*, p. 320.

Chapter 4: Bodies and Apparatuses

  1. Althusser, op. cit.
  2. Quite apart from the problems of a statics of systems—which works against the dynamics of mutations—there are also the traditional problems of economist determinism. Its degree of mobility is low and no theory of apparatuses is likely to remove the heavy constraints it implies. The second storey of the superstructure is ill-equipped for productive tasks. In order to understand why new reproductive apparatuses have to be produced, we have to fall back upon the notion of an upheaval in the material conditions of production and therefore in the social relations of production. At first sight, the most obvious facts do not satisfy these conditions, and no history of ideology, past, present or future, indicates the existence of 'concomitant variations' between the 'dominant ideological apparatus' series and the 'social relations of production' series. In French society, for instance, the 'information apparatus' took over from the educational apparatus as the Number One state ideological apparatus—the role once played by the religious state ideological apparatus. The transition occurred between 1960 and 1980, without the replacement of one ruling class by another and without any modification in the social relations of production. In the Middle Ages, the Church achieved the dominant position in Christendom, but it appeared and was built *before* the feudal mode of production, in the last stages of the slave mode of production. What mutation in class relations corresponds to the rise and success of Islam in the Arabian Peninsula? In such cases of ideological reshaping, there is little point in settling down to stare into the mirror.
  3. Marx, *Capital, Volume One*, Harmondsworth 1976, p. 512, note 27.
  4. 'God duplicates himself and sends his Son to Earth, as a mere "subject" forsaken by him (the long complaint of the Garden of Olives which ends in the Crucifixion), subject but Subject, man but God, to do what prepares the way for the final Redemption, the Resurrection of Christ', Althusser, p. 167.

Book II

Section I

Chapter 1: Incompleteness

  1. E. Benvéniste, *Le Vocabulaire des institutions indo-européennes*, Paris 1969, Vol. II, p. 14.
  2. 'Organisation', *Encyclopedia Universalis*.
  3. Pierre Birnbaum, *La fin du politique*, p. 92.
  4. Tönnies, *Community and Association*.
  5. Pierre Bourdieu, *Esquisse*, p. 300.
  6. Ernest Renan, *Souvenirs d'enfance et de jeunesse*.
  7. Hence the comic aspect of current debates: 'I am quite willing for power to exist, but I reject any delegation of power.' In other words, I accept your triangles, but not the three sides.

8. Kings II 1-10.
9. St Augustine, *The City of God*.
10. J.-T. Desanti, *Les Staliniens*, Paris 1975, pp. 360-369.
11. There is of course no demonstrative system that is not founded upon something undemonstrable. Incompleteness therefore implies, not that something has to be postulated, but that the postulate has to belong to a logical system distinct from the demonstrative system in question.

Chapter 2: Natural Religion

1. A collection can, however, be studied as a collective phenomenon. Cf. René Maunier, 'La Queue comme groupe social' (*Les Annales*, 1940) and, of course, Sartre's analyses of queues.
2. 'Discours au Collège de France', *Archives des sciences sociales des religions*, No. 41, January-June 1976.
3. *Dialogues avec Mitsou Ronat*, Paris 1967.
4. Lucien Febvre, 'Psychologie et histoire', *Encyclopédie Française*, Vol. VIII, 1938; 'La Sensibilité et l'histoire: comment reconstituer la vie affective d'autrefois?', *Annales*, nos. 1-2, 1941.
5. Lucien Febvre, 'Le Besoin de sécurité', *Annales*, 1953, pp. 244-247.
6. Elisabeth Badinter, *The Myth of Motherhood: An Historical View of the Maternal Instinct*, London 1981.
7. *The German Ideology*, p. 31.
8. Marx, 'Economic and Philosophical Mauscripts,' *Early Writings*, p. 348.
9. The family quarrels show how closely they are related. If, like Sartre, one begins with an idealism of the subject (*Being and Nothingness*), one can move into the Marxist idealism of *praxis* (*Critique of Dialectical Reason*) without shifting one's ground or giving any warning. The problematic is the same. The philosophers of Cartesian liberty are quite at home with Marxist 'necessity'. It is, of course, just as easy to move in the opposite direction. Sartre could thus move on to (or back to) an absolute moral subjectivism which showed no break with his Marxist phase. The initial speculative *cogito* (1935-1950) becomes historical *praxis* (1960-1968) and then reverts to the status of a *project*, an abstract historical revolt. Sartre's thought changed its form, but never its nature. That is typical of all philosophical trajectories.
10. Kant, *Critique of Pure Reason*, p. 337.
11. Benvéniste, pp. 179-209.
12. Patristics does not of course form a homogeneous corpus. Both style and doctrine are split along a fairly clear line between Greek and Latin culture, between East and West. The Greek-speaking fathers are more inclined towards metaphysics and ontology. They make good philosophers, but have a leaning towards contemplation. The Latin fathers tend to be jurists and moralists, inclining more towards action and related problems. They make better rhetors than thinkers. In the first case Cicero dominates, in the second the major influence is Plato. A somewhat unfortunate division. The Pelagian debate over Grace has its centre of gravity in the West, the debate over the Holy Ghost in the East. The former concerns freedom and 'works'; the latter revolves around esprit de corps and the status of constituted bodies. The dynamics of individual action are a Western speciality, climaxing in 'Protestantism and capitalism'. The statics of existing groups is an Eastern speciality, culminating in 'the spirit of orthodoxy and totalitarianism'.
13. Marx, 'Excerpts from James Mill's *Elements of Political Economy*', *Early Writings*, p. 260.

14. Ibid.,
15. Marx, *Grundrisse*, Harmondsworth 1973, pp. 331–332.
16. Michel Serres, *Le Parasite*, Paris 1980.
17. Marx, *Capital Volume One*, p. 163.
18. Ibid., p. 143.
19. Ibid., p. 90.

Chapter 3: Counter-Evidence

1. 'Once we have put forward an idea or a theory, our aim should not be to preserve it by seeking supportive evidence. On the contrary, we must look at the facts which seem to disprove it. (...) We can only find a solid basis for our ideas if we try to destroy our own conclusions by providing counter-evidence' (Claude Bernard).
2. Cf. Georges Labica, 'Lénine et la religion', in CERM, *Philosophie et religion*, Paris 1974. See also Lenin, *Socialism and Religion* (1905, six pages).
3. Letter to Annenkov, 28 November 1846.
4. Marx, 'On The Jewish Question', *Early Writings*, p. 218.
5. Ibid., p. 217.
6. Ibid., p. 234.
7. See the Chomsky–Piaget debate in *Théories du langage, théories de l'apprentissage*, Paris 1979.
8. 'I am studying Comte on the side because the British and French make so much fuss over that fellow. What captivates them is the encyclopedic about him, the synthesis. But he is so wretched in comparison with Hegel.' Marx to Engels, 7 July 1866.
9. Cf. P. Arbousse-Bastide, *Le Positivisme politique et religieux au Brésil*, Paris 1952.
10. Cf. Michel Serre's analysis, 'Comte autotraduit dans l'encyclopédie', in *La Traduction*, Paris 1974.

Section II

I. The Economy of Lack

1. Jean Crenier, author of an *Essai sur l'esprit d'orthodoxie* (Paris 1938), contrived to abstract from the body of orthodoxy and from the vocation of heresies to become alternative orthodoxies. Grenier was Albert Camus's master.
2. *Les Deux sources de la morale et de la religion*.
3. Educator, conductor, *duce*, from the Latin *ducere*, to lead, to command. 'Pedagogue' comes from a Greek term meaning to push, to guide. The French term *instituteur* (primary-school teacher) was introduced into the language by the revolutionary Convention and is borrowed from the most solemn of political vocabularies: *instituere civitatem*, to found the state.
4. See Cornford, *From Religion to Philosophy*, London 1912, and J.-P. Vernant, *Mythes et pensées chez les Grecs*, Paris 1965 (especially 'Du mythe à la raison', Vol Ii, p. 95).
5. Henri-Irenée Marrou, *Histoire de l'education dans l'Antiquité*, Paris 1948. On Homer, see pp. 243–269.
6. Henri Guillemin, *L'Arrière-pensée de Jaurès*, Paris 1966, p. 215.
7. On *profanus* and *profanare*, see *Hommages à Georges Dumézil*, Collection Latomas, Vol. 45, Paris 1960, p. 46 ff.

8. G. Belloin, *Et nos rêves*, Paris 1979, p. 93.

9. See Alfred Loisy, *La Naissance du christianisme*, Paris 1933, especially chapters II and III: 'L'Evangile de Jésus' and 'Jésus le Christ'.

10. 'Lenin lives in the soul of every member of our party. Each member of our party is a fragment of Lenin. Our entire communist family is a collective incarnation of Lenin', *Izvestia*, 24 January 1934, cited in Collection 'Kiosque', *Lénine, Trotsky, Staline*, p. 148.

11. I am sure that no one who followed the funeral procession of Pierre Overney, Pierre Goldman or Jean-Paul Sartre will have the indecency to object to this. The fact that such a volatile molecule as the intellectual left or far left could find the concentrated high-point of their existence in such painful events should serve to underline for sceptics the political importance of death.

Chapter 2: The Defence System

1. Historical meteorology—blue skies over Western Europe for almost forty years (1945–1980)—is enough to explain why the trade in hot air, both oral and printed, has risen steadily in that zone. Self-service: who wouldn't prefer our individual comforts to the harsh rigours of organization—*in so far as he had the choice*?

2. Leroi-Gourhan, *La Geste et la parole*, Paris 1964, p. 257.

3. The main original sources are Zosima (ed. Pascoud, Paris 1971), Hesychius of Miletus and, above all, Eusebius of Caesarea's *Vita Constantini*. A full bibliography is given in Gilbert Dragon, *Naissance d'une capitale* (*Constantinople et ses institutions de 330 à 451*), Paris 1974.

4. On this controversial question, see Paul Veyer, *Pain et cirques*, Paris 1976, especially 'La Divinisation des empéreurs et la notion de charisme', pp. 560–589. The best summary (both accurate and synthetic) is still Cerfaux and Tondriau, *Un Concurrent du christianisme: Le Culte des souverains dans la civilisation gréco-romaine*', Paris 1957.

5. Petronius, *Satires*, 175.

6. 'As early as 318 Constantine granted the bishops jurisdiction to remove cases from the normal courts. In such circumstances, the episcopal sentence was executory and no appeal was allowed. This was the origin of the privileges which eventually placed the Church outside and above the common law and gave it an authority capable of compromising that of the prince.' Marcel Simon 1972.

7. Pierre Griolet, 'De Constantin à Charlemagne ou la propédeutique ecclésiale des pouvoirs', in *Histoire des idéologies*, Vol. 1.

Chapter 3: Atopia

1. Alfred Loissy, *La Naissance du christianisme*, p. 113.

2. Emphasis added.

3. Michel Serres.

Chapter 4: Constancy

1. The mythological formulae in inverted commas are taken from Francine Markovits, *Marx dans le Jardin d'Epicure*, Paris 1974.

2. Max Weber, 'Science as a Vocation', in *Essays in Sociology*, London 1945, pp. 129–156.

3. *Economy and Society I*, New York 1968, p. 252.

354

4. *Les vraies richesses*, in *Oeuvres Romanesques*, Paris 1977.

5. Michel Serres, 'Romains et Faulkner traduisant l'Ecriture', *La Traduction* (*Hermès III*) Paris 1974, p. 246.

6. *Surveys from Exile*, Harmondsworth 1973, pp. 146–151.

7. This is a free interpretation of *Le Mythe de l'éternel retour*, Paris 1949. Eliade is actually well aware of the ruses of mythical permanence. See the special issue of *Cahiers de l'Herne*, No. 33, 1978.

8. E. Dodds, *The Greeks and the Irrational*, Berkeley 1951.

9. Roger Bastide, *Le Sacré sauvage*, Paris 1975. Cf. the discussion of Bastide's contribution to *Le Besoin religieux*, Neufchâtel 1973, pp. 145–171.

10. Montesquieu, *Pensées diverses*.

11. 'Magicians or medicine-men appear to constitute the oldest artificial or professional class in the evolution of society'. *The Golden Bough* I, p. 420.

12. J.-P. Vernant, *Les Origines de la pensée grecque*.

13. Seligman (Frazer Lectures, 1933) summarizes the four main criteria that distinguish the 'divine king'. He has power over nature; his person is the dynamic centre of the universe; his acts follow a ritual order; and when he grows old he is put to death. The historical prototype appears to originate on the banks of the Upper Nile in pre-dynastic Egypt (the reth, king of the Shillouk as incarnation of the Nyikang, the founder of the kingdom). Evans-Pritchard questioned the empirical basis of the model and especially the ritual character of the execution in 1848, but Young restored the original to its rights in 1966.

14. The Paris Commune was not the work of the First International, nor the October Revolution of the Second or the Chinese Revolution of the Third. That is to say nothing of the colonial emancipation movements, where there was at best indifference, at worst, hostility.

15. Guy Scarpetta, *Eloge du cosmopolitanisme*, Paris 1980.

16. E.J.Hobsbawm, 'Some Reflections on *The Break-up of Britain*', *New Left Review* 105, September-October 1977.

17. It goes without saying that, because of the inner duality of historical development, the technical vector is essentially different from the cultural vector. Our civilization is not culturally superior to others simply because it has gained technological 'superiority' over them. There are no exceptionally gifted cultures. 'European' ideology or, still worse, Indo-European ideology is based upon a confusion between the two vectors, and no serious theoretician would lower himself to discussing it. Let me make it quite clear that the corollary of the universality of human nature is that all historical cultures are strictly equal. Consequently, no hierarchy of human groups can be established.

Index

356

Capet, Hugues, 264
Capital (Marx), 9, 41, 88, 90–1, 107,
    145, 198, 210, 201, 210–11, 229
    231, 246, 249, 308, 347
Carlyle, Thomas, 221
Carnot, Nicolas Sadi, 104–5, 269,
    348
Carpentier, Alejo, 262
Catechisme positiviste (Comte),
    230–2
Caussidière, Marc, 44
Cavaillès, Jean, 56
Ceausescu, Nicolae, 6–7
Chablakin, 350
Changeux, Jean-Pierre, 228
Charcot, Jean Martin, 99
Charlemagne, 264
Che's Guerrilla War (Debray), 346
Chekhov, Anton, 41
Chomsky, Noam, 190, 192, 228, 352
Churchill, Winston, 262
Cicero, 10, 265, 351
Clausewitz, Karl von, 303, 305, 307
Clausius, 105, 268–9
Clemenceau, Georges, 229
Columbus, Christopher, 134
Communist Manifesto (Marx &
    Engels), 111
Community and Association
    (Tönnies), 173–4, 326
Comte, Auguste, 44, 86, 228–32,
    338, 352
Condillac, Étienne de, 86
*Considérations sur le pouvoir
    spirituel* (Comte), 230
Constant, Benjamin, 303
Constantine, 281–92, 295, 353
Conversations with Allende
    (Debray), 346
Cook, James, 12
Copernicus, Nicolaus, 50, 225
Cortes, Hernán, 92
Cours de Philosophie Positive
    (Comte), 232
Cousin, Victor, 87
A Critique of Arms (Debray), 346
Critique of Dialectical Reason
    (Sartre), 349, 351
Critique of the Gotha Programme
    (Marx), 198, 221, 225, 308, 311

Critique of Pure Reason (Kant),
    120–1
Cyril of Alexandria, 296

Dagron, Gilbert, 286
Danton, Geroges Jacques, 44
Darkness at Noon (Koestler), 349
Darwin, Charles, 74, 85
Daunou, Pierre, 86
Dawkin, Richard, 156
La Décade philosophique, 87
The Decline of the Middle Ages
    (Huizinga), 4
De l'Amour (Stendhal), 88
De Man, Paul, 119
Démocratie et totalitarisme (Aron),
    349
Demosthenes, 40–1
Descartes, René, 16, 23, 61, 122,
    137, 161, 226, 333, 349, 351
Destutt, Comte de Tracy, 34, 85–8
*Deutsch-Französische
    Jahrbücher*, 222
Deutscher, Isaac, 21
Devereux, Georges, 347
Dézamy, Théodore, 249
Dialectics of Nature (Engels), 105
Díaz, Porfirio, 230
Diderot, Dénis, 255
Diocletian, 288–9
Dionysius Exiquus, 264
Discourse on Method (Descartes),
    346
*Discourse on the Origins
    of Inequality* (Rousseau), 12
Dodds, Eric Robertson, 328
Don Quixote (Cervantes), 3
Drieu, Pierre (La Rochelle), 119
Dumézil, Georges, 64, 254
Durkheim, Emile, 44, 85, 120, 126,
    135, 172–3

The Eighteenth Brumaire (Marx),
    91, 326
Einstein, Albert, 170
Eliade, Mircea, 44, 326–7
L'Emergence humaine (Ruffié), 346
Encyclopedists, 86